INTIMATIONS OF MORTALITY

In *Intimations of Mortality*, Barbara Reich offers an empirically based critique of the failures of end-of-life communication and decision-making in the United States. Using England and Canada as occasional foils, Reich explores why US physicians, patients, and families struggle to have the conversations necessary to provide seriously ill and dying patients with medical care consistent with their preferences. Reich also shows how a number of different factors – including payment mechanisms, liability fears, cultural phenomena, communication avoidance, death denial, and clinical uncertainty – impact physician-patient communication and medical decision-making, leave patients and families without the tools they need to make informed choices, and instead leave the default practices in place. Ultimately, this groundbreaking analysis unveils the interconnectedness of the many obstacles to better communication and decision-making at the end-of-life and offers much needed suggestions for improvement.

Barbara A. Reich is Professor of Law who has taught Bioethics, End-of-Life Law, and other Medical Law subjects for more than two decades. She is the author of numerous articles addressing end-of-life issues, including articles about the Theresa Schiavo case, racial disparities in health care delivery, informed consent and shared decision-making, advance directives, and cognitive challenges to making good medical decisions. Barbara is a graduate of Harvard Law School.

Intimations of Mortality

MEDICAL DECISION-MAKING AT THE END OF LIFE

BARBARA A. REICH
Western New England University School of Law

CAMBRIDGE
UNIVERSITY PRESS

CAMBRIDGE
UNIVERSITY PRESS

University Printing House, Cambridge CB2 8BS, United Kingdom

One Liberty Plaza, 20th Floor, New York, NY 10006, USA

477 Williamstown Road, Port Melbourne, VIC 3207, Australia

314–321, 3rd Floor, Plot 3, Splendor Forum, Jasola District Centre, New Delhi – 110025, India

103 Penang Road, #05–06/07, Visioncrest Commercial, Singapore 238467

Cambridge University Press is part of the University of Cambridge.

It furthers the University's mission by disseminating knowledge in the pursuit of education, learning, and research at the highest international levels of excellence.

www.cambridge.org
Information on this title: www.cambridge.org/9781108486804
DOI: 10.1017/9781108762595

First published 2022

A catalogue record for this publication is available from the British Library.

ISBN 978-1-108-48680-4 Hardback

To René

Ich suche nichts, weil ich Dich gefunden habe.

Contents

Preface

Our mortality binds us together as individuals, families, communities, cultures, nations, and denizens of the earth. But each of us must write our own script for how to navigate life with the future certainty of death. How and when we write (and amend) that script very likely will influence both the physical and emotional experiences of how we die. While much of how we will die remains outside of our control, preparation for death throughout life can enhance the experience of life and make the foreknowledge of death less frightening and more familiar. Most people who survive childhood arrive at a point in adulthood where the thought of death is no longer a distant and abstract concept. Whether it is diagnosis with a life-threatening illness or the cumulative effects of aging, something puts each one of us into the position of having to face the road to death and to make decisions along that path. Or not. Some deliberately or unconsciously avoid making these decisions or even contemplating the future – because change is hard and everything must remain as it always was. Death is the ultimate change of circumstances.

We have a system of medical care undergirded with ethical principles and a legal system as backup to these principles that are meant to protect and guide patients through the complex medical decisions that often arise at the end of life. On the surface, both medicine and law look good – a combination of excellent scientific training, the latest technology, an emphasis on patient autonomy and physician beneficence, and related law ensure that patients receive the 'best' medical care. Right? Well, in ideal circumstances, yes. As in many countries and cultures, ethical principles and law in the United States support the right of patients to make medical decisions according to their own values. In most circumstances, the principle of autonomy allows an adult to choose whether to accept or to refuse medical treatment, including therapeutic care and life-prolonging technology. This autonomy principle is protected – in theory – via the legal doctrine of informed consent. So, while one person with a terminal illness might request all available medically appropriate care to prolong life, no matter what the costs or adverse effects, another person might choose no therapeutic care, preferring to focus solely on palliation of symptoms. And a third person might seek a middle ground, agreeing to try therapy for the disease but then to discontinue that therapy when side effects or disease progression interferes too much with quality of life. Each of these paths is a valid choice under the ethical principle of autonomy and the law of informed consent.

And yet, for a country that has enshrined the autonomy principle in its culture and law, the United States struggles mightily with calibrating care to the wishes of individual patients. Comparisons of medical care that patients collectively receive at the end of life with a population-wide snapshot of prior expressed wishes indicate that patients in the United States are receiving far more life-prolonging and otherwise invasive interventions to stave off death than they would prefer. An ever-increasing body of empirical research backs this up: studies suggest that more than one-fifth of medical care provided in the United States is unnecessary, and that the consequent inappropriate use of burdensome or high-intensity medical technology at the end of life adversely impacts patients. Yet most dying patients say that they would prefer comfort care. Combine these two sets of data on actual practice versus patient preferences and we have a system that, statistically and for many individual patients, overutilizes unwanted medical technology at the end of life. This is not to say that physicians get it wrong every time, but this discrepancy suggests that many patients are receiving care that they do not want and that is also medically inappropriate. The reasons for this misalignment are many and complex – and are the primary subject of discussion in this book. The focus is on physician-patient (and family) communication and decision-making, including an attempt to understand the reasons why (according to the data) so many patients receive care at the end of life that they probably would not choose if they were better informed. To make this discussion more useful, I situate this question within the larger context of law, health systems, culture, dysfunctional politics, and cognitive barriers to good decision-making.

Acknowledging the validity of individual preferences for various pathways to death is important, but it ignores the fact that many people avoid entirely the thinking process that is necessary to make robust, well-informed decisions about which pathway to choose because the thought of death is uncomfortable to confront. Many patients avoid making decisions in advance. If the decision not to decide is the result of a voluntary and considered choice to accept mortality by relinquishing attempts to exert control over death and the dying process, then perhaps all is well, at least for the dying person – though the medical technology juggernaut may still result in an undesirable and perhaps harmful prolongation of the process. If, however, the non-decision arises out of a reluctance to confront mortality, then the non-deciders likely do themselves a disservice, not only at the time of death but throughout the life that precedes it.

Modern medical care often can stave off death for quite a while (though often with significant cost to quality of life), and the default model in the United States is to provide therapeutic treatment and life-prolonging interventions unless the patient affirmatively opts out. Why is this the case? The answer to that question is complicated. Conversations about prognosis and the potential utility of various treatments provide an essential opportunity for patients to convey to their physicians their preferences about care at the end of life – and for physicians in turn to explain to patients the potential value of various medical options – their harms and prospective benefits. We may be tempted to assume that the better (though imperfectly) informed decisions resulting from these conversations can help reduce avoidable physical and emotional suffering and lead to care that aligns with patients' well-considered values and preferences. The problem with the prior sentence is that while it may be theoretically correct, it rarely reflects the reality of physician-patient communication and decision-making. Individually, physicians, patients, and families struggle to have candid, substantive, and timely discussions about necessary choices in the face of life-threatening illness. In the absence of these discussions, physicians in our health care culture frequently provide full-on medical interventions, even when patients are actively dying, because no one – patient or family member – has told them to stop.

The common purpose of the following chapters is to understand this communication problem better in all of its multilayered complexity, to situate the challenges of physician-patient communication within the broader health care system, law, and culture in which they occur, and to consider feasible and realistic individual and system-wide improvements to end-of-life decision-making. To that end, this book considers several interrelated layers of inquiry that may appear to belong in separate books but are, in reality, very much intertwined. One question that this book will explore is whether and how the universal access to care along with other health care structures in Canada and the United Kingdom produce superior end-of-life care for patients in these countries. (Of course, this in turn begs the question of what constitutes 'superior' care, but there is some agreement on that question.) Rest assured that this is *not* a book about health care system reform, though some discussion of the topic is necessary to understand the financial, governmental, political, and cultural context in which physicians in the United States provide medical care. The United States is obviously very different from Canada and the United Kingdom, not only because we lack universal access to health care but more broadly because the complexity and dysfunctionality of our health care insurance and regulatory systems, along with intractable political schisms, make reform extremely challenging. Health care reform would be great for many reasons, but it would not effectively resolve our collective difficulties with end-of-life communication and decision-making.

A variety of other systemic and individual factors contribute to a pattern of poor physician-patient communication and high-intensity care at the end of life – what some have called the 'conveyer belt' of medicine. Systemic problems, such as mechanisms of health care reimbursement and liability concerns among physicians, add pressure to provide potentially inappropriate care. At the same time, cultural attitudes toward mortality play a significant role – many admire and praise the model of the patient as a 'fighter' in a 'battle' against death. And denial of mortality is common. Physicians' professional culture, focusing oftentimes too much on cure over care, perpetuates many of these dysfunctionalities. On top of these problems, Black and other racial and ethnic minorities distrust the health care system (with good reason) and may therefore experience an added communication burden regarding end-of-life decisions. And in addition to all of these obstacles, there are the mostly unacknowledged cognitive barriers to ever knowing what the 'best' choice is for many seriously ill patients. Only when physicians, patients, and families acknowledge the rational limitations of decision-making for life-threatening illness can the serious work of communicating and decision-making begin. This book considers all of these obstacles to 'good' end-of-life decisions and suggests what we can do, individually and collectively, to get to 'better'. 'Best' nearly always remains unknowable.

I am not a trained philosopher, an expert in decision theory, or a health care professional. I come at this topic from the perspective of a legal academic with an interest in the multi-causal aspects of poor communication and decision-making by and for adults at the end of life.* Although most of my days are spent teaching and writing about law, this book discusses law only as a framing structure and foundation (along with ethical principles) for the process of decision-making at the end of life. As the book will demonstrate, law does not do a very good job of addressing the problems discussed here. Law, with very narrow and limited exceptions, is not the answer. The book attempts to reach several audiences and so makes some compromises along the way. It is a book written for all interested parties – patients and their caretakers, academics, clinicians, and policy makers – and anyone else who would like to understand the reasons why confronting mortality and making decisions at the end of life is so difficult (apart from the obvious).

There are no quick fixes. The already vast and burgeoning body of literature on the topic of death and dying demonstrates that point quite well. Many experts are hard at work devising ways to excise the excess from medical care in the United States, and I do not pretend to have better answers than they do. But an improved understanding of *what* is happening – systemically and individually among patients and physicians – and *why* it is happening may help physicians, patients, and families communicate more effectively and make decisions along the pathway to death that more closely reflect the authentic and realistic preferences of the patient. Getting to 'better' also may incrementally improve care for the seriously ill at a system-wide level, to the benefit of future patients. Improving care for the dying obviously will require some changes of culture and customary practice in medicine. So I will add

* Throughout the book, I omit consideration of decision-making for severely ill and disabled infants and children. I also sidestep discussion of medical aid in dying (popularly known as "physician-assisted suicide"), mainly because the focus of the book is on communication between physicians and patients rather than the ethics of various end-of-life options.

a caveat: much of the argument in the book rests on a foundation of empirical evidence, but we are each of us an 'n' of one. The critiques and recommendations that follow are not aimed at any individual physician or patient or family member. Many individuals acknowledge the fact of mortality, communicate well, and make end-of-life decisions with courage, grace, and dignity. These same individuals very likely live their lives with the same qualities. The human instinct for survival is very powerful, and patients will quite rightly endure a lot in exchange for more life. The trick is knowing when to say 'when' (and that thinking process can be cultivated in advance).

This is not a book about 'how to die well' but rather a book about 'how to think well about dying'. Thinking well about dying requires two elements: an understanding of the health care system's deficiencies and of how doctors communicate with patients and a willingness to acknowledge mortality as an ineluctable part of life (and to live and make decisions accordingly). For the young and the fortunately healthy, there is little cause to contemplate the prospect of death, at least not often. Perhaps the death of a grandparent, parent, or friend brings mortality into sharp focus for a time, but it tends to recede into the background of daily life. As we grow older, the thought of mortality creeps into mind more frequently until, finally, it is a little bird singing into ears that grow deaf. How we cope with these ever more frequent intimations of mortality throughout our lives colors the days that become the weeks and months and slippery years – and determines how well prepared we are to face death.

Acknowledgments

The title of this book is a riff on Wordsworth's "Ode: Intimations of Immortality from Recollections of Early Childhood" (1807). Portions of this book draw on the following previously published work (some of which was published under my former name, Barbara A. Noah):

- Surrogate Decision-Making: Clinical Uncertainty, Rational Apathy, and the Problem of Trust, 15 Ethics, Medicine & Public Health Journal (Oct.–Dec. 2020)
- Rational Patient Apathy, 49 Seton Hall Law Review 535–628 (2019) (with René Reich-Graefe)
- Potential Utility of an Independent Decision-Making Board for Seriously Ill Patients Lacking Decisional Capacity, 6 Ethics, Medicine & Public Health Journal 63–71 (July–Sept. 2018)
- Removing Obstacles to a Peaceful Death, 23 Elder Law Journal 197–233 (2018) (with Kathy Cerminara)
- The (Ir)rationality of (Un)informed Consent, 34 Quinnipiac Law Review 691–704 (2016)
- Avoiding Overtreatment at the End of Life: Physician-Patient Communication and Truly Informed Consent, 36 Pace Law Review 737–800 (2016) (with Neal Feigenson)
- A Better Death in Britain? 40 Brooklyn Journal of International Law 870–915 (2015)
- Two Conflicts in Context: Lessons from the Schiavo and Bland Cases and the Role of Best Interests Analysis in the United Kingdom, 36 Hamline Law Review 239–264 (2013)
- In Denial: The Role of Law in Preparing for Death, 21 Elder Law Journal 1–31 (2013)
- The Role of Race in End-of-Life Care, 15 Journal of Health Care Law & Policy 349–378 (2012)

• The Role of Religion in the Schiavo Controversy, 6 Houston Journal Health Law & Policy 319–346 (2006)
• Politicizing the End of Life: Lessons from the Schiavo Controversy, 59 University of Miami Law Review 107–134 (2005)

A heartfelt thank you to Matt Gallaway, senior editor at Cambridge University Press, for his enthusiastic support of this project from proposal to press. Also, many thanks to Jadyn Fauconnier-Herry for shepherding the publication process and to Mathivathini Mareesan for supervising the production process. Thank you also to Linda Benson for her truly excellent editing – including her thoughtful substantive questions that improved the book. I also appreciate the willingness of my university to support this project with a semester-long research sabbatical. Special thanks to our law librarians for patiently teaching me how to use the indexing tool in MS Word and for their efficiency in sourcing materials from other libraries.

Thank you to those many physicians who have published their research, their thoughts and struggles with end-of-life communication, and the stories of their encounters with patients and families. Your candor, compassion, self-critical assessment, and the overall window into your profession have greatly informed the discussion in this book. To those physicians with whom I have had conversations about these topics – including Dr. Julia Bonacum, Dr. Diane Dietzen, Dr. Melissa Hession, and especially Dr. Petra Kriz – thank you for your time and generous willingness to answer all of my questions, even the uncomfortable and impertinent ones.

Portions of this book build on previously published work with splendid coauthors, including Kathy Cerminara, Neal Feigenson, and René Reich-Graefe. Thank you to these authors for allowing me to share the results of our collaborations. Also, my sincere thanks to John Tingle and Clayton Ó Néill for reading chapters, answering my many questions, and commenting on the UK health care discussion throughout this book. I am also very grateful to Patti Peppin for reading chapters and for improving my understanding of health care in Canada. Thank you to those additional readers who commented on various chapters, including Monica Aswani, Julia Bonacum, Zack Buck, and Kathy Cerminara. An extra big thank you to those who read multiple chapters or the entire draft, including Petra Kriz who provided insight into the realities of medical practice, Leora Harpaz who shared her own experiences with the health care system and made spot-on suggestions for how to improve the book on a global level, and Rosy Jacobsen who commented on everything from language choice and tone to the arc of the argument. I very much appreciate Kathy Cerminara and Barry Furrow for their support of this project in its early stages, and Neal Feigenson for his advice on the academic publication process and his excellent suggestions about my plan of attack. My daughter, Claudia Jackson, provided research assistance and read and commented on the entire manuscript, along with patiently listening to my blethering on about the book in progress. Thank you, Claudia. All errors and omissions are mine.

Most of all, I am deeply grateful to my husband, René Reich-Graefe, for his incisive comments and suggestions, his sublime insight into the topic of this book, his appetite for conversation about the big, daunting matters and the banal details, and his patience, encouragement, and sense of humor (especially whenever I said, "this chapter is practically going to write itself"). I'm not looking for anything because I found you.

1

The Conundrum

How Much Medical Care Is 'Enough'?

Enough is as good as a feast.

—P. L. Travers, *Mary Poppins* (HarperCollins, 1934)

Most people want to live long and they want to live well. Quantity of life is experienced through the lens of quality – surviving is not enough without thriving. And the whole idea of quality only exists within the broader reality of the scarcity and uncertainty that is inherent in life. We can acknowledge this truth without allowing it to paralyze us. We can live with the knowledge that life is finite and that its end – in both timing and circumstances – is uncertain. Still, living in constant fear of illness and death can wreck an otherwise good span of years. It is only natural that to enjoy the pleasures of life, we tuck away thoughts of mortality rather than dwelling constantly on the truth – that the five minutes I just spent typing this paragraph are five minutes gone from my life, and that I do not know how long it will be before something abruptly, or slowly and inexorably, brings my life to an end.

When confronted with a potentially terminal diagnosis, the lurking uncertainty of how much life is left becomes a rather more immediate question. Most seriously ill patients want to live as long as possible, assuming that quality of life remains acceptable. They are seeking equipoise between surviving and thriving. But aiming for that equipoise between surviving and thriving isn't everyone's choice. Some patients will strike the balance differently, choosing to forgo a good deal of statistical life extension to focus on quality – hoping to continue a relatively active life while avoiding suffering. Others will seek maximal life extension regardless of the impact of medical interventions on the ability to enjoy life. This is an individual decision, but one that should be taken with eyes wide open and with as much available information as is possible. As Isaac Asimov supposedly once said, "Life is pleasant. Death is peaceful. It's the transition that's troublesome."[1] This observation of course begs the question of when that transition starts. The answer to this question is part of the fundamental question that this book attempts to tackle – once a person is

[1] Isaac Asimov (1920–1992).

seriously ill, when is the right time to start thinking about preparing for death and so consider ceasing medical efforts to prolong life? The answer will, of course, vary according to individual preference and circumstance. Acknowledging the reality of death sooner rather than later in life probably makes it easier to address this question when it arrives, but this is only a partial answer.

This decision-making process also requires input from an expert – the physician's role is not only to provide medical care but also to furnish information about the patient's evolving medical situation, an opinion about which options (if any) are worth pursuing, and about when to stop. Physicians have an ethical and legal obligation to talk in a timely and honest way with their patients about diagnosis, treatment harms and benefits, and prognosis. Unfortunately, as explained in much more detail in Chapter 3, many seriously ill patients lack the understanding necessary to make well-informed decisions about therapeutic and end-of-life care – either because their physicians don't provide all the necessary information or because patients cannot or will not process it. Still, at the end of life, it's often difficult to know when death is imminent and when it is still a little way off, and modern life-sustaining technology adds another variable to this prognostic uncertainty. Whatever the individual patient's goal is at the end of life – living as long as possible or ceasing burdensome interventions for a focus on comfort – physicians cannot guarantee a Goldilocks 'just-right' result at the end of life. Expecting physicians to predict the timing of death with precision and to know when to cease treatment or life support so that each patient dies neither a moment 'too soon' nor a moment 'too late' (by the patient's measure) is expecting too much. They can only share best estimates and recommendations, based on statistical averages and factors unique to the patient to guide patients in making hard choices. This in turn requires timely and frank communication with patients and families.

This book focuses on decision-making in the context of life-threatening illness and end-of-life care, so it is important to understand what 'end-of-life care' means. There often is no clear delineation between care for life-threatening illness and care at the end of life, because that end point remains undefined and is, in some ways, a matter of individual physician and patient perception. There are essentially three types of care for seriously ill and dying patients: *therapeutic care* – treatments, tests, and procedures intended to cure or to prolong life by slowing the progress of disease; *palliative care*, intended to ameliorate symptoms from the medical condition itself and from side effects of treatments and to support the patient and family emotionally and spiritually; and *life-sustaining care*, such as mechanical ventilation, artificial nutrition and hydration, and dialysis, which can extend the life of a dying patient. Of course, these types of care sometimes overlap. Patients may receive life-sustaining care in tandem with therapeutic care with the former serving as a bridge to improvement or even recovery and, ideally, all seriously ill patients receive palliative care throughout the course of their illness.

LIFE EXPECTANCY, HEALTH STATUS AND HEALTH CARE SPENDING

We in the United States utilize a lot of health care at the end of life, often to an extent that does more harm than good. Evidence at the system-wide level also indicates a misalignment between what most terminally ill patients say they prefer – limited burdensome care in favor of comfort care – and what many patients actually receive – high-intensity therapeutic and life-prolonging care. Since health care interventions can cause iatrogenic harm[2] in the form of adverse events and debilitating side effects, and life-sustaining technologies can cause harm by prolonging the dying process and increasing suffering, more care at the end of life is not necessarily better. In the late 1990s, the Institute of Medicine adopted the term 'overuse' of medical care and defined it as "a health care service [that] is provided under circumstances in which its potential for harm exceeds the possible benefit."[3] As the literature on overuse has developed, the term is now used to refer to at least two separate categories of medical care: overuse of testing and overtreatment. The term 'overtreatment' refers broadly to medical care that presents an unfavorable harm-benefit calculus for an individual patient, but this calculus should also take individual patient preferences into account. Caution is warranted for multiple reasons when using the term 'overtreatment' to refer to this trend of high utilization at the end of life: the emotional pressures at the end of life make communication and complex decision-making very difficult for patients and families, and it is always easier to categorize care as overtreatment in hindsight. Even so, as most people indicate that they prefer less intensive and invasive care at the end of life, the term is used frequently in the health care literature. Whatever the label, the underlying concern in these circumstances is that patients receive burdensome medical interventions without understanding the potential for harm relative to the prospect of clinical benefit or life extension. In the absence of that understanding, patients are consenting to care with blinders on.

It's important to keep in mind the interrelationship between objective and subjective *quality* of care (which focuses on outcomes for patients) and *value* of care (which considers cost in relation to achieved outcomes). Value in health care is typically defined as patient outcomes, such as quality and safety, per dollar spent. Research confirms that spending more on treatments and tests at the end of life does not necessarily improve quality of care or quality of life and, in fact, may have the opposite effect. Recent studies have concluded that dramatic spending differences on end-of-life care among US counties have very little measurable effect on quality. To be clear, the focus of this book is on improving communication and quality of care at the end of life, not on system-wide cost reduction. To the extent that part of the 'waste' in health care spending arises from provision of inappropriate treatments, improvements in end-of-life

2 Iatrogenic harm is harm caused by a treatment or diagnostic test. The word "iatrogenic" comes from the Greek words *iatros* (physician) and *genesis* (origin).

3 Mark R. Chassin & Robert W. Galvin, Institute of Medicine National Roundtable on Health Care Quality: The Urgent Need to Improve Health Care Quality, 280 JAMA 1000–1005 (1998).

communication and decision-making might collaterally also result in a reduction of unnecessary and potentially harmful spending. It remains to be seen whether improvements in this regard, if implemented across a wide segment of the dying population, would reduce costs overall – but the evidence suggests that cost savings would be an added benefit of achieving the central goals discussed here. In any event, eliminating waste from the health care system, while a worthy goal, does not guarantee care at the end of life that aligns with individual patient preferences. And eliminating waste certainly does not guarantee that individual patients' expressed preferences will actually be informed in any meaningful way or based on the patient's clear-eyed assessment of how he or she wants to exit life.

To describe what the phenomenon of overtreatment actually looks like at both the individual and system-wide levels, it's necessary to start with some high-level data about life expectancy, utilization, and cost before looking at specific examples. In 2018, the most recent year for which Centers for Disease Control and Prevention (CDC) statistics are available, life expectancy in the United States was 78.7 years, and more than 2.8 million people died in the United States during that year. The leading causes of natural death were heart disease and cancer.[4] The COVID-19 pandemic has reduced US life expectancy by a population-wide average of a year in the first half of 2020, and by 2.7 years for Blacks and 1.9 years for Latinx individuals.[5]

The concept of overuse implicates two dimensions of health care – the actual treatments, tests, and procedures provided to patients and the amount of health care dollars paid for this care. Health care in the United States is very costly in terms of both how it is priced (much higher than in other high-income countries) and how much of it we use. The United States currently spends the highest amount annually per patient and the highest amount as a percentage of its gross domestic product among high-wealth countries. Health spending in the United States reached 17 percent of GDP in 2019 compared with an average 8.8 percent among other countries in the Organization for Economic Cooperation and Development (OECD).[6] Yet overall health status in the United States is poor compared with the health of populations in other comparable countries (though US residents rank themselves very highly when self-reporting their health status). We have a shorter life expectancy and higher rates of heart disease, obesity, and cancer than other high-wealth

[4] Centers for Disease Control and Prevention, NCHS Data Brief, No. 355 (January 2020), www.cdc.gov/nchs/data/databriefs/db355-h.pdf. These numbers do not include deaths due to medical error. Because the CDC draws its data from cause-of-death codes on death certificates and there is no code for death from medical error and systems failures, these deaths are not formally counted. Estimates suggest that medical error is the third-leading cause of death in the United States. Martin A. Markary & Michael Daniel, Medical Error – the Third-Leading Cause of Death in the U.S., 353 British Med. J. (2016) DOI: 10.1136/bmj.i2139. It remains to be seen where COVID-19 deaths rank on the list of causes of death.

[5] Elizabeth Arias et al., Provisional Life Expectancy Estimates for January Through June, 2020, Vital Statistics Rapid Release Report No. 010 (Feb. 2021), www.cdc.gov/nchs/data/vsrr/VSRR10-508.pdf.

[6] Organisation for Economic Cooperation and Development (OECD) Statistics, National Center for Health Statistics, www.oecd.org/els/health-systems/health-data.htm.

countries, but we think that we're in great shape.[7] A recent analysis of published research on waste in the health care system confirms the high level of US spending on health care and estimates that about 25 percent of this is unnecessary spending resulting from failures in coordination of care, overtreatment and low-value care, pricing problems, fraud and abuse, and administrative complexity.[8] In spite of spending more on health care than other countries, US life expectancy compares poorly with the OECD average life expectancy in 2017 of 80.8 years.[9]

When we overutilize care on an individual patient basis or system wide, we are simultaneously overpaying in the sense that we are paying for unnecessary care, regardless of how it is priced. Since overtreatment and overpaying are interdependent, reducing unnecessary treatment should (at least in theory) have an independent and positive effect on the health care budget's bottom line. Although this book focuses on quality of care and good decision-making by and for the dying, not on cost cutting, the interdependency between utilization and payment is worth keeping in mind, especially because these spending and utilization trends will worsen with time. On average, older adults require more health care than younger adults, so utilization of health care tends to increase with every decade of life.[10] The US Census Bureau projects that by 2035, adults aged 65 and older will outnumber children aged 18 and younger.[11] As the baby-boomer population[12] ages, the demands on an already inefficient, inequitable, and financially unsustainable US health care system will increase.

Various studies document the disconnect between high health care spending and quality health care that produces a healthier population. Despite its heavy spending, the United States ranks last for overall quality of care among eleven high-wealth countries, according to a 2017 report from the Commonwealth Fund.[13] The "Mirror,

7 James Banks & James P. Smith, International Comparisons in Health Economics: Evidence from Aging Studies, 4 Annual Rev. Econ. 57–81 (2012).

8 William H. Shrank et al., Waste in the US Health Care System: Estimated Costs and Potential for Savings, 322 JAMA 1501–1509 (2019).

9 Organisation for Economic Cooperation and Development (OECD) Statistics, National Center for Health Statistics, www.oecd.org/els/health-systems/health-data.htm. The direct connection between health care spending and life expectancy is causally complex – a life expectancy differential based on death tallies in a given year can have many causal explanations, including suicide, drug overdose, traffic and gun fatalities, and now a pandemic.

10 David Lassman et al., US Health Spending Trends by Age and Gender: Selected Years 2002–10, 33 Health Aff. 815–822 (2014).

11 Jonathan Vespa, The U.S. Joins Other Populations with Large Aging Populations, March 13, 2018, www.census.gov/library/stories/2018/03/graying-america.html.

12 "Baby boomer" refers to the generation of people born between 1946 and 1964.

13 E.C. Schneider et al., "Mirror, Mirror 2017: International Comparison Reflects Flaws and Opportunities for Better U.S. Health Care" (2017), www.commonwealthfund.org. In 2021, as the book was in production, the latest report was published. In "Mirror, Mirror 2021: Reflecting Poorly," the United States remained last of the eleven studied nations overall. Canada fell from ninth to tenth place, while the United Kingdom lost its first position, falling to fourth place overall. The authors explained that "[t]he U.K.'s drop in rank from #1 to #4 is associated with that country's lower performance on several domains (such as access to care and equity) compared to 2017." The United States continues to spend the most on health care as a percentage of its GDP, yet it places last overall

Mirror" report includes comparisons among eleven high-wealth countries, including some with single-payer health care systems, in an attempt to determine which country's health care system is the fairest of them all. The researchers studied the health care systems in five domains: care process, access, administrative efficiency, equity, and health care outcomes. The United Kingdom with its government-sponsored universal access system ranked first overall, first in equity (a measure of how the system serves the wealthiest and the poorest patients), and first in care process. The United Kingdom also ranked third in the domains of access and administrative efficiency but tenth on health care outcomes. This last ranking is striking because the United Kingdom achieved the fastest reduction in "mortality amenable to health care" (deaths from preventable and treatable causes) in the preceding decade. Overall, the UK rankings suggest that it is possible to provide cost-effective and high-performing health care for all residents, but universal coverage does not necessarily guarantee high overall performance, as the data from Canada demonstrate. Canada, which also boasts universal access to health care, ranked ninth overall, ninth in equity and health care outcomes, tenth in access, and sixth in the domains of care process and administrative efficiency.

By contrast, the United States doesn't look very good in the mirror – it ranked eleventh overall and eleventh in outcomes and in access and equity, tenth in administrative efficiency, and fifth in care process. The United States also has the highest rate of mortality amenable to health care among countries studied and was the least improved over the prior decade on that measure. Because a substantial number of US residents still lack stable and affordable access to health care, overall health status is poorer – increasingly so with age. The United States also compares badly with other countries with respect to infant mortality and life expectancy at age 60 but performs better in certain care contexts such as thirty-day in-hospital mortality after heart attack or stroke. The United States also compares favorably with several top performers on the five-year relative survival rate for breast cancer and is about average on the five-year relative survival rate for colorectal cancer. But it is notable that the ranking of the United States in nearly all domains of health care remains at the bottom of the group, despite the fact that it spends the most per capita and as a percentage of GDP of any of the countries studied.[14] Other reports have reached similar conclusions.[15]

and last in all domains of care except for care process (where it improved to second place). Eric Schneider et al., "Mirror, Mirror 2021: Reflecting Poorly," www.commonwealthfund.org (2021).

14 When I share this report with my students in a course called Health Care Finance & Delivery, most are shocked to learn that the United States ranks last. This destruction of their illusions about American exceptionalism in health care is a bit painful for them but encourages their interest in understanding why it is so and what we can do about it.

15 Institute of Medicine, US Health in International Perspective: Shorter Lives, Poorer Health (2013) www.nationalacademies.org/hmd/Reports/2013/US-Health-in-International-Perspective-Shorter-Lives-Poorer-Health.aspx.

Much of the heavy spending in the United States arises from higher pricing of health care goods and services – not from providing superior medical care to its residents. The United States pays substantially more for drugs, tests, treatments, administrative costs, and clinician labor than most other countries, driving up spending.[16] A combination of increasing prices, increased treatment intensity, and an aging population (though the United States has the lowest percentage of population older than age 65 among the eleven) accounts for a substantial portion of the high level of spending in the United States. [17] And, as explained further in the next chapter, we also have a reimbursement system and a business-oriented health care culture that rewards intensity of health care services at the end of life.

QUALITY AND UTILIZATION OF MEDICAL CARE AT THE END OF LIFE

The "Mirror, Mirror" report evaluated the comparative quality of health care overall rather than focusing on care for the dying. We have all read surveys of 'the best' in various categories – the best places to retire, the best law schools, the best microbreweries. Where is the best place to die? There's a survey for that, too. In its 2015 report, the Economist Intelligence Unit (EIU) published its latest "Quality of Death Index," which ranks palliative care (including end-of-life care) across the world. Within the top fifteen countries, the United Kingdom ranked first (and was also first in previous rankings), followed by Australia, New Zealand, Ireland, Belgium, Taiwan, Germany, the Netherlands, the United States in ninth place, France, Canada in eleventh, Singapore, Norway, Japan, and then Switzerland. The rankings are based on scores derived from twenty quantitative and qualitative indicators across five categories: palliative and health care environment, human resources, affordability of care, quality of care, and community engagement. Although Canada ranked slightly behind the United States overall, it ranked ahead on several factors including quality of palliative care and availability of human resources – physicians, nurses, and other professionals with expertise in palliative care.[18]

The Quality of Death Index considered multiple dimensions of end-of-life care and found that countries with the highest ratings shared several common features: a well-implemented national palliative care policy framework, high levels of public

16 Irene Papanicolas et al., Health Care Spending in the United States and Other High-Income Countries, 319 JAMA 1024–1039 (2018); Gerard F. Anderson et al., It's the Prices, Stupid: Why the United States Is So Different from Other Countries, 22 Health Aff. 89–105 (2003); Gerard F. Anderson et al., It's Still the Prices, Stupid: Why the U.S. Spends So Much on Health Care, A Tribute to Uwe Reinhardt, 38 Health Aff. 87–95 (2019). For more on pricing and utilization, the Dartmouth Atlas of Health Care provides a trove of additional information, though based solely on Medicare and Medicaid data. www.dartmouthatlas.org/.

17 Joseph L. Dieleman et al., Factors Associated with Increases in US Health Care Spending, 1996–2013, 318 JAMA 1668–1678 (2017).

18 Economist Intelligence Unit, 2015 EIU Quality of Death Index, https://eiuperspectives.economist.com.

spending on health care services, well-developed palliative care training for clinicians, support to reduce the financial burden of palliative care for patients, widely available opioid analgesics for pain management, and a robust public awareness of palliative care and its benefits. The United States does reasonably well on some of these measures but rather poorly on others. How can it be that the United States spends so much on health care at the end of life yet is ranked last internationally among these countries in overall health care systems and outcomes and only ninth in quality of care for the dying in the EIU report? The simple answer is that spending more per patient and providing more care overall does not guarantee higher-quality care – quite the opposite. (The more nuanced and multilayered answer to this question, beyond the spending versus quality gap, will occupy a good deal of the rest of this book.) As the EIU report explained: "Cultural shifts are needed . . . from a mindset that prioritises curative treatments to one which values palliative care approaches that regard dying as a normal process and which seeks to enhance the quality of life for dying patients and their families."[19]

Data compiled by organizations like the EIU provide insight into questions about the availability of palliative care, the consistency of clinician training in palliative care, the degree of public education about its benefits, and similar systemic questions. Excellence in these matters, however, still doesn't necessarily translate into high-quality end-of-life care for every individual patient. Quality of death rankings, by necessity, tend to oversimplify a complex inquiry. At a systemic level, reimbursement incentives, cultural norms, and health care infrastructure also impact quality of care at the end of life, for better or for worse, and there are many measures of quality in end-of-life care. While access to palliative care and opioid-based pain medications is a good indicator of quality in a health care system, the intensity of care, place of death, and other measures also provide some insight into how well a system is functioning.

Empirical studies document very high levels of health care utilization at the end of life in the United States. In one study, researchers looked at differences among seven countries in utilization of care and costs of care for a cohort of patients aged 65 and older who died from cancer.[20] Canada spent the most per patient, with the United States spending a bit less, and the United Kingdom spending about half of the US amount. The study also found that in the last 180 days of life, US patients had far higher rates of ICU admission – about 40 percent of patients spent time in the ICU compared with less than 18 percent of patients in other countries. And nearly 28 percent of US patients in the study cohort were admitted to an ICU in the last thirty days of life.[21] It is striking that the United Kingdom ranks first in quality of death and yet

19 Ibid.

20 Justin E. Bekelman et al., Comparison of Site of Death, Health Care Utilization, and Hospital Expenditures for Patients Dying with Cancer in 7 Developed Countries, 315 JAMA 272–283 (2016) (analyzing data from 2010).

21 Ibid. Canada spent an average of $21,840 per patient compared with the United States spending $18,500, while England spent only $9,342 per patient.

spends far less per patient at the end of life – the explanation lies in the fact that the culture and practice of UK end-of-life care emphasize palliation of symptoms rather than intensive treatment.

Looking at the broader population of older patients, the data indicate that nearly 30 percent of Medicare beneficiaries spent time in an ICU in the final month of life,[22] and about 20 percent of all patients were admitted to an ICU near the time of death.[23] One-third of Medicare dollars spent for patients in their last year of life are spent in the final month. Intensive therapies and technologies such as care in an ICU, mechanical ventilation, cardiopulmonary resuscitation, and chemotherapy provided in the final month of life account for nearly 80 percent of these costs.[24] There is certainly a lot of nuanced judgment inherent in a decision to admit (and keep) a terminally ill patient in an ICU. No single factor – the patient's age, overall health status, disease, functional status – offers an easy basis to assess the appropriateness of critical care. Some critical care physicians will refuse to admit patients for whom they believe ICU care cannot provide a benefit. Others will admit patients to the ICU at the request of the family or as the path of least resistance. Even so, health care providers recognize the risks of very intensive treatment, in the form of avoidable suffering and preventable iatrogenic harm,[25] which can hasten death, significantly increase suffering, and reduce quality of life in a patient's final days.

Why all the intensive care in the United States? Part of the explanation has to do with availability of beds: the United States has far more ICU beds per capita compared with other wealthy countries, and hospitals naturally want those beds to 'pay'. Because of inconsistencies in defining what constitutes an ICU bed, statistics come in the form of ranged estimates. The United States has twenty to thirty-one ICU beds per 100,000 people whereas Canada has only thirteen beds per 100,000 and the United Kingdom only three to seven beds per 100,000.[26] In the United States, dying patients, including elderly patients, are far more likely to receive care in an ICU than in other countries, despite the fact that many of these patients have little chance of making a meaningful recovery. In contrast, patients of advanced age and low functional status are often refused ICU admission in other Western countries.[27] This US pattern of routine ICU admission runs contrary to the guidelines of the US Society of Critical Care Medicine, which recommend prioritizing ICU admission for

[22] Joan M. Teno, et al., Change in End-of-Life Care for Medicare Beneficiaries: Site of Death, Place of Care, and Health Care Transitions in 2000, 2005, and 2009, 309 JAMA 470–477 (2013).

[23] Jacqueline M. Kruser et al., Assessment of Variability in End-of-Life Care Delivery in Intensive Care Units in the United States, 2 JAMA Network Open DOI: 10.1001/jamanetworkopen.2019.17344 (2019).

[24] Baohui Zhang et al., Health Care Costs in the Last Week of Life: Associations with End of Life Conversations, 169 Archives Internal Med. 480–484 (2009).

[25] Matthijs Kox & Peter Pikkers , "Less Is More" in Critically Ill Patients: Not Too Intensive, 173 JAMA Internal Med. 1369–1372 (2013).

[26] Meghan Prin & Hannah Wunsch, International Comparisons of Intensive Care: Informing Outcomes and Improving Standards, 18 Curr. Opin. Crit. Care 700–706 (2012).

[27] Paul E. Marik, The Cost of Inappropriate Care at the End of Life: Implications for an Aging Population, 32 Am. J. Hospice & Palliative Med. 703–708 (2015).

patients with reversible medical conditions who have a reasonable chance of recovery rather than admitting all patients with life-threatening illness to an ICU.[28]

There are many other examples of high-intensity, low-value care near the end of life. For example, 25 percent of Medicare beneficiaries have surgery in the final three months of life,[29] and 8 percent in the last week of life.[30] Patients also often receive treatment for nonfatal conditions such as non-melanoma skin cancer without reference to life expectancy.[31] Nursing home patients with advanced dementia are more likely to receive mechanical ventilation when they are transferred to hospitals with higher numbers of ICU beds. There is no evidence that mechanical ventilation benefits these patients, but research suggests that hospitals that have increased their ICU capacity are more likely to provide this intensive intervention to patients who are unlikely to benefit from it.[32] Overall, rates of prolonged mechanical ventilation are increasing despite the fact that patients who require vents to breath have very poor outcomes, if they survive at all.[33]

Rates of late-stage chemotherapy use provide another measure of intensity of treatment at the end of life. One study reported that nearly 39 percent of cancer patients in the United States received chemotherapy in the last 180 days of life, compared with only about 29 percent of patients in Canada. In the last thirty days of life, more than 10 percent of cancer patients in the United States and nearly 9 percent of patients in Canada received chemotherapy.[34] The benefits of chemotherapy for end-stage cancer patients are questionable at best. For many patients with metastatic cancer from solid tumors, chemotherapy after diagnosis can prolong life and improve quality of life by reducing symptoms, but the trade-offs are significant. The toxic effects of chemotherapy – nausea, weakness, vomiting, pain, weight loss, fever, and more – are substantial and these effects routinely require palliative measures. What's more, there is good evidence that chemotherapy at the end of life confers little if any life-prolonging benefit and nearly always reduces quality of life for patients dying from cancer. Chapter 7 explores these matters in more detail.

[28] Joseph L. Nates et al., ICU Admission, Discharge, and Triage Guidelines: A Framework to Enhance Clinical Operations, Development of Institutional Policies, and Further Research, 44 Crit. Care Med. 1553–1602 (2016).

[29] Michael J. Nabozny et al., Constructing High-Stakes Decisions: It's Better to Die Trying, 263 Ann. Surg. 64–70 (2016).

[30] Alvin C. Kwok et al., The Intensity and Variation of Surgical Care at the End of Life: A Retrospective Cohort Study, 378 The Lancet 1408–1413 (2011).

[31] Eleni Linos, Treatment of Nonfatal Conditions at the End of Life: Nonmelanoma Skin Cancer, 173 JAMA Internal Med. 1006–1012 (2013).

[32] Joan M. Teno et al., Association of Increasing Use of Mechanical Ventilation Among Nursing Home Residents with Advanced Dementia and Intensive Care Unit Beds, 176 JAMA Internal Med. 1809–1816 (2016).

[33] Christopher E. Cox et al., Expectations and Outcomes of Prolonged Mechanical Ventilation, 37 Crit. Care Med. 2888–2894 (2009).

[34] Justin E. Bekelman et al., Comparison of Site of Death, Health Care Utilization, and Hospital Expenditures for Patients Dying with Cancer in 7 Developed Countries, 315 JAMA 272–283 (2016) (analyzing data from 2010). England did not report chemotherapy use in the study.

High utilization of care at the end of life for some patients is unsurprising – it makes sense that many dying individuals will require substantially more medical care at this point in their lives than previously. Any presumption that heavy end-of-life spending clearly indicates waste is too facile – the reality is much more complex because, for example, the timing of death is often unpredictable, and of course some patients *do* survive very serious illnesses. About 30 percent of Medicare dollars spent annually go to care for the 5 percent of Medicare beneficiaries who die each year.[35] The problem is that it is difficult to predict prospectively which of all Medicare patients are in fact in their final year of life and which other patients may be seriously ill, utilizing a lot of care, but not dying within a year. Therefore, it is also difficult on a global basis to try to cut waste in the last year of life based on prognosis, given the inherent fallibility of prognostic estimates.[36]

Most patients state that they would prefer to die at home, but in the United States, England, and Canada, many patients die instead in hospital. In Canada, both in-patient and home hospice care are not as widely available as in the United States, which explains why more Canadians die in hospital. One Canadian study found that 45 percent of cancer deaths occur in hospitals (with variation by province and territory), while many of those admitted could have received palliative care in a less acute setting but did not, suggesting an unmet need for community-based services.[37] Overall, nearly 60 percent of Canadians die in hospital.[38] In England, deaths in hospital are trending downward, with about 46 percent of patients dying in hospital.[39] On this measure, at least, it is encouraging to see that in the United States, the trend toward dying at home or in a long-term care facility has continued. For the first time since early in the twentieth century, more Americans now die at home than in hospital – in 2017, more than 30 percent of people in the United States died at home, compared with just fewer

35 Matthew A. Davis et al., Identification of Four Unique Spending Patterns Among Older Adults in the Last Year of Life Challenges Standard Assumptions, 35 Health Aff. 1316–1323 (2016); Amber E. Barnato et al., Trends in Inpatient Treatment Intensity Among Medicare Beneficiaries at the End of Life, 39 Health Services Research 363–375 (2004).

36 Liran Einav et al., Predictive Modeling of U.S. Health Care Spending in Late Life, 360 Science 1462–1465 (2018). The researchers found that Medicare beneficiaries with the highest predicted mortality actually accounted for less than 5 percent of total Medicare spending, and that fewer than 10 percent of Medicare beneficiaries who actually died within the year had a predicted mortality probability of more than 50 percent.

37 Canadian Institute for Health Information, End-of-Life Hospital Care for Cancer Patients (2013). However, the rate of ICU utilization for cancer patients in Canada is relatively low (11 percent) and only about 3 percent of patients receive chemotherapy in their last two weeks of life; most patients admitted to hospitals with late-stage cancer receive only palliative care, but the fact that about one-third of these patients were actually in the hospital for two weeks or longer before death suggests that there would be time to arrange outpatient care prior to death.

38 Statistics Canada, Deaths, by Place of Death (Hospital or Non-Hospital), Table: 13–10-0715–01 (providing data from 2018).

39 Public Health England, Percentage of Deaths that Occur in Hospital (providing data from 2018).

than 30 percent in hospital.[40] This trend suggests that patient preferences to die at home receive more consideration than previously. Still, the US remains the heaviest utilizer of high-intensity care at the end of life among the countries studied.

Patients who wish to die at home and who die instead in hospital (or worse, in an ICU) provide an example of inappropriate care – but even this example is not as straightforward as it might seem. A patient may be admitted to hospital because of unmanageable symptoms and then be unable to get home again due to lack of adequate home hospice care, disagreement among family members, or poor clinical advice and practice. Short of a 'do not hospitalize' order, rigidly enforced, patients who wish to die at home may nevertheless end up dying in hospital. In any event, death at home as a metric of quality of care deserves some scrutiny and skepticism. Dying at home is not an entirely reliable metric of low-intensity care or good symptom management. Patients who die at home may still have spent time in an ICU before death and may have received chemotherapy or other debilitating treatments as outpatients until close to death. Medicare covers home hospice visits, but nothing approaching twenty-four-hour care. Few patients and families can afford to pay for twenty-four-hour home care out of pocket, so much of the burden of actual caregiving, from administering medications to keeping the patient clean, falls on family members. At the very end, this can mean that a spouse is left with the task of dripping liquid morphine into a dying spouse's mouth and worrying that he is perhaps dripping in too much (or not enough). Dying at home also increases the likelihood that the patient will experience an abrupt escalation of unmanageable symptoms that would be more effectively addressed in hospital.[41]

Despite the fact that Medicare patients have relatively reliable access to hospice care (with geographic variations), Medicare data demonstrate that Americans underutilize hospice. Although the use of hospice services has been increasing since the early 2000s, just over half of terminally ill Medicare patients received one day or more of hospice care in 2018. Only about 30 percent of Medicare decedents with cancer and just over 15 percent of those with dementia received hospice care; 40 percent of those in hospice received care for only fourteen days or fewer.[42] A large subset of dying patients utilize hospice, at best, for a comparatively short time. The benefits of hospice care are well documented in the medical literature, but, for a variety of reasons, physicians in the United States tend to avoid recommending hospice until the very end of a dying patient's illness. Chapter 7 returns to this topic in more detail, but it's worth mentioning here that the underutilization of

[40] Sarah H. Cross & Haider J. Warraich, Changes in the Place of Death in the United States, 381 New Eng. J. Med. 2369–2370 (2019). The remainder of people died in nursing facilities, hospice facilities, assisted living facilities, and the like.

[41] Richard Leiter, Is Dying at Home Overrated? N.Y. Times, Sept. 3, 2019, www.nytimes.com.

[42] National Hospice and Palliative Care Organization, Facts and Figures, 2020 Edition (Aug. 2020), www.nhpco.org.

hospice represents one of the unfortunate consequences of our system's default toward high-intensity treatment at the very end of life.

So, we overuse intensive and burdensome medical care in the United States, resulting in preventable harm to patients (not to mention unnecessary spending) and physicians know it. They acknowledge that they are providing unnecessary medical care for a variety of reasons. In one survey of more than 2,000 physicians, the respondents estimated that more than one-fifth of all medical care was unnecessary. A subset of more than a quarter of these respondents put the number much higher – estimating that at least 30 percent to 45 percent of care was unnecessary. When asked why they thought that overtreatment was so prevalent, the most commonly cited reasons were fear of malpractice claims (about 85 percent), patient pressure (59 percent), and difficulty accessing medical records (about 38 percent).[43] This refreshingly candid assessment of causes of unnecessary treatment is a good start – that physicians are aware of the drivers of over-utilization opens the door to discussion of how to mitigate their impact.

Another study of patients in one large academic health care system also suggests that more than one-fifth of medical care provided to critically ill patients is probably 'unnecessary' and therefore potentially inappropriate care. The study defined unnecessary care to include situations in which the burdens of care grossly outweigh the benefits, the patient cannot survive outside an ICU, the patient is permanently unconscious, treatment cannot achieve the patient's goals, or death is imminent.[44] All of these interventions have costs to the patient as well as to the health care system – patients endure iatrogenic harm and physical and emotional suffering from these treatments and technologies, and the system pays the overall economic price. The good news is that the medical and health policy communities are paying more attention to the problem. For the past several years, researchers have published systemic reviews of evidence of overuse of care in a wide variety of contexts and have begun to consider how to respond to the problem.[45] The US health care system is not alone in struggling with this system-wide problem.[46]

The US Institute of Medicine (IOM) 2014 report "Dying in America" makes similar points as the EIU report, with plenty of data to raise concerns about over-utilization of burdensome care at the end of life:[47] physicians are slow to refer

43 Heather Lyu et al., Overtreatment in the United States, 12 PLoS ONE, https://doi.org/10.1371/journal.pone.0181970 (2017).

44 Thanh N. Huynh et al., The Frequency and Cost of Treatment Perceived to Be Futile in Critical Care, 173 JAMA Internal Med. 1887–1894 (2013).

45 Daniel J. Morgan et al., 2019 Update on Medical Overuse: A Review, 179 JAMA Internal Med. 1568–1574 (2019).

46 Shannon Brownlee et al., Evidence for Overuse of Medical Services Around the World, 390 The Lancet 156–168 (2017).

47 Institute of Medicine, Dying in America: Improving Quality and Honoring Individual Preferences Near the End of Life (2014), www.nationalacademies.org/hmd/Reports/2014/Dying-In-America-Improving-Quality-and-Honoring-Individual-Preferences-Near-the-End-of-Life.aspx.

patients for palliative care and hospice, physicians often fail to initiate conversations about end-of-life choices, and they need more training in communication skills. Medicare fee-for-service payment creates perverse incentives to provide inappropriate treatment and services to patients who might not otherwise choose them, putting quality at risk. The IOM report urges more public education about end-of-life care, services, and efforts to try to normalize discussion about death and dying, along with improved integration of patient care to incorporate palliative care earlier in treatment and to encourage a seamless transition to hospice. The report also advocates emphasis on improved communication between physicians and patients about end-of-life options and patient preferences.[48]

The IOM report also notes several encouraging developments in end-of-life care in the United States, including well-established palliative and hospice care education for health care providers and ongoing research to document the benefits of a palliative approach to maximize quality of life for dying patients. Even so, the report concludes that all of this improved knowledge has not resulted in improved patient care: "Of people who indicate end-of-life care preferences, most choose care focused on alleviating pain and suffering. However, because the default model of hospital treatment is acute care, advance planning and medical orders are needed to ensure that these preferences are honored."[49] Numerous studies suggest that most patients prefer to avoid pain and suffering, even at the expense of longer life,[50] but for many patients, this is not how life ends.

Overtreatment of patients at the end of life is widely recognized as problematic in American medical practice, both in the medical literature and among specialist practice groups. Professional initiatives such as "Choosing Wisely" promote physician-patient communication and better clinical decision-making among physicians by emphasizing the need for care that is evidence based and not duplicative, avoids harm, and is truly necessary.[51] Multiple cancer care guidelines developed as part of Choosing Wisely focus on reducing the use of unnecessary tests and treatments and generally avoiding "low-value" cancer care, suggesting that oncologists are very aware of the problematic nature of overutilization of burdensome care for cancer patients.[52] JAMA's "Less is More" initiative publishes research on overuse across a variety of medical specialties, providing evidence-based recommendations to avoid

48 Ibid.

49 Ibid.

50 Alfred F. Connors et al., A Controlled Trial to Improve Care for Seriously Ill Hospitalized Patients: The Study to Understand Prognoses and Preferences for Outcomes and Risks of Treatments (SUPPORT), 274 JAMA 1591–1598 (1995); Emily B. Rubin et al., Seriously Ill Patients' Willingness to Trade Survival Time to Avoid High Treatment Intensity at the End of Life, 180 JAMA Internal Med. 907–909 (2020).

51 Choosing Wisely, www.choosingwisely.org.

52 Alison S. Baskin et al., Scope and Characteristics of Choosing Wisely in Cancer Care Recommendations, 6 JAMA Oncology 1463–1465 (2020).

waste and iatrogenesis in medical care.[53] Unfortunately, the pattern of overuse of burdensome care for dying patients in the US continues largely unabated.

WHAT IS THE GOAL AND HOW MIGHT WE GET THERE?

Now that we've waded through all of that preliminary data, it's useful to take a step back and ask how the very subjective experience of dying and the quality of that experience can be reduced to objective, measurable criteria. What does 'quality' end-of-life care actually mean? Is more care better or, to the contrary, is dying a situation in which less is almost always more? Empirical (and anecdotal) evidence suggests that, usually, less is more, but it is not appropriate to assume that this is the answer for all patients. As Chapter 3 will explain, our autonomy-based system of informed choice generally allows patients to request and receive any and all care to prolong life, as long as it has *some* potential for clinical effectiveness.

The data on utilization of care for the dying in the United States suggest a significant misalignment between the type and quantity of care provided and the wishes of the average patient. Overall, there is a system-wide tendency to provide a substantial amount of care that is not medically appropriate or consistent with what patients would choose if they were fully informed and able to comprehend the known downside risks compared with the potential upside benefit of late-stage therapeutic interventions and life-prolonging technologies. Many dying patients receive at least some medical care that confers no benefit (not even life extension) and instead increases suffering. These well-documented trends, along with surveys of physicians, indicate that a substantial number of physicians keep mum and knowingly provide medical interventions that they know or suspect will not benefit patients. It is indisputable that our current medical system is geared toward the provision of more treatments and life-prolonging technology, even for dying patients, rather than de-escalation of care. Unfortunately, patients frequently lack the necessary information to judge whether and when they should opt for de-escalation because physicians and patients often fail to have timely, honest conversations about the reality of the patient's medical situation and appropriate end-of-life options.

The difficult question is how much of all of this end-of-life care is appropriate in an effort to prolong life and at what point should the focus turn from prolonging life (at all cost – to the patient and the system) to ensuring a 'good death'. The answer to this question, as with all complex questions, is "it depends" – on the medical situation that each patient faces and on each patient's individual preferences. Looking at statistical averages and trends doesn't answer the bigger question – to what extent do *individual* patients receive care for terminal illness that actually aligns with their individual preferences? Much of the discussion that follows

53 JAMA, Less is More, https://jamanetwork.com/collections/44045/less-is-more.

contains generalizations about end-of-life care and decision-making, but the reality is not so monolithic. Patients' age, race, insurance status, state of residence, and idiosyncratic preferences all impact the way that they access medical care, how they are perceived by health care providers, and how they experience care at the end of life. The reality is that these factors only begin to explain why end-of-life communication so often fails to help patients achieve their ideal of a good death. Overall, 'the system' and its participants – physicians, patients, hospitals, insurers, plus the influence of culture and the overarching fear of death – often prevent patients from making informed, authentic-to-themselves decisions about treatment and care for terminal illness.

Finally, patients with life-threatening illness are frequently asked to make complex, high-stakes medical decisions while struggling with the added impact of anxiety, low health literacy, and family pressures. On top of these fundamental barriers to good communication and decision-making, the inherent clinical uncertainty in matters such as prognosis and future treatment efficacy often causes patients (and their physicians) to default to high-intensity treatment. Together with various aspects of clinical uncertainty (discussed in detail in Chapter 8), the cognitive biases of both patients and physicians make it extremely challenging for seriously ill patients to process and comprehend the risks and benefits of, and alternatives to, whatever therapeutic or life-prolonging treatments physicians are offering. And that's only when the physician and patient have actually engaged in some substantive discussion and evaluation of choices. These additional aspects of decision-making impact both physicians and patients, and they render the classic goal of informed consent unachievable in all but the rarest of circumstances.

The chapters that follow will explore the various drivers of unnecessary, inappropriate, and unwanted medical care more systematically and will consider ways to mitigate their impact. To be clear, the goal is twofold: to understand how to improve communication in ways that will help patients avoid medical care that provides no quantitative (life-prolonging) benefit and that will often come with a high cost of avoidable suffering and to promote care that reduces suffering and improves quality of life at the end. These twin goals generally serve the interests of all patients, including those who make informed decisions to request all interventions to prolong life. The discussion that follows will return, again and again, to physician-patient communication, how to make it better, and why it will rarely approach anything like the ideal of perfectly informed decision-making. It is nearly impossible individually and clearly impossible at a system-wide level to make perfect in-advance decisions, given the various manifestations of uncertainty. In this context, the book includes discussion of why, from a cognitive perspective, patients and their physicians struggle to say "no" to unnecessary care. It sounds like a bit of a grim picture, but there is cause for optimism for those patients who are willing to fully engage with impending death – not necessarily to accept death but to give a nod to its certainty, to know when to say "enough."

2

The US Health Care 'System'

The Good, the Bad, and the Probably Unfixable

America's health care system is neither healthy, caring, nor a system.

—Walter Cronkite (1916 – 2009)

Health care finance and delivery systems in all of their wonderful complexity exert a significant but often hidden impact on the practice of medicine, including end-of-life care. The US health care finance and delivery system is highly disjunctive and disorganized. In fact, calling it a 'system' suggests a level of organization, coordination, and working toward a common purpose that simply doesn't exist in US health care. Understanding what is going on with end-of-life care in the United States, on both the patient end and the provider side requires a basic grasp of our system of access to health care, payment for care, and regulation of the practice of medicine. The significantly different health care systems in Canada and the United Kingdom (which actually deserve to be called 'systems') here serve as comparative foils for the US approach. The dense and descriptive content of this chapter provides essential context for an understanding of how and why physicians and patients in the United States often make suboptimal decisions in the face of life-threatening illness.

Two fundamental orbits of the health care system deserve consideration. First, payment and insurance systems wield a substantial and far from salutary influence on health care access and utilization. Unlike other economically prosperous countries that ensure universal access to health care, the United States has a profusion of federal and state insurance programs, along with many, many private insurers, that complicate both access to care and the financing of health care. Patients who do not have reliable access to health care are less likely to receive high-quality end-of-life care. Second, federal and state law governing the practice of medicine and patients' rights also impacts care for seriously ill patients. Much of the relevant law governing end-of-life care originates in state legislatures and courts and varies in important respects from one state to another. The highly decentralized finance and delivery of health care together with the diffuse structure of health care regulation makes top-down federal reforms to health care very challenging to implement. Any reforms designed to improve care for patients with life-threatening illness face the immediate barrier of attempting to conquer a radically fragmented health care system.

HEALTH INSURANCE AND PAYMENT – THE US 'SYSTEM'

Recall from Chapter 1 that the United States spends the most as a percentage of its GDP on health care compared with other high-wealth nations. Yet, even with all of this spending, many people lack access to health care. President Barack Obama's Patient Protection and Affordable Care Act (ACA), modeled on a state program from Massachusetts, sought to extend health coverage to uninsured individuals and to make the purchase of insurance by individuals more affordable, yet, as of this writing, we still have a large number of uninsured residents in the United States. Just before the ACA went into effect at the end of 2010, more than 16 percent of US residents (49.9 million) had no health insurance. By 2016, five years in, the ACA had resulted in historic lows in uninsured people, with 10 percent of Americans aged 18–64 lacking insurance, and a total uninsured rate of 8.6 percent for all Americans, but the trend from there has been less encouraging. By 2018, 10.4 percent of individuals who were not yet eligible for Medicare were uninsured, an uptick of almost half a million people compared with 2017. This lost ground resulted in large part from the Trump administration's decisions to quietly remove information about ACA enrollment from government websites and to eliminate the tax penalty for failing to comply with the so-called individual mandate – the requirement that everyone who was not otherwise covered under government or employer-sponsored health insurance purchase insurance coverage. Even so, we now have more insured individuals than prior to 2010 when implementation of the ACA began. Overall, the ACA has led to significant increases in both public and private insurance coverage, with almost 20 million more people insured.[1] But these relatively improved levels of coverage pale in comparison with other wealthy countries in which nearly all residents enjoy the benefit of access to affordable health care. In addition, unlike the systems in Canada and the United Kingdom most Americans have some cost-sharing and out-of-pocket expenditures even if they are insured (and *a lot* of cost sharing if they are in a high-deductible plan), although the amount and type of these costs vary.[2]

Substantial state-to-state disparities in health insurance coverage still exist, despite the positive impact of the ACA. Before the ACA's enactment in 2010, Massachusetts was the only state to mandate insurance for all of its citizens – and to provide the requisite financial subsidies to help lower-income residents afford to purchase health insurance as individuals if they otherwise lacked access to coverage.[3] At one

[1] Kaiser Family Foundation, Jennifer Tolbert et al., Key Facts About the Uninsured Population (2019), www.kff.org.

[2] The Commonwealth Fund, The US Health Care System, https://international.commonwealthfund.org/countries/united_states/.

[3] New Jersey and New York City have since joined the ranks of states and cities that provide support for universal health insurance coverage. New Jersey Health Insurance Market Preservation Act, https://nj

point pre-ACA, nearly 99 percent of Massachusetts residents not yet eligible for Medicare were covered through a combination of employer-sponsored coverage, individual plans under compulsory purchase rules ('the individual mandate'), and an expanded Medicaid program. This (by US standards) astonishing rate of coverage was accomplished via state legislation under then-Governor Mitt Romney. As the 2012 Republican nominee for president, Romney later faced attacks from conservatives for this supposedly 'liberal' program. The most recent numbers show Massachusetts with the lowest percentage of residents lacking insurance, compared with Texas with the highest uninsured population.[4] Even Texas has made gains – prior to the implementation of the ACA, nearly one-quarter of Texas residents (including many children) lacked health insurance of any kind, but Texas still ranks last in the country for rates of insurance.[5] Although the ACA has helped reduce coverage disparities from state to state, wide variations in insurance coverage remain.

During the Trump administration, the Republican-controlled Congress did not manage to repeal the ACA[6] but did enact a series of incremental changes to reduce the Act's efficacy, by eliminating some subsidies for states that have expanded their Medicaid programs under the ACA, permitting the sale of so-called skinny plans (with bare bones coverage), and diluting protections for patients with preexisting conditions (which is nearly everyone). The efforts to kneecap the ACA partially succeeded – the number of people who lack health insurance coverage once again is increasing and premium costs are rising substantially in many states.[7] In November 2020, just after the national election, the Supreme Court heard argument on yet another challenge to the ACA, which claims that the individual mandate provision cannot be severed from the rest of the legislation and that the entire Act is therefore constitutionally invalid. In late 2019, a federal appeals court panel ruled that the ACA's individual mandate is unconstitutional, since Congress had removed the tax penalty.[8] The oral argument took place one week after the presidential election and the case enjoyed the enthusiastic support of the Republican Party, which still seeks to repeal the ACA despite its popularity with Americans.[9] The

.gov/treasury/njhealthinsurancemandate/index.shtml; Susan Jaffee, NYC Guarantees Health Care to All, 393 The Lancet e3–e4, Jan. 26, 2019.

4 US Census Bureau, Katherine Keisler-Starkey & Lisa N. Bunch, Health Insurance Coverage in the United States (2019), www.census.gov.

5 Ibid.

6 National Federation of Independent Business v. Sebelius, 567 US 519 (2012). The Court upheld the individual mandate to buy insurance enforced by a tax penalty by a vote of 5–4, based on Congress's taxing power. In 2017, Republicans eliminated the tax penalty that enforced the individual mandate.

7 The 2019 coverage data show a continuous drop in coverage over the first three years that the forty-fifth president was in office. US Census Bureau, Health Insurance Coverage in the United States: 2019, www.census.gov/library/publications/2020/demo/p60-271.html.

8 Texas v. US, 945 F3d 355 (5th Cir. 2019).

9 California v. Texas (argued November 10, 2020).

Supreme Court once again declined to invalidate the Act, though on the narrowest of procedural grounds.[10]

SOURCES OF HEALTH INSURANCE COVERAGE

Most people with private insurance receive it as an employee benefit.[11] Employers purchase insurance for an employee group and pay some of the cost while employees have pretax income deducted as a contribution to the cost. However, most employment in the United States is 'at will', meaning that employment can end at any time and, with it, insurance coverage for employees and their dependents (although they may purchase insurance through a separate federal program that allows for up to eighteen months of additional coverage, for a steep price).[12] What's more, employment-based health insurance is not mandatory, and many employers opt not to provide health insurance as an employee benefit, particularly for hourly-wage and part-time workers.[13] While individuals have the option to purchase insurance directly through an ACA marketplace, they may pay higher premiums than those covered by employer group plans since employers usually contribute some (often a significant portion) of the premium costs for covered employees. All of these variables add up to a sense of precarity that's quite at odds with the whole idea of insurance. The loss of jobs due to the impact of the COVID-19 pandemic illustrates this point – many people with employer-sponsored health insurance have seen this insurance benefit disappear (for themselves and their dependents) along with their source of income.

A number of federal insurance programs also cover various populations. First, the federal Medicaid program is a jointly funded and administered federal/state program that covers those with lower incomes and the "medically needy," a term that is defined differently in various states. It is a social safety net program in which eligibility is based primarily on economic need and coverage goes to very low-income individuals and their children and people with certain disabilities. While state programs are subject to federal oversight in terms of eligibility, funding, and benefits, there is wide variation from state to state as to who qualifies for Medicaid and what services and benefits are covered. Medicaid tends to be far more generous in coverage in politically liberal states than in conservative states, and the failure of

10 *California* v. *Texas*, slip op. No. 19–840. Argued November 10, 2020 – Decided June 17, 2021, together with No. 19–1019, *Texas et al.* v. *California et al.*

11 Congressional Research Service, US Health Care Coverage and Spending, Mar. 21, 2019, https://crsreports.congress.gov/product/pdf/IF/IF10830.

12 COBRA Coverage and the Marketplace, www.healthcare.gov/unemployed/cobra-coverage/.

13 The ACA requires that employers with fifty or more full-time employees either provide insurance or participate in the Employer Shared Responsibility Payment (ESRP) assessment process, but smaller employers still have no obligation to offer subsidized insurance to their employees. Internal Revenue Service, Employer Shared Responsibility Provisions, www.irs.gov/affordable-care-act/employers/employer-shared-responsibility-provisions.

some politically conservative states to accept the Medicaid expansion option under the ACA further exacerbates these disparities in state Medicaid coverage.[14] Additional federal programs, including the Children's Health Insurance Program (CHIP) that was added in 1997 to supplement Medicaid, the Veterans' Affairs Tricare Program, and the Indian Health Service, provide government-subsidized coverage to particular subpopulations.

In addition to these programs, the United States has Medicare, a federal entitlement program that covers all legal US residents (who have resided in the United States for at least five years) aged 65 and older and insures more than 17 percent of the entire population. Because much of the published research concerning end-of-life care relies on Medicare data records and because most people who die have reached the age of Medicare eligibility, a good deal of the discussion that follows about how health care finance influences end-of-life communication and decision-making will rely on Medicare-based data. For now, a few general points about Medicare are worth noting. Medicare includes hospital insurance (Part A), Supplemental Medical Insurance (Part B), and pharmaceutical benefits (Part D), along with coinsurance purchased by eligible program beneficiaries. Part A is funded primarily through payroll taxes, while Part B is available to those who enroll and pay a Part B premium, which is supplemented with tax funding. Part C, now called "Medicare Advantage," allows beneficiaries to elect an alternative program delivered by managed care organizations (mostly health maintenance organizations) instead of traditional Part A and B Medicare. Most people who elect traditional Medicare also purchase a 'gap' policy from a private insurer to cover what would otherwise be unreimbursed deductibles and co-payments under Medicare. For people with lower incomes, a gap policy may be unaffordable, leaving them at risk of financial instability or bankruptcy in the case of a severe illness.

HEALTH CARE PAYMENT, INCENTIVES FOR OVERUTILIZATION, AND QUALITY OF CARE

Payment systems may influence whether and how often physicians order particular tests, treatments, and procedures for their patients. There is a well-documented trend to provide medically unnecessary care in circumstances where doing so will increase revenue for health care institutions or individual physicians.[15] The Medicare fee-for-service (FFS) reimbursement model is a substantial driver of these problems: it encourages overuse of care by paying physicians more when they provide more treatments, procedures, and tests. FFS reimbursement increases

[14] Larisa Antonisse et al., The Effects of Medicaid Expansion Under the ACA: Updated Findings from a Literature Review (2019), www.kff.org/medicaid.

[15] Heike Hennig-Schmidt et al., How Payment Systems Affect Physicians' Provision Behaviour – An Experimental Investigation, 30 J. Health Economics 637–646 (2011) (finding that physicians provided more services with fee-for-service incentives).

costs, leads to fragmented and duplicative care, and causes harm to patients. Physicians are, of course, also influenced by other factors such as organizational structures, professional culture, and the medical needs of patients.[16] Chapter 6 explores the many influences on physician behavior and their impact on end-of-life communication and care.

Medicare – a single-payer system that can negotiate steep discounts with its clinical providers – pays for many types of services on a prospective payment model. It generally reimburses hospitals on the basis of diagnosis-related group (DRG) payment categories. The Centers for Medicare and Medicaid Services (CMS) administers the program and determines what fees it will pay for each DRG, based on the intensity of services required for a particular group of patients with a particular diagnosis. The DRG payment calculation process is quite complex, but, for purposes of this discussion, the basic concept will suffice. Physicians caring for Medicare patients are reimbursed based on a system called the resource-based relative value scale (RVS), in which points are assigned based on the time and intensity of the physician's services, plus consideration of medical practice expenses and malpractice insurance expenses. This RVS scale is then used to calculate a fee schedule for physician payment. The more productive the physician is in terms of patient load and procedures, the more she is paid under RVS reimbursement.[17] Although the RVS system contains costs at one level by paying physicians a nonnegotiable fee, it does little to reduce the volume of services physicians provide – physicians can increase their income by providing more services at the RVS rate.

The US Medicare program has begun a partial transition from fee-for-service payment, including (among other strategies) a system of penalties for poor quality of care and rewards for high-quality care. On the penalty side, the CMS penalizes hospitals for readmissions within thirty days of initial hospitalizations (often the result of inadequate coordination of care).[18] CMS has also implemented a Value-Based Purchasing Program for hospitals that adjusts payments to hospitals up or down based on the hospital's overall performance score, which is calculated by outcome measures and patient satisfaction.[19] While patient satisfaction is important, it can be a double-edged sword. Physicians sometimes feel pressure to give patients what they want to improve ratings and bring increased reimbursement. If what a patient wants is timely communication and high-quality care, there is no problem; however, when a patient demands a treatment, test, or procedure that is not medically necessary or appropriate, the physician may risk sacrificing quality to earn a good patient rating. Both the penalty system and the Value-Based Purchasing

[16] Christopher Robinson et al., Effect of Financial Relationships on the Behaviors of Health Care Professionals: A Review of the Evidence, 40 J. L. Med. & Ethics 452–466 (2012).

[17] Barry R. Furrow et al., Health Law §§ 8–12, 8–13 (3rd ed. West 2015).

[18] CMS, Hospital Readmissions Reduction Program (HRRP), www.cms.gov/Medicare/Medicare-Fee-for-Service-Payment/AcuteInpatientPPS/Readmissions-Reduction-Program.

[19] CMS, Hospital Value-Based Purchasing, www.cms.gov/Medicare/Quality-Initiatives-Patient-Assessment-Instruments/Value-Based-Programs/HVBP/Hospital-Value-Based-Purchasing.

Program adjust payments to hospitals for acute care for the entire hospital, rather than only for those conditions used to calculate the metrics on which the penalties and program are based.[20] Medicare Accountable Care Organizations (ACOs), through which physicians and hospitals coordinate care to avoid duplicative and unnecessary care (and share in the savings when they succeed) also show promise in reducing spending while maintaining quality.[21] The Merit-Based Incentive Payment System (MIPS) rewards physicians by tying payments to care that is both high quality and cost efficient.[22] The problem with MIPS is that it adds extra administrative requirements on top of the existing FFS system. While the results of these first efforts are mixed, the government, as the country's largest health care payer, is finally making links between quality of care and reimbursement methods, understanding that the older FFS model incentivized overutilization of care, including at the end of life. Although the ACA set a goal to move 90 percent of Medicare's payment into value-based models, there is as yet limited evidence that the changes in reimbursement structure have improved quality of care or reduced utilization of unnecessary care.

While concerns about FFS payment models have gained the attention of academics and policy makers, individual physicians are still frequently reimbursed on a fee-for-service model with its consequent incentives to order tests, treatments, and procedures that are not medically necessary.[23] The fate of experimental reimbursement reforms that promote quality over quantity remains unclear. So, it's difficult to predict whether reduction of FFS payments will make much of a difference in the context of treating life-threatening and terminal illness. End-of-life care is delivered on an ad hoc, as needed (or requested) basis. Terminally ill patients who land in the hospital or the ICU can receive a wide array of tests and interventions, as well as consultations from multiple specialists, along with life-prolonging technologies such as ventilation and dialysis. These sorts of fragmented and diverse treatments cannot easily be reimbursed on a 'bundled' payment basis in the way that a targeted cardiac surgery or a total joint replacement is now often reimbursed. There is, however, a continuing effort to implement value-based payment programs and other sorts of global payment structures that pay for quality rather than volume of services.[24]

[20] J. Brian Cassel et al., The Business Case for Palliative Care: Translating Research into Program Development in the US, 50 J. Pain & Symptom Management 741–749 (2015) (explaining that these penalty and purchase programs are part of the substantial shift toward paying for quality versus quantity and noting that by the end of 2018, half of Medicare payments would be calculated based on quality or value).

[21] CMS, Next Generation Accountable Care Organization (NGACO) Model: Evaluation of First Two Performance Years (2016–2017), https://innovation.cms.gov/innovation-models/next-generation-aco-model.

[22] CMS, Merit-Based Incentive Payment System, https://qpp.cms.gov/mips/overview.

[23] Samuel H. Zuvekas & Joel W. Cohen, Fee-For-Service, While Much Maligned, Remains the Dominant Payment Method for Physician Visits, 35 Health Aff. 411–414 (2016).

[24] Kenton J. Johnston, Building a Better Clinician Value-Based Payment Program in Medicare, 325 JAMA 129–130 (2021).

HEALTH CARE ACCESS AND PAYMENT – THE CANADIAN SYSTEM

Systems matter in health care. A brief consideration of health care systems in Canada and the United Kingdom serves as a useful comparator and provides the basis for later discussion about their relative influence on quality and quantity of care for seriously ill and dying patients. Unlike the United States, both the United Kingdom and Canada have systems in place to make health insurance and health care available to all residents. To be sure, these systems have their flaws and struggles – perfect systems of human organization do not exist – but they generally succeed in providing access to a basic package of health care benefits for all.

The United States and Canada share a border, but there are stark differences in the two countries' health care systems. A country's approach to health care access speaks volumes about its cultural attitudes toward egalitarian care and collective responsibility for the health of all residents. In Canada, a national health insurance program provides universal coverage for all legal residents and is funded with general tax revenue. The system is called "Medicare" but, unlike US Medicare, the term refers to the universal coverage system for residents of all ages. The Canadian federal government sets and administers national standards for the health care system through the Canada Health Act of 1984, and it provides funding. The early steps in the momentous move to a federal-provincial partnership in the provision of health care occurred in the 1960s. Reflecting the underlying accord to provide health care across the country, the 1984 legislation adopted five principles of operation: universality of coverage by the provinces for services by hospitals and physicians, portability to other provinces and countries, reasonable accessibility to services free of barriers (such as co-payments), comprehensive services, and public administration of the program.[25]

The Medicare program is a form of single-payer insurance, but each of the thirteen provinces' and territories' plans vary. In effect, each province is a single purchaser of medical services for its residents. Under the Canada Health Act, each province administers its own plan and must provide comprehensive coverage to all residents. Although private insurance coverage for services covered under provincial plans is illegal, most Canadians purchase private supplementary insurance to cover items and services (such as prescription drugs and dental care) that are not covered under the provincial plans. By making the purchase of private insurance for services covered by Medicare illegal, the Canadian government built in a bulwark against the potential for system fragmentation and inequality of health care based on wealth. Although many other inequalities remain in the system, the ban of full-coverage private health insurance at least prevents the development of a satellite private-pay system of potentially superior care for those with higher incomes.

Fees are set via periodic negotiations between provincial ministries of health and provincial medical associations. The Canada Health Act also bans balance billing,

[25] Canada Health Act, https://laws-lois.justice.gc.ca/eng/acts/c-6/page-1.html.

meaning that physicians cannot bill patients directly for a fee that exceeds the negotiated fee.[26] Canada pays for hospital care on a global lump-sum payment basis, while physicians themselves are primarily independent contractors, and about three-quarters of their contracts use a fee-for-service payment model.[27] Canadians pay virtually no co-payments and have their choice of primary care physicians, although (as in the United States) there may be long wait times to get a space in a particular physician's practice.[28]

While universal access to care exists in theory, Canadians often have to wait for nonemergency care due to shortages of technology and personnel in certain specialties. Canada puts significant resources into primary care, but the availability of high-technology diagnostic equipment such as CT and MRI devices is suboptimal. Waiting times for key procedures such as hip replacement, cataract surgery, and cardiovascular surgery are long, and physicians and patients recognize that the waiting time for some procedures is unreasonable.[29] Despite these problems, life expectancy in Canada exceeds that in the United States, with men living on average to age 79.9 and women to 84.1,[30] compared with 76.2 and 81.2 for men and women respectively in the United States.[31] In general, some of the most expensive medical conditions to treat are chronic conditions – diabetes, cardiovascular diseases, chronic lung disease, and the like – so a health care system that places its emphasis and resources on primary care and disease management is making a good investment.[32]

The Canadian system is attentive to both quality and cost-effectiveness. Canadian physicians must furnish data to the Canadian Institute for Health Information, an independent, government-financed organization that collects health data from all provinces and territories to promote excellence in clinical decision-making and to avoid waste in the form of unnecessary or duplicative treatment.[33] Health Canada, the federal governmental department that is responsible for public health, publishes information on all topics of health, including Medicare, public health, food safety, prescription drugs, and more, and provides centralized funding and meta-level

26 Goran Ridic et al., Comparisons of Health Care Systems in the United States, Germany, and Canada, 24 Materia Socio Medica 112–120 (2012).

27 Canadian Institute for Health Information, Physicians in Canada, www.cihi.ca/en/physicians-in-canada.

28 Sara Allin & David Rudoler, The Canadian Health Care System, Commonwealth Fund, https://international.commonwealthfund.org/countries/canada/.

29 Goran Ridic et al., Comparisons of Health Care Systems in the United States, Germany, and Canada, 24 Materia Socio Medica 112–120 (2012).

30 Statistics Canada, Life Tables, 2016-18, https://www.statcan.gc.ca/en/start. Canada calculates life expectancy using the three most recent years' data to avoid annual random data fluctuations.

31 Centers for Disease Control and Prevention, NCHS Data Brief, No. 355 (January 2020), https://www.cdc.gov/nchs/data/databriefs/db355-h.pdf.

32 Joseph L. Dieleman et al., US Spending on Personal Health Care and Public Health, 1996–2013, 316 JAMA 2627-2646 (2016).

33 Canadian Institute for Health Information, www.cihi.ca/en.

administration of all health-related activities in Canada. While the Canadian system is far from perfect, it is commendable in its ability to provide universal coverage for primary and specialist care and to contribute to significantly longer life expectancies.

HEALTH CARE ACCESS AND PAYMENT – THE NATIONAL HEALTH SERVICE IN THE UNITED KINGDOM

In the United Kingdom, the government directly funds health care for all citizens and legal residents through a single system financed almost entirely by taxes and contributions to the National Insurance system, a payroll tax program akin to Social Security in the United States. The UK's National Health Service (NHS) was founded in 1948 and is a pure 'socialized medicine' system, in the sense that the UK government not only funds all care but also directly delivers health care services via the NHS. Coverage is broad and largely free at the point of service, but there are significant exceptions – for dental care, some eye care, eyeglasses, and a standard prescription drug co-payment, for example. The NHS is divided into four segments – England (the largest of the NHS administrative groups), Wales, Scotland, and Northern Ireland. General practitioner (GP) physicians are paid via a mixture of capitation (a fixed fee per patient for care over a given period of time) to cover basic services and fee-for-service payments for additional services. The capitation rate per patient reflects patient age, gender, local population health characteristics, and other factors. Some GPs are employed in practices or as locums (filling a position temporarily) and receive salaries. Most specialists work as salaried employees at NHS hospitals and are also permitted to work in private practice at private hospitals. Only about 10 percent of Britons buy private health insurance with the remainder receiving care from the NHS. Private insurance allows patients better access to non-NHS care, especially for elective medical procedures, but it usually does not cover mental health, maternity care, emergency care, and general practice, so even those with private insurance will usually receive a substantial portion of their care from the NHS.[34]

Although the NHS is another imperfect health care system (particularly as it has been systematically underfunded by the Tories during Britain's still-in-effect austerity measures adopted in the aftermath of the 2008 financial crisis)[35] and concerns about rationing and patient safety abound, the system and relevant regulatory bodies take quality and safety seriously. The Care Quality Commission (CQC) monitors the NHS for compliance with basic safety standards and seeks to ensure quality of

[34] Ruth Thorlby & Sandeepa Arora, The English Health Care System, Commonwealth Fund, https://international.commonwealthfund.org/countries/england/.

[35] There are ongoing efforts to address funding challenges confronting the NHS. The NHS's "Five Year Forward" process models different tax-funding approaches to ensure adequate and accessible care for all covered individuals. www.england.nhs.uk/five-year-forward-view/next-steps-on-the-nhs-five-year-forward-view/funding-and-efficiency/.

care. All health care providers (institutional and individual) must register with the CQC and must abide by "fundamental standards" of quality.[36] In addition, the National Institute for Health and Care Excellence (NICE), which operates in England and Wales, develops guidelines for quality health care practices and clinical pathways to care for patients with particular conditions, and these guidelines include systems for collecting and evaluating outcomes data.[37]

Culturally, the British strongly support the NHS and point to it as one of the UK's great achievements, but critics point out that there are weaknesses.[38] For one thing, access to medical care for all of a country's residents does not guarantee good health. The effects of other forms of social inequality (substandard housing, nutrition, education, etc.) can negate the benefits of equitable access to care.[39] One of the many roles of NICE is to assess the cost-effectiveness of certain treatments and medicines, and this process has generated controversy in the United Kingdom – as it likely would in the United States. While both cost-effectiveness assessments and clinical pathways have the potential to improve care for the dying in the United States, the more explicit rationing inherent in these processes would likely be unwelcome to many US patients who are accustomed to having many expensive but potentially ineffective therapies covered, at least if they have generous employer-sponsored coverage and once they age into Medicare.

Since systems matter, it's important to note that, overall, people in the UK are the most satisfied with their health system's performance, affordability of care, effectiveness of care, and their regular doctor. More than 61 percent of UK survey respondents believe that the system works well and needs only minor fixes, compared with about 34 percent in Canada and only about 29 percent in the United States. More than 25 percent of respondents in the United States believe that the US system needs to be rebuilt completely, compared with about 10 percent of Canadians and just 3 percent of UK respondents.[40] Although this is only one survey, its conclusions seem consistent with public sentiment in general about these health care systems, as reflected in news articles, political debate, and my own research on-site in all three countries. Another survey a few years later also concluded that 63 percent of the public was satisfied with the NHS overall, and 72 percent expressed satisfaction with

36 Ruth Thorlby & Sandeepa Arora, The English Health Care System, Commonwealth Fund, https://international.commonwealthfund.org/countries/england/.

37 National Institute for Health and Care Excellence, What We Do, www.nice.org.uk/about/what-we-do.

38 Nicholas Timmins, Healthcare for Everyone: The Trials and Tribulations of the NHS Model, 366 Brit. Med. J. 15645 (September 2019).

39 A recent study concluded that one-third of premature deaths in England are linked to social inequality not related to timely and adequate access to medical care. Dan Lewer et al., Premature Mortality Attributable to Socioeconomic Inequality in England Between 2003 and 2018: An Observational Study, 5 Lancet Pub. Health e33–e41 (2020).

40 Irene Papanicolas et al., An Analysis of Survey Data from Eleven Countries Finds That "Satisfaction" with Health System Performance Means Many Things, 32 Health Aff. 734–742 (2013).

GP services.[41] The level of satisfaction dropped a bit, to 57 percent in 2018, driven mainly by concerns about staffing and funding.[42] As one expert in health law explained, "Our NHS is engrained into the political and social establishment of the UK. It is probably the most important public institution in the UK and the most politically sensitive. All governments have a deep reverence for it as part of the national character and culture."[43]

HEALTH CARE AS A RIGHT

Access to health care is indisputably one important constituent piece of life, liberty, and the security of the person. In every other high-wealth country, access to health care for all residents is considered to be the responsibility of an equitable society, not a privilege for the financially fortunate. The role of government in ensuring this access is not seriously questioned. Many commentators have argued that access to health care is a fundamental element of a just society,[44] and that it is part of the pantheon of universal human rights.[45] By contrast, in the United States, health insurance prior to age 65 is a consumer good, available to some but not to others. Patients behave as consumers, including shopping around for the 'best' physician or treatment center when they have the means to do so, and a long-standing ethos of personal responsibility for health acts as a counterforce to changes that would result in access to health care (including high-quality care at the end of life) for all. Some people take the position that they should have no responsibility for the health care costs of others. There are two competing attitudes toward the concept of insurance. The distributive justice theory of insurance holds that insurance is intended to spread risk over a large, heterogeneous population, varied with respect to both health and wealth, so that some who are more fortunate inevitably subsidize others who are less fortunate. The fortunate insured who enjoy good health pay premiums into the insurance pool from which the less fortunate, less healthy insured draw resources. Given that continued health is far from certain, the fortunate insured also acknowledge that they or their dependents can at any time become the less fortunate ones in need of access to health care. If we compare this vision with the actuarial fairness model of insurance, we see a very different picture. In this model, insurance is a means of spreading risk as actually *experienced* by individuals, or by smaller,

[41] Ruth Robertson, Public Satisfaction with the NHS and Social Care in 2016, www.kingsfund.org.uk/sites/default/files/media/BSA_final_Kings_Fund_Mar_2017.pdf.

[42] Ruth Robertson, Public Satisfaction with the NHS and Social Care in 2017: Results and Trends from the British Social Attitudes Survey, www.nuffieldtrust.org.uk/research/public-satisfaction-with-the-nhs-and-social-care-in-2017.

[43] John Tingle, Lecturer in Law, Birmingham University, via email (June 11, 2020).

[44] Wendy K. Mariner, Toward an Architecture of Health Law, 35 Am. J. L. & Med. 67–87 (2009).

[45] Joseph C. d'Oronzio, A Human Right to Healthcare Access: Returning to the Origins of the Patients' Rights Movement, 10 Cambridge Q. Healthcare Ethics 285–298 (2001).

homogenous groups over a length of time, so that each insured over his or her lifetime only pays for the risks he or she is most likely to incur individually.[46]

The distributive justice way of thinking about insurance provides the underlying rationale for the universal coverage insurance programs in many countries – the idea that those who are more fortunate must not only pay to minimize personal risk but also help the less fortunate. Yes, the healthy among us pay for insurance coverage that we don't use or use only minimally, while the sick on average use way more health care than their individual premiums pay for. Yet, we who are healthy are the lucky ones, right? Of course, that luck could run out at any moment. We could also think about this approach as the 'golden rule' model of insurance – do unto others as you would have them do unto you. It all comes down to culture: the philosophy of individual responsibility has, at least until now, remained more popular in the United States than the idea of group responsibility for the less fortunate.[47] It's worth noting though that when the vast majority of us become the less fortunate late in life and in end-of-life situations, we then happily enjoy the benefits of the universal entitlement system called Medicare. In the United States, our current system suggests that we want the best health care and as much of it as possible, while paying as little for it as possible in the form of premiums and taxes, even if it means that some 'other people' will go without decent access to health care.

On top of this attitudinal problem, the US system is held hostage by a small but powerful group of elites who collectively spend billions of dollars annually to control – via lobbying, campaign contributions, and corporate executive positions – whether and how health reform happens.[48] Unlike in the United Kingdom and Canada, the system of insurance and consequent access to health care in the United States is heavily influenced by private market concentration, allowing a few players to control prices in a distinctly profit-driven, unnecessarily complex, and heavily fragmented health care system. It is no wonder that prices continue to rise and that the less fortunate among us struggle to remain insured or to obtain and afford any insurance at all.

This personal responsibility attitude comes with enormous cost. As with most everything in American life, the availability of health care and the treatment of serious illness reflect a culture riddled with divisions between those who are fortunate in financial and physical health and those who are not.[49] There are two worlds of health and medical care – one for low-income, uninsured (and underinsured) patients and another for well-off, better-educated, well-insured, and

46 Deborah A. Stone, The Struggle for the Soul of Health Insurance, 18 J. Health Politics, Pol'y & L. 287–317 (1993).

47 Erin C. Fuse Brown et al., Social Solidarity in Health Care, American-Style, 48 J. L. Med. & Ethics (2020).

48 Olivier J. Wouters, Lobbying Expenditures and Campaign Contributions by the Pharmaceutical and Health Product Industry in the United States, 1999–2018, 180 JAMA Internal Med. 688–697 (2020).

49 Donald M. Berwick, The Moral Determinants of Health, 324 JAMA 225–226 (June 12, 2020).

medically connected patients.[50] Worse still, there is a well-documented correlation between poverty and ill health,[51] making it more likely that those most in need of medical care are least able to access or afford it. Prior to Medicare eligibility, the type and quality of a person's insurance coverage may dictate whether a seriously ill patient has access to a recommended treatment, to good palliative care, or to hospice. For uninsured patients, the safety net is almost nonexistent. In the United States, wide variations in insurance coverage, along with variable financial means to make up the gap between covered and uncovered medical costs, means that the 'green screen' – the ability to pay – functions as a barrier to optimal care for many patients. Patients who worry about high medical bills frequently delay seeking necessary medical care. By the time people in the United States age into Medicare eligibility at 65, those who spent much of their lives with minimal access to health care (a disproportionate number of whom never reach eligibility age) may be unable to reap the full benefits of health care coverage – preventive care and proper management of chronic conditions comes too late. Even Medicare beneficiaries can face unreimbursed charges and surprise medical bills, high prescription drug costs, and more. About two-thirds of personal bankruptcy filings in the United States are the result of medical issues – either situations where patients were unable to pay medical bills or became bankrupt due to lost income because of illness.[52]

Health equity between White patients and Black and Latinx patients remains elusive. The correlation between minority race and lower income means that people of color are less likely to be insured prior to Medicare age, and simultaneously live with more risks to health (for example, inadequate housing, unsafe drinking water, and similar indicia of systemic inequality and racism). On top of this, for many years, empirical evidence has demonstrated that race adversely affects the quantum and quality of health care provided to minority patients.[53] There is irrefutable evidence of racial bias in health care delivery.[54] Despite more focused attention by government, public health experts, and health policy experts,[55] there is little evidence of progress toward equity in overall health.[56] Structural racism and racist policies have

[50] Duraldo D. Brooks, et al., Medical Apartheid: An American Perspective, 266 JAMA 2746-2749 (1991).

[51] Michael Marmot, The Health Gap: The Challenge of an Unequal World, 386 The Lancet 2442–2444 (2015).

[52] David U. Himmelstein et al., Medical Bankruptcy: Still Common Despite the Affordable Care Act, 109 Am. J. Public Health 431–433 (2019). The study estimates that 530,000 families file for bankruptcy each year for reasons related to medical care and bills.

[53] Marian E. Gornick et al., Effects of Race and Income on Mortality and Use of Services Among Medicare Beneficiaries, 335 New Eng. J. Med. 791–799 (1996).

[54] M. Gregg Bloche, Race and Discretion in American Medicine, 1 Yale J. Health Pol'y L. & Ethics 95–131 (2001).

[55] Institute of Medicine, Unequal Treatment: Confronting Racial and Ethnic Disparities in Health Care (2002), https://pubmed.ncbi.nlm.nih.gov/25032386/.

[56] Frederick J. Zimmerman & Nathaniel W. Anderson, Trends in Health Equity in the United States by Race/Ethnicity, Sex, and Income, 1993–2017, 2 JAMA Network Open 1-10 (2019).

perpetuated racial disparities in access to care, in how health care is delivered, and in health outcomes that persist two decades into the twenty-first century.[57]

INFORMED CONSENT AND END-OF-LIFE LAW IN THE UNITED STATES

In addition to our multiplayer, public/private insurance system (which still leaves many people without even basic coverage), a potpourri of state and federal laws govern medical practice, quality, liability, payment, and patients' rights. A brief overview of these laws in the United States, Canada, and the United Kingdom provides a basis for later, more detailed discussion about how well law works to promote quality end-of-life care and to support complex medical decision-making. The United States, the United Kingdom, and Canada are all common law systems, meaning that both legislation and court decisions provide sources of law. The United Kingdom is a unitary law system (with some devolved legal administration in Northern Ireland, Scotland, and Wales), while Canada and the United States are federations, in which the provinces/territories and states, respectively, regulate the practice of medicine and end-of-life decision-making.

Each of the fifty US states has implemented its own statutes addressing health care, sometimes causing confusion and conflict. Physicians are licensed by states through their individual boards of medicine, and these state boards exert control over practice standards, physician discipline, and even various aspects of drug prescribing. For example, recent attention to opioid prescribing and its role in increasing rates of addiction to prescription and illegal drugs has led to varying state restrictions on prescribing and requirements to track physicians and pharmacies to reduce over-prescription of opioids and other addictive drugs. Access to proper opioid medications is obviously a matter of serious concern for very ill patients, particularly those suffering from cancer, and it is crucial to strike a proper regulatory balance.

In the United States, the right of patients with decisional capacity to make treatment decisions is well established in both common law judicial opinions and as codified in many state statutes. Broader constitutional values of liberty and privacy also reinforce the right of autonomy and self-determination in medical care. The ethical principle of patient autonomy is protected by the law of informed consent. Patients have a right of both informed consent and informed refusal, including to refuse care that would otherwise prevent the patient's death. Chapter 3 will discuss these matters in more detail.

State laws impact end-of-life care and communication in other significant ways. For example, in the context of end-of-life care for patients who have lost decisional

57 Zinzi D. Bailey et al., How Structural Racism Works – Racist Policies as a Root Cause of US Racial Health Inequities, 384 New Eng. J. Med. 768–773 (2020).

capacity, standards of proof required to withdraw or withhold life-sustaining treatment from incapacitated patients also vary by state. All states require the highest standard of civil proof – clear and convincing evidence – but the implementation of this standard varies. Some states, such as Missouri and Michigan, require clear and convincing evidence that the patient would refuse the precise life-supportive measure being used or contemplated under the precise medical conditions in which he finds himself. In these states, only a detailed written advance directive or well-documented and detailed conversations with a physician or surrogate decision-maker will satisfy the evidentiary standard. In the absence of such proof, the patient will continue to receive the life-prolonging care in question and, sometimes, additional proffered care. In other states, the law requires clear and convincing evidence that the patient, based on her values and preferences, would refuse proffered treatment or would discontinue ongoing treatment. In many states, a statutory hierarchy of decision-makers for the incapacitated patient, usually the spouse first, followed by the majority of adult children, can use a 'substituted judgment' process to express their understanding of what the patient would choose but must satisfy the particular state's standard of proof on this question (if there is a dispute that requires court resolution). Many state laws also allow patients to formally appoint a health care agent to make decisions. Chapters 9 and 10 discuss end-of-life decision-making for incapacitated patients in more detail.

As a further example of the variety and more than occasional incoherence of American end-of-life law, many but not all states have legal requirements for advance directives to be considered valid. Some states do not explicitly require a particular form but recognize duly executed forms from other states. Other states refuse to recognize out-of-state forms. Physicians generally are protected from liability if they follow a patient's wishes in an advance directive but are not legally required to do so. Some states, such as Massachusetts, focus on the formal appointment of health care decision-making agents rather than requiring particular advance directive forms. A number of states are in the process of implementing some statutory version of Physician Orders for Life Sustaining Treatment (known as the POLST paradigm) in which patients and health care providers document care preferences with respect to the use of life-prolonging technology. These documents become part of the patient's formal medical record. A few states also require that physicians provide patients and families with information about rights and options regarding end-of-life care. Chapter 9 also explores the limitations of advance care planning to improve the care of dying patients.

Although the law governing medical treatment and decision-making is mostly left to the states, the federal Patient Self-Determination Act, enacted in 1990, requires that most hospitals, nursing homes, and certain other health care institutions provide patients with information about advance directives and their right to make treatment decisions, including the right to refuse unwanted medical treatment. It also requires that facilities educate clinicians and others about these rights. Critics and skeptics have noted the Act's very limited effectiveness in accomplishing its goals.[58] Finally, the US Supreme Court has made a couple of forays into end-of-life jurisprudence, via decisions in the *Cruzan* case (discussed in Chapter 5) and a pair of companion cases related to medical aid in dying.[59]

INFORMED CONSENT AND END-OF-LIFE LAW IN CANADA

In Canada, the law similarly protects the right of patients with decisional capacity to make choices about their medical care, including end-of-life care. As in the United States, the right of informed refusal includes the right to refuse treatments even when withdrawal or withholding of treatment will result in the patient's death from underlying conditions.[60] The Canadian Charter of Rights and Freedoms also recognizes the Canadian people's interests in liberty and security of the person,[61] and this provision has been interpreted by Canadian courts to include bodily integrity as implicated in medical treatment decisions.[62]

Most Canadian law dealing with end-of-life matters derives from common law court decisions. Notable exceptions include Quebec's Civil Code,[63] which separately recognizes certain relevant rights via statutory provisions. Several provinces, such as Ontario[64] and British Columbia,[65] have also comprehensively addressed matters of informed consent via statute. In addition, most of the provinces and territories have enacted legislation specifying requirements for surrogate decision-making and advance directives, including health care directives, powers of attorney for personal care, and similar documents.[66] As in the US, Canadians may set out in advance their preferences for care at the end of life, should they lose the ability to make decisions themselves, and they may appoint a person to serve as a surrogate decision-maker to make these decisions.[67] Finally, provincial and territorial statutes have delegated the regulation of physician practice in Canada to professional

58 US Government Accountability Office, GAO-95-135, Patient Self-Determination Act: Providers Offer Information on Advance Directives But Effectiveness Uncertain (1995), www.gao.gov/assets/hehs-95-135.pdf.

59 Washington v. Glucksberg, 521 US 702 (1997); Vacco v. Quill, 521 US 793 (1997).

60 Jocelyn Downie et al., eds., Canadian Health Law and Policy 387–389 (4th ed. LexisNexis Canada 2011).

61 Constitution Act 1982, §7 ("Everyone has the right to life, liberty and security of the person and the right not to be deprived thereof except in accordance with the principles of fundamental justice.").

62 Fleming v. Reid, O.J. No. 1083, 4 O.R. (3d) 74 (Ontario C.A.) (1991).

63 Quebec Civil Code, §§ 10–11 recognizes the concept of bodily integrity and informed consent, providing in part that "No one may be made to undergo care of any nature, whether for examination, specimen taking, removal of tissue, treatment or any other act, except with his consent. Except as otherwise provided by law, the consent is subject to no other formal requirement and may be withdrawn at any time, even verbally."

64 Ontario Health Care Consent Act 1996, www.ontario.ca/laws/statute/96h02.

65 British Columbia Health Care (Consent) and Care Facility (Admission) Act, www.bclaws.ca/EPLibraries/bclaws_new/document/ID/freeside/00_96181_01.

66 Downie et al., eds., Canadian Health Law and Policy, 188–189.

67 Ibid., 394–395.

organizations. The provincial and territorial laws govern matters such as who may practice medicine within the province or territory, conflicts of interest in the practice of medicine, and the quality of health services.

Overall, the law governing end-of-life care and informed consent in Canada is less of a morass than that in the United States, but differences between provinces and territories abound. While the fragmentation of health care delivery and regulation poses challenges to system-wide improvement, Canada is willing to consider federal statutory requirements in certain circumstances, often while leaving details of implementation to the provinces. The recent national legalization of Medical Aid in Dying (MAiD) and the inclusion of voluntary euthanasia within the meaning of that term reflect a political and legal system that is both structurally capable of sweeping change and culturally willing to, first, adopt public positions and debate compromises and, second, accept and implement change, with appropriate caution.

INFORMED CONSENT AND END-OF-LIFE LAW IN THE UNITED KINGDOM

As in the United States and Canada, patients in the United Kingdom have a right of self-determination and autonomy in medical decision-making that is protected both by Article 8 of the European Convention on Human Rights and as adopted by the United Kingdom in its Human Rights Act of 1998.[68] However, the legal system and its impact on medical practice in the United Kingdom differs significantly from that of the United States. Instead of a state-by-state patchwork of statutes and common law opinions, there is a fairly unified approach to end-of-life decision-making in England, Wales, and Northern Ireland, and substantively similar standards in Scotland (though with variations in required procedures). Although no legislation directly regulates end-of-life care, aspects of the Mental Capacity Act of 2005 (as revised and updated in 2019) apply in England and Wales, and are relevant to patients who have lost decisional capacity.[69] The Health Act of 2006 regulates, among other things, accountability in the management and prescription of controlled drugs.[70] In addition, the Human Rights Act of 1998 contains provisions that have been interpreted by courts as relevant to the right of human dignity and the right to die.[71] These statutes aside, the vast majority of end-of-life law in the United Kingdom comes from common law precedent, while guidance documents provide additional guardrails for the practice of medicine in the United Kingdom. The General Medical Council, the NHS, and NICE have all developed and published

68 Human Rights Act (1998), www.legislation.gov.uk/ukpga/1998/42/contents.

69 Mental Capacity Act 2005, www.legislation.gov.uk/ukpga/2005/9/contents; Mental Capacity (Amendment) Act 2019, www.legislation.gov.uk/ukpga/2019/18/enacted.

70 Health Act 2006, www.legislation.gov.uk/ukpga/2006/28/contents.

71 Human Rights Act 1998, www.legislation.gov.uk/ukpga/1998/42/contents.

numerous practice guidelines. In 2008, the Department of Health in England adopted a systematic ten-year plan to improve the quality of end-of-life care.[72]

Patients with decisional capacity have the right to make treatment decisions, including a right of informed consent and of informed refusal of care. Rather than being codified via statute, these rights are protected via court precedents in tort law, specifically via claims of battery and negligence.[73] Under current English law, the physician retains the ultimate authority to make treatment decisions for incapacitated adults rather than the patient's family,[74] a very different model than in the United States. Even the courts do not dictate what happens except to the extent of pronouncing on the lawfulness of the treatment that the physician proposes.[75] However, the authority of the physician is limited: the physician must do what is in the patient's best interests.[76] Courts have interpreted 'best interests' to include not only medical interests but also the patient's own wishes, values, and preferences prior to loss of decisional capacity. So the concept of best interests in England includes explicit elements of concern for the patient's autonomous preferences. The Mental Capacity Act and accompanying guidance documents also include relevant provisions that require doctors to act in the best interests of incapacitated patients.[77] The discussion that follows will return to the concepts of patient autonomy and of best interests – ethical principles that guide medical care in the United States as well – but with different mechanisms of implementation and mixed results.

ASSESSING THE POSSIBILITY OF FUTURE REFORM

The US health care system presents many obstacles to the delivery of high-quality care for seriously ill and dying patients, and the complex and decentralized structure of health care finance and delivery makes efficient reform very challenging. Top-down solutions do not appear to be an option, at least not without the cooperation of warring political factions willing to put aside their differences and agree to act from a sense of goodwill to improve the lot of all of their constituents. State-by-state variation of law that directly impacts end-of-life care also presents a structural obstacle to national reform with uniform rules. There are many moving parts to address – for example, the various federal insurance programs and, at last count, 952 private health insurance companies operating in the United States.[78] Realistically,

72 Department of Health, End of Life Care Strategy: Promoting High Quality Care for All Adults at the End of Life (2008), https://www.gov.uk/government/publications/end-of-life-care-strategy-promoting-high-quality-care-for-adults-at-the-end-of-their-life.

73 Jonathan Herring, Medical Law and Ethics 152 (7th ed. Oxford University Press 2018).

74 Ibid., 154; Dominic Bell, The Legal Framework for End of Life Care: A United Kingdom Perspective, 33 Intensive Care Med. 158–162 (2007).

75 Bell, The Legal Framework for End of Life Care.

76 *Re* A., *1 FLR* 549 (2000).

77 Mental Capacity Act 2005, as amended, §4, www.legislation.gov.uk/ukpga/2005/9/contents.

78 Insurance Information Institute, Facts and Statistics: Industry Overview, www.iii.org.

as later discussion in this book will illustrate, rational health care system optimization at the federal level is difficult to imagine given the politicization of health insurance, access to care, and other health care matters and the broader impact of political and cultural polarization in this country. Nevertheless, there are ways to improve end-of-life communication and decision-making for individual patients that render these broader structural challenges somewhat less relevant.

Although this chapter provides a broad sketch of the different approaches to access to health care and the protection of patient rights, the discussion going forward will focus on those aspects of health care systems that directly influence end-of-life communication and decision-making. Portions of what follows will consider approaches to end-of-life care in the United States in comparison with the UK, particularly England,[79] and with Canada, countries with notable cultural differences and consequentially different structural approaches to medical practice and health care delivery. In both England and Canada, residents have access to health care via universal entitlement programs, funded and administered by the government using tax revenue, but this book is not about whether universal health care per se improves end-of-life decision-making and care. Rather, the question is whether societies that are sufficiently willing to consider the needs of the collective (rather than focusing solely on individual needs and wants) are better able to support individual physicians and patients in the quest for high-quality end-of-life care. There is much to learn from these two countries, though the functionality of their respective health care systems is, as with any human system, far from perfect. These universal health care programs operate in societies in which cultural norms, the role of physician and patient, and related matters create opportunities for improved care but also trigger concerns about respect for individual preferences and about cost-efficient utilization of scarce resources. Overall, the evidence suggests that the English system in particular performs very well in care for the dying – though whether this high quality results from external influences like the NHS or from individual physician and patient willingness to confront death and make good end-of-life choices (or the confluence of both) is less obvious.

[79] Although the NHS operates throughout the United Kingdom, laws that are relevant to end-of-life care and decision-making vary among England, Wales, Scotland, and Northern Ireland. For reasons of expediency, much of the discussion ahead focuses on the law in England.

3

Autonomy and Informed Consent in the Real World

The risk of a wrong decision is preferable to the terror of indecision.

– Maimonides

The twentieth century ushered in a dazzling array of modern medical technologies including many effective new treatments for disease and novel preventative therapies that have helped extend the average lifespan dramatically. From penicillin and polio vaccines to statins to immunotherapies and robotic surgery, we enjoy the benefits of science and medicine. While life expectancy at birth in the United States in 1900 was just over 47 years,[1] we now live, on average for 78.7 years.[2] Thirty-plus years of additional life bring all of the pleasures of longer life but also more deaths from cancer (primarily a disease of old age), heart disease, and other forms of illness and frailty. Despite this notably longer span of life, however, people in the United States experience high levels of disease and disability in their later years – comparable with those who reside in much poorer countries.[3] At the same time, modern life-sustaining technologies such as dialysis, mechanical ventilation, implantable cardiac devices, and artificial nutrition also can prolong life when normal bodily functions fail.[4] All of these medical treatments and technologies can save or at least prolong our already lengthened lives, but they also present added decisional dilemmas for seriously ill patients, their families, and their physicians.

[1] Centers for Disease Control and Prevention, Life Expectancy at Birth, at 65 Years of Age, and at 75 Years of Age, www.cdc.gov/nchs/data/hus/2010/022.pdf.

[2] Centers for Disease Control and Prevention, Fast Stats – Life Expectancy, www.cdc.gov/nchs/fastats/life-expectancy.htm.

[3] Collin F. Payne, Aging in the Americas: Disability-free Life Expectancy among Adults Aged 65 and Older in the United States, Costa Rica, Mexico, and Puerto Rico, 73 J. Gerontol. B. Psychol. Sci. Soc. Sci. 337–348 (2018).

[4] Life-sustaining medical technology, particularly ventilators, also created a need for the law to define "death" for various legal and medical purposes (homicide, estates and trusts law, organ harvesting, and more). Report of the Ad Hoc Committee of the Harvard Medical School to Examine the Definition of Brain Death, 205 JAMA 85–88 (1968).

The resulting complex medical decisions and the more than occasional conflicts that surround them in turn have triggered a need for legal regulation of and intervention in end-of-life decision-making. When there is a disagreement about a medical decision (between patients, families, and physicians), the law has a limited role to play. In addition to informed consent law, other aspects of law define who should be making decisions for patients who cannot decide for themselves – more about that in Chapter 9, which considers the added complexities of surrogate decision-making. The law also may become relevant in those unfortunate cases where controversy about a patient's care leads to litigation, a topic for exploration in Chapter 5 via consideration of three cases from the United States, the United Kingdom, and Canada.

PATHWAYS TO DEATH AND DECISIONAL OPPORTUNITIES

At the risk of stating the obvious, not all deaths are alike. While each death is, in its own way, unique, there are various scenarios, and identifying them is useful to frame discussion about end-of-life communication and decision-making. We can and should prepare emotionally for death in whatever form it arrives, but there are variables – including foreseeability, abruptness, and the degree of clinical and prognostic uncertainty – that require different things of us. At one level of course, all deaths are foreseeable, but the foreseeability of a particular type of death inversely correlates with the amount of opportunity to prepare for it in some way.

At one end of the death scenario spectrum is sudden and unforeseen death – from an accident, a stroke, or a ruptured aneurysm, for example. Here, no decisions need to be made except, perhaps, regarding the formal declaration of death (if the patient is on 'life support' – a misnomer in these cases) and organ donation, and the only common practical preparation is in-advance funeral planning. Next along the spectrum are deaths that are abrupt but foreseeable – such as death during surgery, a final stroke after a series of previous strokes, or a fatal arrhythmia after years of heart problems. In this scenario, preparation for a foreseeable but not immediately expected death might include discussions with physicians and family about patient preferences and completion of advance care planning documents. However, as in the first scenario, once the patient is declared legally and medically dead, there is little more to discuss and decide. Next, there is highly foreseeable but non-abrupt death from a diagnosed terminal illness – the inexorable and predictable death from pancreatic cancer, for example, or the relentless progression of neurological diseases like amyotrophic lateral sclerosis (ALS). Then there are deaths from diseases, such as certain types of cancer, that are sometimes curable and sometimes not – prolonged situations in which clinical and prognostic uncertainty occupy a large amount of emotional and intellectual bandwidth in decision-making. Finally, there is death due to entropy – the progressive frailty of old age or dementia – a kind of death that is foreseeable but far less predictable in its course as the body (and sometimes the mind) gradually winds down. It is primarily in these last three scenarios that patients are presented with both time and options that often involve difficult choices regarding therapeutic treatment and life-sustaining technologies. It is also in these last three scenarios that patients are most directly tasked with the hard work of acknowledging approaching death while making complex medical decisions.

Simple consent by a patient with decisional capacity to a straightforward procedure is radically different from decisions about end-of-life care. When an otherwise healthy patient is asked to make an informed decision to consent to, for example, a surgical procedure to remove an inflamed appendix, the surgeon will describe the purpose of the surgery, its risks and benefits, and alternatives to the procedure, if any, and the patient then will sign a consent form indicating a willingness to undergo the surgery. Post-surgery, the patient will return to his former life and no longer be a patient. By contrast, when patients are presented with complex information about prognosis, treatment efficacy, and comparative harms and benefits, they must make difficult choices and simultaneously cope with the emotional and physical distress that comes with news of a life-threatening diagnosis – and the end of living a 'non-patient' life.

There are two broad categories of end-of-life decisions. First, patients diagnosed with life-threatening conditions must make multiple decisions along the pathway of progressive disease about which treatments to pursue. Sometimes, only one therapeutic approach is appropriate, so the choice is simply treatment or no treatment (although this decision can still present serious complexities). More often, there are multiple avenues of treatment, each with its own probabilities of potential harms and benefits, and the patient must try to comprehend and weigh complex and novel medical concepts before deciding which path to take. Choosing one path often excludes the pursuit of others, adding to the patient's sense of disorientation and uncertainty in what is already a high-stakes situation. As part of this process, patients also may have to think about how to respond should the disease worsen or the side effects of therapy become intolerable. Second, at some point, it may become apparent that cure is not an option and that death is approaching. At this point, the focus switches from decisions about therapeutic care to the question of how to achieve a 'good death' (not as an outcome but as a process). What constitutes a good death surely means different things to different people but has some elements in common, such as avoiding physical suffering. Other qualities of a good death include dying in a chosen place of death (often in the familiar environment of home), maintaining independence and control, maintaining dignity, having someone present, and having a sense of closure or spiritual peace.[5]

Good communication also ranks high among concerns of dying patients and their families. When asked what is most important to them at the end of life, one group of patients ranked pain management as most important, followed by spiritual peace,

[5] Sarah Hales et al., The Quality of Dying and Death, 168 Archives Internal Med. 912–918 (2008).

presence of family, being mentally aware, and having their treatment choices followed.[6] This last factor requires, of course, that physicians and patients can effectively communicate and discuss the question of treatment choices, arrive at 'good' decisions (more about what 'good' means in this context later), and see these choices through. Another study of comments from focus groups asked patients who had survived time in an ICU, these patients' family members, and family members of patients who had died in an ICU, to describe 'high-quality' palliative care. The overwhelming emphasis of the comments from all three groups centered on communication, in particular timely, jargon-free, honest, and compassionate communication about what was happening with the patient. These interviewees also emphasized the importance of coordination of communication, complained about hearing inconsistent information from different physicians, and hoped for complete enough information to be able to make meaningful decisions about care. Some patients and families had good experiences in this regard; others did not. Overall, patients and families wanted truthful information about the medical situation, conveyed with sensitivity. All interviewees also emphasized the importance of pain management and attention to the dignity and humanity of the patient.[7] When asked, seriously ill patients and their families are well able to articulate what is important in delivering high-quality end-of-life care.

None of these decisions happen in a vacuum, nor should they. Decisions about therapeutic care, life-sustaining care, and palliative care all require the expert guidance of treating physicians, making the quality and timing of communication between physician and patient critical. Good decision-making matters (and not only at the end of life). Medical care that doesn't align with patient preferences has serious costs that extend well beyond medical bills. Patients can suffer harm in the form of avoidable, often debilitating side effects and suffering when they receive unwanted medical care. But to avoid this harm, patients must specifically say "no" to proffered care, and this is rarely easy. The surviving-versus-thriving balance, the idea of some perfect equipoise of prolonging life with meaningful quality, is the highest-stakes calculus (with accompanying decisions) that many of us will ever make. That ideal balance will differ among patients, making the physician's communication task multilayered and driven by a totality of factors that move way beyond clinical benefits and harms. The conversation ideally must cover not only the medically appropriate options and their respective harms, benefits, and alternatives but also discussion of what the patient is seeking to achieve – or willing to endure. On top of all of this emotional, existential, and technical complexity, the inherent and unavoidable uncertainty in these decisions threatens many patients with a kind of

6 Karen E. Steinhauser et al., Factors Considered Important at the End of Life by Patients, Family, Physicians, and Other Care Providers, 284 JAMA 2476–2482 (2000).

7 Judith E. Nelson et al., In Their Own Words: Patients and Families Define High-Quality Palliative Care in the Intensive Care Unit, 38 Critical Care Med. 808–818 (2010).

decisional overload and paralysis. That paralysis, where it comes from, and what to do about it is the subject of Chapter 8.

Timely, honest, and humane communication between physicians and patients and families can result in improved quality of life for dying patients, and a reduction in unwanted and inappropriate medical care. Care that comports with patient preferences and goals can include the entire range of options from reducing high-burden treatment with an emphasis on comfort care to providing all life-prolonging care in cases where the patient's goal is maximal life extension. Unfortunately, there are many internal, emotional, and cognitive barriers to these sorts of conversations, along with external (systemic) pressures on physicians to avoid them and instead provide highly invasive medical care to dying patients. Physician-patient communication and informed consent as it would function in a perfect world don't reflect the reality of end-of-life care, which is rather less than ideal in many instances. A more detailed understanding of what is happening – and not happening – between physicians and patients as they make complex medical decisions will illustrate the high stakes for patients in the form of missed opportunities to prepare for death and to avoid unwanted and burdensome medical interventions in their final weeks and days.

AUTONOMY AND BENEFICENCE: TWO FINE WORDS IN SEARCH OF MEANING

In the United States, according to legal and ethical principles, medical care should accord with the individual patient's preferences, and this includes a well-established common law right to refuse therapeutic care and life-prolonging technologies, even when it will result in earlier death.[8] Patient autonomy, as implemented via the legal doctrine of informed consent, is the primary ethical principle that governs medical decisions,[9] including those made on behalf of patients who have lost the ability to make decisions for themselves. The rejection of old-school paternalism in favor of patient autonomy is now well accepted in the medical community, though in practice, subtle but powerful exercises of paternalism are still at work, particularly in the sharing of information with patients.[10] Until recently, although it was accepted that patients could and should make decisions about medical care as part of their right of self-determination, physicians remained as gatekeepers to the patient's information about prognosis and therapeutic efficacy, and therefore also to access to medical treatment. Now, however, in the age of the Internet and 'Dr. Google', patients have more information than ever before. As physicians

[8] Bartling v. Superior Ct., 163 Cal.App.3d 186 (1984); Bouvia v. Superior Ct., 179 Cal.App.3d 1127 (1986); Barry R. Furrow et al., Health Law §16–3 (3rd ed. West 2015).

[9] "Every human being of adult years and sound mind has a right to determine what shall be done with his own body." Schloendorff v. Society of New York Hospital, 105 N.E. 92, 93 (1914).

[10] There are good arguments for placing some limits on individual autonomy. Alexander McCall Smith, Beyond Autonomy, 14 J. Contemp. Health L. & Pol'y 23–39 (1997).

attempt to guide patient care in a way that serves patients' values and goals, they retain an obligation of professional agency – that is, a duty to ensure that treatments, tests, and life-prolonging technologies that patients receive are in fact medically appropriate.[11] Chapter 6 will explain how physicians face multiple external pressures to provide care that they know, or at least suspect, is not in the best interests of their patients.

There certainly is value in assessing whether the cost of medical care for individuals or groups of patients is an efficient use of health care dollars, and also whether the medical interventions are likely to accomplish the goal of extending life or improving the patient's quality of life. Both of these measures are objective standards, at least in theory, but the ethical value of patient autonomy requires a separate inquiry into whether proposed treatment is consistent with the patient's preferences. This is a subjective measure in which the quality of medical care is evaluated according to its consistency with the individual patient's values, preferences, and goals. Patient autonomy as a high ideal sounds great, but one of the biggest challenges to getting the medical decision-making process 'right' is to actually identify the patient's values and preferences as they relate to the medical situation at hand, and to use them as guideposts for treatment recommendations and an overall collaborative and robust decision-making process. This inquiry requires time, skill, and diligence in conversation with the patient. It also requires that the physician accurately tell the patient what is happening (diagnosis and prognosis), and what decisions are needed, so that the patient understands what she has heard, can think about her situation in the context of her values, and the conversation continues as the patient's situation evolves. There is a good amount of evidence that some or all of this doesn't happen for many seriously ill patients.

In ideal circumstances, patients can express their preferences directly to their physicians, based on their own values and goals as applied to the medical decision on the table. As long as a patient retains decisional capacity, the their choice may be objectively irrational, unreasonable, or unwise, but the autonomy principle mostly protects these choices. There are some exceptions to this general rule, some limits and boundaries to patient autonomy. Physicians have no obligation to provide medical care that simply cannot physiologically accomplish its desired goal or to provide care that does not comport with accepted medical practices.[12] Physicians may also refuse to provide requested care (such as medical aid in dying) if they object on the basis of conscience,[13] and this includes, in most states, conscience-based refusals to comply with the advance directive of a patient who has lost decisional capacity.[14] These

11 Madison K. Kilbride & Steven Joffe, The New Age of Patient Autonomy: Implications for the Physician-Patient Relationship, 320 JAMA 1973–1974 (2018).

12 Furrow et al., Health Law §16–55.

13 Ibid. § 16–63.

14 Thaddeus M. Pope, Legal Briefing, Conscience Clauses and Conscientious Refusal, 21 J. Clinical Ethics 163–80 (2010).

exceptions aside, patients can request any and all medically appropriate care and (subject to insurance coverage or ability to pay) can receive it.

Various public figures have announced their individual preferences and goals with respect to the end of life, and it's instructive to look at a range of thinking on this very personal and subjective question. In 2014, Brittany Maynard, a 29-year-old woman with a fast-growing and inevitably fatal brain tumor, spoke out about the lack of a medical aid in dying (MAiD) option in her home state of California – and moved to Oregon to obtain this life-ending assistance in order to avoid the severe suffering associated with the last stages of her illness.[15] Her dignified advocacy for a pragmatic option to avoid suffering at the very end of life drew attention to the question of MAiD around the country and later led to the passage of a law permitting MAiD in California. The late radio and television host Larry King, who had publicly railed against the prospect of death, sought to extend his life for as long as possible. In a colorful interview, the then 81-year-old King described the various measures he took to stave off aging and acknowledged that he finds his own death unimaginable. As King explained, "I can't get my head around one minute being there and another minute absent." He also wished aloud to attend (or maybe just observe from above?) his own funeral, musing that "I would like the ceremony to begin, 'Today we are honoring a 160-year-old man who was caught in bed by an irate husband.'"[16] Ezekiel Emanuel, an eminent oncologist and bioethicist, has expressed yet another preference – to live a reasonably long life but to die before the usual disabilities of age overwhelm his functionality and ability to contribute to the world. Emanuel persuasively critiques the American desire for immortality, but his personal vision of dying while still relatively in his prime dismisses the possibility of enjoying life at a very old age:

> Living too long is also a loss. It renders many of us, if not disabled, then faltering and declining, a state that may not be worse than death but is nonetheless deprived. . . . It transforms how people experience us, relate to us, and, most important, remember us. We are no longer remembered as vibrant and engaged but as feeble, ineffectual, even pathetic.[17]

All three of these individuals described their individual preferences, as is their right – to avoid suffering by curtailing the dying process; to live as long as possible no matter what the physical or psychic cost; to die at the optimal time, navigating the narrow

15 George F. Will, Affirming a Right to Die with Dignity, Wash. Post (Aug. 28, 2015), www.washingtonpost.com/opinions/distinctions-in-end-of-life-decisions/2015/08/28/b34b8f6a-4ce7-11e5-902f-39e9219e574b_story.html.

16 Mark Leibovich, Larry King Is Preparing for the Final Cancellation, N.Y. Times Mag. (Aug. 26, 2015), www.nytimes.com/2015/08/30/magazine/larry-king-is-preparing-for-the-final-cancellation.html. Mr. King did not get his wish. He died in January 2021 of COVID at the age of 87.

17 Ezekiel Emanuel, Why I Hope to Die at 75, *The Atlantic* (Oct. 2014), www.theatlantic.com/magazine/archive/2014/10/why-i-hope-to-die-at-75/379329/.

gap between premature and 'too late' death. And yet, these three approaches to mortality also share a common theme: the desire to exert control over that which ultimately cannot be controlled – a desire for dominion over death (and the way that one is remembered) that is often fundamentally at odds with the frequently unpredictable and uncontrollable reality of dying.

To evaluate whether individual patients are receiving care that is consistent with their preferences, physicians have to consider the patient's level of understanding about the medical interventions she accepts (or rejects), not just the expected medical outcomes of those decisions. In other words, in the US system, the patient calls the shots, even if the patient's choice among reasonable clinical options is not what the physician would recommend (or choose for herself).[18] However, given the wide knowledge gap and resulting information asymmetry between highly trained physicians and the average patient, the patient depends on the physician to provide relevant information about the options. Without that information, presented in a way that the patient can understand and that allows the patient to discriminate among options and choose a 'best' option, consent to treatment is a hollow exercise of autonomy – a signature on a page that documents cooperation and assent, but not real understanding of what the patient is signing up for. All of this then begs the question – when do patient's expressed preferences actually represent their well-considered wishes? Do patients truly know what is best for them? Can terminally ill patients ever know what's best without the benefit of hindsight, which is never available to them? In many situations, this fundamental lack of predictability – the unavoidable reality of clinical uncertainty – makes patient preferences as a guiding principle something of a mirage. Nevertheless, autonomy is what we've got – it's the bedrock of our modern health care decision-making process.

Despite the emphasis in the United States on the principle of autonomy, US law also includes references to and consideration of the principle of beneficence. The ethical principle of beneficence, which operates alongside the primary principle of autonomy, requires that physicians provide only that care that is in their patient's best interests – medically and otherwise.[19] Many state laws acknowledge a place for best interests analysis in making treatment decisions for incapacitated patients.[20] If the patient is unwilling or unable to make decisions about her medical care, and no information is available about the patient's wishes, and no surrogate decision-maker is available, the physician is obligated to act in the patient's best interests. The ethical principle of beneficence has two sides to it – an affirmative fiduciary duty to

18 For a thoughtful discussion of the boundaries of patient autonomy, see John Lantos et al., Clinician Integrity and Limits to Patient Autonomy, 305 JAMA 495–498 (2011).

19 John C. Fletcher et al., Introduction to Clinical Ethics 12 (2nd ed., University Publishing Group, 1997) (describing beneficence as the "obligation to benefit patients . . . and to further their welfare and interests").

20 For example, state law in Massachusetts instructs health care proxies to make decisions for incapacitated patients based on what the patient would choose but, if this is unknown, instructs the proxy to decide what is in the patient's best interests. Mass. Gen. Laws Ch. 201D, § 5 (1997).

do what is best for the patient and a duty to avoid doing things that will harm the patient. These duties and the decisions required to implement them may appear straightforward – at first glance – but the idea of beneficence raises some thorny questions. Is it always in a patient's best interests to live longer no matter the suffering and other existential cost to the patient? To try treatments that have a small probability of benefit and a high risk of harm? On the other hand, can it ever be said that it's in a patient's best interests to die, or to die sooner by the withholding or withdrawal of life-supportive technology? Permanently unconscious patients, for example, may live on indefinitely with lots of supportive medical care, but is it in such a patient's best interests to receive this care? In these cases, in the absence of sufficient evidence that the patient would refuse life-prolonging treatment, families and courts may default to continued care. US law generally favors continuing life-supportive measures when the patient's wishes are unknown or in dispute.[21] Even so, courts sometimes try to fold patient wishes into the concept of best interests by concluding that based on what is known of the patient's values and what was important to him, it is in the patient's best interests to do (or cease doing) what the patient probably would have chosen.[22] As Chapter 5 explores in more detail and Chapter 9 considers in the context of surrogate decision-making, many individuals – and some courts – support the default position of continued care for permanently unconscious and otherwise incapacitated patients, with little consideration of the patient's quality of life.

AUTONOMY IN THE REAL WORLD

Patient goals for care fall into two general categories. Therapeutic goals include cure, prolonging survival, and palliation of symptoms, while personal goals may include dying at home, surviving to celebrate an important life event, getting affairs in order, or resolving an old conflict. Within the realm of therapeutic goals, some terminally ill patients wish to receive all possible interventions to prolong life, even if these increase suffering. Other patients, apparently a large majority, prefer to avoid pain and suffering as much as possible, even if this means not living as long. If the goal is to align medical care with patient preferences, how often do we get this goal-concordant care right? This is not a simple question to study,[23] but the evidence suggests that significant numbers of patients receive care that is not consistent with their goals. Recall from Chapter 1 that most patients say they prefer limited care and comfort care at the end of life, but that many patients actually receive high-intensity

[21] Furrow et al., Health Law §16–33.

[22] In re Conroy, 486 A.2d 1209 (NJ 1985) (describing a sliding scale of wholly subjective (patient preference) to wholly objective (best interests) standards for making decisions for incapacitated patients without advance directives).

[23] Alison B. Turnbull & Christiane S. Hartog, Goal-Concordant Care in the ICU: A Conceptual Framework for Future Research, 43 Intensive Care Med. 1847–1849 (2017).

therapeutic and life-prolonging care. Rather than making general, conclusory statements about these questions, it again makes sense to dig into the medical literature for actual evidence of how physicians and patients communicate, what care is provided, and what factors influence the quality of communication and decision-making in the quest to achieve goal-concordant care.

Empirical research into the question of whether end-of-life care aligns with patient preferences has demonstrated a need for improvement. In one fairly encouraging study, only one out of eight patients aged 65 and older received care in the final months that was inconsistent with their wishes. Patients who died at home were more likely to receive care that comported with their goals, whereas death in a hospital or nursing home was more likely to be associated with receiving care that was inconsistent with patient preferences.[24] In a less focused but still useful measure, some studies evaluate family members' perspectives on care that a loved one received at the end of life. Care that is rated as good or excellent would seem more likely to also be consistent with patient goals. (Of course, this assumes that the family members being surveyed understood enough about the patient's goals and regarded adherence to those goals as an important quality factor.) In one such study, evaluating late-stage care of cancer patients, family members were more likely to describe care as "excellent" in situations where the patient received three or more days of hospice care, avoided ICU admission in the last thirty days of life, and died outside of the hospital.[25]

Many dying patients do not have conversations with their physicians about their prognosis or treatment preferences. In fact, many dying patients appear not to know (or at least not to have been formally informed) that they are dying. In one study of ICU patients and their surrogate decision-makers, fewer than 40 percent of those surveyed reported that their physicians had talked with them about their prognoses or preferences for life-sustaining treatment. Of the patients who wanted only palliative care rather than life-prolonging measures, only 29 percent thought that their care was consistent with this goal.[26] In another study that looked at whether patients received goal-concordant care, only 68 percent of patients received end-of-life care that was consistent with their preferences. That number alone is quite troubling, but the details are even more so. In the studied group of patients with advanced cancer, patients were asked to choose between "a course of treatment that focused on extending life as much as possible, even if that meant more pain and discomfort" or "a plan of care that focused on relieving pain and discomfort, even if that meant not living as long." Seventy-two percent of the patients chose treatment focusing on relieving pain and

24 Nita Khandelwal et al., How Often Is End-of-Life Care in the United States Inconsistent with Patients' Goals of Care?, 20 J. Palliative Med. 1400–1404 (2017).

25 Alexi A. Wright et al., Family Perspectives on Aggressive Cancer Care Near the End of Life, 315 JAMA 284–292 (2016).

26 Janet Teno et al., Decision-Making and Outcomes of Prolonged ICU Stays in Seriously Ill Patients, 48 J. Am. Geriatrics Soc. S70–S74 (2000).

discomfort and 28 percent chose life-extending treatment. Overall, only 39 percent of patients recognized that they were terminally ill at the start of the study, so the remaining group was making decisions without knowing (or at least overtly acknowledging) their terminal prognoses and therefore were unlikely to discuss their end-of-life preferences or concerns with anyone, including their treating physicians. Patients who *were* aware that they were terminally ill and who had discussions with physicians about their wishes regarding end-of-life care were more likely to receive care that was consistent with their preferences. Unfortunately, 13 percent of the group who had chosen care that minimizes suffering (72 percent of the entire cohort) nevertheless received life-prolonging care, suggesting that even when patients say "no" to invasive care, this wish is not always respected. Other patients who recognized that they were terminally ill nevertheless chose and received care intended to prolong life as much as possible. Patients, of course, have the right to make this choice, but the study also suggested that patients in this group didn't live any longer than patients who chose to focus on symptom relief, and that they experienced higher rates of distress and poorer quality of life.[27] Given the predictable suffering of terminally ill patients who choose life-prolonging care and the limited utility of this care in actually prolonging life, physicians can help patients avoid unnecessary suffering by being more forthright about how the final days and weeks of life are likely to unfold with and without life-prolonging technology.

The accurate implementation of decisions about cardio-pulmonary resuscitation serves as another bellwether of good communication and comprehension of patient preferences. In a large group of seriously ill, hospitalized patients who had directly or via a surrogate decision-maker expressed a preference for or against resuscitation, physicians frequently did not understand what the studied patients actually wanted. Physicians got it right 86 percent of the time for those patients who wanted CPR but were correct only 46 percent of the time when patients preferred *not* to have CPR attempted. All patients included in the study had conveyed their wishes regarding resuscitation, but there were frequent misunderstandings and a clear bias in favor of believing that patients wanted CPR, even when they did not. Patients who were older and had a worse functional status and prognosis were more likely to be understood in their rejection of CPR, suggesting that physicians were perhaps projecting their own values about the appropriateness of resuscitation attempts onto individual patients.[28] Conversations about code status also must be precise and detailed. Terms like "full code" and "partial code" can cause confusion.[29]

27 Jennifer W. Mack et al., End-of-Life Discussions, Goal Attainment, and Distress at the End of Life: Predictors and Outcomes of Receipt of Care Consistent with Preferences, 28 J. Clinical Oncology 1203–1208 (2010).

28 Neil S. Wenger, et al., Physician Understanding of Patient Resuscitation Preferences: Insights and Clinical Implications, 48 J. Am. Geriatrics Soc. S44–S51 (2000).

29 Karl Steinberg & Thaddeus Mason Pope, "Do You Want Everything Done?" Clarifying Code Status, PSNet (December 2019). "Full code" refers to complete efforts to reverse cardiac arrest, including intubation, chest compressions, and medications. "Partial code" refers to a situation where a patient

Patient and families need to understand that CPR frequently entails not only chest compressions but also ventilator support. Patients may be willing to accept one but not the other. The frequency of physician misunderstandings about patients' resuscitation preferences, particularly the tendency to get it wrong with patients who preferred no CPR, means of course that patients risk receiving an unwanted and painful medical intervention at or near the point of death.

The autonomy problem at the end of life goes beyond the pattern of patients receiving unwanted care. It also includes situations where patients demand care beyond what is medically appropriate. It's probably fair to say that no patient wants burdensome care that will not advance her cause – toward cure, improved quality of life, or prolongation of life. While physicians are not obligated to provide care that is scientifically futile – care that simply cannot accomplish its goal – there is quite a lot of pressure to provide medical care that has only a remote chance of helping the patient. For this reason, as data from Chapter 1 demonstrated, we see cancer patients requesting and receiving chemotherapy within days of death, and physicians attempting resuscitation of patients with multiple medical conditions that are incompatible with life. In cases where medical care has at least some minimal potential to 'work' (and is therefore not scientifically futile), the qualitative problem of ethical futility (now often referred to as "potentially inappropriate care") comes into play.[30] For dying patients, the matter of potentially inappropriate care arises often in the course of trying to decide when to transition from therapeutic and life-prolonging care to palliative care alone. This question often coincides with the decision point about resuscitation status, especially if the patient is hospitalized. In particular, decisions about CPR and continuing or ceasing life-prolonging technology (for example ventilation, dialysis, and artificial nutrition and hydration) raise moral questions about the sanctity of life and involve implicit judgments about quality of life. Chapter 5 explores these questions in more detail.

Definitions of potentially inappropriate care vary and are value and context specific. The medical, ethics, and legal communities have long recognized the definitional challenges. One way to consider whether a particular medical therapy will or will not work for a given patient involves physician experience. If the medical intervention under consideration has not worked for the last 100 similarly situated patients, it is unlikely to work for this particular patient.[31] This concept might help guide decision-making about whether to try a particular treatment or, on the contrary, to conclude that trying that therapy is inappropriate care. But this approach does not presume that it is impossible that the treatment would work, only that

may agree to some aspects of full code but rejects others – e.g., accepts chest compressions but not intubation.

30 Gabriel T. Bosslet et al., An Official ATS/AACN/ACCP/ESICM/SCCM Policy Statement: Responding to Requests for Potentially Inappropriate Treatments in Intensive Care Units, 191 Am. J. Respiratory & Critical Care Med. 1318–1330 (2015).

31 Lawrence J. Schneiderman, Defining Medical Futility and Improving Quality of Care, 8 Bioethical Inquiry 123–131 (2011).

beneficial results are highly improbable. As critics have pointed out, it is unclear how similar and representative the 100 cases must be.[32] Lawrence Schneiderman and colleagues have taken the position that medical care that only maintains life in permanently unconscious patients or that will not enable a patient to survive without intensive medical interventions should generally be considered 'futile'[33] – but many individual patients and families may disagree with this position. For some patients and families, the fact that recovery to some level of independent function is impossible does not render life-prolonging treatment futile per se because of the inherent value of life, even in cases of permanent unconsciousness or complete medical dependency. In the US medical-legal system, these beliefs generally are respected. Since there is an array of viewpoints regarding what quality and functionality of life are of innate value and ought to be preserved, we in the United States will never agree on a definition of ethically futile care.

Recall from Chapter 1 that physicians acknowledge that they sometimes provide potentially inappropriate care. How should physicians respond to patient and family requests for medical interventions that they believe are inappropriate? The AMA's Council on Ethical and Judicial Affairs has stated that "Physicians are not required to offer or provide interventions that, in their best medial judgment, cannot reasonably be expected to yield the intended clinical benefit or achieve agreed-on goals for care. Respecting patient autonomy does not mean that patients should receive specific interventions simply because they (or their surrogates) request them."[34] But this statement doesn't do much to resolve the physician's dilemma. In general, rather than thinking about whether requested care is 'futile' (whatever that may mean in the specific patient's context), commentators have suggested an approach that is, in essence, a physician gut check. When physicians feel inclined to deny a patient request for care, "they are usually acting from a profound sense that further treatment would be fundamentally wrong.... In many of the situations in which questions of futility arise, providers believe that the treatment in question would not be in the patient's interests, even from the patient's perspective." In such cases, physicians should attempt to understand what the patient hopes to achieve with the treatment and correct any unrealistic expectations.[35] This is excellent advice, but it requires an emotionally challenging conversation with the patient and a truthful explanation of the patient's medical situation, including prognosis – something that, as we shall see, physicians sometimes are reluctant to pursue. Policy statements on how to respond to requests for potentially inappropriate care elaborate on and

32 Robert D. Truog et al., The Problem with Futility, 326 New Eng. J. Med. 1560–1564 (1992).

33 Lawrence J. Schneiderman et al., Medical Futility: Its Meaning and Ethical Implications, 112 Annals Internal Med. 949–954 (1990).

34 Am. Med. Ass'n, Council on Ethical and Judicial Affairs Code of Medical Ethics, Opinion 5.5, Medically Ineffective Interventions (2016).

35 Truog et al., The Problem with Futility.

reinforce this advice,[36] but, again, physicians must be willing to rather intimately engage with patient and family at a time when emotions and fears already run high.

Various attempts to define potentially inappropriate care provide some useful conceptual tools, but putting these tools into practice by discussing the idea of inappropriate care with patients and then refusing to provide this care is not easy for physicians, for a variety of reasons. It must be very difficult to explain to a cancer patient why further chemotherapy doesn't make sense and why refocusing medical efforts on palliation of symptoms is the better path. Similarly, discussing "Do Not Attempt Resuscitation" (DNAR) orders with seriously ill patients and their families is without a doubt rarely, if ever, a comfortable conversation. Many patients do not understand what CPR entails – such as chest compressions that can break the ribs – and they vastly overestimate its potential effectiveness, perhaps because CPR is portrayed inaccurately on television.[37] In reality, in-hospital cardiac arrest is relatively common, and only 17 percent of patients who receive CPR survive to discharge. Of that group, only about half remain neurologically intact or have only minor impairments.[38] So, it is necessary to have these conversations to avoid becoming complicit in allowing patients to put themselves through the wringer in their last days of life with unavailing interventions. Low- or no-value care not only depletes limited medical resources and increases medical bills, it also – most importantly from an autonomy perspective – harms the patient physically and existentially. It is not 'care' at all. It's difficult to say precisely how much unnecessary care at the end of life results from patient and family requests and how much is the result of physician unwillingness to be candid about the likely ineffectiveness of certain medical interventions in prolonging life or improving quality of life. But there is clearly a causal connection between inappropriate care at the end of life and poor communication between physicians and patients.

The over-arching goal is proportionality – providing therapeutic and life-prolonging care to patients for whom it is a benefit in their unique circumstances. But what is a benefit today can become a burden tomorrow. When the patient is dying, medical treatment can get in the way of a patient-preferred natural death. More institutions are recognizing this fact explicitly with some even re-naming DNAR to "AND" (Allow Natural Death).

36 Gabriel T. Bosslet et al., An Official ATS/AACN/ACCP/ESICM/SCCM Policy Statement: Responding to Requests for Potentially Inappropriate Treatments in Intensive Care Units, 191 Am. J. Respiratory & Critical Care Med. 1318–1330 (2015).

37 Susan J. Diem et al., Cardiopulmonary Resuscitation on Television – Miracles and Misinformation, 334 New Eng. J. Med. 1578–1582 (1996) (finding a 75 percent survival rate after the cardiac arrest and a 67 percent survival rate to discharge and noting that 65 percent of cardiac arrests occurred in children, teenagers, or young adults who are not representative of real-life age distributions for this event).

38 Mary Ann Peberdy et al., Cardiopulmonary Resuscitation of Adults in the Hospital: A Report of 14,720 Cardiac Arrests from the National Registry of Cardiopulmonary Resuscitation, 58 Resuscitation 297–308 (2003); Mark H. Ebell & Anna M. Alfonso, Pre-arrest Predictors of Failure to Survive After In-Hospital Cardiopulmonary Resuscitation: A Meta-Analysis, 28 Family Practice 505–515 (2011).

INFORMED CONSENT LAW AND PRACTICE – PAPERING OVER POOR COMMUNICATION

Where does the US law of informed consent fit into this picture? Under the legal doctrine of informed consent, physicians have an obligation to provide patients with timely and accurate information that will enable patients to make informed decisions about medical treatments,[39] including end-of-life care.[40] The common law of informed consent law in all fifty states requires (with minor variations) that physicians discuss with the patient the risks, benefits, and alternatives to the proposed medical intervention, including the option to do nothing,[41] to 'wait and see'. The scope of required disclosure varies by jurisdiction but typically follows one of two models, with states about evenly divided between the two. In states that have adopted the *professional* standard of disclosure, physicians must proactively disclose all information that a reasonable physician would disclose under the circumstances. In jurisdictions that follow the *patient-oriented* standard, the physician must disclose in advance what a reasonable patient would want to know under the circumstances.[42] Under both standards, physicians also must answer patients' questions and requests for information that may be beyond the scope of usual disclosure.

While most patients indicate that they would like to participate in medical decision-making, the US law of informed consent and the ethical principle of self-determination on which it is based allow patients to reject information as well as to receive it.[43] In cases of waiver, the patient still must understand enough of his situation to understand what information he is waiving, leaving physicians to attempt to thread the needle between respecting a patient's right not to know and saying too much about what it is that the patient is giving up knowing.[44] To be clear, patients are not merely participants in their fate – they are the deciders. Patients may waive the right to receive adequate levels of information about their condition and treatment but only if they understand that they're deliberately keeping themselves in the dark – which in itself is a decision. Separately, in some circumstances, physicians may exercise a 'therapeutic privilege' to withhold information from a patient in cases where the information may be harmful to the patient.[45] This exception to informed

[39] Canterbury v. Spence, 464 F.2d. 772 (DC Cir. 1972) (explaining that a patient's "dependence upon the physician for information affecting his well-being, in terms of contemplated treatment, is well-nigh abject"); Cobbs v. Grant, 502 P.2d 1 (Cal. 1972).

[40] Alan Meisel et al., The Right to Die: The Law of End-of-Life Decisionmaking §2.06[A] (3rd ed. Aspen 2020).

[41] Hippocrates supposedly said, "To do nothing is sometimes a good remedy."

[42] Furrow et al., Health Law. Although the two standards have varying effects on the plaintiff's burden of proof in an action for battery or negligent failure to obtain informed consent, these effects are not relevant for purposes of this discussion.

[43] Alan Meisel & Mark Kuczewski, Legal and Ethical Myths About Informed Consent, 156 Archives Internal Med. 2521–2526 (1996).

[44] Furrow et al., Health Law §3–15(c).

[45] Canterbury v. Spence, 464 F.2d. 772 (D.C. Cir. 1972).

consent requirements threatens to swallow the rule because physicians often worry that providing too much information (or too soon) will increase anxiety to the point that it becomes counterproductive for the patient's well-being. For this reason, courts have policed the therapeutic privilege and set out substantive requirements to prove that its use was justified in a particular patient's case.[46] Therapeutic privilege is *not* a broad exemption that would justify the withholding of prognostic information for large numbers of seriously ill patients, although the AMA's ethics statement on the question gives physicians considerable leeway to decide when and how much information to disclose to patients.[47]

In the context of life-threatening and terminal illness, several decisional elements require physician-patient communication and informed consent, including harms of proposed treatments, anticipated benefits of treatments, and comparative harm-benefit trade-offs when there are multiple treatment pathways for the patient's condition. Let's imagine a patient who has been diagnosed with metastatic colon cancer, and that the standard treatment for this condition is surgery followed by chemotherapy. Providing a laundry list of common and rarer potential harms associated with chemotherapy will satisfy the harms aspect of informed consent disclosure: for example, nausea, hair loss, fatigue, anemia, weight loss, and neuropathy. However, this list does not give the patient information about how to weigh these risks – how serious they might be, how frequently they arise, whether this *particular* patient, given her unique attributes, is more likely to experience certain potential harms or, for that matter, whether the patient even understands what neuropathy means. Disclosure should also include an estimated benefit to the patient of receiving treatment. Assuming that the chemotherapy being prescribed is standard for the cancer in question, the hope is that it has some potential for efficacy, but how much potential? To what end? What is the best-case scenario for what life will be like for the patient after surgery and chemotherapy? How likely is that best case to materialize? What's the worst-case picture? Metastatic cancer is rarely curable, but chemotherapy and other systemic treatments can slow its progress and ameliorate some of the symptomatic effects of tumor growth. This process of sorting and weighing of potential harms and prospective outcomes requires a longer conversation between physician and patient, and it is difficult to know whether or how often this occurs.

Once a patient reaches the end-stage of illness, the conversation and disclosure focus shifts from cure or prolongation of life to how to manage the pathway to death. These discussions present another set of challenges because physicians also must now discuss with patients and families the options of stopping therapeutic

46 Furrow et al., Health Law §3–15(d).

47 Am. Med. Ass'n, Code of Medical Ethics, Opinion 2.1.3 ("The obligation to communicate truthfully about the patient's medical condition does not mean that the physician must communicate information to the patient immediately or all at once. Information may be conveyed over time in keeping with the patient's preferences and ability to comprehend the information.").

interventions, of withholding or withdrawing life-prolonging technology, and of focusing solely on palliation of symptoms. This discussion often will include the possibility of a DNAR order, if the patient has not completed one already, along with decisions about interventions like mechanical ventilation, dialysis, and artificial nutrition, depending on the situation. These conversations, by definition, are equally or even more complex and emotionally taxing (for all parties) than consent to treatment because the conversation turns from whether to when and how the patient will die. Complicating matters further, many patients and families do not understand their options at the end of life. In one older survey of outpatients in Oregon, 69 percent of those surveyed understood that patients have a right to refuse unwanted medical treatment, even if the refusal will hasten death, but only 46 percent of those surveyed knew that they could request withdrawal of life-prolonging treatment already in place, and only 41 percent understood that it was legal to prescribe pain medication, even if the medication itself might hasten death.[48] In these circumstances, palliative care team members can educate patients and family members about their choices and help address their concerns and fears. Chapter 7 considers the many benefits of integrated therapeutic and palliative care.

The failures of informed consent law are well documented in the literature, although the doctrine continues to serve at least some sort of hortatory function. Numerous commentators have observed that the paradigmatic ideal of informed consent is, in reality, utopian or illusory.[49] As George Annas has observed, informed consent is "more accurately termed informed choice"; because of the doctrine's "implications for power and accountability,"[50] critical evaluation of its limitations is essential. Annas argues that courts have not gone far enough in requiring physicians to discuss relevant information with patients. In fact, some courts have not required that a physician disclose the patient's prognosis unless the patient asks and conclude that prognosis need only be disclosed if it is material in the patient's particular case,[51] which is rather astonishing. Peter Schuck, in discussing the "informed consent gap" between what idealists such as judges and medical ethicists envision and what realists such as physicians and social scientists know to be true, argues that the gap

[48] Maria J. Silveira et al., Patients' Knowledge of Options at the End of Life: Ignorance in the Face of Death, 284 JAMA 2483–2488 (1999).

[49] Carl E. Schneider, The Practice of Autonomy: Patients, Doctors, and Medical Decisions (Oxford University Press 1998) (critiquing the operation of informed consent in practice but not advocating that it be abandoned); Carl E. Schneider, After Autonomy, 41 Wake Forest L. Rev. 411–444 (2006); Peter H. Schuck, Rethinking Informed Consent, 103 Yale L.J. 899–959 (1994); Angela Fagerlin et al., An Informed Decision? Breast Cancer Patients and Their Knowledge About Treatment, 64 Patient Ed. & Counselling 303–312 (2006).

[50] George J. Annas, The Rights of Patients p. 113 (Southern Illinois University Press 2004).

[51] Annas, The Rights of Patients p. 119. For an example, see Arato v. Avedon, 858 P.2d 598 (Cal. 1993). The patient, who died of pancreatic cancer, underwent a grueling and ineffective chemotherapy treatment and did not order his business affairs. Under either standard of disclosure – what a reasonable physician would disclose or what a reasonable patient would want to know, prognosis seems like important information to offer to the patient.

is essentially structural and "reflects the constraints imposed by human psychology, the physician-patient relationship, the tort law system, and an increasingly cost conscious health care delivery system." He concludes that informed consent as envisioned by the idealists is mostly unachievable and that attempting to close the consent gap by imposing more onerous obligations via tort law would fail and might actually widen the gap.[52] Most of the critiques of informed consent doctrine agree that there is no practical, cost-effective way to narrow the gap between the ideal of disclosure, comprehension, and fully informed, authentic choice and the actual practice of consent between physicians and patients. Although perfection (as in all human affairs) is unachievable, there is room for improvement. As discussed in Chapter 11, there are limits to what can be accomplished on a system-wide basis, but there are clearly steps that individual physicians and health care organizations can take that will promote better conversations and more meaningful consent.

The ideal of informed consent is a process aimed at empowering the patient, not a signature on a piece of paper. The term itself is a misnomer because the goal of the process is patient comprehension more than technical consent. Yet many of us have experienced the deficiencies of informed consent in action. As a member of a very active institutional review board (IRB) earlier in my career, I heard researchers speak of "consenting 100 subjects." 'Consent' is an intransitive verb – it does not take a direct object. It is not something that physicians or researchers *do to* a person. It is also common to hear stories of patients being whisked off for a test or procedure with only a brief description of what to expect, as the consent form and pen are simultaneously thrust into their hands. A signed form is intended to document the informational conversation that preceded it. Without that conversation, there is nothing to document except perhaps, the patient's lack of objection – her assent – to whatever medical care she receives next.

In addition, decisions about care for life-threatening illness and end-of-life care are often more complex than typical informed consent scenarios. For example, explaining to a patient the risks, benefits, and alternatives to a cardiac catheterization procedure or the surgical resection of a skin cancer would involve a focus almost exclusively on medical risks and benefits and alternative treatments. In contrast, an informed consent discussion about whether to begin a third round of chemotherapy when the first two have failed, or to sign a DNAR order, or to begin artificial nutrition and hydration is much more complex and emotionally challenging. Of course, chemotherapy and CPR and enteral feeding each have medical risks and benefits, but for the discussion to be truly informed, the physician should also discuss the probability of a good outcome, and the broader contextual 'risk' of, in some cases, prolonging the dying process with little or no upside benefit to the patient and the real possibility of downside costs including increased suffering. This in turn requires the physician and patient or surrogate to acknowledge that the patient is dying,

52 Peter H. Schuck, Rethinking Informed Consent, 103 Yale L.J. 899–959 (1994).

perhaps soon. This discussion will be unavoidably emotional for all involved, but simply asking the patient, "If your heart stops, do you want us to attempt to restart it again? If not, sign here" really does a disservice to the patient and makes a mockery of the entire practice of informed consent. It might technically satisfy consent requirements and so avoid civil liability, but it utterly ignores the objective of helping patients make decisions in keeping with their subjective goals and preferences within the broader reality of their medical situations.

Informed consent practices in the United States tend to perpetuate a stunted and overly mechanistic view of the physician's role in guiding end-of-life decision-making. Physicians in the United States are rarely called upon to make the actual decision about whether to withdraw life-sustaining medical treatment. Even if the patient or surrogate requests that the physician decide, the physician has an ethical obligation to do so based on an understanding of the particular patient's values and goals. In the US system, physicians are usually informational and treatment fiduciaries, not decision-making agents for their patients. Because the autonomy principle focuses on the patient's preferences and choices, the physician can avoid the more complex discussion of whether continuing treatment, initiating new treatment, or accepting life-supportive measures serves the patient's best interests. This leaves the patient in the lurch:

> Responsibility for medical care has landed on the shoulders of patients with a resounding thud. Patients have the choice of telling physicians what to do in relation to health care decisions. The tone of medical practice has shifted from paternalistic to consultative, in which the physician lays the possibilities before the patient, with the potential pluses and minuses of each, and the patient makes the choice.[53]

Under most circumstances, if a patient or surrogate decision-maker requests continued treatment or life-prolonging interventions, the physician can simply acquiesce and provide it. As Chapter 6 explains, there are multiple incentives to do just that. But when the requested intervention is arguably not in the patient's best interests, mere acquiescence debases the physician's role. Because the physician is responsible for the patient's well-being, the physician has an ethical and legal duty to help the patient or surrogate decision-maker understand the risks, potential outcomes, and alternatives associated with the requested intervention, not just its purpose. In some circumstances, physicians, while acknowledging that the decision remains the patient's, have an ethical obligation to speak up and opine as to what, from the physician's perspective, appears to be in the patient's best medical interests and to discuss this opinion in the context of the patient's preferences.

The law sends conflicting signals to physicians regarding the management of patient care at the end of life. On the one hand, physicians *do* have an ethical and

[53] Timothy J. Paterick et al., Medical Informed Consent: General Considerations for Physicians, 83 Mayo Clinic Proc. 313–319 (2008).

legal duty to avoid providing treatments that are harmful to patients or are inconsistent with their wishes. Some courts have recognized this obligation and have awarded damages against physicians and institutions for providing unwanted treatment.[54] Other courts do not view an effort to prolong a patient's life – even when contrary to the patient's expressed wishes – as a compensable injury to the patient.[55] Most state statutes also insulate physicians from liability for patient deaths that result from withdrawal of life-sustaining treatment as dictated by a patient's advance directive or requested by a surrogate decision-maker. On the other hand, despite this apparent support for the implementation of patient preferences, most states also have enacted conscience clause legislation, which allows a physician to transfer the care of a patient when compliance with that person's advance directive would conflict with the physician's conscience.[56] Chapter 9 includes a deeper dive into the role of advance care planning in making decisions for patients who have lost the ability to choose for themselves, but it's worth noting here that advance directives do little to resolve the conflicting signals that the law sends to physicians.

The problem with informed consent law is obvious – the protection of the autonomy principle that informed consent law provides is only as good as the quality and accuracy of the information on which consent is based and the patient's ability to comprehend and process that information and then to make a choice consistent with his individual values. Compliance with informed consent law alone does not ensure that patients' decisions are *actually* informed. The ideal of informed consent lacks meaning when the patient can't comprehend, or just doesn't receive relevant information. Comprehension is essential, but even with genuine effort to ensure that the patient understands what he is agreeing to, there are significant impediments to meaningful informed consent, including medical illiteracy and medical jargon, cognitive barriers to comprehension, and clinical uncertainty. Chapter 8 explores these barriers in detail. So, legal informed consent may not ensure that patients receive care consistent with their individual goals of care. Meaningful communication requires more – from both physicians and their patients. Physicians, as professional repeat-players, have to be willing and prepared to undertake the difficult conversations that help patients and families understand their options, including the option of

54 Estate of Leach v. Shapiro, 469 N.E.2d 1047 (Ohio Ct. App. 1984) (recognizing a civil cause of action for wrongful continuation of life supportive measures).

55 Anderson v. St. Francis–St. George Hosp., Inc., 671 N.E.2d 225 (Ohio 1996) (rejecting a "wrongful living" claim based on hospital's resuscitation of patient after he had succeeded in having a DNR order placed in his chart and holding that "continued living" is not a compensable injury); Allore v. Flower Hosp., 699 N.E.2d 560 (Ohio Ct. App. 1997) (refusing to recognize a battery claim for intubation and ventilation of a dying patient contrary to his advance directive and the statements of his health care proxy and citing *Anderson* with approval and critiquing the court's decision in *Leach*).

56 For example, New Hampshire's statute says: "If a physician . . . because of his or her personal beliefs or conscience, is unable to comply with the terms of the advance directive or surrogate's decision, he or she shall immediately inform the qualified patient, the qualified patient's family, or the qualified patient's agent. The qualified patient, or the qualified patient's agent or family, may then request that the case be referred to another physician" N.H. Rev. Stat. Ann. § 137-J:7(I)(d).

de-escalating acute care and focusing on palliation of symptoms. Patients need guidance to move beyond ticking a few boxes or signing a form – which usually won't be adequate to help them understand the complex and ongoing decision-making calculus that serious medical illness often requires. As discussed next, the broader challenge to informed consent at the end-of-life is the frequent lack of contextual information that allows patients to situate a particular decision into their medical 'big picture'.

THE REALITY OF PHYSICIAN-PATIENT COMMUNICATION

In an ideal world, physicians will have the time, communication skills, and emotional resilience to initiate truthful and nuanced conversations with patients about their medical reality – what the diagnosis means, best estimates of prognosis, the relative merits of available treatment options, and how all of this information fits with the patient's values and preferences. The physician and patient will discuss options via a process of shared decision-making. In this decision-making model, physician and patient engage in a back-and-forth discussion in which the physician shares medical information, the patient shares her values and concerns, and the two together reach a decision about which treatment pathway, on balance, best promotes the goal of effective treatment consistent with the patient's preferences. The process of shared decision-making, when done well, allows the patient access to relevant medical information but also, crucially, allows and expects the physician to exercise her responsibility for the patient's overall well-being. Within the shared decision-making model, the physician not only offers options to the patient but also opines about which options are most likely to promote the patient's goals.[57]

The ideal patient will be able to comprehend and retain all of this novel information in spite of the emotional turmoil that comes with very bad news about her medical situation (while also probably feeling physically unwell). This patient will then be able to manipulate complex information – such as comparing the statistical likelihood of 'success' between different treatments and simultaneously considering the competing harms of those treatments, all in the context of a well-defined and probably evolving set of goals (cure, remission, life-prolongation, palliation of symptoms) and, after careful consideration, will make an informed decision about how to proceed. To have realistic goals, the patient will need accurate and timely information about what goals are at least potentially achievable based on scientific evidence and the physician's prior experience. In this ideal world, there will be one physician (or team of clinicians) consistently in charge of the patient's care, who is available for follow-up conversations and will coordinate information and decision-making with other clinicians involved in caring for the patient.

[57] Glyn Elwyn et al., Shared Decision Making: A Model for Clinical Practice, 27 J. Gen. Int. Med. 1361–1367 (2012); Michael J. Barry & Susan Edgman-Levitan, Shared Decision Making – The Pinnacle of Patient-Centered Care, 366 New Eng. J. Med. 780–781 (2012).

This physician will be able to consistently tread the fine line between empathy for the patient and emotional involvement that may become counterproductive for them both. There will be timely follow-up conversations as the patient's medical situation evolves. Even in these ideal circumstances, the decisions that patients must make and the conversations required to support them are emotionally and intellectually challenging for all involved – and that's if things go really well.

The reality is that, in many instances, physicians and patients fail to have timely, thorough, and honest conversations about care for life-threatening illness and about what choices remain when cure is not an option. A variety of factors tend to impede these conversations on the physician side, including lack of communication training, emotional resistance, fear of liability, and a reluctance to deprive patients of hope. Chapter 6 explores these factors in detail. For these reasons, physicians may be wary about providing reasonably complete or even truthful information about the patient's prognosis and the potential efficacy of proposed treatments. Patients, for their part, are sometimes reluctant to ask too many questions which might result in uncomfortable and unpreferred answers. They may worry about taking up too much of the physician's time, or they may not know what questions to ask. Within this don't ask/don't tell culture, physicians may hesitate even to raise the topic of prognosis or to discuss withdrawal or withholding of therapeutic or life-sustaining medical care, unless the patient or family initiates the conversation and signals an interest in ongoing discussion. In the absence of detailed, candid discussions, physicians in our health care culture tend to assume that patients want full-on medical interventions even when patients are actively dying.[58] So, seriously ill patients find themselves caught up in the medical technology juggernaut without an easy escape route, at least not without the help of physicians. While it is true that patients living with a long illness have more time to adapt to the fact that they will eventually need to face death and consider de-escalating therapeutic care, even these patients need truthful and timely information to make informed choices. Those patients who become suddenly and acutely ill or who receive a new diagnosis of a life-ending medical condition have the added challenge of little time to adjust to their new and unwelcome circumstances, while also feeling really crummy.

Physicians can and must learn how to initiate and carry on these difficult conversations – not an easy task with distressed patients and family members and in a stressful practice environment. As the experts in the room, physicians have an ethical obligation to talk with patients about all reasonable options and how they might comport with patient preferences. Patients rely on physicians to broach the topic, and the evidence suggests that these conversations generally help rather than frighten or depress patients. Conversations about life-threatening illness and end-of-life care

58 Rachelle E. Bernacki & Susan D. Block, Communication About Serious Illness Care Goals: A Review and Synthesis of Best Practices, 174 JAMA Internal Med. 1994–2003 (2014) (explaining that "our health care system is oriented toward providing life-sustaining treatment, unless a patient actively chooses against it").

contain yet another layer of complexity. Most patients want to know whether their disease is curable and, if not, how long they can expect to live.[59] Even so, the autonomy principle and the law of informed consent recognize the right of patients not to participate in their medical decisions (although the patient always participates to the extent that he cooperates with whatever treatment the physician recommends). It is ethically appropriate to withhold information from patients at their explicit request (via the patient 'waiver' of informed consent mentioned earlier in this chapter) because doing so is another way of respecting patient autonomy. However, while physicians have no ethical or legal obligation to force patients to engage in these discussions, there is no excuse for sidestepping the conversation altogether – for the majority of patients who need and want information in order to make good decisions. In situations where the patient hasn't specifically declined to discuss his or her medical situation, the physician has an ethical and professional responsibility to be proactive in initiating discussions about treatment options and end-of-life care.

Professional standards and guidelines recommend advance care planning and discussions of prognosis for patients whose life expectancy is one year or less.[60] One guideline for the management of terminal cancer recommends a personalized approach, noting that this

> requires stepping back from the paradigm of applying one line of therapy after the other and focusing primarily on disease-directed interventions. Instead, we need to move toward developing a treatment plan that is consistent with evidence-based options (including disease-focused and palliative care) and the patient's informed preferences for how we pursue and balance these options throughout the course of illness.[61]

Another guideline also stresses the importance of truthful and timely communication.[62] Simply put, cancer patients – and all seriously ill patients – cannot make informed decisions about whether to pursue "one line of therapy after the other" without knowing whether they are terminally ill and, if so, how long they can (statistically) expect to live.

59 Areej El-Jawahri et al., Associations Among Prognostic Understanding, Quality of Life, and Mood in Patients With Advanced Cancer, 120 Cancer 278–285 (2014) (75 percent of patients with advanced cancer wanted to know as much as possible about their cancer diagnosis and treatment); Valerie Jenkins et al., Information Needs of Patients with Cancer: Results from a Large Study in UK Cancer Centres, 84 British J. Cancer 48–51 (2001) (87 percent of a large sample of cancer patients wanted to be told everything about their medical situation including bad news); Constantine Alifrangis et al., The Experiences of Cancer Patients, 104 Q. J. Med. 1075–1081 (2011) (only 66 percent of patients in the United Kingdom wanted to be given a prognosis and 12 percent said that they would not want to be told that they had a short time to live).

60 Nancy Berlinger et al., The Hastings Center Guidelines for Decisions on Life-Sustaining Treatment and Care Near the End of Life (2nd ed. Oxford University Press 2013).

61 Jeffrey M. Peppercorn et al., American Society of Clinical Oncology Statement: Toward Individualized Care for Patients With Advanced Cancer, 29 J. Clinical Oncology 755-760 (2011).

62 Timothy Gilligan et al., Patient-Clinician Communication: American Society of Clinical Oncology Consensus Guideline, 35 J. Clinical Oncology 3618–3634 (2017).

Unfortunately, physicians often avoid or delay disclosing details about patients' prognoses, and they resist initiating discussions about discontinuing therapeutic care and focusing on palliation of symptoms. In one study of patients with metastatic cancer, only about 16 percent of patients had an accurate awareness of their prognosis.[63] With respect to patients with likely incurable cancers, another study found that while two-thirds of physicians tell their patients at the initial visit that they have an incurable form of cancer, only one-third ever discuss life expectancy at any point in the relationship.[64] Yet another survey of physician disclosure habits found that while 65 percent of physicians would discuss prognosis with patients who are asymptomatic but have four to six months to live, most physicians would wait until patients have symptoms to discuss DNAR status, hospice, and preferred site of death.[65] Given the unpredictability of the course of serious illness, delaying discussion of these matters will inevitably mean that some patients miss the singular opportunity to make important and deeply personal choices about how they will spend their last months and weeks of life.

Physicians also tend to overestimate the remaining life spans of seriously ill patients and to convey prognoses in overly optimistic terms. In one study, researchers found that in predicting patients' remaining life expectancies, physicians were correct only 20 percent of the time and were overoptimistic 63 percent of the time. They also noted that a closer doctor-patient relationship was associated with overoptimistic predictions.[66] While it is rather nice to think that physicians have a harder time giving bad news to patients whom they feel close to, they do their patients no favors by withholding information that is directly relevant to decisions about future treatment and future remaining life. In fact, outside the very narrow confines of therapeutic privilege or waiver, these physicians breach their ethical duty to the patient.

A review of empirical research concerning physician honesty regarding prognosis revealed that although most clinicians believe that truth-telling is important, many avoid the discussion or provide less than full disclosure to patients. The ethical value of truth-telling is defined as honest communication about prognosis or other end-of-life issues and, like autonomy and beneficence, should guide medical care and decision-making.[67] In spite of this ethical imperative, quite a few physicians admit that even when cancer patients specifically request prognostic estimates, they

63 Pang-Hsiang Liu et al., Physicians' Propensity to Discuss Prognosis Is Associated with Patients' Awareness of Prognosis for Metastatic Cancers, 17 J. Palliative Med. 673–682 (2014).

64 Belinda E. Kiely et al., Thinking and Talking About Life Expectancy in Incurable Cancer, 38 Seminars in Oncology 380–385 (2011).

65 Nancy L. Keating et al., Physician Factors Association with Discussions About End-of-Life Care, 116 Cancer 998–1006 (2010).

66 Nicholas A. Christakis & Elizabeth B. Lamont, Extent and Determinants of Error in Doctors' Prognoses in Terminally Ill Patients, 320 Brit. Med. J. 469–473 (2000).

67 Karen Hancock et al., Truth-Telling in Discussing Prognosis in Advanced Life-Limiting Illness: A Systematic Review, 21 Palliative Med. 507–517 (2007).

withhold their opinion or provide a deliberately inaccurate figure in many cases. In a study that looked at how physicians communicated expected survival times to patients with terminal cancer, physicians were frank with patients only 37 percent of the time, provided deliberately inaccurate survival estimates about 40 percent of the time, and preferred to offer no estimate (deliberately withholding information) for about 23 percent of the patients studied. The authors concluded that "for all of these patients, physicians were able and willing to formulate objective prognoses, whether accurate or not, but had difficulty communicating them, even to insistent patients."[68] A surprising number of physicians admit to deliberately deceiving patients when discussing prognoses. In a survey of physicians, one in ten physicians admitted to *lying* to a patient within the previous year, and more than half acknowledged that they had been unreasonably optimistic about a patient's prognosis,[69] which is, at best, a lie of omission. It is more than a bit ironic that some physicians believe that they can preserve patient trust by withholding crucial and objective information. In such cases, it is unsurprising that physicians hesitate to state a firm prognosis, even when pressed to do so.

Conducting truthful and timely conversations on a regular basis requires time, exacts an emotional toll, and demands a level of skill and compassion that is not easy for physicians to achieve and maintain. They are seeking to strike a fine balance – providing patients with enough appropriate information to guide their decisions while supporting them emotionally, communicating kindly and humanely and without hurry, and allowing time for tears and questions and grief. In cases where the recommendation is de-escalation of burdensome care, physicians worry that patients will feel abandoned. In modern medicine, time pressure alone creates a barrier to good communication. A plethora of training courses and advice articles teach physicians how to communicate bad news, and they certainly provide tools, talking points, even suggested phrasing for physicians who struggle with communication. But the physician who is too emotionally involved, or not empathetic enough, or who fears a 'scene' with the patient or family and so avoids communicating truthful information about the patient's situation still needs to be willing to undertake this training and to try to implement it. The advice provided in this sort of training may, for some physicians, feel unnatural and forced. Practice helps, of course, but these conversations will always be more difficult for some physicians than for others.[70] Chapters 6 and 8 explore more deeply the many reasons why physicians are reluctant to talk with patients about poor prognoses and other bad news.

68 Elizabeth B. Lamont & Nicholas A. Christakis, Prognostic Disclosure to Patients with Cancer Near the End of Life, 134 Annals Internal Med. 1096–1105 (2001).

69 Lisa I. Lezzoni, et al., Survey Shows That at Least Some Physicians Are Not Always Open or Honest with Patients, 31 Health Aff. 383–391 (2012).

70 Maria J. Friedrichsen et al., Breaking Bad News in the Transition from Curative to Palliative Cancer Care – Patient's View of the Doctor Giving the Information, 8 Support Care Cancer 472–478 (2000).

Even the best physician communicators will encounter patients who are less willing or able to comprehend and accept information about prognosis and treatment efficacy. The physician may effectively convey diagnosis, prognosis, and other relevant information clearly but the patient may not take it in. When patients receive the initial news of, for example, a cancer diagnosis, it is difficult to listen, comprehend, and retain medical information in the emotions of the moment.[71] There are patients with metastatic cancer who, for example, express excitement that immunotherapy treatment doesn't cause hair loss. Given the gravity of the medical situation and the other potentially dangerous side effects associated with immunotherapy, the emphasis on lack of hair loss is startling. Whether deliberate or the result of emotional and information overload, this sort of patient misunderstanding is, like bad decision-making overall, multi-causal. Some forms of communication and comprehension problems can be overcome, at least with most patients. Taking time, avoiding medical jargon, shared decision-making, and the use of decision aids to explain treatments and harms in a factual and comprehensible way, all can improve patient understanding of prognosis and treatment options. Chapter 11 explores some of these approaches in more detail. But patients who remain in denial about their prognosis may simply refuse, consciously or unconsciously, to process what they have heard and make decisions accordingly. Sherwin Nuland has observed that a fair number of terminally ill patients never get to the 'acceptance' stage of Elisabeth Kübler-Ross's five stages of grief.[72] They remain in a state of denial of impending death until the very end.[73]

The evidence also suggests that patients who have end-of-life discussions with their physicians do not report added sadness or worry, beyond what they naturally experience in the face of a terminal illness. To the contrary, as one study of cancer patients demonstrated, these conversations are positively associated with patients' accepting that their illness is terminal, choosing comfort care over life-prolonging technologies, and completing a DNAR order. As in many other studies, patients in this studied group who did not have end-of-life conversations were significantly more likely to receive burdensome medical care in their last days of life and to experience a diminished quality of life.[74] Avoiding discussions about the patient's situation may in fact perpetuate anxiety by prolonging the process of accepting the prognosis and deciding about future care.[75] For many people, probably most, acceptance of terminal illness, processing the reality of impending death, and then

[71] Kristina Chapman et al., Lay Understanding of Terms Used in Cancer Consultations, 12 Psycho-Oncology 557–566 (2003).

[72] Elisabeth Kubler-Ross, On Death & Dying (Simon & Schuster 1969). The five stages are denial, anger, bargaining, depression, and acceptance.

[73] Sherwin B. Nuland, How We Die p. 228 (Knopf 1994).

[74] Alexi A. Wright et al., Associations Between End-of-Life Discussions, Patient Mental Health, Medical Care Near Death, and Caregiver Bereavement Adjustment, 300 JAMA 1665–1673 (2008).

[75] Rachelle E. Bernacki & Susan D. Block, Communication About Serious Illness Care Goals: A Review and Synthesis of Best Practices, 174 JAMA Internal Med. 1994–2003 (2014).

being able to make important decisions, all take time. When patients are deprived of that time, they lose out. The short-term benefit of 'not having to think about it' becomes meaningless when the truth finally becomes known, especially when the patient has lost the opportunity to make and implement treatment decisions that align with his preferences and to otherwise get his affairs in order. All of the patient's family and friends may similarly lose the opportunity to come to terms with losing the patient in the near future and to have important conversations with him.

It is also important to avoid shortcuts in these conversations. For example, statistical life expectancy based on past experience with similar populations provides a snapshot of population trends, but it's difficult to assess its relevance to any particular patient's situation. There is often no way to predict whether a particular patient will outlive the statistical projection for life expectancy or die much sooner than the average.[76] This form of clinical uncertainty, however, is no excuse to avoid discussion – it is only important to explain to the patient the limitations of statistics (and to do so symmetrically, rather than emphasizing only the possibility of outliving the average). Similarly, prognosis for meaningful recovery in many medical circumstances, such as for stroke patients, requires a discussion between physician and patient of complex variables such as the likelihood that the patient will regain a degree of physical function that is acceptable to the patient. A meta-analysis of data from multiple studies on the recovery of stroke patients who were receiving mechanical ventilation found that prognosis was generally poor, with 58 percent of these patients dying within thirty days, but that a minority of patients survived without severe disability. The authors of this study caution that physicians can be unrealistically optimistic *or* pessimistic in various circumstances.[77] The question of clinical and prognostic uncertainty and their consequences looms large in the context of decision-making for patients with life-threatening illness, something that Chapter 8 explores in depth.

On top of these considerations, conversations between physicians and patients need to cover more ground than simply discussing prognosis. Patients themselves overestimate their chances of survival and often mistakenly believe that certain interventions such as 'palliative chemotherapy', with its accompanying serious toxicity and other adverse effects, can potentially provide a cure. Physicians should recognize that patients frequently fail to understand that certain invasive treatments lack curative value, either because this information is not included in the consent discussion or because it is impossible to predict with any accuracy the effects of the

[76] George A. Diamond, Future Imperfect: The Limitations of Clinical Prediction Models and the Limits of Clinical Prediction, 14 J. Am. Coll. of Cardiology A12, A12-22 (1989). Courts also have recognized the limitations of statistical prognoses in the context of defining boundaries of informed consent. Arato v. Avedon, 858 P.2d 598 (Cal. 1993) ("[S]tatistical life expectancy data had little predictive value when applied to a particular patient with individualized symptoms, medical history, character traits, and other variables.").

[77] Robert G. Holloway et al., Prognosis and Decision Making in Severe Stroke, 294 JAMA 725–733 (2005).

treatment on a particular patient. Regarding chemotherapy for metastatic cancer, one study found that 69 percent of patients with lung cancer and 81 percent of patients with colorectal cancer incorrectly believed that the chemotherapy they were receiving might possibly cure their disease,[78] rather than simply slowing its progression. In another similar study of patients with incurable cancer, half of the patients believed that the goal of therapy was curative.[79] In yet another study of patients who were newly diagnosed with metastatic lung cancer, researchers compared two groups – one group received standard oncology care while the other received standard oncology care plus palliative care and support from the beginning of their participation in the study. Among the total number of patients participating, almost one-third believed that their cancer was curable. Nearly all patients understood that the goals of therapy were life extension and improvement of symptoms, but nearly 70 percent of these patients also expressed a therapeutic goal of 'getting rid' of all of the cancer. Because palliative care includes not only symptom management but also educating patients and families about the disease, its prognosis, and the harms and benefits of therapies, it can help patients and families make informed decisions about treatment, including declining treatment that will likely provide little or no benefit. In the study, the group of patients who received palliative care support soon after diagnosis had a much more accurate understanding of their terminal prognoses and were substantially less likely to have chemotherapy at the end of life. Only 10 percent of the palliative care group had late-stage chemotherapy compared with half of the standard oncology care group.[80]

As this last study illustrates, the problem with unrealistic expectations of cure is that patients will be more likely to consent to treatment that may possibly palliate symptoms or even extend life but is also likely to cause significant toxic effects that will impair quality of remaining life. These concerns are even more troubling when physicians offer patients truly experimental treatments, or therapies that have not been proven to work for their particular form of disease – something that one oncologist called "desperation oncology."[81] Patients who understand that chemotherapy under these circumstances cannot cure their illness and will at best slow its progress may weigh the value of this treatment differently and may be more likely to

78 Jane C. Weeks et al., Patients' Expectations About Effects of Chemotherapy for Advanced Cancer, 367 New Eng. J. Med. 1616–1625 (2012) (noting that, "[p]aradoxically, patients who reported higher scores for physician communication were also at higher risk for inaccurate expectations" regarding the curative potential of chemotherapy).

79 Areej El-Jawahri et al., Associations Among Prognostic Understanding, Quality of Life, and Mood in Patients With Advanced Cancer, 120 Cancer 278–285 (2014).

80 Jennifer S. Temel et al., Longitudinal Perceptions of Prognosis and Goals of Therapy in Patients with Metastatic Non-Small-Cell Lung Cancer: Results of a Randomized Study of Early Palliative Care, 29 J. Clinical Oncology 2319–2326 (2011) (10 percent in the palliative care group versus 50 percent in the standard care group).

81 Gina Kolata, Desperation Oncology: When Patients Are Dying, Some Cancer Doctors Turn to Immunotherapy, N.Y. Times, Apr. 26, 2018, www.nytimes.com/2018/04/26/health/doctors-cancer-immunotherapy.html.

decline it. The conversation between physician and patient that is needed to evaluate the patient's level of understanding in these circumstances is likely to be as challenging as any conversation about poor prognosis. Simply presenting patients with statistics about likely prognosis and the efficacy and side effects of various treatment options is no substitute for the broader responsibility to the patient to discuss the reality of the patient's particular situation (as far as it can be known) and the relative merits of the available options. The challenge for physicians is to present information that will allow patients and families to make informed decisions and to guide those decisions with the physician's expert judgment about the best course of action without overwhelming patients with unwanted or confusing data. Physicians need to take the lead on these conversations, beginning with an understanding of what the patient would like to know and following up with honest answers.[82]

Without truthful information about prognosis or the probable value of medical interventions, the ideal of patient autonomy doesn't mean much, except in those narrowly defined waiver cases where the patient opts to leave decisions to the physician. And there is an obvious danger in this choice. As Nuland observed, "Many a patient worn down by the ravages of illness or overwhelmed by the immediacies of a dire situation will be unwilling or emotionally unable to use his autonomy. The need to be cared for and to be relieved of responsibilities is not easily dealt with under such circumstances, and it may lead to wrong decisions."[83] When a patient opts out of participating in his treatment decisions, the very human tendency of physicians to err on the side of caution may mean that the patient receives more medical interventions, with all of their attendant harms, than he would otherwise want. Nuland exhorts every patient to "study his or her own disease and learn enough about it to recognize the onset of that time when further treatment becomes a debatable issue," adding that "it should not be beyond the capacities of any but a small percentage of people to accomplish" this task.[84] With respect, this vision of patient participation is probably more than a bit optimistic, given the challenges of mortality denial, medical literacy problems, the desire to retain hope (about which Nuland writes so movingly), and the cognitive obstacles to comprehension and authentic decision-making. Even so, the physician has the responsibility to educate the patient, and providing patients with accessible literature about their condition and treatments may help with this process.

YET ANOTHER CHALLENGE: STATISTICS AND INNUMERACY

On top of all of the professional complexity of deciding whether and when and how to convey truthful information to patients about their illness, physicians need to try

[82] Constantine Alifrangis et al., The Experiences of Cancer Patients, 104 Quarterly J. Med. 1075, 1079–80 (2011).

[83] Nuland, How We Die p. 229.

[84] Ibid., p. 260.

to avoid muddying the waters in describing potential treatment efficacy or prognosis. For example, patients will perceive very different messages if the physician, when discussing a surgical intervention, describes it as giving a patient "a 50 percent chance at a better outcome" versus that same intervention increasing the patient's chance "of improved outcome from 5 percent to 7.5 percent."[85] Most patients are not equipped to comprehend and ask skeptical questions about the presentation of statistical outcomes so it is up to the physician to explain things clearly.[86]

Physicians themselves may struggle with how to interpret statistics, and they receive very little training on the subject in medical school.[87] In one study of physician comprehension of the concept of 'false positives' in medical tests, researchers asked an array of physicians and medical students the following question: "If a test to detect a disease whose prevalence is 1/1000 has a false positive rate of 5 percent, what is the chance that a person found to have a positive result actually has the disease, assuming you know nothing about the person's symptoms or signs?" Of the sixty-one participants in the study, only fourteen provided the correct answer, which is 2 percent. About three-quarters of the participants answered the question incorrectly. The most common incorrect answer was the furthest from the statistical reality: 95 percent. The study authors recommended increased training for physicians in evaluating the value of diagnostic testing.[88] As a commentator on the study explained, the common answer of 95 percent is "radically, catastrophically wrong." If one in 1,000 people have a given disease, a 5 percent false positive rate means that, out of the 999 others, about fifty would test positive for the disease even though they do not have it. So, a total of fifty-one people would receive positive results but only one of those fifty-one actually has the disease in question (one true positive test result versus fifty false positives). Therefore, if the test result is positive, the correct statistical chance of having the disease is five out of 51 or about 2 percent, not 95 percent.[89] The problem with incorrect understanding of false positives (and statistics in general) is that patients may be subjected to potentially harmful treatment for a disease that they do not actually have or may agree to a treatment that they incorrectly believe has a decent chance of helping.

Similarly, there is a misperception that cancer screening saves lives. For cancers that can be prevented or cured with early detection, this is clearly correct. Colonoscopy to detect precancerous and early stage cancerous polyps saves lives,

85 Robert G. Holloway et al., Prognosis and Decision Making in Severe Stroke, 294 JAMA 725–733 (2005).

86 Ellen Peters et al., Numeracy Skill and the Communication, Comprehension, and Use of Risk-Benefit Information, 26 Health Aff. 741–748 (2007). For a fabulous example of an exception to this generalization, see Stephan Jay Gould, The Median Isn't the Message, 15 Virtual Mentor 77–81 (2013).

87 Daniel Morgan, What the Tests Don't Show, Wash. Post, Oct. 5, 2018.

88 Arjun K. Manrai et al., Medicine's Uncomfortable Relationship with Math: Calculating Positive Predictive Value, 174 JAMA Internal Med. 991–993 (2014).

89 Morgan, What the Tests Don't Show.

as do Pap smears to detect the early cell changes that come with human papilloma virus (HPV) infection that can cause cervical cancer. Unfortunately, not all cancers, even when detected early, are curable. In a study of physicians, nearly half of those surveyed incorrectly believed that detecting more cases of cancer in screened populations proves the value of screening. The study authors provide the following scenario to describe the problem of lead-time bias:

> Imagine a group of patients in whom cancer was diagnosed because of symptoms at age 67 years, all of whom die at age 70 years. Each patient survives for only 3 years so the 5-year survival for the group is 0 percent. Now imagine that the same group undergoes screening. Screening tests by definition lead to earlier diagnosis. Suppose that with screening, cancer is diagnosed in all patients at age 60 years, but they nevertheless die at age 70 years. In this scenario, each patient survives 10 years, so the 5-year survival for the group is 100 percent. Yet, despite this dramatic improvement in survival (from 0 percent to 100 percent), nothing has changed about how many people die or when.

What *has* changed in the example is that the earlier-screened patients have to live for seven more years with the knowledge that they have a cancer that will kill them. As the study authors observe, what actually matters is evidence of reduced mortality rates rather than increased survival time.[90] What does all of this mean for those of us who aren't math whizzes? Many physicians do not fully understand the statistics that underlie their recommendations to patients. While it is important that physicians have truthful and timely conversations with patients about recommended therapeutic interventions and their chances for 'success', it's also important that the physicians themselves can correctly understand statistical information and accurately convey that information to patients. Experts have offered advice on how to communicate statistical information to patients in ways that reduce the risk of misunderstanding,[91] but physicians themselves first have to understand the statistics.

Overall, patient willingness to endure intensive therapy in exchange for increased survival varies widely; however, to make autonomy and informed consent meaningful, patients must receive specific, comprehensible information about prospective harms and benefits of treatment, including estimated survival benefit. When discussing these very complex calculations, physicians also should remind patients that they are providing information about statistical averages based on past experience with past cancer patients. There is (usually) no way to know whether any particular patient will meet or exceed the statistical survival benefit or rather fall well short of it. Chapter 8 further explores this interplay between statistical predictions and patient decision-making.

90 Odette Wegwarth et al., Do Physicians Understand Cancer Screening Statistics? A National Survey of Primary Care Physicians in the United States, 156 Annals Internal Med. 340–349 (2012).

91 Gerd Gigerenzer & Adrian Edwards, Simple Tools for Understanding Risks: From Innumeracy to Insight, 327 British J. Med. 741–744 (2003).

THE ALLURE OF HOPE

To be clear, physicians are not withholding information from patients for any nefarious reason (beyond perhaps wanting to avoid emotionally difficult conversations), but many express reluctance to convey statistical details about prognosis based on concern that the information would seem too abrupt and would interfere with patients' hope.[92] Consider for a moment what 'hope' actually means for terminally ill patients. While much of the literature on prognostic disclosure mentions the concern that patients who are told that they will die from their illness will 'lose hope', this phrase is often used without much reflection about its meanings or implications. Preserving hope by deception or evasion is troubling for several reasons. First, while it may be difficult for patients to hear bad news about prognosis, the costs of keeping this information from the patient are high – patients are far more likely to accept burdensome treatments that may offer little chance of advancing the patient's cause by prolonging life or remission of disease. Second, the deceit involved may, when revealed, cause the patient to lose trust in the physician. Although the wish to protect patients from distress may be well intentioned, "a conspiracy of silence usually results in a heightened state of fear, anxiety and confusion – not one of calm and equanimity."[93] Misguided attempts to preserve hope by avoiding discussion of reality deprive patients of the opportunity to voice their own fears, to prepare for death by speaking previously unspoken words to loved ones, and to get their affairs in order.

Of course, it is natural that seriously ill patients hope for a new discovery, a miracle cure – but these are extremely rare. Occasionally there is a great leap of progress toward effective therapy, even a game changer. Immunotherapy, for example, has dramatically altered the treatment landscape for many cancer patients, and oncologists have rapidly integrated immunotherapy technology into treatment as the gold standard for certain cancers. I'm not discounting the value of hope of a cure or a better-than-expected course of disease and length of survival, but it should be realistic hope. With adequate disclosure and comprehension of prognosis, patients can still hope, but within the realm of reason. For example, once a patient understands that 85 percent of patients with her disease die within five years, she might still rationally and reasonably hope that she might be among the fortunate 15 percent who survive much longer. She can also acknowledge that she has no way of knowing in advance whether she will fall into the statistical 85 percent or the 15 percent group, and she'd better prepare herself and her loved ones for the statistically more likely outcome and live her remaining life accordingly. This is hope with eyes wide open. Unfortunately, the medical system is built around

[92] Elisa J. Gordon & Christopher K. Daugherty, "Hitting You Over the Head": Oncologists' Disclosure of Prognosis to Advanced Cancer Patients, 17 Bioethics 142–168 (2003).

[93] Lesley J. Fallowfield et al., Truth May Hurt But Deceit Hurts More: Communication in Palliative Care, 16 Palliative Med. 297–303 (2002).

delivering the possible long-shot cure, what Atul Gawande calls "a multi-trillion dollar edifice for dispensing the medical equivalent of lottery tickets – and have only the rudiments of a system to prepare patients for the near certainty that those tickets will not win."[94] The problem with this hope for a highly improbable lottery win is that the patient can only buy one ticket, and the cost is existential – patients may not realize how the gamble might adversely impact what is left of their lives.

There also are concepts of hope that don't focus on long disease remission or cure. As Sherwin Nuland has explained, for patients with advanced disease, hope can be redefined to mean something different from hope of a cure. Terminally ill patients who actually know that they are dying may recast hope for more realistically achievable goals: the hope of dying at home without suffering, or the hope of celebrating one last Christmas or other family occasion.[95] Other patients may find hope in checking an item or two off of a 'bucket list'.[96] For all patients, hope may include achieving a sense of peace with the idea of simply not being here any longer, while dying in the knowledge that, by their own personal standards, they have lived life well.

THE IMPACT OF RACE AND RACISM

Conversations between physicians and patients with life-threatening illness are inherently difficult. Patients need to trust physicians in order to overcome the physician-patient information asymmetry and to accept physician recommendations. For racial minority patients, the overarching obstacles to high-level communication and decision-making operate within a broader realm of personal and systemic distrust. On the system level, historical research abuses such as the United States Public Health Services Study of Untreated Syphilis in Black Males (the Tuskegee Syphilis Experiment), in which Black men with syphilis were not given treatment even after it became available,[97] or the appropriation of the genetic material of a Black patient for profit,[98] continue to cast a large shadow over interactions between minority race patients and what is still a predominately White health care system. In addition, a large number of racial minority patients will also have experienced a medical system that has often overtly treated them as second-class citizens, or worse. Many commentators have concluded that the lack of trust in the medical system makes complex medical decisions even more difficult. Minority race patients must rely on the expertise of physicians as they navigate the

94 Atul Gawande, Being Mortal pp. 171–172 (Picador 2014).

95 Nuland, How We Die pp. 233, 239–241.

96 Vyjeyanthi S. Periyakoil et al., Common Items on a Bucket List, 25 J. Palliative Med. 652–658 (2018). The authors recommend discussions with patients about their bucket lists as a means to engage patients in conversation and informed decision-making.

97 Vicki S Freimuth, African Americans' Views on Research and the Tuskegee Syphilis Study, 52 Social Science and Med. 797–808 (2001).

98 Rebecca Skloot, The Immortal Life of Henrietta Lacks (Broadway 2010).

ongoing process of treatment while feeling uncertain about whether those same physicians are fully trustworthy.[99]

Given the profound and persistent inequities in the US health care system, and the history of mistreatment of Blacks and other underrepresented groups, it is no wonder that these patient populations distrust the medical system. Consider one incontrovertible example: several studies have demonstrated that Blacks are less likely than Whites to receive surgical treatment of early-stage lung cancer, and, consequently, have a lower overall survival rate for the disease.[100] One study followed nearly 11,000 lung cancer patients over the course of eight years and controlled for variables including disease stage, insurance coverage, socioeconomic status, access to care, and coexisting illness. The investigators found that Black patients underwent surgical resection of the cancer only 64 percent of the time, compared with a rate of nearly 77 percent for White patients in the studied group. The five-year survival rate for the Black group was correspondingly lower – about 26 percent versus 34 percent for White patients – whereas the five-year survival rate among patients who *had* undergone surgery was the same in both racial groups. Most strikingly, however, surgical resection is *the* optimal treatment for early-stage lung cancer, leaving little room for the argument that some other, less common but equally effective, treatment was indicated for any particular patient.[101] Two physicians, commenting on this study, lament that the results "suggest that there is a difference in how physicians manage cancer that is based on the patient's race, regardless of other attributes, and that the consequence of these lapses in care is reduced survival among blacks. Evidence that bias on the part of physicians (either overt prejudice or subconscious perceptions) influences access to optimal cancer care is disheartening."[102] For the minority patient, her loved ones, and her community, it is a disaster, and, of course, it feeds more justified distrust. There are too many similar examples of bias in health care to recount here, but the evidence is overwhelming.

The problem of distrust in the medical system originates in the past but lingers in the present due to ongoing racism within and outside of the medical system.[103] In

99 Laura S. Sullivan, Trust, Risk, and Race in American Medicine, 50 Hastings Ctr. Rep. 18–26 (2020).

100 Peter B. Bach et al., Racial Differences in the Treatment of Early-Stage Lung Cancer, 341 New Eng. J. Med. 1198–1205 (1999); Howard P. Greenwald et al., Social Factors, Treatment, and Survival in Early-Stage Non-Small Cell Lung Cancer, 88 Am. J. Pub. Health 1681–1684 (1998) (finding that White patients were 20 percent more likely to undergo surgery than Black patients and were 31 percent more likely to survive five years, commenting that "[p]oor general health and adverse health behavior (such as smoking), which often coincide with low income and membership in minority groups, may lead to lower rates of surgery as providers judge disadvantaged patients to be relatively poor surgical risks").

101 Bach et al., Racial Differences in the Treatment of Early-Stage Lung Cancer.

102 Talmadge E. King Jr. & Paul Brunetta, Racial Disparity in Rates of Surgery for Lung Cancer, 341 New Eng. J. Med. 1231–1233(1999).

103 Dinushika Mohottige & L. Ebony Boulware, Trust in American Medicine: A Call to Action for Health Professionals, 50 Hastings Ctr. Rep. 27–29 (2020).

a very recent survey, substantial percentages of Black and Latinx patients report experiencing racism in the health care system.[104] The effects of racism, implicit bias, and inequalities in the health care system play out in the form of very different patterns of end-of-life care for Black and other racial and ethnic minorities. Empirical research demonstrates that racial/ethnic minority race and lower socioeconomic status are associated with poorer patient ratings of health care quality and provider communication at the end of life.[105] External quality ratings for cancer care also document worse performance on various quality metrics for end-of-life care in cancer centers that serve a primarily minority population.[106] The data also document several relevant racial variations in the context of end-of-life decision-making and care. For example, Black and Latinx patients, having both personally and culturally experienced the denial of proper medical care compared with their White peers,[107] are less likely to receive palliative care and to utilize hospice[108] and are more likely to request life-sustaining treatments and CPR compared with White patients.[109] The implications of this pattern are deeply worrying – it indicates that patients who distrust the medical system as a whole are likely to resist suggestions to cease therapeutic interventions and pivot to palliation of symptoms and hospice care, even for their own benefit (because they cannot erase the sense of doubt and resulting possibility that they're being counselled into giving up on a longer life too early). This is a terrible burden to shoulder at life's end. Chapter 7 explores racial variations in the utilization of palliative and hospice care in more detail.

In addition to matters of trust, other factors, including religious beliefs and cultural differences from the Western norm, influence attitudes about patient autonomy in medical decision-making.[110] Because the quality of communication between physician and patient strongly influences the quality of care that the patient receives, inaccurate social and cultural assumptions will interfere with

[104] Paige Nong et al., Patient-Reported Experiences of Discrimination in the US Health Care System, 3 JAMA Network Open, DOI:10.1001/jamanetworkopen.2020.29650 (2020).

[105] Lisa C. Welch et al., End-of-Life Care in Black and White: Race Matters for Medical Care of Dying Patients and Their Families, 53 J. Am. Geriatric Soc. 1145–1153 (2005).

[106] Garrett T. Wasp, End-of-Life Quality Metrics Among Medicare Decedents at Minority-Serving Cancer Centers: A Retrospective Study, 9 Cancer Med. 1911–1921 (2020).

[107] M. Gregg Bloche, Trust and Betrayal in the Medical Marketplace, 55 Stanford L. Rev. 919–954 (2002).

[108] Amresh Hanchate et al., Racial and Ethnic Differences in End-of-Life Costs: Why Do Minorities Cost More than Whites? 169 Arch. Intern. Med. 493–98 (2009).

[109] Etienne Phipps et al., Approaching the End of Life: Attitudes, Preferences, and Behaviors of African-American and White Patients and Their Family Caregivers, 21 J. Clin. Oncology 549–554 (2003); Kimberly Johnson et al., What Explains Racial Differences in the Use of Advance Directives and Attitudes Towards Hospice Care? 56 J. Amer. Geriatrics Soc. 1953–1958 (2008); Amber E. Barnato, et al., Racial and Ethnic Differences in Preferences for End-of-Life Treatment, 24 J. Gen. Intern. Med. 695–701 (2009).

[110] Leslie J. Blackhall et al., Ethnicity and Attitudes Toward Patient Autonomy, 274 JAMA 820–825 (1995).

communication, and quality is likely to suffer.[111] In recognition of this problem, medical education and training in physician-patient communication needs to recognize the value and practices of 'cultural competence' – the awareness that patients of different racial, ethnic, and religious backgrounds may have different goals and values, and a corresponding ability to communicate effectively with these patients.[112] Cultural competence education only treats the symptoms rather than confronting the root causes of racism, but it is a start. The potent combination of well-justified distrust in the medical system and cultural non-Eurocentric differences may very well undermine the bond between physician and patient at a time when truthful, empathic, and complete communication matters the most.

'DOING EVERYTHING' VERSUS TRYING FOR 'JUST RIGHT'

The advent of modern life-supportive technologies and therapies allows physicians to keep patients alive when their bodies would otherwise succumb to an underlying illness or injury. When therapeutic and life-sustaining technologies are used to assist a patient through a difficult illness or injury and return to health, there is rarely any question about their appropriateness. When a patient's illness has progressed to the point where there is no hope of cure or even improvement, however, the use of these technologies in a situation that merely prolongs dying while increasing suffering poses complex ethical dilemmas. As Isaac Asimov observed, "The saddest aspect of life right now is that science gathers knowledge faster than society gathers wisdom."[113] The same can be said for medicine – medicine can now accomplish much more than it could in the past, but is the use of medical technology in an attempt to prolong life always wise? In the context of terminal illness, people frequently believe that more therapeutic care leads to longer life and improved physical well-being. We have all heard grieving families assure others that the doctors 'did everything they could'. 'Doing everything' may help to alleviate feelings of helplessness on the part of families (and physicians), but it is not necessarily in the patient's best interests, nor is it necessarily consistent with what the patient would choose, if fully informed of her prognosis and the opportunity costs of high-intensity care at the end of life. What most patients hope for is that physicians will do everything that will provide a benefit (as the patient perceives it) and nothing that will cause avoidable harm without accompanying benefit. Patients, if they are thinking about the calibration of end-of-life care, mainly hope that the physician gets their care 'just right', as defined by the patient. This is asking a lot of physicians,

[111] Insoo Hyun, Waiver of Informed Consent, Cultural Sensitivity, and the Problem of Unjust Families and Traditions, 32 Hastings Ctr. Rep. 14–22 (2002).

[112] Nancy Berlinger & Annalise Berlinger, Culture and Moral Distress: What's the Connection and Why Does It Matter? 19 AMA J. Ethics 608–616 (2017).

[113] Isaac Asimov Book of Science and Nature Quotations (Isaac Asimov & Jason A. Shulman, eds.) (Weidenfield & Nicholson 1988).

who cannot provide assurances of a 'just right' outcome. Moreover, it can never be known, even in hindsight, whether this optimal balance was achieved.

In this era of highly technological medical care, physicians and patients often feel complementarily reluctant to engage in detailed discussions about the patient's values, preferences, and concerns or, worse, even to acknowledge openly that the patient is dying.[114] The task of communicating with critically ill patients is emotionally difficult and time consuming and hard to get right. In the end, it's all about trying to strike the optimal medical balance in each individual case – which can never be described in advance by any kind of global, one-size-fits-all measure. Calibrating care for dying patients therefore requires timely, detailed, and honest physician-patient communication. Unless and until physicians and patients can have these conversations, many patients will continue to receive burdensome medical care that they otherwise would have refused if they had known in advance its implications for the quality of their last weeks and days. While there are many physicians who communicate well with patients and the discussion in this chapter doesn't apply to all physicians, the empirical research on the subject of physician-patient communication reveals common and unsettling shortcomings in current practices. Much of the discussion that follows attempts to unpack and explain the many causes of communication failure.

114 Timothy E. Quill, Initiating End-of-Life Discussions With Seriously Ill Patients: Addressing the "Elephant in the Room," 284 JAMA 2502–2507 (2000).

4

The Denial of Death and Its Sequelae

The fear of death follows from the fear of life.
A man who lives fully is prepared to die at any time.
—Edward Abbey[1]

A highly unscientific empirical analysis of one week's obituaries in my local newspaper revealed the following data: of the ninety-four individuals featured that week, only sixteen died (this includes those who died, died peacefully, or died suddenly). The rest passed away (peacefully or without elaboration), were called safely home, were taken too soon, entered into eternal rest, were reunited with loved ones, came to the end of his or her life adventure, or otherwise departed. Euphemism certainly has its place, and it is understandable that many people will opt for euphemism in obituaries. Nevertheless, it is striking how few of the authors of these announcements chose the most concise and descriptive word for the event.

This study of obituaries is instructive in broader terms. Our culture makes it quite difficult to acknowledge death, even when it has indisputably occurred or is imminent. Death and serious illness lead to awkward condolences and downcast eyes. Broader recognition of mortality and of how it gives life meaning is even more challenging – though the greats throughout history have frequently made this point. Franz Kafka, for example, wrote in a letter: "The meaning of life is that it stops." There is an understandable, but ultimately self-defeating, duality at work in the context of denial of death, which often becomes apparent at the onset of serious illness. Many people avoid thinking about mortality until a serious illness or advancing infirmity makes consideration of impending death unavoidable. Once faced with a potentially life-ending diagnosis, however, people (understandably) try to exert tremendous control over the illness and the dying process.

[1] Edward Abbey, A Voice Crying in the Wilderness p. 36 (St. Martins Griffin, 1989).

As individuals, we have different attitudes toward the prospect of death, especially our own. Consider some poetic takes on death. Some openly express fear:

I that in heill wes and gladnes,
Am trublit now with gret seiknes,
And feblit with infermite;
Timor mortis conturbat me.

Our plesance heir is all vane glory,
This fals warld is bot transitory,
The flesche is brukle, the Fend is sle;
Timor mortis conturbat me.[2]

Others, perhaps especially those who genuinely believe in an afterlife, can live with some serenity in the face of mortality:

Death is nothing at all.
It does not count.
I have only slipped away into the next room.
Nothing has happened.

*****

Life means all that it ever meant.
It is the same as it ever was.
There is absolute and unbroken continuity.
What is this death but a negligible accident?

Why should I be out of mind because I am out of sight?
I am but waiting for you, for an interval,
somewhere very near,
just round the corner.

All is well.
Nothing is hurt; nothing is lost.
One brief moment and all will be as it was before.
How we shall laugh at the trouble of parting when we meet again![3]

The reality is that most of us try not to dwell too much on death – because "[n]either the sun nor death can be looked at steadily."[4] It is something that happens to old people, or to other people, or even if it's going to happen to us eventually, that event is a long way off, and there is no need to consider it in the moment. Yet, we all are, at least occasionally, uncomfortably aware of the passage of time. Time flies, time

2 William Dunbar, Lament for the Makaris (15th century). *Timor mortis conturbat me* is a Latin refrain in this medieval English poem: "The fear of death distresses me."
3 Henry Scott-Holland, Death Is Nothing At All (1847–1918).
4 François de La Rochefoucauld, Reflections; or Sentences and Moral Maxims (1678).

drags, time stands still, but most of us notice at some point that a calendar year seems to go by much more quickly than it used to. Every passing year becomes a smaller fraction of an entire life. I recall my elderly father looking at me one New Year's Eve, with wide eyes, asking, "Where did the year go?" We have all experienced the elasticity of time and, in our later years, will experience its acceleration. At the end of life, time may slow with suffering. Even so, a few hours or days at this point in life potentially hold enormous value – as an opportunity to experience one final time the joy of love, friendship, and family, to say things long unsaid, and to say good-bye.

There are many different ways to measure time. There are the usual units of time – years, months, moon phases, weeks, days, hours, minutes, and seconds. There are mornings and evenings, weekdays and weekends, planting and harvest, and the four seasons. There are also the large-scale units – eons, eras, epochs, millennia, and centuries. Then there are the more mundane, banal measures of the passage of time. T. S. Eliot's Prufrock "measured out [his] life with coffee spoons."[5] For me, it's tubes of toothpaste. I usually buy my preferred brand in a two-pack and, when I am about halfway through the second tube, I make a mental plan to buy more toothpaste. As I was brushing my teeth one morning and noting that I was halfway through the second tube, I remembered an estate sale that I'd visited in my neighborhood. The agents running the sale had put price stickers on *every* object in the house, even partially consumed bottles of shampoo and tubes of toothpaste. Apart from the fact that scoring a bargain on a dead person's half-used tube of toothpaste seems grotesque, the collection of personal care items for sale provided a rather poignant reminder that, at some point, it all stops – mid-toothpaste tube, most likely. None of us has any way of gauging how many more tubes we will need to buy, even though we know that we brush twice daily and use one tube every four weeks. Some will stock up on toothpaste so that there will be more tubes in the house than their remaining years of teeth cleaning will require, but stockpiling toothpaste – or anything else – doesn't buy immortality or help much with the fear of death.

In the early and middle decades of a natural life-span, we tend to orient our thoughts toward an unknown but comfortably unquantifiable future. By middle age, we become uncomfortably aware that the time-bound future is becoming ineluctably shorter, and we may stop looking forward as frequently and start looking back more often. This past, while no doubt filled with the usual (or unusual) perturbations of life, has an allure. For those of us who are fortunate to be born and to live in a first-world country with comfortable access to the necessities of life, and who are also fortunate enough to live into late middle age, the past (if we are lucky) is filled with good memories of people and experiences. It's always true that at any age, the future (however measured) becomes shorter with every day lived, but it's easier to ignore this fact in youth and perhaps, for some, in middle age. Once we experience a clear demarcation line, however, such as diagnosis with a life-threatening illness, the end of

5 T. S. Eliot, The Love Song of J. Alfred Prufrock in Collected Poems 1909–1962 (Harcourt, 1917).

the future becomes more visible, prominent, and real. The fear of death, which is always with us, comes roaring to the forefront of consciousness.

Every human culture has long struggled with the foreknowledge of death, the inevitable by-product of human sapience. The idea that death makes no exception for anyone, no matter how powerful, wealthy, and determined, resonates from the oldest of literature through modern music. From 'Timor Mortis' poems to Shakespeare's golden lads and chimney sweepers,[6] to Kansas singing "Dust in the Wind," humankind has always acknowledged the fact of mortality. Extended human longevity, however, is a new development – a product of the twentieth century. The evolution of medical care in particular – from care focused on the emotional, spiritual, and physical needs of the dying to high-tech efforts to stave off death – has, paradoxically, exacerbated the fear and denial of death that permeates our culture. Instead of appreciating significantly more lifetime than our forebears ever had, we seem to appreciate that we now have significantly more time and leisure to worry about dying.

Beginning in the mid-to-late nineteenth century, dying was transformed from an accepted (though generally unwelcome) life passage into a medical crisis, with the resultant medicalization of the deathbed. Around the middle of the nineteenth century, "[t]he most apparent manifestation of the medicalization of death took place when the doctor replaced the priest as master of ceremonies."[7] Before then, it was common for physicians to leave their dying patients in the care of family members and clergy when they could no longer offer any useful treatment. By the mid-1800s, however, expectations and practices began to change, and physicians often remained with their dying patients until the end. Although this change in practice predated any new ability to treat dying patients, cultural attitudes toward the deathbed were shifting. Despite their inability to provide any curative care, physicians began to believe that they had a "responsibility to hold out some, even if very limited, course of action to the dying patient, to help her overcome a sense of helplessness."[8]

In the past, patients and families nearly always had firsthand experience with death – even in the early twentieth century – a world war and the 1918 flu pandemic made death an everyday reality. As Joan Didion also has observed, at the turn of the twentieth century, "the act of dying had not yet been professionalized. It did not typically involve hospitals. . . . Death was up close, at home. The average adult was expected to deal competently, and also sensitively, with its aftermath."[9] Now that many more deaths occur in hospitals and long-term care facilities, many adults have

6 William Shakespeare, Cymbeline, Act IV, Scene 2. ("Fear no more the heat o' the sun, / Nor the furious winter's rages; / Thou thy worldly task hast done, / Home art gone, and ta'en thy wages; / Golden lads and girls all must, / As chimney-sweepers, come to dust.").

7 Shai Lavi, How Dying Became a "Life Crisis," 137 Daedalus 57–65 (2008).

8 Ibid.

9 Joan Didion, The Year of Magical Thinking pp. 60–61 (Vintage Books, 2006).

no practical experience and competence in dealing with death. With the progress of modern medicine, patients began to believe that with sufficient effort (medical and otherwise), there could also be hope of a 'solution' to the 'problem' of dying.

Until relatively recently, religious faith played a dominant role in the lives of many, if not most, people. Most faiths, including Christianity, offer the promise of eternal life after bodily death, at least if the individual has taken the appropriate steps to achieve salvation. For those who have faith, the promise of an afterlife must surely provide some comfort in the face of death. Yet, Christianity also acknowledges the fear of death.[10] When society had all the rituals of organized religion, there was a pre-approved and accepted pathway, a collective set of instructions about how to live right and, finally, enter Paradise. While many people still embrace religious beliefs, others, in today's more secular age, lack the framework of organized religion to navigate the prospect of death. With the 'safety net' of formal religion gone,[11] the fear of death may be partially grounded in an uncomfortable realization – that it is up to the individual to determine how to live life well and how to reconcile herself to mortality.

Religious faith does not necessarily guarantee a serene acceptance of death. Surprisingly, some research suggests that religious beliefs and traditions do not decrease fear of death, although these studies produced mixed results.[12] In fact, one study indicates that terminally ill patients who identify with a religious faith or practice are more likely than agnostic or atheist patients to seek burdensome care at the end of life. The study found a correlation between high levels of religious belief and preferences for intensive life-prolonging care, including ventilation and resuscitation. While unable to fully explain this result, the study authors speculated that these preferences might arise from a sense that the sanctity of life requires the patient to submit to all available efforts to prolong it – and that suffering at death furthers a religious purpose.[13] There are also patients and families who hope for a miracle despite a patient's poor prognosis. Belief in miracles is quite common in the United States,[14] leading to situations in which patients seek all possible life-prolonging care to give their deity time to intervene.

CULTURAL INDICIA OF THE FEAR OF DEATH

In American culture, the denial of death and aging undergirds quite a lot of popular thinking, and our medical system operates within this denialist culture. The luxury

10 The Book of Psalms contains a plea for more time before the singer confronts his death: "Hear my prayer, O Lord, and give ear unto my cry; hold not thy peace at my tears: for I am a stranger with thee, and a sojourner, as all my fathers were. O Spare me, that I may recover strength, before I go hence, and be no more." Psalm 39:12–13 (King James Version).

11 Peter D. Heinegg, ed., Mortalism: Readings on the Meaning of Life p. 10 (Prometheus 2003).

12 Timothy P. Daaleman & Larry VandeCreek, Placing Religion and Spirituality in End-of-Life Care, 284 JAMA 2514–2517 (2000).

13 Andrea C. Phelps et al., Religious Coping and Use of Life-Prolonging Care Near Death in Patients with Advanced Cancer, 301 JAMA 1140–1147 (2009).

14 Eric W. Widera et al., Approaching Patients and Family Members Who Hope for a Miracle, 42 J. Pain & Symptom Mgmt. 119–124 (2011).

of time, in the form of longer average life-spans, together with the promise of new therapies, has created the illusion that there is time to procrastinate, to delay confronting mortality, perhaps even the hope of postponing death indefinitely. Some researchers now talk of doubling the human life-span, even of a 'cure for death', and of aging as a 'disease' that should be treated.[15] Daniel Callahan and others have criticized this mind-set, arguing that research "should not, even implicitly, have eradication of death as its goal" because it supplants emphasis on the importance of relieving suffering at the end of life and it "promotes the idea among the public and physicians that death represents a failure of medicine."[16] But research into life-span extension continues, now with lots of funding from tech billionaires, and with little regard for the consequences of the distorted message it sends or for its overall logical futility.[17] As one commentator quipped, "[o]nce regarded as an unyielding, utterly unforgiving, brute feature of existence, death is increasingly portrayed as a bad lifestyle option."[18] This quest for a modern fountain of youth denies the reality of mortality and ignores the fact that more days or years of life do not necessarily guarantee more quality of life or more contentment with what life brings.

Cultural portrayals of older people provide more evidence of ambivalence about aging. We hear phrases like 'sixty is the new forty' and see advertisements for 'adult communities' depicting vigorous, tanned septuagenarians playing golf and tennis. As a society, we celebrate youth and physical perfection, and we seek it for ourselves. There are advertisements everywhere for pills and treatments for all sorts of ills associated with aging – a brain oxygen-boosting miracle for memory; human growth hormone treatment to grow more youthful; dietary supplements to increase energy, strength, and sex drive. We also spend enormous amounts on beauty and anti-aging products and services – from plastic surgery and injectable muscle-paralyzing toxins to hair color products and skin creams.[19] The results may create the appearance of youth and may therefore support the fiction that aging happens to other people, but no amount of Botox is going to dissipate the fear of death. Negativity about aging permeates our society and makes efforts to embrace aging and, eventually, dying very difficult. Old age is rarely revered anymore in Western societies, and older people internalize negative stereotypes of aging, which can affect perception of quality of life.[20]

15 Thomas Donaldson, Prospects of a Cure for "Death," Alcor Life Extension Foundation, https://alcor.org/Library/html/ProspectsOfACureForDeath.html; Lawrence M. Fisher, The Race to Cash in on the Genetic Code, NY Times, Aug. 29, 1999 (quoting William Haseltine, then CEO of Human Genome Sciences, as saying that "[d]eath is a series of preventable diseases"), www.nytimes.com/1999/08/29/business/the-race-to-cash-in-on-the-genetic-code.html.

16 Daniel Callahan, Death and the Research Imperative, 342 New Eng. J. Med. 654, 654–55 (2000).

17 Ariana Eunjung Cha, Tech Titans' Latest Project: Defy Death, Wash. Post (Apr. 4, 2015), www.washingtonpost.com/sf/national/2015/04/04/tech-titans-latest-project-defy-death/.

18 Leigh Turner, Antiaging, 292 JAMA 2155–2156 (2004).

19 Laurie Essig, American Plastic: Boob Jobs, Credit Cards, and Our Quest for Perfection (Beacon Press, 2010).

20 Els van Wijngaarden et al., A Captive, a Wreck, a Piece of Dirt: Aging Anxieties Embodied in Older People With a Death Wish, 80 OMEGA – J. of Death and Dying 245–265 (2019).

Paradoxically, alongside this anti-aging juggernaut, there is now an industry of death and dying. Death memoirs are nothing new, but they appear to have multiplied and moved online in recent decades.[21] Some of these memoirs contemplate what it means to be a patient captive to medicine and disease or describe a brave 'battle' and a consequent appreciation of life.[22] Others explain how the experience of terminal illness casts the sufferer into the role of an outsider, no longer a member of society in the usual sense. In one such book, the author also explains the reasons for his refusal of surgery and other treatment for his cancer, adding that "[n]aturally it is appropriate to show a patient who chooses metastasis instead of the technological prolongation of death a certain admiration, even though, strictly speaking, he hardly deserves it, for he really has only a choice between two evils and it is almost purely a question of taste as to which he prefers."[23] The author neatly presented the stark choice he faced – no treatment and no side effects and certain death versus treatment and side effects and certain death. The mere fact that he could state the choice so succinctly makes him an outlier, not to mention that he refused therapeutic treatment and died in his late 50s. The increasing practice of publicly sharing one's innermost thoughts and graphic experiences of illness via social media seems paradoxical when juxtaposed with the general unwillingness to engage in conversation about end-of-life preferences or to acknowledge and accept aging and the prospect of death. In the United States and elsewhere, there are multitudes of death memoirs and manuals, sharing websites and blogs on the experience of terminal illness. Many of these sources provide solace for ill patients and their families – a community of suffering and support – but all of this together suggests that, as a society, we postpone thinking about death until it's unavoidable.

The battle metaphor appears frequently in the context of discussions about treatment for life-threatening illness – particularly cancer. Observers praise those who choose to pursue all avenues for extending and preserving life as 'fighters'. There is also talk of a person's 'losing the battle with cancer'. The metaphor has several problematic implications. First, it suggests that a cancer patient who dies from his disease has somehow failed – to be smart enough, brave enough, or tough enough to outwit and defeat the cancer. This implies that better choices by the patient would have resulted in 'victory' when, in fact, for many cancers and other life-ending diseases, there is simply no victory to be had.[24] The battle metaphor may

[21] The German language even has a typically succinct compound word for such books – Krebsbüchlein, which roughly translates as "little cancer book."

[22] Edward E. Rosenbaum, A Taste of My Own Medicine (Random House, 1988); John Gunther, Death Be Not Proud (Modern Library, 1953).

[23] Peter Noll, In the Face of Death pp. 3–4 (Viking, 1989).

[24] Lee M. Ellis, et al., Losing "Losing the Battle with Cancer," 1 JAMA Oncology 13–14 (2015); Jane Demmen et al., A Computer-Assisted Study of the Use of Violence Metaphors for Cancer and End of Life by Patients, Family Carers and Health Professionals, 20 Int'l J. Corpus Linguistics 205–231 (2015) (patients, caregivers, and health care professionals all use metaphors such as "fight," "battle," and "war" with varying but statistically similar degrees of frequency).

also subtly pressure patients to keep fighting – accepting more medical treatments rather than focusing on palliation of symptoms – to continue the narrative that they are brave or perhaps to appease family members and friends. For this reason, the family of a person with a terminal illness can do that patient the favor of asking what she really wants – to continue treatment or to focus on comfort – and give the patient 'permission' to choose, even if they think that they might lose the loved one earlier than would otherwise be the case. (As explained further in Chapter 7, it is by no means clear that a shift to palliation of symptoms while ending attempts at cure shortens life for those in the final stages of terminal illness.) This conversation will be difficult but, for some patients, it may provide the freedom to cease attempts at a cure.

Even when a patient realizes that he has come to this decision point, the prospect of leaving a loved one behind, perhaps disappointing her by giving up the 'fight', adds yet another variable to a difficult thinking process. Martin Ginsburg, the husband of Ruth Bader Ginsburg, wrote her the following letter as he was dying from cancer:

> My dearest Ruth,
>
> You are the only person I have loved in my life. Setting aside a bit parents and kids, and their kids. And I have admired and loved you almost since the day we met at Cornell some 56 years ago. What a treat it has been to watch you progress to the very top of the legal world. I will be in Johns Hopkins Medical Center until Friday, June 25th, I believe. And between then and now, I shall think hard on my remaining health and life, and whether on balance the time has come for me to tough it out or to take leave of life because the loss of quality now simply overwhelms. I hope you will support where I come out, but I understand you may not. I will not love you a jot less. –Marty[25]

Justice Ginsburg shared this letter publicly, which suggests that she understood and accepted her dearly loved spouse's decision to cease active treatment.

Apart from the problematic aspects of the battle metaphor, a patient fighting the 'war' may not have consciously considered and understood for what cause he is fighting – for maximal survival, for quality of life and avoidance of suffering, for equipoise between the two – or is he perhaps sticking to the fight narrative for the sake of beloved family? Do these patients even realize that there are different avenues to the end? The battle metaphor implies that fighting cancer with the full force of treatments and life-prolonging technologies is the only heroic (and reasonable, non-assailable) choice – that the only thing to do is to fight to the death. This is simply false. There is nothing wrong with choosing therapeutic and life-prolonging technologies to delay death, if the decision to do so represents the informed and carefully considered values of the patient, and if there are available medical options to pursue this goal. The problem confronting our system of care for the dying is that,

[25] Michael S. Rosenwald, 'My dearest Ruth': The remarkable devotion of Ruth Bader Ginsburg's husband, Wash. Post, Oct. 25, 2018.

in many cases, the choice to fight is neither informed nor medically wise – at least in terms of the adverse impact of treatments on an ever-diminishing quality and quantity of life.

THE IMPACT OF DEATH DENIAL ON LIFE

All of the previous discussion describes *how* we behave with the knowledge of our mortality. Philosophers and scholars also have attempted to explain *why* we behave this way and what consequences flow from the denial of death. As has been observed throughout the ages, humans, unlike other animals, are conscious of their own mortality, which can create unsettling feelings of ambivalence. Our superiority in this regard by definition brings with it the fear of death – thanatophobia for those who like fancy words. The cultural anthropologist Ernest Becker captured the human paradox most eloquently:

> Man is literally split in two: he has an awareness of his own splendid uniqueness in that he sticks out of nature with a towering majesty, and yet he goes back into the ground in order blindly and dumbly to rot and disappear forever. It is a terrifying dilemma to be in and to have to live with. The lower animals are, of course, spared this painful contradiction, as they lack a symbolic identity and the self-consciousness that goes with it .... But to live a whole lifetime with the fate of death haunting one's dreams and even the most sun-filled days – that's something else.[26]

The fear of death (in the absent of an immediate and known threat to survival) is not innate in humans; it is learned. Until around age 3, children have no fear of death, and not even much comprehension of what death is. This fear, in adults, manifests itself at the end of life as fear of physical pain and suffering and loss of control, emotional suffering at the thought of being gone, missing the opportunity to be part of the lives of those who remain, and causing loved ones sadness and grief. Fear also has an existential component – the fear of facing what is unknown, what comes after death (if anything).[27]

Becker made it his life's work to think and write about human consciousness of mortality. He argued that much of our individual nature and ultimate character is, by necessity, built around the denial of mortality. Even when it is lurking in the background of our minds, it serves a purpose – to perpetuate our self-preservation instinct. The terror (as Becker preferred to call it) of death is normal, and it is continually with us, though we repress it much of the time. This repression is necessary to function in the world without being paralyzed by fear, but it creates what Becker called an "impossible paradox." While the fear of death is always with us,

[26] Ernest Becker, The Denial of Death p. 26 (The Free Press, 1973). Becker added, more succinctly, "We are gods with anuses." Ibid. at p. 51.

[27] Richard T. Penson et al., Update: Fear of Death, 10 The Oncologist 160–169 (2005).

we are often oblivious to this fear in our conscious, daily lives.[28] We are therefore also oblivious to the waste we constantly create (waste of time, waste of meaningful interaction with others, wasteful consumption) rather than acknowledging on a daily basis that death could come as soon as tomorrow. Everything that is good in life flows from this knowledge – that life is finite and, therefore, that every day of life has unique value.

Although we repress the fear of death much of the time, the knowledge that life will come to an end creates in all of us a search for meaning in life. Becker hypothesized that the terror of death drives much of human behavior, and later social psychology experiments have proved him correct. Because we are aware of our future death and experience terror at the thought of it, we try to manage that terror by imagining ourselves as "significant contributors to an ongoing cultural drama."[29] So, Becker wrote of 'heroism' – of the desire to stand out, to be special, to be valued and remembered. This heroic quest drives some people to seek external indicia of achievement – money, awards, fame, sex partners, mountains climbed, bottles of vintage champagne emptied, Picassos owned – none of which ultimately allays the underlying fear of death and dying. It all only amplifies that there is an end. As Becker observed, "just as there are useless self-sacrifices in unjust wars, so too is there an ignoble heroics of whole societies: it can be the viciously destructive heroics of Hitler's Germany or the plain debasing and silly heroics of the acquisition and display of consumer goods, the piling up of money and privileges."[30] On what Becker called the "more noble side" of this desire for heroism, people will sacrifice their lives or well-being for the sake of others. Those who adopt the battle metaphor in their medical treatment may also be seeking a form of heroism in life. Becker ultimately suggested that part of the human reaction to the fear of death is to chase heroism, but that there are better and worse ways of doing so. The only way to really live is to listen to the "rumble of panic underneath everything. . . . Whatever is achieved must be achieved . . . without deadening, with the full exercise of passion, of vision, of pain, of fear, and of sorrow."[31] In the absence of this kind of eyes-wide-open life, we suffer more at the thought of our own death.

Meanwhile, there are those who work to make the world a better place – in theory, a more noble form of heroism – while vigorously marketing their efforts, seeking out awards and other recognition, and all the while failing to recognize the irony in their actions. As someone very dear to me once said, "I'm trying very hard to be a person of very low ambition" – and there's irony, even in that! The remarkable thing is that, a few months after Becker's death (at the age of 49, from cancer), his magnum opus, *The Denial of Death*, won a Pulitzer Prize. There is now a foundation in his name

[28] Becker, The Denial of Death, p. 17.
[29] Sheldom Solomon et al., The Worm at the Core: On the Role of Death in Life p. 211 (Random House, 2015).
[30] Becker, The Denial of Death, pp. 6–7.
[31] Ibid., p. 284.

that works to educate people about the denial of death.[32] What would he have thought of this, I wonder?[33]

Most of us have some desire to leave behind at least a small and lasting footprint on the earth. The idea of legacy is a form of Becker's heroism. Those who stand out will be remembered (in theory, and for good or ill). In any event, his ideas about chasing heroism are reminders that the concept of legacy is a double-edged sword. Imagine someone who has used his life to do something that he is both good at and that makes life feel worthwhile – someone who discovers and uses a genuine talent in a way that improves the world around him. Toward the end of such a life, knowing that one has spent time doing something worthwhile, and well, must provide some solace. The tribute to Led Zeppelin at the Kennedy Center Honors in 2012[34] surely left the artists contemplating the idea of legacy. John Paul Jones, Robert Plant, and Jimmy Page sat in the audience as Ann and Nancy Wilson performed an exuberant cover of "Stairway to Heaven," one of the great anthems of my generation. The expressions on the faces of the remaining original artists[35] alternated between contemplative and delighted. To watch your best work being performed and fêted must bring feelings of satisfaction, but also of loss. The celebration of a career implicitly acknowledges its ending. This is legacy in one of its better manifestations, but it still creates ambivalence. Many others will look back over life and acknowledge (or try to avoid acknowledging) that they missed their chance to use a talent or skill to the fullest during their time on the planet. T. S. Eliot's Prufrock seems to struggle with this feeling of wasted opportunity:

> *I have seen the moment of my greatness flicker,*
> *And I have seen the eternal Footman hold my coat, and snicker,*
> *And in short, I was afraid.*[36]

To look back on a life of missed and wasted opportunities – the reluctance to love generously; to work hard; to treat others well; to take conscious, meaningful risks and, with risk, to invite failure – probably makes the thought of death even more daunting.

Becker's admonition to use life well while consciously acknowledging the fear of death doesn't align well with modern culture. The advent of social media and rampant consumerism in particular allow those who wish to avoid mortal thoughts a continuous outlet, a form of ventilation for all of the fleeting, frightening, toxic thoughts that bedevil sleep in the wee small hours of the morning. Søren

32 Ernest Becker Foundation – Illuminating Denial of Death, www.ernestbecker.org.

33 Becker's final book, *Escape from Evil*, was left unfinished; when he was near to death, he requested it to remain unpublished. His wife and publisher decided, "with some initial anguish over the risk of irreverence," not to abide by his request. Ernest Becker, Escape from Evil p. xv (The Free Press 1975).

34 Search "Led Zeppelin Kennedy Center Honors long version" and you will find it on YouTube.

35 John Bonham's son, Jason, is actually playing drums in the performance.

36 T. S. Eliot, The Love Song of J. Alfred Prufrock, The Waste Land and Other Poems (Harcourt Brace 1934).

Kierkegaard's concept of busyness seems to explain quite a lot of what we do to avoid thinking about difficult truths:

> [I]n the press of busyness, there is neither time nor quiet to win the transparency that is indispensable if a man is to come to understand himself. . . . Nay, the press of busyness into which one steadily enters further and further, and the noise in which the truth continually slips more and more into oblivion, and the mass of connections, stimuli, and hindrances, these make it ever more impossible for one to win any deeper knowledge of himself.[37]

Kierkegaard's words read like a prescient description of the modern experience of being sucked in by social media. Self-aware humans know when they are wasting precious time and, at least subconsciously, are troubled when they do so. But denial of mortality, the careful avoidance of acknowledging that life ends, lets us fritter away time with useless distractions, because there will always be time 'later' to do the important stuff. Worse still are those who struggle to find enough activity to create the busyness that they crave. One of the saddest phrases I've ever heard is "Oh, it passes the time." Some people are literally killing time because they haven't anything worthwhile to do or don't want to do anything worthwhile. For those who engage with life in all its dimensions, "[t]here never seems to be enough time to do the things you want to do."[38]

Unfortunately, busyness can include not only time-wasting but sometimes also bad behavior – anger and conflict can nicely occupy the mind when the fear of death takes hold. As John Steinbeck wrote,

> Humans are caught – in their lives, in their thoughts, in their hungers and ambitions, in their avarice and cruelty, and in their kindness and generosity too – in a net of good and evil. I think this is the only story we have and that it occurs on all levels of feeling and intelligence. Virtue and vice were the warp and woof of our first consciousness and they will be the fabric of our last. . . . A man, after he has brushed off the dust and chips of his life, will have left only the hard clean questions: was it good or was it evil? Have I done well – or ill?[39]

Steinbeck puts his finger on one of the underlying reasons why many people resist thinking about their mortality. As life gets longer – and thus shorter – it becomes more difficult to avoid asking and answering these big questions. We can only ignore all the bad behavior, all of the wasted time and busyness in our pasts for so long – only for as long as we can tell ourselves that we have an open, unlimited window of time in which to correct past mistakes. At the end of life, when we are facing death, we reap what we have sown – not only with others but also within ourselves.

Becker was hardly the first to point out that failing to acknowledge the fear of death has negative consequences. The Roman philosopher Lucretius observed that

[37] Søren Kierkegaard, Purity of Heart Is to Will One Thing (1847).

[38] Jim Croce, Time in a Bottle, You Don't Mess Around with Jim (ABC Records, 1972).

[39] John Steinbeck, East of Eden p. 411 (Penguin, 1952).

the fear of death encouraged superstitious beliefs, dependence on religion, and the pursuit of trivial things such as money and power. The Greek philosopher Epicurus suggested that the cure for this fear required two simple steps: acknowledge the fear of death and then appreciate that it is an irrational fear, because dead people feel nothing, experience nothing, and fear nothing.[40] These two steps will allow us to live life without fear. Sounds good, right? The problem is we cannot think or pray our way out of this fear of death, at least not entirely.[41] But the effort to live fully and with open acknowledgment of impending death, even if not entirely successful, bears its own fruit. It is possible to live useful and meaningful lives (measured by our own standards) without being in constant mortal terror, while still acknowledging mortality – and to save the terror for when death actually approaches, to accept that the end is then imminent, and to make decisions accordingly.

TO BE A ROCK AND NOT TO ROLL

Life holds the promise of pleasure, contentment, and, sometimes, joy. Life also invariably entails a series of losses and of attempts to stave off the feelings that loss brings. From the earliest days of childhood, we experience loss – the loss of a friendship or the death of a pet – and later, in adulthood, the loss of a job, of true love, a goal unfulfilled, the end of a satisfying career. And at some point, as we grow older, we also lose the sense that life and our days on the planet are infinite or at least not foreseeably coming to an end. Each loss in life is akin to a small death. Coping with loss is one of life's primary endeavors, and learning to acknowledge and accept life's continual and inevitable losses will, at least in part, determine how we approach death.

The denial of death has real consequences, not only at the end of life but throughout it. On the physical side, death denial, anti-aging culture, and modern medicine have played a significant role in transforming the natural process of dying into a technologically driven and often illogically overzealous quest to prolong the lives of terminally ill patients. The denial of mortality also has serious psychological and emotional consequences. Chapter 8 considers the cognitive and behavioral explanations for mortality denial and their consequent impact on decision-making at the end of life. Overall, it's no surprise that many people avoid thinking about dying until the matter becomes urgent and may try to avoid it even then. Modern medicine offers ample opportunity for engaging in more busyness in that regard. Holding firm against the denial tide pays dividends that increase with age – like a wise investment that grows steadily, in spite of life's vicissitudes.

40 Sheldon Solomon et al., The Worm at the Core: On the Role of Death in Life pp. 215–217 (Random House 2015) (discussing the work of Lucretius and Epicurus).

41 Philip Larkin, Aubade, Collected Poems (Farrar Straus and Giroux, 2001).

5

Disorders of Consciousness and the Meaning of Life

I would rather be ashes than dust!
I would rather that my spark burn out in a brilliant blaze
    than it should be stifled by dry-rot.
I would rather be a superb meteor, every atom of me in magnificent glow,
    than a sleepy and permanent planet.
The function of man is to live, not to exist.
I shall not waste my days trying to prolong them.
I shall use my time.

—Jack London[1]

Patients in a permanent vegetative state (PVS) exist in the netherworld between life and death. They breathe independently, their hearts beat without assistance, and their bodies are warm to the touch. With medical support, these patients can live for many years. Yet, consciousness, the *sine qua non* of human existence, is irrevocably lost. These patients cannot and never will again see, feel, and respond to the world around them. Their capacity for love is gone, their ability to communicate is gone, and they remain entirely dependent on medical care for their bodily needs. Patients in PVS require artificial nutrition and hydration because they can no longer ingest food and fluids by mouth. They require bathing, turning, and cleaning of bodily waste because they can no longer perform these basic activities of self-care. Modern medicine can keep the motor running, but the patient remains in neutral – a physical vessel now lacking the spark of consciousness.

In most cases involving PVS and other disorders of consciousness (DOC),[2] the patient will quite rightly receive life-sustaining treatment after the immediate event that caused the condition so that physicians can assess the patient and begin to understand the longer-term implications of the patient's medical situation. The broader dilemma arises when the patient's condition doesn't improve and family members and health care providers consider the question of whether to withdraw

[1] Irving Shepard, Jack London's Tales of Adventure p. vii. (Doubleday, 1956).
[2] James L. Bernat, Chronic Disorders of Consciousness, 367 Lancet 1181–1192 (2006).

life-sustaining care and to allow the patient to die. Before the advent of modern medical technology, these patients died rather quickly and humanely from their underlying physical disabilities.[3] Now, enteral feeding, antibiotics for infection, and related life-prolonging measures create a daunting ethical dilemma. What to do on behalf of permanently unconscious patients who are only alive because technology makes them so? Clinical uncertainty adds to the dilemmas created by medical technology that keeps these patients alive. How can we know that the patient might not wake up tomorrow? Those who seek to keep these patients alive embrace their lack of actual knowledge about the future of these patients to maintain the status quo. Although there is a general medical consensus that withdrawal of care from patients in a confirmed, permanent vegetative state is ethically acceptable, the families of these patients may struggle to accept the prognosis or may believe that the patient's life retains value and ought to be preserved, regardless of its quality. The emotional and moral burden of deciding to withdraw life-prolonging treatment – something that is onerous for all surrogate decision-makers who face choices about whether to prolong the life of a loved one – may also weigh the family down.

Clearly, PVS patients lack any capacity to make any medical decisions for themselves. In the absence of an advance directive that addresses the question, a family member, as surrogate decision-maker, must decide how to proceed with the patient's care. Once a diagnosis of PVS is confirmed according to neurological testing protocols, families may still struggle to reach agreement about whether to continue life-prolonging care for the patient. If hospital personnel and processes such as ethics consultation (Chapter 10 discusses this and other dispute resolution mechanisms in detail) cannot resolve the disagreement, a family member or the hospital itself may seek judicial resolution of the question. Fortunately, these disputes are rare, but ethical and legal conflicts concerning permanently vegetative patients have challenged judicial systems and created public controversy in several countries, sometimes to the point of becoming a *cause célèbre* in the culture wars. The interim public debate and ultimate resolution of these cases reveal quite a bit about the culture of a country's attitudes toward death, its tools for communicating about end-of-life matters, and its ability to engage in reasoned debate around ethically challenging cases.

Decisions about whether to continue providing care to patients in PVS are especially difficult (in the absence of clear knowledge of the patient's wishes as previously expressed in an advance directive or conversations with family or health care providers) precisely because these patients are neither actively dying nor progressing toward recovery. PVS is one of the most ethically challenging scenarios of end-of-life decision-making, in no small part because the condition produces wide divergence of opinion as to the 'correct' path. One person may conclude that there is

3 Linda Ganzini et al., Nurses' Experiences with Hospice Patients Who Refuse Food and Fluids to Hasten Death, 349 New Eng. J. Med. 359–365 (2003) (in which surveyed nurses reported that patients usually died a 'good death' – with a median rating of 8 out of 9 on a quality of death scale – within two weeks of stopping eating and drinking).

nothing worse than languishing in a state of permanent unconsciousness, potentially for years, while another may believe that the withdrawal of life-prolonging care is morally wrong in the case of a patient who could live for many years – despite the patient's inability to engage with the world in any way. In such a controversial context, it's instructive at a systemic and cultural level to consider how three countries have responded – legally and culturally – to one of the more ethically complex situations in end-of-life communication and decision-making. The interplay between politics, culture, and decision-making for patients in PVS that this chapter describes serves as a preview for the broader discussion of surrogate decision-making and the limited utility of advance directives in Chapter 9.

Conflicts about the care of patients in PVS vary in configuration, but when these disputes land within the jurisdiction of the courts, public debate about the fate of the patient in question tends to inflame an already tragic situation. The US case of Theresa Schiavo raised broader questions about the law of informed refusal and surrogate decision-making. It also put a spotlight on the pernicious impact of the American culture wars on an already disquieting medical conflict.[4] The *Schiavo* case, in which the patient's parents disagreed with her husband's decision to withdraw life-prolonging care, brought public debate to the boiling point. While the law regarding withdrawal of medical care from patients in PVS is well settled in the United States, the *Schiavo* case provides a remarkable example of how deeply the culture wars can impact medical decision-making at the end of life, and of how public pressure can derail the thoughtful and timely resolution of an end-of-life dispute. The case of Anthony Bland in the United Kingdom was decided by the House of Lords in a much more deliberate and measured process and without undue prolongation of the dispute through legal and political maneuvering. Despite the fact that the patient's family was in agreement to withdraw life-prolonging care, the *Bland* case also provoked intense public discussion. After careful consideration, the House of Lords ultimately affirmed the family's wishes. In Canada, a judicial decision concerning the case of Hassan Rasouli led to a ruling from the Supreme Court of Canada that confirmed the role of the family in decision-making for patients who lack capacity to make their own choices. In the *Rasouli* case, the patient's wife wanted life-prolonging care continued, but Mr. Rasouli's treating physicians considered it medically inappropriate. The dispute resolution process in these three cases serves as a bellwether for the quality of societal discourse regarding intractable end-of-life care disputes in the three countries. The openness, honesty, and ethical integrity of societal discourse on these matters in turn can impact the ability of individuals to comprehend, discuss, and make decisions about their own medical dilemmas (or those of family members). Distorted and manipulative public debate about high-profile disputes has potential consequences for individuals who face their own hard choices at the end of life.

4 Kathy L. Cerminara, Collateral Damage: The Aftermath of the Political Culture Wars in *Schiavo*, 29 Western New Eng. L. Rev. 279–308 (2007).

THE PERMANENT VEGETATIVE STATE

Patients in PVS and other disorders of consciousness (such as coma and the minimally conscious state) are not dead under death by neurologic criteria (DNC, commonly known as 'brain death'). The Uniform Determination of Death Act, adopted in most US states, defines death as either "(1) irreversible cessation of circulatory and respiratory functions, or (2) irreversible cessation of all functions of the entire brain, including the brain stem."[5] Although there have been recent proposals to clarify the criteria for DNC and how it is determined,[6] accepted clinical practice permits patients on life support with completely absent brain function to be declared legally dead. The bodily functions of patients who are diagnosed with DNC are, pending this determination, sustained by medical technology including mechanical ventilation and drugs to support blood pressure. Because patients in these conditions are legally dead, cessation of this supportive technology is uncontroversial from a legal and ethical perspective, though family members may initially find it hard to understand that a person with a warm body and a beating heart is dead.

In contrast, the types of injury to the brain that result in PVS can leave the patient's heartbeat and breathing intact, with no need for mechanical ventilation. PVS is a form of unconsciousness that differs from coma, and can be caused by either a traumatic brain injury or anoxia (lack of oxygen), leaving the patient with "severe brain damage, and in which coma has advanced to a state of wakefulness without detectable awareness."[7] (The permanent vegetative state is also distinguished clinically from the minimally conscious state "in which the patient exhibits definite responsiveness that is cognitively driven, rather than unconscious reflexive responses."[8]) Once physicians conclude that the vegetative state is irreversible, the patient is understood to have a prognosis of no recovery of any degree of consciousness, hence the term 'permanent vegetative state'. An initial diagnosis of persistent vegetative state is just that – a diagnosis. Prognosis comes later. Patients who suffer traumatic brain injuries are considered to be in a permanent vegetative state after one year, whereas the vegetative state of patients whose brain injury is anoxic is considered permanent after three months.[8]

Because patients in PVS experience waking and sleeping cycles, involuntarily open their eyes, move their limbs, and utter sounds,[9] family members and other

5 Uniform Law Commission, Determination of Death Act (1980), www.uniformlaws.org/committees/community-home?CommunityKey=155faf5d-03c2-4027-99ba-ee4c99019d6c.

6 Ariane Lewis et al., It's Time to Revise the Uniform Determination of Death Act, 172 Annals Internal Med. 143–144 (2020).

7 Roger N. Rosenberg, Consciousness, Coma, and Brain Death, 301 JAMA 1172–1174 (2009).

8 Multi-Society Task Force on PVS, Medical Aspects of the Persistent Vegetative State (Pt. I), 330 New Eng. J. Med. 1499–1508 (1994).

9 Ibid.; Christopher M. Booth et al., Is This Patient Dead, Vegetative, or Severely Neurologically Impaired?, 291 JAMA 870–879 (2004).

nonmedical observers sometimes find it difficult to accept that the patient lacks any capacity for thought, emotion, communication, or other activities associated with consciousness. These patients typically can breathe without assistance but can never again experience or interact with their environment in even the most minimal way. With medical care, including a surgically implanted feeding tube to provide artificial nutrition and hydration (ANH), PVS patients can live for many years.

There is cause for caution in reaching conclusions about the prognosis of patients who appear to be in a vegetative state. Diagnosis of the nature and extent of unconsciousness is complex, though recent technological developments have allowed physicians to test the diagnosis of PVS. Studies suggest that about 40 percent of patients who have been diagnosed with PVS are in fact minimally conscious.[10] In one small study, 19 percent of recently diagnosed patients demonstrated signs of consciousness when their brain activity was measured with an electroencephalogram (EEG) test.[11] In addition to EEG evaluation, new brain imaging technologies such as functional magnetic resonance imaging (fMRI) technology allow physicians to identify localized neural activity in the brain that was previously undetectable through observable patient responses. In rare circumstances, apparently unconscious patients are able to answer yes/no questions by activating different parts of their brains that control motor imagery versus spatial imagery. In theory, this process would allow these patients to answer questions about their treatment preferences. The few patients in these studies who demonstrated some responsiveness had suffered traumatic brain injuries. It appears that patients with anoxic brain injuries, which affect the brain globally, are less likely to retain any ability to interact with the world.[12] These tests have rightly called into question the accuracy of diagnoses of PVS, raising questions about the appropriateness of withdrawal of life-sustaining measures from these patients.[13] Of course, the broader question is whether even those patients who might be able to communicate in a basic way when being

[10] Caroline Schnakers et al., Diagnostic Accuracy of the Vegetative and Minimally Conscious State: Clinical Consensus Versus Standardized Neurobehavioral Assessment, 9 BMC Neurology 35 (2009).

[11] Damian Cruse et al., Bedside Detection of Awareness in a Vegetative State: A Cohort Analysis, 378 The Lancet 2088–2094 (2011) (assessing sixteen patients recently diagnosed with PVS and finding that three of these patients could demonstrate some brain response to commands).

[12] Martin M. Monti et al., Willful Modulation of Brain Activity in Disorders of Consciousness, 362 New Eng. J. Med. 579–589 (2010).

[13] J. Andrew Billings et al., Severe Brain Injury and the Subjective Life, 40 Hastings Ctr. Rep. 17–21 (May/June 2010); Martin M. Monti et al., Willful Modulation of Brain Activity in Disorders of Consciousness, 362 New Eng. J. Med. 579–589 (2010) (finding that five out of fifty-four patients with DOC were exhibiting some awareness and cognition); Damian Cruse et al., Bedside Detection of Awareness in a Vegetative State: A Cohort Analysis, 378 The Lancet 2088–2094 (2011); Adrian M. Owen et al., Detecting Awareness in the Vegetative State, 313 Science 1402 (2006); Adrian M. Owen et al., Using Functional Magnetic Resonance Imaging to Detect Covert Awareness in the Vegetative State, 64 Arch. Neurol. 1098–1102 (2007).

scanned for brain activity, who are minimally conscious, would choose life-prolonging treatment.

THERESA SCHIAVO

Several major cases involving young adults in PVS have shaped US jurisprudence addressing disputes over withdrawal of life-sustaining treatment from patients who are not actively dying. Each of these disputes involved uncertainty about the quality or quantity of evidence of the permanently incapacitated patient's wishes, both because none of the patients had an advance directive and because a family member or the state was disputing the appropriateness of a health care agent's decision.[14] One of the most recent of these cases concerned the care of Theresa Schiavo in Florida.

In 1990, a sudden cardiac arrest left Theresa Schiavo, at age 26, with a severe anoxic brain injury leading to PVS.[15] Beginning in 1998, Theresa's husband, Michael Schiavo, having accepted the reality of Theresa's prognosis, sought permission from the Florida courts to have her feeding tube removed so that she could die peacefully. Michael based his request on Theresa's previously expressed wishes and values, explaining that Theresa would never have wanted to continue to exist in a vegetative state after all hope of recovery had objectively vanished. This testimony was consistent with the requirement in Florida law that decisions for incapacitated patients should attempt to reflect what the patient would choose were she able to do so herself.[16] Theresa's parents vigorously objected to this request, arguing that the evidence of Theresa's wishes was insufficient and that its source was suspect. During the controversy, those who argued for Theresa's continued treatment pointed to suspected marital problems between the couple, and to Michael Schiavo's decision to live with and father two children with another woman several years after Theresa's brain injury. These private family matters became a point of argument for conservative religious groups who intervened in the case.[17] In Theresa's case, the diagnosis of PVS was confirmed with multiple brain scans and upon autopsy, but disputes about the nature of Theresa's medical condition still made reaching consensus difficult. Theresa's parents and others involved her care questioned whether she was indeed in a permanent vegetative state, believing that her facial expressions and movements

14 Guardianship of Schiavo, 780 So.2d 176 (2001) (disputing, among other things, whether it was appropriate for the patient's husband to continue to serve as her surrogate decision-maker); Cruzan v. Director, Missouri Dept. of Health, 497 U.S. 261 (1990); In re Quinlan, 355 A.2d 647 (1976).

15 The description of events in the *Schiavo* case is adapted from Barbara A. Noah, Politicizing the End of Life: Lessons from the Schiavo Controversy, 59 U. Miami L. Rev. 107–134 (2005); Barbara A. Noah, The Role of Religion in the Schiavo Controversy, 6 Houston J. Health L. & Pol'y 319–346 (2006).

16 The Florida statute requires that before a proxy decision-maker may exercise an incapacitated patient's right to withdraw life-prolonging measures, the decision must be supported by "clear and convincing evidence that the decision would have been the one the patient would have chosen if the patient had been competent." Fla. Stat. §765.401(3).

17 Too Vigorously Assisted Suicide, Nat'l Review (Mar. 21, 2005), www.nationalreview.com/2005/03/too-vigorously-assisted-suicide-editors/.

indicated some degree of awareness. Despite the fact that Michael was the judicially appointed guardian for Theresa, her parents' continued objections were sufficient to delay the implementation of Michael's request. Even so, in a series of judicial decisions, state and federal courts repeatedly confirmed the legal propriety of acceding to Michael's request, finding the evidence of Theresa's wishes legally sufficient to support the removal of ANH.[18]

During the ongoing legal disputes about the appropriateness of continuing Theresa's life-supportive measures, her feeding tube was removed and replaced *twice* before it was removed for a third and final time. For more than seven years, the legal battle continued between Theresa's husband and parents, with astonishing levels of intervention from the Catholic Church, pro-life groups, the Florida state legislature, then-Governor Jeb Bush, and the US Congress. The Catholic Church took the position, via a papal declaration, that artificial nutrition and hydration are 'ordinary care' and must be provided under all circumstances.[19] The ensuing events included motions for a new trial, a visit to Theresa's bedside by a conservative US senator, death threats against the judge who issued the orders to remove Theresa's feeding tube, special legislation from the Florida legislature giving then-Governor Jeb Bush the power to 'stay' the removal of Theresa's already removed tube (meaning in this context to order the tube reinserted), a subpoena from Congress for Theresa and Michael Schiavo to 'testify' before it, and political grandstanding by conservative members of Congress on the pro-life aspects of the case.[20] Protesters at the facility where Theresa resided attempted to storm the place and bring her water.[21] Individuals offered Michael Schiavo millions of dollars to turn over his guardianship of Theresa to her parents. A memo written by an aide to a Florida Republican senator suggested that the *Schiavo* case offered a great political opportunity that would appeal to the Republican base.[22] These ongoing displays of cynicism were breathlessly reported on a continuous basis by cable news. One has to wonder what Theresa would have thought about being used as a pawn by strangers.

Finally, in 2005, after numerous state and federal court hearings, the Florida court once again ordered that the clinicians at the facility caring for Theresa remove her feeding tube. On March 18, 2005, the facility complied with the court order and additional legal maneuvering ensued, including motions filed with the US Supreme Court and several Florida courts. Ultimately, all of the courts that heard the parents' appeals declined to overturn the order directing removal of Theresa's feeding tube for the third and final time. Fifteen years after her cardiac arrest, in 2005, Theresa

18 Kathy Cerminara & Kenneth Goodman, Key Events in the Case of Theresa Marie Schiavo, https://science.jburroughs.org/mbahe/BioEthics/Articles/SchiavoTimeline.pdf.

19 Noah, The Role of Religion in the Schiavo Controversy.

20 Noah, Politicizing the End of Life.

21 Abby Goodnough, Protesters Hold Vigil for Schiavo at Hospice, N.Y. Times (Mar. 20, 2005).

22 Mike Allen, Counsel to GOP Senator Wrote Memo on Schiavo, Wash. Post (Apr. 7, 2005), p. A1, www.washingtonpost.com/wp-dyn/articles/A32554-2005Apr6.html?sub=AR.

Schiavo died.[23] Photos and video showing Theresa in her much-diminished state are still littered across the Internet. Her privacy and dignity were sacrificed for political gain and traction in the culture wars.

ANTHONY BLAND

In the United Kingdom, the case of Anthony Bland took a very different path from the *Schiavo* dispute. On April 15th, 1989, 17-year-old Anthony Bland was caught up in the melée of the Hillsborough football ground disaster, where ninety-six football fans died and hundreds of others were injured in a crowd crush.[24] His lungs were crushed and punctured and the supply of oxygen to his brain was interrupted, leaving him in a permanent vegetative state. Like Theresa Schiavo, the injury to Anthony's brain was anoxic, rather than traumatic (though it resulted from trauma), so the brain injury was global rather than localized. Unsurprisingly, given his age, Anthony had never indicated his wishes with respect to this situation, but his father gave evidence that his son would not choose to be left dependent on life-supportive care in these tragic circumstances. Unlike in the *Schiavo* case, the entire family concurred, and the hospital then sought a judicial declaration that it could legally discontinue all life-sustaining treatment including artificial nutrition and hydration. There was also indisputable evidence that Anthony's cerebral cortex was badly damaged, showing no signs of electrical activity and having, over time, become more liquid than solid. All of the consulting physicians agreed that there was no objective hope of improvement.[25]

The petition to remove ANH from a patient in PVS raised a novel question for the courts in the United Kingdom. Both the High Court and the Court of Appeal supported the application to remove ANH and allow Anthony to die. On appeal, the House of Lords, then the UK's highest court,[26] ruled that withdrawal and withholding of medical treatment, including ANH, from patients who lack decisional capacity and who have no advance directive was permissible. The official solicitor appointed as Anthony's guardian ad litem argued that removal of artificial nutrition and hydration would constitute murder. All members of the House of Lords disagreed with this characterization, on varying grounds. They reasoned that nonconsensual treatment violates the principle of autonomy and that it is only appropriate to treat incapacitated patients without their consent when their best

23 Cerminara & Goodman, Key Events in the Case of Theresa Marie Schiavo.

24 BBC News, How the Hillsborough Disaster Unfolded (Apr. 26, 2016), www.bbc.com/news/uk-19545126.

25 Airedale N.H.S. Trust v. Bland [1993] AC 789.

26 At the time of the Bland ruling, the United Kingdom's highest appeals court consisted of a sub-chamber of the House of Lords. The trial court in this case is called the High Court of England and Wales. The intermediate level is called the Court of Appeal. Since October 1, 2009, the highest court has been called the Supreme Court of the U.K. It is staffed by twelve justices (beginning with the justices of the former judicial chamber of the House of Lords).

interests require it. In other words, inserting a feeding tube without consent is a violation and the remedy is to remove it, unless the best interests of the patient require it to remain. The court applied what was, in effect, the obverse of the reasoning used in the Florida courts, which makes no presumption of a violation of patient rights with the initial insertion of the feeding tube and only permits its removal if they conclude that removal is consistent with the patient's preferences.

As to permanently unconscious patients, the court concluded that the patient's interest in being kept alive had ended (thus no longer justifying treatment), even though discontinuation of life support also does nothing to advance the patient's interests. (Perhaps, though, one might argue that a patient's interest in living with, and dying in, dignity may still be advanced by the removal of a feeding tube from one in a permanent vegetative state.) The court argued that, in these cases, the duty to provide life-sustaining care ceases. As Lord Goff explained, "if the justification for treating a patient who lacks the capacity to consent lies in the fact that the treatment is provided in his best interests, it must follow that the treatment may, and indeed ultimately should, be discontinued where it is no longer in his best interests to provide it."[27] Lord Browne-Wilkinson went further, arguing that withdrawal of treatment in Anthony's case was not only lawful but also legally required to avoid committing the tort of battery. The court went on to explain that

> the object of medical treatment and care was to benefit the patient, but since a large body of informed and responsible medical opinion was of the view that existence in the persistent vegetative state was not a benefit to the patient, the principle of the sanctity of life, which was not absolute, was not violated by ceasing to give medical treatment and care involving invasive manipulation of the patient's body, to which he had not consented and which conferred no benefit upon him.[28]

Implicit in this statement is the conclusion that although the court respects the principle of the sanctity of life, maintaining life alone, without consent and possibility against the patient's wishes, may not be in a patient's best interests if the treatment in question does nothing to improve the patient's condition. Lord Hoffman expressly rejected the majority view of the US Supreme Court in the *Cruzan* case[29] and instead took the position that 'best interests' includes "not only recovery or the avoidance of pain (neither of which apply in this case) but also a dignified death. On this issue I respectfully agree with the dissenting judgments of . . . Brennan and Stevens JJ in Cruzan."[30]

27 Airedale N.H.S. Trust v. Bland [1993] AC 789.

28 Airedale N.H.S. Trust v. Bland [1993] AC 789. For a cogent critique of the illogic in the court's position, see Sheila McLean, Old Law, New Medicine pp. 148–149 (Pandora, 1999).

29 Cruzan v. Missouri Dept. of Health, 497 U.S. 261 (1990). This case, which predated the *Schiavo* litigation, also involved a family's request to withdraw life-sustaining treatment (ANH) from their daughter who was in a permanent vegetative state.

30 Airedale NHS Trust v. Bland [1993] A.C. 789 (Hoffman, L. J.) (citing Cruzan v. Director, Missouri Dept. of Health, 497 U.S. 261 (1990)).

Less than four years after his injury, in March 1993, Anthony Bland's feeding tube was removed and he was allowed to die. There was, naturally and necessarily, a good deal of public awareness, discussion, and controversy surrounding the *Bland* case during and after its litigation and resolution. In particular, commentators questioned the validity of arguments centered on the patient's best interests, given that PVS patients experience neither benefits nor (physical) burdens of treatment,[31] but the bulk of public reaction about the case appeared to accept that withdrawal of ANH was ethically acceptable.[32] Despite the public debate and a lack of consensus among health care providers about whether to continue to provide ANH to Anthony Bland, the case never devolved into the kind of political and societal circus that surrounded the *Schiavo* case in the United States.

HASSAN RASOULI

In Canada, the case of Hassan Rasouli presented a different sort of challenge to the courts. In October 2010, Mr. Rasouli underwent surgery to remove a benign tumor in his brain. After the surgery, he developed a severe brain infection that left him unconscious. He was dependent on mechanical ventilation and a feeding tube. After a diagnosis of PVS and a confirming opinion, the treating physicians sought to discontinue life-prolonging treatment and to provide only palliative care. Mr. Rasouli's wife, Ms. Parichehr Salasel, who was also his surrogate decision-maker under relevant provincial law, argued that it would be inconsistent with the family's Muslim faith to withdraw medical care – that as a Muslim, Mr. Rasouli would wish to receive medical care until all signs of life were gone. Ms. Salasel, herself a physician, also disagreed with the diagnosis of PVS and believed that her husband showed signs of consciousness. (Mr. Rasouli's condition was later upgraded to 'minimally conscious'.) Ms. Salasel applied to the Superior Court in Ontario for an order to block withdrawal of care. Meanwhile, the treating physicians requested a declaratory order supporting their plan to withdraw life-prolonging care, arguing that continued treatment provided the patient with no benefit and that treatment in these circumstances was inhumane. The Superior Court of Ontario held that Ontario's Health Care Consent Act (HCCA) requires consent for treatment and that the 'treatment package' in this case included the withdrawal of life-prolonging interventions such as mechanical ventilators and feeding tubes and the implementation of palliative care to ease the patient's death.[33]

[31] Andrea J. Fenwick, Applying Best Interests to Persistent Vegetative State – A Principled Distortion? 24 J. Medical Ethics 86–92 (1998).

[32] Paquita de Zulueta & Francesco Carelli, Permanent Vegetative State: Comparing the Law and Ethics of Two Tragic Cases from Italy and England, 2 London J. Primary Care 125–129 (2009).

[33] Rasouli (Litigation Guardian of) v. Sunnybrook Health Sciences Centre and Cuthbertson (2011 ONSC).

The Supreme Court of Canada affirmed this judgment and that of the intermediate court and held that in Ontario, physicians will most often need consent from a surrogate decision-maker to stop an incapacitated patient's life-prolonging treatment. If a patient's surrogate decision-maker wants treatment to continue, the physician cannot unilaterally overrule this decision. At the same time, if the physician believes that the surrogate decision-maker's choice in a case is inconsistent with either a patient's wishes or his best interests, the physician can apply to Ontario's Consent and Capacity Board (CCB) for clarification and a ruling.[34] Ontario is unique among the Canadian provinces and territories in having created an independent CCB to resolve disputes regarding, among other things, surrogate decision-making for patients who have lost the ability to make medical choices. Part of Chapter 10 considers the role of the CCB in Ontario as well as the potential for this sort of mechanism to be implemented in certain US states.

The ruling in the *Rasouli* case turned on statutory interpretation – the meaning of 'treatment' in Ontario's HCCA. It did not address the merits of whether continued treatment was in Mr. Rasouli's best interests. Justice Karakatsanis, one of two dissenting justices, argued that when the medical decision concerns treatment that is no longer medically beneficial or is in fact potentially harmful, then other factors should come into play. In particular, she suggested that the nature of the patient's condition, the professional obligations and views of the treating physicians, and the overall impact of continued treatment on the health care system are also relevant to the decision. Justice Karakatsanis also disagreed with the majority's conclusion that treatment within the HCCA includes withdrawal of treatment and suggested that common law standards of medical care were sufficient to protect the interests of the patient in medical futility disputes. In cases of disagreement between physicians and family members, the family member can ask a court to review the decision and to consider at that time both the patient's values and preferences and the bodily integrity and human dignity of the patient.[35] Commentators have observed that the majority ruling in the *Rasouli* case creates a baseline entitlement for patients to receive treatment, even when a physician is unwilling to provide it, leaving the physician to apply to the CCB for support.[36] With the prospect of a family veto to physician proposals to withdraw life-prolonging care, there also is less incentive for physicians to initiate difficult conversations about the medical benefit of the treatment in question and its ability to further the patient's interests.

The *Rasouli* case received plenty of news coverage at the time, and members of the public rallied to the cause. There was, however, no governmental interference in the case, no politicization of a tragic situation. Mr. Rasouli's family later sued physicians

34 Cuthbertson v. Rasouli, 2013 SCC 53, [2013] 3 S.C.R. 341. The physicians in the case chose not to consult the CCB.

35 Ibid.

36 Hilary Young, Why Withdrawing Life-Sustaining Treatment Should Not Require "*Rasouli* Consent," 6 McGill J. Law & Health 54–104 (2012).

involved in his care, claiming that they used intimidation and threats to try to persuade the family to consent to withdrawal of care. The lawsuit was dismissed by Ontario's highest court.[37] It is unclear whether Mr. Rasouli is alive as of this writing.

SOME COMPARISONS AND OBSERVATIONS

In these three cases that consider the withdrawal of life-prolonging care from patients with disorders of consciousness, the configuration of the disagreement varied, but the underlying sources of conflict and the ethical questions at issue were very much the same. In both the *Schiavo* and *Rasouli* cases, the family members who objected to removal of life-prolonging care disputed the diagnosis of PVS. In Theresa Schiavo's case, the diagnosis was correct and was confirmed by medical imaging while she was alive as well as by autopsy. In Hassan Rasouli's case, his wife's belief that Mr. Rasouli was exhibiting some awareness was borne out by further examination and his diagnosis changed from PVS to minimally conscious. In Anthony Bland's case, physicians all agreed that he was indeed in a permanent and irreversible vegetative state, and medical imaging of his brain supported this conclusion. Uncertainty or disagreement about diagnosis and prognosis in these cases understandably upends efforts to achieve agreement about withdrawal of life-prolonging measures. Even so, each jurisdiction has a well-established surrogate decision-making process and must try to get the decision right, or at least not obviously wrong in the face of uncertainty.

All three cases also raised questions of whether continued life-prolonging care was in the patient's best interests. None of the three patients had advance directives to guide decision-making. In the *Schiavo* case, some evidence was presented that Theresa would refuse care under the circumstances; similarly, in both *Bland* and *Rasouli*, the relevant family members spoke about what they believed would be the patient's choice. Even so, opinions as to patient preferences as part of an autonomy-driven decision-making process weren't sufficient to resolve the disputes. All three cases also considered – to varying degrees – the patient's quality of life and best interests. The opinions in the *Bland* case most prominently emphasized best interests, concluding that continued existence in a confirmed permanent vegetative state provides no benefit to the patient. The Supreme Court majority opinion in *Rasouli* focused primarily on the technical reading of the statute in question, thereby sidestepping the best interests question.

It's also worth noting that the highest courts in each country decided the *Bland* and *Rasouli* cases. By contrast, the *Schiavo* dispute was litigated mainly in state courts in Florida, one state of fifty. The structural fragmentation of litigation on these matters in the United States makes achieving consensus and a uniform

[37] Tom Blackwell, Court Tosses $2M Lawsuit by Family of Brain-Damaged Man Accusing Doctors of Threats and Assault, Nat'l Post (Mar. 4, 2015), https://nationalpost.com/news/canada/court-tosses-2m-lawsuit-by-family-of-brain-damaged-man-accusing-doctors-of-threats-and-assault.

approach to hard cases even harder. In addition, US courts rarely decide the substance of end-of-life disputes. They tend to focus on procedure and standards of proof and to dispose of these cases on purely procedural or formal grounds. *Schiavo* is a somewhat unusual example in which a US court actually decided the merits of the question: Did the evidence of Theresa's wishes meet the state's standard of proof and would she therefore choose to discontinue life-prolonging treatment in her circumstances? The courts answered yes to both questions in several separate appeals.

Surprisingly, it is also not always clear in US states what the role of the court ought to be in deciding disputes about medical care. Many courts will focus on standards of proof of the patient's wishes and the nature of evidence that would be enough to meet the required standard. Courts may also opine on whether judicial review of certain decisions is required, and whether to appoint a decision-maker or instead make the substantive decision itself. There is wide variation from state to state on these questions,[38] which creates both ambiguity and uncertainty in a decisional scenario that is already fraught with ambivalence. By contrast, medical decision-making in England and Wales benefits from the extensive guidance of the Mental Capacity Act (not in existence at the time of the *Bland* case), as to substantive and procedural standards for resolving treatment disputes for incapacitated patients,[39] and Ontario's CCB has similar substantive and procedural standards to guide its decision-making. Chapter 10 considers the operation of the MCA and the CCB in more detail.

It is never a comfortable thought process to consider whether death is preferable to life – even a life with little or no consciousness. It is even more difficult when the matter under consideration is not one's own life and death, but that of another person. These cases suggest that some courts and the cultures in which they operate are more willing to fully and open-heartedly engage in this difficult calculus (on behalf of those who cannot) than others. Court opinions from England suggest more pragmatism and activism in confronting difficult end-of-life choices. They ask whether it makes sense to maintain the status quo for a patient or to take the irrevocable step of allowing the patient to die by withdrawing life-prolonging care. Beginning with the *Bland* case, and continuing in successor cases,[40] there is evidence of a genuine willingness to consider openly not only the express wishes of the patient (if they are known) but also the patient's best interests and quality of life.

38 Barry R. Furrow et al., Health Law §§ 16-44-16-48 (3rd ed. West 2015).

39 The Mental Capacity Act of 2005 (as amended) applies to England and Wales, www.legislation.gov.uk/ukpga/2005/9/contents.

40 National Health Service Trust A. v. M. and N.H.S. Trust B. v. H., 1 All E.R. 801 (2001) (concurring with the House of Lords in *Bland* taking into account the European Convention on Human Rights and Fundamental Freedoms (ECHR)); Danuta Mendelson & Timothy Stoltzfus Jost, A Comparative Study of the Law of Palliative Care and End-of-Life Treatment, 31 J. L. Med. & Ethics 130–143 (2003).

This willingness is now also a legal necessity under the current legal rules in England and Wales. If the patient was unable to consent when life-prolonging treatment was initiated (which would be justified by either presumptive consent or a best interests analysis at the time of the initial intervention), and that treatment can only be continued based on the consent of a surrogate decision-maker or a conclusion that it is in the patient's best interests, then it is crucial to engage fully in an assessment of best interests (in the absence of surrogate consent). The fact that the physician is the formal decision-maker for incapacitated patients by law in England and Wales[41] may make the consideration of quality of life structurally more routine and less emotionally fraught (though physicians no doubt struggle with these questions). The physician can, to some extent, step away from deep divisions within a patient's family and by shouldering the responsibility may be able to reduce or relieve feelings of guilt and regret that a family decision-maker might otherwise experience. It is difficult to imagine how such a process would be received in the United States. While at least one state statute permits the unilateral withdrawal of life-prolonging care over the objections of family members,[42] it is not widely accepted that physicians should make decisions for incapacitated patients.

The English courts' willingness to speak directly of the patient's best interests and to acknowledge that it is not always in a patient's best interests to continue receiving care that keeps him alive would cause consternation among many people in the United States, particularly those who describe themselves as 'pro-life'. In the *Bland* case, Lord Browne-Wilkinson expressed the view that physicians have a *responsibility* to withdraw life-sustaining medical care when such treatment is considered contrary to the patient's interests:

> [I]f there comes the stage where the responsible doctor comes to the reasonable conclusion (which accords with the views of a responsible body of medical opinion) that further continuance of an intrusive life-support system is not in the best interests of the patient, he can no longer lawfully continue that life-support system: to do so would constitute the crime of battery and tort of trespass to the person.[43]

In *Bland*, the Lord Justices concluded that ANH interfered with the natural trajectory toward death that would otherwise have been the patient's fate.[44] This view has been confirmed repeatedly as a matter of law and policy in the practice of medicine in the United Kingdom. In a more recent case, Aintree Hospital v. James, the

41 In the absence of an advance directive or other prior statement to guide the decision and in the absence of a legal proxy decision-maker, GMC guidance makes the physician the responsible decision-maker. General Medical Council, Decision Making and Consent §§ 88-89 (9 Nov. 2020). The physician, when deciding for an incapacitated patient, must still consider the patient's past and present wishes and beliefs (to the extent they can be known) and must consult with the patient's health care team and anyone who cares for the patient or is interested in his or welfare. Mental Capacity Act § 4(6)-(7) (2005).

42 Texas Advance Directives Act, Section 166.046(e) (1999) (discussed in more detail in Chapter 10).

43 Airedale NHS Trust v. Bland [1993] AC 789 (Browne-Wilkinson LJ).

44 Airedale NHS Trust v. Bland [1993] AC 789 (Hoffman LJ).

Supreme Court further refined the best interests analysis. Lady Hale wrote that "the focus is on whether it is in the patient's best interests to give the treatment, rather than on whether it is in his best interests to withhold or withdraw it." The wishes of the patient remain relevant – the opinion added that the best interests standard also contained an element of substituted judgment that should include the patient's wishes and could also include "altruistic sentiments and concern for others" along with broad consideration of the patient's welfare, "not just medical but social and psychological."[45] This hybrid analysis that factors in both the patient's best interests and the patient's values and wishes is conceptually challenging, but worth the effort, because it maintains respect for the now-incapacitated patient's autonomy.[46]

In the United States, a strong emphasis on the sanctity of life (and societal discomfort with assessing quality of life) coupled with the primacy of patient and surrogate autonomy makes it less likely that a court will reach the conclusion that it is in the patient's best interests to withdraw life-prolonging care. The sanctity of life principle places equal value on all life – no matter its quality. The principle may be most associated with religious beliefs – that life is a gift from God – but some argue that no religious foundation is necessary to conclude that all human life deserves protection. To proponents of the sanctity principle, even when a patient wishes to end life (by refusing further life-sustaining interventions or by some form of voluntary hastened death), it is wrong to give the patient what she asks for. However, there's no consensus around this view. To the contrary, some argue that keeping a person alive for months or years on life support offends the person's dignity and elevates mere biological existence over a life with meaning.[47] For purposes of this discussion, how an individual patient views sanctity of life represents part of that patient's unique, autonomous persona and should guide how others make decisions for that patient. The problem arises when outside forces – governments, courts, religious groups – attempt to impose a particular view regarding sanctity of life across an entire population rather than asking whether the sanctity of life principle accords with a particular patient's beliefs. As Ronald Dworkin observed of those who espouse the principle,

> The struggle to stay alive, no matter how hopeless or how thin the life, expresses a virtue central to *their* lives, the virtue of defiance in the face of inevitable death. It is not just a matter of taste on which people happen to divide, as they divide about surfing or soccer. None of us wants to end our lives out of character.[48]

45 Aintree University Hospital v. James [2013] UKSC67; Jonathan Herring, Medical Law and Ethics pp. 527–528 (7th ed. Oxford University Press 2018) (explaining that the presumption in favor of preserving life is "subservient to an assessment of the best interests viewed from the perspective of individual patients").

46 In the United States, compare In re Conroy, 486 A.2d 1209 (1985) (adopting a sliding scale of decision-making between complete emphasis on the incapacitated patient's wishes and complete reliance on best interests based on the available evidence of patient preferences).

47 Ronald Dworkin, Life's Dominion pp. 194–195 (Knopf 1993).

48 Ibid., p. 213.

Some patients believe that showing respect for the sanctity of life requires fighting to the end, while others believe that allowing life to end quietly, perhaps at home, and without undue perturbations, promotes both sanctity and human dignity. This is not a question on which our society (or probably any society) will reach agreement, but the autonomy principle, if we're serious about implementing it, doesn't require agreement.

Disagreements about whether and when further treatment or life-sustaining measures are medically or ethically appropriate raise questions about the subjective value of the medical intervention along with questions about the probability that the medical intervention will be effective.[49] A professional judgment that continued life support is inappropriate for patients in PVS might make sense to many (or most) medical professionals, but more than a few family members of these patients will dispute this conclusion. The subjective value of continued treatment is in the eye of the beholder. In the case of PVS patients, it is clear that ANH keeps patients alive but does not improve their condition. So, is ANH in these cases 'effective'? Without information about an individual patient's beliefs regarding continued life-prolonging measures, it is difficult to know when to cease providing support to a person whose condition will never improve. In these circumstances, US courts (and health care providers) are often reluctant to opine about an incapacitated patient's best interests or, underlying that inquiry, the patient's quality of life.[50] Rather than confronting hard questions about best interests and quality of life, courts in these cases generally will choose to 'err' on the side of continued treatment,[51] focusing on the sanctity of life. A purely biologic view of life – for which consciousness isn't required – certainly presents a simple bright-line rule for US courts,[52] but this approach fails to answer the more difficult questions presented in these cases.

49 Robert D. Truog et al., The Problem with Futility, 326 New Eng. J. Med. 1560–1564 (1992).

50 Cruzan v. Director, Missouri Dept. of Health, 497 U.S. 261 (1990) ("[W]e think a State may properly decline to make judgments about the 'quality' of life that a particular individual may enjoy, and simply assert an unqualified interest in the preservation of human life to be weighed against the constitutionally protected interests of the individual."); Conservatorship of Wendland, 28 P.3d 151 (2001) (upholding a trial court decision to continue life-sustaining treatment despite a surrogate decision-maker's request to withdraw it because the surrogate "offered no basis for such a finding other than her own subjective judgment that the conservatee did not enjoy a satisfactory quality of life and legally insufficient evidence to the effect that he would have wished to die"); In re Conservatorship of Helga M. Wanglie, No. PX-91-283, Dist. Ct. Probate Div. (Minn. 1989) (upholding the surrogate's request for continued treatment of the patient, who was in a permanent vegetative state and who died more than a year later of sepsis).

51 Cruzan v. Director, Missouri Dept. of Health, 497 US 261 (1990) ("An erroneous decision not to terminate [life-supportive measures] results in a maintenance of the status quo; the possibility of subsequent developments such as advancements in medical science, the discovery of new evidence regarding the patient's intent, . . . at least create the potential that a wrong decision will eventually be corrected. . . . An erroneous decision to withdraw life-sustaining treatment, however, is not susceptible of correction.").

52 In re Baby K, 16 F.3d 590 (4th Cir. 1994) (resolving, on technical statutory grounds, a dispute about continued life supportive measures for an anencephalic infant and thus defaulting to protection of purely biologic life).

This thinking imposes serious costs on permanently unconscious patients and nicely sidesteps the most difficult questions. The problem with erring in favor of continued treatment is that it is just as likely to offend an individual's autonomy and bodily integrity as would erring in the opposite direction and withdrawing treatment. A decision to maintain the status quo by continuing life-supportive measures may help assuage feelings of helplessness on the part of families and caregivers, and it may align with the interests of pro-life organizations, but it is not necessarily in the individual patient's best interests, nor does it necessarily reflect what the patient would choose. In fact, if we are honest, a decision to continue life-prolonging measures for a permanently unconscious patient – in the absence of evidence that the patient would prefer this – is done *not* in the patient's best interests but for the sake of others who believe that it's morally imperative.[53]

A couple of final points deserve mention here. Another question that arises repeatedly in the case of patients in PVS or with other disorders of consciousness is whether artificial nutrition and hydration, delivered via a surgically implanted tube or intravenously, is medical treatment or simply 'ordinary care'. All three courts that ruled in the cases discussed here treated ANH as a form of technological medical care that could be withdrawn in appropriate circumstances, but the question remains controversial among the lay public. Family members may be (understandably) distressed at the thought of their loved one dying from dehydration and starvation. What is medical technology to physicians and courts is a fundamental requirement for life in the eyes of some families. At least in part for this reason, the parents of Theresa Schiavo, who were devout Catholics, objected to the removal of Theresa's feeding tube. Improved communication about the nature of artificial nutrition and hydration may help some families understand the technological nature of the intervention but is not likely to move those who believe that it is required, either as a matter of religious faith or because it is 'ordinary care'.

In addition, the withdrawal of artificial nutrition and hydration (or any other life-prolonging technology) is considered as factually, ethically, and legally distinct from hastening death or euthanasia. The court in the *Bland* case took pains to characterize a doctor's removal of life-prolonging measures as an omission (not motivated by a desire to bring about the patient's death) rather than an act intended to cause the patient's death. As Lord Goff explained:

> I agree that the doctor's conduct in discontinuing life support can properly be categorised as an omission. . . . [D]iscontinuation of life support is, for present purposes, no different from not initiating life support in the first place. In each case, the doctor is simply allowing his patient to die in the sense that he is desisting from taking a step which might, in certain circumstances, prevent his patient from dying as a result of his pre-existing condition; and as a matter of general principle an

53. Lois Shepherd, In Respect of People Living in a Permanent Vegetative State – and Allowing Them to Die, 16 Health Matrix 631–691 (2006).

> omission such as this will not be unlawful unless it constitutes a breach of duty to the patient.[54]

There is much agreement in US courts on this question, and medical ethics commentators have argued that withdrawing life support is not 'killing' the patient but rather allowing the patient to die of the underlying disease or injury that required the initiation of life support in the first place. It is ceasing to place an artificial obstacle in the way of what would otherwise be a natural death.[55] Yet, there will always be some who resolve the ambivalence created by medical technology in what turns out to be hopeless cases by taking the absolute view that withdrawal of life-sustaining care from a patient who is not actively dying is homicide, even if the underlying action is grounded in respect for the patient's dignity and values.

CAN WE AGREE TO DISAGREE?

With the continual advancement of life-supportive technologies, we add to our arsenal for delaying death. We can prolong the life of patients in PVS and, because we can, we do, whether or not the patient in question would wish it, at least in cases where there is disagreement about the question. Numerous countries and cultures struggle with the questions presented here and arrive – at various speeds and with various degrees of careful debate – at the same answer – that it can be ethically appropriate and legally permissible to withdraw life-prolonging technology from permanently unconscious patients. The debate and resolution of disputes about patients in PVS provides a window into the law and culture of a country. In the United States, the *Schiavo* litigation illustrates a legal and cultural struggle that, to some degree, has made itself felt in all ensuing end-of-life conflicts. Disputes concerning Canada's Hassan Rasouli and the UK's Anthony Bland serve as useful comparators – not only with respect to how these disputes were resolved but also as evidence of different degrees of cultural discomfort with making decisions about the futures of patients in this tragic medical situation. The United States, as the most politically and culturally balkanized of the three countries, seems to struggle the most when an end-of-life conflict makes headlines.

In the United States, discourse on end-of-life matters is both hampered and enriched by its heterogenous culture. The racial, ethnic, religious, and cultural diversity that is the hallmark of the United States also makes it difficult to reach a collective, societal consensus on end-of-life matters. Mainstream political discourse in the United States is heavily divided on these questions. Many hold the view that life begins at conception and that all life is sacred, even if the person in

[54] Airedale NHS Trust v. Bland [1993] AC 789 (Goff LJ) (distinguishing from this situation the case of "an interloper who maliciously switches off a life support machine").

[55] In Re Conroy, 486 A.2d 1209, 1224 (1985) (explaining that the refusal of medical treatment "merely allows the disease to take its natural course; if death were eventually to occur, it would be the result, primarily, of the underlying disease").

question is permanently unconscious. Others vehemently disagree. Our piecemeal and erratic state and federal legislative and judicial processes resolve individual disputes. The mechanisms of legal adjudication go some way to creating consensus by recognizing some fundamental rights of decision-making, but when an individual's wishes are unclear and a dispute reaches the judicial system, cultural and political balkanization adds fuel to the ensuing conflict. We struggle to establish even a baseline national consensus on the questions raised in the litigation described here. This divisiveness, with respect not only to end-of-life care but also reproductive autonomy and other matters, is often referred to as the 'culture wars'.[56]

In the US culture wars, truth sometimes falls victim to zeal. A decade or so ago, attempts by the Obama administration to enact a provision to compensate physicians for discussing end-of-life advance care planning with Medicare patients were derailed by fabricated and fear-mongering 'death panel' accusations.[57] Despite repeated corrections of false statements regarding the content and intent of these regulatory proposals, polls showed that a substantial percentage of those surveyed incorrectly believed that reforms in the Affordable Care Act included panels that would opine on patients' fitness to receive health care or would promote euthanasia.[58] These reforms to promote end-of-life planning ultimately were implemented,[59] though organizations such as the National Right to Life Committee argued that payment for advance care planning would create a bias against life-prolonging treatment and could exert pressure on some people to forgo medical treatment to reduce costs.[60] Some Americans suffer the affliction "of ignoring volumes of evidence in favor of the flashes that meet the eye, the hunches that seize the gut."[61] Overall, the bald falsity of the 'death panels' claim (first introduced into mainstream political discourse by former vice-presidential candidate Sarah Palin) is evidence that those who oppose a particular law (or judicial decision) that protects the principle of individual autonomy but might not comport with 'pro-life' values will stop at nothing to block its implementation.

[56] Conscience clauses, for example, those that permit pharmacists to refuse to fill prescriptions for certain contraceptives, the 'morning-after pill', chemical abortifacients, and drugs used for medical aid in dying, provide another hot-button example of the culture wars in action.

[57] Earl Blumenauer, My Near Death Panel Experience, N.Y. Times, Nov. 15, 2009, at WK12 (describing US Rep. Blumenauer's efforts to implement Medicare reimbursement for this service and political uproar that followed, including a series of blatant lies about the proposal offered up by its opponents), www.nytimes.com/2009/11/15/opinion/15blumenauer.html.

[58] Associated Press, The Associated Press-GfK Poll: Health Care Reform (Sept. 25, 2012), http://surveys.associatedpress.com/data/GfK/HealthReform_2012_Topline_1st%20release.pdf.

[59] Starting on January 1, 2016, Medicare began reimbursing physicians for advance care planning conversations with their patients. Dept. of Health & Human Services, Medicare Program: Revisions to Payment Policies Under the Physician Fee Schedule, 80 Fed. Reg. 70886 (Nov. 16, 2015).

[60] Pam Belluck, Medicare Plans to Pay Doctors for Counseling on End of Life, N.Y. Times, July 8, 2015, at A1, www.nytimes.com/2015/07/09/health/medicare-proposes-paying-doctors-for-end-of-life-counseling.html.

[61] Benjamin Anastas, The Foul Reign of Emerson's "Self-Reliance," N.Y. Times Mag., Dec. 2, 2011 at MM58, www.nytimes.com/2011/12/04/magazine/riff-ralph-waldo-emerson.html.

In the end, how a country – its courts and its culture – debates and resolves difficult end-of-life cases will to some extent be a result of the willingness of individual physicians, patients, and families to have uncomfortable, emotional, and conflict-laden conversations. In countries and cultures where greater (though not unanimous) societal opinion supports the withdrawal of life-prolonging care from permanently unconscious patients, there is perhaps more willingness to recognize that these patients – as humans, as social individuals, and as legal persons – retain an interest in dignity. That dignity, as exercised, may include a principled refusal to lie inert and permanently unable to interact with the world. Americans, like all human beings individually and all cultures and nations collectively, must have these conversations. Some individuals and cultures and nations can manage these conversations better than others. In the United States, we live in a culture in which the very public politicizing and manipulative behavior of some makes end-of-life decision-making more difficult for all.

6

More Barriers to Good Communication

Wanna fly, you got to give up the shit that weighs you down.

—Toni Morrison, Song of Solomon[1]

Health care policy experts in the United States have been studying for years how to improve the experience of dying and how to avoid overutilization of inappropriate and unwanted medical interventions at the end of life, but progress toward these goals is slow. In fact, the problems described in preceding chapters appear to be getting worse in some respects. As Chapter 3 explained, the law of informed consent is relevant to these problems but doesn't do much to solve them. Informed consent law and the underlying ethical principles of autonomy and beneficence impose a duty to inform patients of the risks and benefits of treatment such as late-stage chemotherapy and life-sustaining care (including the risk of harms and the likelihood of success measured by cure, extended life expectancy, or palliation of symptoms). But the mechanical process of legal consent rarely helps to improve patient understanding of the complexity and magnitude of the decisions she faces. Only honest, timely, and thorough two-way communication between physician and patient can accomplish this goal, and always imperfectly. Putting aside the flawed legal mechanism of informed consent for the moment, it's useful to consider the causes of inadequate physician-patient communication as a starting point for thinking about how to improve complex medical decision-making.

Various aspects of the medical system and professional culture (some of which appear less consequential in the United Kingdom and Canada) exert tremendous pressure on US physicians to offer burdensome medical interventions to seriously ill and dying patients. Some of these same factors discourage physicians from discussing the downside risks of the 'all in' pathway for patients with incurable illness, or from initiating conversations about terminating therapeutic treatment or life-prolonging technologies when they may no longer benefit the patient. A more

[1] Toni Morrison, Song of Solomon p. 179 (Knopf, 1977).

thorough understanding of the barriers to good physician-patient communication can help to frame the broader problem and to understand its magnitude.

COMMUNICATION AVOIDANCE AND ITS CAUSES

As the evidence in Chapter 3 demonstrates, physicians sometimes avoid 'bad news' conversations with patients and may attempt to preserve hope by omitting details or being untruthful about prognosis, and the consequences of avoidance can be dire for patients. Patients simply must have an accurate and ongoing understanding of their medical situation, reasonable treatment options, and prognosis to make informed decisions – if that is what they seek to do. For patients with cancer and other complex illnesses, evolving circumstances may require sequential conversations – initial diagnosis, discussion of treatment options with a curative intent, prognosis, and when relevant, discussion of ceasing curative therapy in favor of focusing on palliation of symptoms. If a patient wants to opt out of these conversations and put his treatment into the physician's hands (a waiver of participation in decision-making in informed consent lingo as described in Chapter 3), the patient still needs *some* information about his situation to understand the implications of the waiver. Without these conversations, few patients will have an accurate understanding of their prognoses and treatment options. In one study of patients with stage IV incurable gastrointestinal cancer, only 5 percent of patients completely understood the four aspects of their terminal disease status: that they were terminally ill, that their disease was incurable, the advanced stage of their disease, and that they could expect to live only months as opposed to years. The study authors advised discussion of prognosis with patients on an ongoing basis to help patients and families make informed decisions about end-of-life care.[2] When patients do not understand that death is imminent, they are more likely to agree to continuing burdensome medical care. Many patients do just that.[3]

A literature review concerning physician honesty and communication with patients regarding prognosis sets out reasons why clinicians withhold information and are reluctant to discuss prognosis and other end-of-life matters. Physicians reported discomfort with broaching the topic or responding to patients' requests to talk about prognosis, stress from dealing with patients' and their families' emotions, inadequate training in prognostication, uneasiness with discussing death, and thoughts about their own mortality.[4] While physician discomfort in these matters is understandable, most of these reported explanations concern physicians' own

[2] Andrew S. Epstein et al., Discussions of Life Expectancy and Changes in Illness Understanding in Patients with Advanced Cancer, 34 J. Clinical Oncology 2398–2403 (2016).

[3] David C. Goodman et al., Trends in Cancer Care Near the End of Life (2013) www.dartmouthatlas.org/downloads/reports/Cancer_brief_090413.pdf.

[4] Karen Hancock et al., Truth-Telling in Discussing Prognosis in Advanced Life-Limiting Illness: A Systematic Review, 21 Palliative Med. 507–517 (2007).

well-being and are inconsistent with their roles as professionals who are responsible for the welfare of their patients. This is not to discount what physicians are facing – the emotional load of delivering bad news to patients regarding poor prognosis or treatment failure is well documented and can lead to moral and emotional distress, frustration,[5] 'compassion fatigue', or just overall burnout.[6] This sort of physician suffering, while well recognized, isn't easily remedied, although self-care strategies that focus on both professional and personal dimensions sound useful.[7] It is part of the life of a physician: "For you will be invincible / and vulnerable in the same breath / which is the breath of your patients."[8]

There seems to be a disconnect between professionalism and human feelings that will be hard to bridge until physicians learn to make room for and embrace their emotions rather than trying to suppress them.[9] Teaching physicians to embrace their emotions will very likely improve communication enormously by allowing the patient to see the physician as a human being, not a technocrat, and so generate trust via connection.[10] Realistically, this sounds like a large hill to climb, especially because other aspects of medical education and professional culture emphasize the importance of clinical skills and knowledge and the detached exercise of clinical judgment. For physicians who see death on a regular basis, it is natural to develop a certain amount of emotional armor. The challenge is then how to keep that armor sufficiently intact while carrying out the responsibility of communicating with patients and families about the choices they face.

Several of the studies in the literature review also examined whether disclosure had a negative impact on patients, citing concerns about emotional harm to the patient, preserving hope, establishing and preserving trust in the physician-patient relationship, and respect for family requests to withhold information from the patient.[11] Physicians mistakenly believe that discussions about poor prognosis will make patients depressed or deprive them of hope. In fact, the evidence suggests the opposite.[12] The vast majority of patients do not find these conversations distressing.[13] Once hope of a cure is gone, patients can 'redefine hope' (or, to avoid euphemism,

[5] Diane E. Meier et al., The Inner Life of Physicians and Care of the Seriously Ill, 286 JAMA 3007–3014 (2001).

[6] Wendy Dean et al., Clarifying the Language of Clinician Distress, 323 JAMA 923–924 (2020) (explaining the importance of understanding the component parts of what is generally called 'burnout').

[7] Sandra Sanchez-Reilly et al., Caring for Oneself to Care for Others: Physicians and Their Self-Care & 11 J. Support Oncol. 75–81 (2013).

[8] John Stone, Gaudeamus Igitur, in On Doctoring: Stories, Poems, Essays pp. 326–330 (Richard Reynolds & John Stone, eds.) (Simon & Schuster 1995).

[9] Donald M. Berwick, What "Patient-Centered" Should Mean: Confessions of an Extremist, 28 Health Aff. W555–w565 (2009).

[10] Parker Palmer, A New Professional: The Aims of Education Revisited, 39 Change 5–12 (2007).

[11] Hancock et al., Truth-Telling in Discussing Prognosis in Advanced Life-Limiting Illness.

[12] Alexi A. Wright et al., Associations Between End-of-Life Discussions, Patient Mental Health, Medical Care Near Death, and Caregiver Bereavement Adjustment, 300 JAMA 1665–1673 (2008).

[13] Ezekiel J. Emanuel et al., Talking With Terminally Ill Patients and Their Caregivers About Death, Dying, and Bereavement, 164 Arch. Int. Med. 1999–2004 (2004).

realign their expectations with reality) with the help of physicians who are willing to sit with them, talk honestly about what the future holds, and elicit and respond to their questions and fears. As one physician explained, "Patients want us to be truthful, compassionate, and clear, and to stay the course with them."[14]

Other reasons for conversation avoidance vary, but many physicians cite the lack of adequate training for facilitating difficult conversations. In one survey of physicians, 68 percent reported not being trained to discuss end-of-life issues.[15] In another survey, while 99 percent of physicians agreed that end-of-life conversations with patients are important, only 29 percent had any formal training about how to conduct these conversations.[16] By contrast, medical training focusing on performing invasive procedures is well organized and includes demonstrating the procedure, observing the medical student or resident as she performs the procedure, providing feedback, and encouraging self-assessment as learning progresses. A comparable kind of structured training for communication with patients and families remains rare.[17] Of course, some medical specialties (such as geriatrics, oncology, and critical care) by definition require physicians to have end-of-life conversations more frequently. As repeat players, some of these specialists will therefore have enough experience to feel confident about talking with patients and families, even without formal training, but many others struggle with the task.

Physicians also may think that clinical uncertainty justifies conversation avoidance (more about this in Chapter 8). Predicting the timing of death is often quite challenging from a scientific perspective,[18] and newer therapies that slow disease progression further complicate the matter.[19] Research demonstrates that clinical uncertainty about the pathways and progress of disease influences physician disclosure, with some studies indicating that longer estimated survival also has some delaying effect on when physicians will discuss prognosis with patients. Although a majority of physicians believe that patients and family should be told the truth about the prognosis, in reality physicians tend to avoid the topic or to withhold details, sometimes in response to family requests not to tell the patient the truth, or because physicians themselves feel hopeless about their inability to cure the

14 Thomas J. Smith et al., Giving Honest Information to Patients with Advanced Cancer Maintains Hope, 24 Oncology 521–525 (2010).

15 The John A. Hartford Foundation, "Conversation Stopper: What's Preventing Physicians from Talking with Patients About End-of-Life and Advance Care Planning?" Poll (Apr. 2016), www.johnahartford.org/dissemination-center/view/advance-care-planning-poll.

16 Terry Fulmer et al., Physicians' Views on Advance Care Planning and End-of-Life Care Conversations, 66 J. Am. Geriatrics Soc. 1201–1205 (2018).

17 Jennifer A. Woo et al., Clinical Challenges to the Delivery of End-of-Life Care, 8 J. Clin. Psychiatry 367–372 (2006).

18 Laura Van Metre Baum & Debra Friedman, The Uncertain Science of Predicting Death, 3 JAMA Network Open (2020) doi:10.1001/jamanetworkopen2020.1736.

19 Haider J. Warraich et al., How Medicine Has Changed the End of Life for Patients with Cardiovascular Disease, 70 J. Am. Coll. Cardiology 1276–1289 (2017).

patient.[20] Although it is true that no one can predict precisely how long a patient has to live, it is possible to estimate a prognosis for many diseases and to provide the patient with an honest range of possible outcomes.[21] Even in situations where prognosis is difficult to predict with much accuracy, the terminal nature of some illnesses is certain and the physician can explain at least this fact to the patient clearly and without hedging. Instead of doing so, physicians often ignore 'the elephant in the room' and focus on reacting to one crisis after the next.[22] Although the natural tendency may be to avoid specific discussions of prognosis to 'protect' patients and families from distress, this avoidance also protects the physician from having to give bad news and navigate the ensuing emotional fallout.

All of these reasons help explain physician guardedness in discussions with patients; it is a natural reaction in emotional situations to say less rather than more. Physicians are only human, but they are also highly trained professionals with expert knowledge on whom their patients rely. The aversion to frank discussion increases the risk that patients will pursue aggressive and debilitating treatments in the hope of prolonging life without fully understanding the implications of that choice. These patients, in the final chapter of life, now pay the price of avoidable suffering and reduced opportunity to attend to important personal matters before death. Overall, given that a clear majority of cancer patients desire frank information about prognosis and the potential for cure,[23] physician reluctance (or complete failure) to provide this information appears to be at least as much about the physician's own struggles and avoidance as it is about protecting the patient from emotional distress or the loss of hope. Even when these patient-oriented concerns are genuine and well meant rather than self-protective, they have an inherent element of paternalism – the physician simply assumes that emotional distress should be avoided (when it is nearly always unavoidable in matters of impending death) and that the patient wants to engage in false hope or unrealistic optimism.

All that said, many physicians express frustration, self-criticism, and regret about their own failures to have candid conversations with patients. Here are just a few of the many examples published in recent years. One neurologist wrote about his patients with brain tumors: "I had guarded conversations about their future – trying to provide hope, but not too much hope. On several occasions, I operated yet again

[20] Karen Hancock et al., Truth-Telling in Discussing Prognosis in Advanced Life-Limiting Illness: A Systematic Review, 21 Palliative Med. 507–517 (2007).

[21] Jennifer W. Mack & Thomas J. Smith, Reasons Why Physicians Do Not Have Discussions About Poor Prognosis, Why It Matters, and What Can Be Improved, 30 J. Clinical Oncology 2715–2717 (2012).

[22] Tanya H. Tajouri & Timothy J. Moynihan, The Elephant in the Room – Your Patient is Dying: A Teachable Moment, 174 JAMA Internal Med. 185 (2014).

[23] Lesley J. Fallowfield et al., Truth May Hurt But Deceit Hurts More: Communication in Palliative Care, 16 Palliative Med. 297–303 (2002) (87 percent of patients with cancer in a UK study wanted all information, including bad news); Roger J. Sullivan et al., Truth-telling and Patient Diagnoses, 27 J. Med. Ethics 192–197 (2001) (72 percent of American cancer patients in the study wanted full information about their condition and treatments while 85 percent of these patients would want their families to receive all information).

when I should not have done. This was not because the law dictated that I give my patients a choice, but because it was so unbearably painful to spell out the truth to them."[24] An emergency medicine physician confessed:

> I recently tortured an 88-year old woman with advanced dementia .... Her family brought her to the hospital because she had a high fever and was more confused than usual. I knew that she was near her end. ... I asked her daughter ... what I always ask families managing a relative's final days: "Do you want us to do procedures that may well be painful and will not improve her quality of life? Or do you want us to let her go in peace?" ... Faced with this choice, some families allow nature to run its course. They decline medical interventions beyond comfort care (such as pain medicine and oxygen). ... Other families consider it imperative to opt for all possible medical interventions. Unfortunately, this includes invasive procedures that cause transient or lasting discomfort. In my experience, most families choose the second option. That includes my patient's family, who asked that I "do everything" possible to treat her. So I did. ... Eventually, her heart stopped. I gave her CPR that broke some of her ribs. Then the nurses and I forced a breathing tube down her throat. ... None of this helped my patient. She died within a day. Had her family chosen "comfort care only," she could have spent her last moments peacefully surrounded by loved ones. Instead, she died in anxious misery. And those procedures were so rough on her frail body that she may have even lived longer without them.[25]

This family's demands and the physician's obvious reluctance to treat the patient aggressively is a fine example of the mess that we're in. The physician began by asking the family the right question – sort of. (The better question would have been "What would your mother want done in this situation, if we could ask her?") Then he apparently didn't follow up with information about the consequences of the two options. Nor did he (apparently) make a recommendation or opine about the chances that 'doing everything' would actually help the patient in ways that might outweigh the costs of additional suffering occasioned by the 'everything'. The way the physician poses the question to the family suggests that there are only two options – all or nothing – when in fact, even for patients with end-stage dementia, there is usually a middle way that avoids painful and fruitless procedures but is still 'doing something'.

Why don't these physicians say 'no' and decline to provide care that is more likely to harm than help their patients? Simply put, these conversations are hard, not least because patients and families are correspondingly reluctant to hear bad news for both obvious and more complex reasons. Chapter 8 explores the patient side of the physician-patient communication dynamic. Despite seeing serious illness and death

[24] Henry Marsh, An Oncologist Asks When It's Time to Say "Enough," N.Y. Times, Oct. 15, 2019 (reviewing Azra Raza, The First Cell And the Human Costs of Pursuing Cancer to the Last), www.nytimes.com/2019/10/15/books/review/the-first-cell-azra-raza.html.

[25] Geoffrey Hosta, Doctors Are Torturing Dementia Patients at the End of Their Life. And It's Totally Unnecessary, Wash. Post (Nov. 28, 2019), www.washingtonpost.com/opinions/2019/11/28/doctors-are-torturing-dementia-patients-end-their-life-its-totally-unnecessary/.

on a regular basis, many physicians remain uncomfortable with the spiritual and emotional needs of dying patients, and with their own emotions. When physicians feel close to patients, the hard work of disclosing bad news can be especially stressful, but honest conversation is a fundamental moral and legal duty of physicians.[26] After all, physicians continue living for the foreseeable future, while their dying patients do not. If a physician's life's work centers on the prevention and alleviation of suffering, helping dying patients avoid suffering caused by unnecessary medical interventions seems to be of ultimate importance – the last thing (apart from palliative care) that the physician can do for the patient.

PHYSICIAN PROFESSIONAL CULTURE – THE 'DO EVERYTHING' MENTALITY

For the most part, physicians are still trained in a culture of cure at all costs and tend to view a patient's death, even an inevitable death, as a professional failure. Physicians as part of their training naturally become desensitized to blood, bones, and body parts, but they need not become desensitized to death. More specifically, the physician can adopt an objective attitude toward disease that allows her to diagnose and treat the patient without becoming overwhelmed with the horrors of terminal illness and death. Even so, while they may witness death on many occasions, physicians are not like other scientists: "whereas a scientist is interested in death, a doctor is against it."[27] The Hippocratic Oath suggests a more nuanced view of the physician's role that considers not only the potential for effective treatment but also the burdens of treatment: "I will follow that system of regimen which, according to my ability and judgment, I consider for the Benefit of my patients, and abstain from whatever is deleterious and mischievous."[28]

Within this milieu, physicians sometimes exhibit a striking reluctance to cease curative care for their patients, to acknowledge their patients' imminent dying, and to focus on symptom management instead of continuing to treat the illness aggressively. Commentators have noted that physicians' attitudes toward these issues can vary according to their specialty. Surgeons, for example, may have difficulty relinquishing control over postsurgical patients because they fear retrospective censure about the appropriateness of the decision to perform the surgery, or because of guilt if the patient is faring poorly. Surgeons may also wish to avoid appearing to lack confidence in themselves or may worry that losing a surgical patient will harm their statistical success numbers.[29] In one survey of surgeons who regularly performed high-risk operations,

[26] Jennifer W. Mack & Thomas J. Smith, Reasons Why Physicians Do Not Have Discussions About Poor Prognosis, Why It Matters, and What Can Be Improved, 30 J. Clinical Oncology 2715–2717 (2012).

[27] August M. Kasper, The Doctor and Death in The Meaning of Death p. 262 (Herman Feifel, ed.) (McGraw-Hill, 1959).

[28] Oath of Hippocrates (Circa 400 B.C.), Harvard Classics Vol. 38 (P.F. Collier and Son, 1910).

[29] Soumitra R. Eachempati et al., The Surgical Intensivist as Mediator of End-of-Life Issues in the Care of Critically Ill Patients, 197 J. Am. Coll. Surgeons 847–853 (2003).

respondents were provided with a vignette in which a patient and family request withdrawal of life-supportive measures from the patient who is faring poorly seven days after a procedure in which the surgeon had made a surgical error. Under these circumstances, only 33 percent of respondents indicated that they would agree to a request to withdraw life support. In a comparison hypothetical case with no surgical error, only 41 percent of surgeons would agree to withdraw life support. Surgeons, when making this decision to abide by the patient and family request, were highly influenced by the fact of their own surgical error coupled with unfounded optimism about prognosis.[30] The survey suggests that surgeons may allow their emotions to interfere with their willingness to abide by postsurgical requests to withdraw life support.

Oncologists also may struggle with the idea of stopping therapeutic interventions for their patients, either out of a desire to 'beat the cancer' or because the conversation that precedes the decision is so difficult for oncologist and patient alike. One physician tells a story of an oncologist who was upset about his patient's decision to stop chemotherapy and enroll in a hospice program. The oncologist confronted the hospice physician and said, "We might as well just be walking away, and we might just as well shoot [the patient] now."[31] In reality, it seems that many oncologists struggle with the ambivalence that comes with navigating the patient's hopes and telling the patient the truth, and some are quite explicit in the recognition of their specialty's faults. One oncologist recently published a book that examines the treatment of cancer with an experienced and critical eye.[32] The author expresses frustration with the frequent utilization of cancer therapies well beyond the point where these toxic therapies will provide any benefit for the patient. (The book's reviewer, a neurosurgeon, repeats the classic joke about oncologists: "Why should you never give an oncologist a screwdriver? Because they will open the coffin and carry on treating the patient."[33]) The author is unsparing in her criticism of the specialty's failure to be frank with patients about their prognosis – and the consequent continued utilization of useless (but not painless or otherwise costless) therapies. She asks, "Why are we so afraid to tell the stories of the majority who die? Why keep promoting the positive anecdote?" It is good to see someone (and she is not alone)[34] asking these very provocative questions.

Another related driver behind the overutilization of medical interventions is the technology juggernaut – the idea that if technology is available, why not use it? As one commentator has explained, physicians surrender to enormous pressures to test and treat aggressively. He suggests that physicians "need to teach our patients that

30 Margaret L. Schwarze et al., The Role of Surgeon Error in Withdrawal of Postoperative Life Support, 256 Ann. Surgery 10–15 (2012).

31 Kevin B. O'Reilly, End-of-Life Care: Pain Control Carries Risk of Being Called a Killer, Am. Med. News (Apr. 16, 2012), https://hollowhorn.files.wordpress.com/2018/02/20120416pallkill.pdf.

32 Azra Raza, The First Cell: And the Human Costs of Pursuing Cancer to the Last (Basic Books, 2019).

33 Marsh, An Oncologist Asks When It's Time to Say "Enough."

34 Siddhartha Mukherjee, The Emperor of All Maladies: A Biography of Cancer (Scribner 2010).

more medicine is not better medicine, that it is poor health care for doctors to order too many tests or too many interventions, and that costly efforts do not equal better health care."[35] This is excellent advice, but it is not easy for physicians to explain to patients why, sometimes, less is more, particularly at the end of life. Unfortunately, these sorts of conversations take time and, if rushed or misunderstood by patients, can result in patients feeling that the physician doesn't think they are worth full-on treatment efforts or worse, that they are being somehow deliberately deprived of 'the best' medical care.

There are additional complexities at work in these situations. One study demonstrates clear differences between 'cowboys' – "those who consistently and unambiguously recommended intensive care beyond ... current clinical guidelines" and 'comforters' – "those who consistently recommended palliative care for the very severely ill." Although the study found some evidence that patient demands for care, liability concerns, and financial considerations impact physician decision-making, most of the variation in clinical approach in this study was actually driven by mistaken physician beliefs about the usefulness of particular therapies.[36] The conclusion is disheartening – some physicians provide burdensome care to patients despite the lack of clinical evidence of efficacy. An old joke illustrates the common complaint that many physicians lack humility: It was an unusually busy day at the gates of Heaven and Saint Peter was hard at work, processing the entry of a long line. Because those waiting were all saints, they waited patiently, and waited, and waited. At one point, a man in a white coat with a stethoscope around his neck walked past the line, nodded to Saint Peter, and entered through the gates. One of the waiting saints asked, "Hey, who was that, jumping the queue?" Saint Peter answered, "Oh, that's just God. He thinks he's a doctor."[37]

The medicalization of dying has created more than just conundrums about the appropriate use of medical technology. Modern medical training still focuses on cure and treats the patient's illness as a problem to be solved rather than more broadly defining 'care' to include the possibility of stopping therapeutic care and focusing on palliation of symptoms. Although this situation is gradually changing with better education about palliative care, the emphasis on technology as the primary mechanism of medical care has gradually supplanted, or at least marginalized, other fundamental aspects of caregiving, such as personal contact, intimate

35 Sean Palfrey, Daring to Practice Low-Cost Medicine in a High-Tech Era, 364 New Eng. J. Med. e21 (1–2) (March 2011).

36 David Cutler et al., Physician Beliefs and Patient Preferences: A New Look at Regional Variation in Health Care Spending, 11 Am. Economic J.: Economic Policy 192–221 (2019).

37 In case readers think that law professors shouldn't be telling doctor jokes, here's a lawyer joke to even the score. Question: "What's the difference between a lawyer and a vulture?" Answer: "Removable wingtips." Why are there so many doctor and lawyer jokes in the first place? They capture the tropes of certain high-powered professions, they highlight the gap between the way things are and the way they ought to be, and they provide some comic relief, because there are rarely happy occasions for consulting either type of professional.

communication, and spending quality time with grieving patients and their families. Physicians lament the lost art of caregiving as the technology of medicine and the time demands of modern practice leave little time for addressing each patient's personal needs. Many patients – experiencing fear and confusion about the nature of their disease and its treatment or simply sensing that their physicians are pressed for time – hesitate to ask questions or to express their sense of despair or fear.[38] Physicians are also constantly pressed for time, making communication with patients, especially careful listening, more difficult. (A recent study found that physicians interrupted patients within an average of eleven seconds at the beginning of patient visits.[39]) Notwithstanding the ever-increasing bureaucratic and technocratic provision of modern medical care, the ideal of medical care extends to the very point of death, well beyond when cure has ceased to be an option.

Medical education should teach new physicians clearly and unequivocally that medical care is not necessarily always about prolonging life. The common training of physicians focuses on fighting disease, remaining detached, continuing to search for a solution to a problem, but perhaps at the cost of also losing sight of the patient and her goals as a human being. By reorienting the notion of medical care to include the possibility of stopping therapeutic care and focusing on the alleviation of suffering, young physicians in training can learn to rein in their technological imperative impulses and offer the patient other sorts of care to ease the dying process. As Chapter 7 describes in detail, it's important for both physicians and patients to recognize that ceasing therapeutic care or life-prolonging measures when they are no longer beneficial is not a failure of care. The opposite is true. The conversations needed, and the emotions that inhere in those conversations, ask much of physicians because providing comfort to dying patients and their families requires physicians to move beyond the idea of cure to a broader notion of medical care. This broader notion of care can reduce suffering and better comport with patients' true preferences, both of which are surely desirable outcomes at the end of life. In the words of a well-regarded physician, the goal is "[t]o cure sometimes, to relieve often, to comfort always."[40]

BY THE WAY, A WORD ABOUT HOW PHYSICIANS DIE

As Chapter 3 explained, many physicians behave in ways that create a breeding ground for death denial, even when a patient is terminally ill. By avoiding conversations about prognosis or likely treatment efficacy, or by preserving hope with

[38] Arthur Kleinman, On Caregiving, Harvard Magazine 25 (July-Aug. 2010) (explaining that "[t]he structure of training and of service delivery discourages and even disables the art").

[39] Naykky Singh Ospina et al., Eliciting the Patient's Agenda – Secondary Analysis of Recorded Clinical Encounters, 34 J. Gen. Intern. Med. 36–40 (2019).

[40] William E. Cayley Jr., Comfort Always, 13 Fam. Practice Mgmt. 74 (2006) (quoting Dr. Edward Trudeau).

exaggerated optimism, the physician allows the patient's denial to continue, even to flourish. In consequence, patients often will agree to far more burdensome treatment, CPR, and life-sustaining technologies than physicians themselves would choose in similar circumstances.

Physicians themselves are far less likely to live in denial of death, although they share the common discomfort with death, in spite of much more firsthand acquaintance with it. In fact, when facing death, physicians frequently refuse invasive treatment, including CPR, preferring instead to accept the prognosis and spend their remaining time feeling as well as possible. As one physician explained,

> It's not a frequent topic of discussion, but doctors die, too. And they don't die like the rest of us. What's unusual about them is not how much treatment they get compared to most Americans, but how little. For all the time they spend fending off the deaths of others, they tend to be fairly serene when faced with death themselves. They know exactly what is going to happen, they know the choices, and they generally have access to any sort of medical care they could want. But they go gently.[41]

In one study, in which physicians were asked whether they would want CPR if diagnosed with Alzheimer's disease or various other advanced chronic diseases at various ages, most physicians at all projected ages stated that they would decline CPR, particularly with advancing age.[42] Another study also found that physicians preferred significantly less burdensome medical care at the end of life – including intensive care, resuscitation, and ventilation – than patients in the same study would choose.[43] Yet another study noted that physicians who preferred hospice for themselves were more likely to discuss hospice with terminally ill cancer patients.[44] And in a study that looked at physician attitudes toward advance directives and their own end-of-life preferences, nearly 90 percent of those surveyed would choose not to be resuscitated at the end of life. The authors of this study theorize that physicians who regularly witness the suffering of patients who receive high-intensity care at the end of life don't want to endure similar suffering themselves. At the same time, physicians' tendency to be optimistic for their patients leads to escalation of care until it becomes clear (very late in the process) that the patient is dying.[45]

41 Ken Murray, How Doctors Die: It's Not Like the Rest of Us, But it Should Be, Zocalo Public Square (Nov. 30, 2011), www.zocalopublicsquare.org/2011/11/30/how-doctors-die/ideas/nexus/.

42 Teresa A. Hillier et al., Physicians as Patients: Choices Regarding Their Own Resuscitation, 155 Archives Internal Med. 1289–1293 (1995).

43 Gregory P. Gramelspacher et al., Preferences of Physicians and Their Patients for End-of-Life Care, 12 J. Gen. Internal Med. 346–351 (1997).

44 Garrett M. Chinn et al., Physicians' Preferences for Hospice if They Were Terminally Ill and the Timing of Hospice Discussions With Their Patients, 174 J. Am. Med. Ass'n Internal Med. 466 E1–E2 (2014).

45 Vyjeyanthi S. Periyakoil et al., Do Unto Others: Doctors' Personal End-of-Life Resuscitation Preferences and Their Attitudes Toward Advance Directives, 9 PLOS One e98246 (2014).

It is difficult to imagine an entirely benign explanation for this disconnect – that physicians offer and provide to patients end-of-life care that they would not choose for themselves. To be clear, an informed choice by a patient to request resuscitation, intubation, artificial nutrition, dialysis, palliative chemotherapy, and other potentially life-prolonging measures is a valid choice – but only if it is truly informed. The lack of candor suggested by the data in Chapter 3, together with the fact that many physicians themselves would refuse and do refuse burdensome technological interventions at the end of life, is deeply troubling. Why would physicians not tell patients what they know and what they themselves would say 'no' to? Why would physicians be enablers in a system that puts patients – people in emotional and physical distress and with enormous informational deficits compared with the experts – through the wringer at the end of life?

FINANCIAL INCENTIVES AND THE BUSINESS OF MEDICINE

Unlike in the UK's NHS and Canada's Medicare system, there is comparatively little in the way of structural guardrails to prevent overutilization in either employer-sponsored private insurance or the US Medicare program. Within much of the US medical payment structure, the impact of moral hazard (the lack of incentive to guard against personal financial risk) on both physicians and patients regarding reimbursement encourages utilization of unnecessary tests, unproven or likely unhelpful treatments, and life-prolonging technologies for patients at the very end of life. If tests, treatments, and life-prolonging measures don't cost the doctor or the patient, then why not use them? Even for drugs such as oral chemotherapy agents that have high out-of-pocket costs, patients will pay the price if they are able – when the treating physician recommends and prescribes the drug – and there are many such drugs, even under Medicare.[46]

As explained in Chapter 2, fee-for-service payment mechanisms are still common in the United States, resulting in a system in which physicians earn more when they do more – tests, procedures, and consultations. Even within fee-for-service payments, there are disparities in reimbursement that put a thumb on the scale in favor of burdensome treatments. While physicians are well compensated for performing invasive procedures,[47] they receive less compensation under Medicare for 'evaluation and management procedures' including taking the patient's medical history, discussing diagnosis and treatment options, and conversations with patients and family members about treatment plans.[48] Still, performing more evaluation and

[46] Juliette Cubanski et al., The Out-of-Pocket Cost Burden for Specialty Drugs in Medicare Part D in 2019, www.kff.org/medicare/issue-brief/the-out-of-pocket-cost-burden-for-specialty-drugs-in-medicare-part-d-in-2019/.

[47] Jennifer A. Woo et al., Clinical Challenges to the Delivery of End-of-Life Care, 8 J. Clin. Psychiatry 367–372 (2006).

[48] Centers for Medicare and Medicaid Services, Evaluation and Management Services Guide (Jan. 2020), www.cms.gov/outreach-and-education/medicare-learning-network-mln/mlnproducts/downloads/eval-mgmt-serv-guide-icn006764.pdf.

management tasks boosts income for medical providers. Overall, less than 5 percent of Medicare funds go to primary care.[49] Yet primary care physicians are well positioned to work with patients to avoid unwanted care at the end of life (which is often reimbursed on a fee-for-service basis) and to engage with patients in advance care planning so that patients receive the care that they want (or, at least, have a better chance of doing so). Primary care physicians also receive little or no compensation for helping patients with what they may need most – assessing home care needs, making home visits to manage medications, and addressing other social needs.[50]

Physicians face a variety of financial conflicts of interest in the practice of medicine, all of which can bias decision-making and lead to breach of duty to their patients. The American Medical Association's Code of Medical Ethics prohibits physicians from putting their own financial interests ahead of patient interests,[51] but there's evidence that financial considerations influence physicians' clinical decision-making.[52] For example, one study found that oncologists adjust chemotherapy-prescribing practices in response to changes in Medicare reimbursement. The study documented that when Medicare reduced reimbursement for outpatient chemotherapy drugs, oncologists switched to drugs for which they received higher reimbursement and gave chemotherapy to more patients with lung cancer. The study authors speculate that this change in practice patterns reflected a desire to avoid loss of income from chemotherapy.[53]

It is natural to want to maintain one's income rather than see it reduced. US physicians are paid more than physicians in other countries, mainly because fees for medical services are higher. In the United States, primary care physicians earn on average more than $27,000 more per year compared with UK physicians and over $61,000 more than those in Canada. Orthopedic surgeons in the United States earn over $118,000 more per year than those in the United Kingdom and at least $233,000 more per year than orthopedic surgeons in Canada.[54] These differences are striking, given that all are treating similar human bodies with similar medical conditions.

49 Rachel Reid et al., Primary Care Spending in the Fee-for-Service Medicare Population, 179 JAMA Intern. Med. 977–980 (2019).

50 Jennifer E. DeVoe, The Incompatibility of Patient-Centered Care with Fee-for-Service Payment, 180 JAMA Intern. Med. 1572–1573 (2020).

51 Am. Med. Assn. Code of Medical Ethics, Opinion 11.22 also states that "[p]hysicians should not provide wasteful and unnecessary treatment that may cause needless expense solely for the physician's financial benefit or for the benefit of a hospital or other health care organization with which the physician is affiliated. Where the economic interests of the hospital, health care organization, or other entity are in conflict with patient welfare, patient welfare takes priority."

52 Christopher Robertson et al., Effect of Financial Relationships on the Behaviors of Health Care Professionals: A Review of the Evidence, 40 J. L. Med. & Ethics 452–466 (2012).

53 Mireille Jacobsen et al., How Medicare's Payment Cuts for Cancer Chemotherapy Drugs Changed Patterns of Treatment, 29 Health Aff. 1394–1402 (2010).

54 Miriam J. Laugesen & Sherry A. Glied, Higher Fees Paid to U.S. Physicians Drive Higher Spending for Physician Services Compared to Other Countries, 30 Health Aff. 1647–1656 (2011).

The high cost of medical education in the United States (compared with the United Kingdom and Canada) presents another potential roadblock to systemic reform that might result in reducing physicians' income. The price of medical school in the United States has skyrocketed in the past several decades,[55] and even application fees and testing fees are high.[56] Medical students in the United States typically borrow $200,000 to fund medical school and receive meager pay during residency. While scholarships exist and some medical schools are offering tuition-free education, the profession is increasingly open mainly to wealthy students who can afford to spend many years studying while paying high tuition and earning little income.[57] Any reform that might result in lower pay for physicians after such an investment of time and money will encounter major pushback in the United States.

In the United States, professional medicine functions as a business like any other, and, at times, this seller/consumer mind-set can disrupt the physician-patient relationship.[58] From the administration and management perspective, even not-for-profit hospitals want to keep beds full to avoid running a deficit, laying off staff, or reducing compensation. Hospitals that have market power, the latest technology, and high occupancy rates are more profitable than other hospitals.[59] Despite recent declines in profit margins, many hospitals have been able to increase profits using various techniques – some of them questionable. One of the surest methods to increase reimbursements (and profits) is for hospitals to provide technologically intensive services that are reimbursed at higher rates (to the detriment of patients for whom the services delivered are more intensive than necessary). Once a hospital has invested in a new and expensive technology (positron emission tomogrophy (PET), for example), it has a strong incentive to utilize this technology at every opportunity to increase profit. Hospitals also can simply raise prices and change the mix of patients they serve, attempting to bring in more privately insured patients and fewer of the publicly insured.[60] Medicare and Medicaid, along with consolidated health insurers, reimburse for medical care at lower rates than private insurance, given that, as bulk purchasers of medical services, they have the bargaining power to negotiate. For this reason, some hospitals strive to avoid publicly insured patients as much as possible, and the American system to some extent allows this practice. The result is a two-tiered system of care that favors the well off and well insured and discriminates

55 S.Ryan Greysen et al., A History of Medical Student Debt: Observations and Implications for the Future of Medical Education, 86 Academic Med. 840–845 (2011).

56 Lorena Millo et al., The Cost of Applying to Medical School – A Barrier to Diversifying the Profession, 381 New Eng. J. Med. 1505–1508 (2019).

57 David A. Asch et al., The Cost, Price, and Debt of Medical Education, 383 New Eng. J. Med. 6–9 (2020).

58 John Noseworthy, The Future of Care – Preserving the Patient-Physician Relationship, 381 New Eng. J. Med. 2265–2269 (2019).

59 Michael Rosko et al., Predictors of Hospital Profitability: A Panel Study of the Early Years of the ACA, 44 J. Health Care Finance (Winter 2018).

60 Dan P. Ly & David M. Cutler, Factors of US Hospitals Associated with Improved Profit Margins: An Observational Study, 33 J. Gen. Intern. Med. 1020–1027 (2018).

against the under- and uninsured (who are also more often people of color or low-income individuals or both). In addition to trying to avoid certain patients, hospitals make concerted efforts to maximize billings and collection of payment.[61] Compared with the NHS and the Canadian system, the focus on profit in US health care is striking, and its effects on quality of care are quite worrisome.

The highly disjunctive health insurance and delivery system of the United States also requires much more coordination so that we end up, unsurprisingly, with multiple layers of regulation, administration, and supervision. This dysfunctional system requires a lot of administrators to keep it running, and US hospitals have plenty of them – twice as much of the average US hospital budget is devoted to administration compared with hospitals in Canada. In fact, in the United States, more than 25 percent of hospital spending goes to administration.[62] The more complex the health care system, the more costly and unwieldy it becomes. The comparatively simple structure of the US Medicare program – with its simpler benefit structure and payment processes – spends only 5 percent of premiums on administration.[63]

With the focus in the United States on profitability, it's no surprise that physicians who are paid a salary also receive bonuses for productivity volume, but this form of reimbursement can conflict with the professional duty to provide proportionate care to patients rather than all care possible.[64] Many other physicians in the United States are independent contractors whose pay is based in part on the volume of services delivered. High productivity also pays the salaries of all of those administrators and keeps the institution profitable. In the words of one hospital-based physician who wishes to remain anonymous, "the administrators are parasites, feeding off of our hard work." The productivity pressure is made worse by the fact that physicians are worn down by mounting regulatory and clerical responsibilities.[65] Physicians may try to treat patients with appropriate and proportional interventions, but the external pressure to 'produce' can be overwhelming.

It probably goes without saying that less of this profit manipulation is possible in the UK's single-payer system or in Canada's federal/provincial universal coverage system. In Canada, the process of paying hospitals is very different from that in the United States. With the federal funding that they receive, Canadian provinces and territories

61 Sidney M. Wolfe et al., It Is Time to Liberate Hospitals from Profit-Centered Care, 33 J. Gen. Intern. Med. 980–982 (2018).

62 David U. Himmelstein et al., A Comparison of Hospital Administrative Costs in Eight Nations: US Costs Exceed All Others by Far, 33 Health Aff. 1586–1594 (2014). The US also ranks tenth out of eleven countries studied for administrative efficiency. Eric C. Schneider et al., Mirror, Mirror 2017: International Comparison Reflects Flaws and Opportunities for Better US Health Care, www.commonwealthfund.org/publications/fund-reports/2017/jul/mirror-mirror-2017-international-comparison-reflects-flaws-and.

63 Robert P. Kocher, Reducing Administrative Waste in the US Health Care System, 325 JAMA 427–428 (2021).

64 Thomas L. Schwenk, What Does It Mean to Be a Physician? 323 JAMA 1037–1038 (2020).

65 John Noseworthy, The Future of Care – Preserving the Patient-Physician Relationship, 381 New Eng. J. Med. 2265–2269 (2019).

pay the global operating budgets of hospitals and provide separate grants for capital costs and improvements. Therefore, there is far less incentive to seek profit in all possible ways.[66] Structural elements also may explain why the United Kingdom ranks so high with respect to end-of-life care. Physicians in the United Kingdom whose practice is hospital based are employees of the NHS and, as salaried professionals, may as a matter of professional culture more readily comply with official practice guidance, even when it comes from a governmental authority. General practitioners are self-employed but reimbursed by the NHS for services provided. More broadly, the NHS considers all patients as equal residents of the United Kingdom who deserve equal care based on a theory of collective social responsibility for the health of all, with physicians as the intermediaries in this endeavor.[67] In spite of these high ideals, the system's function is far from perfect, but the patients in question truly appreciate reliable access to health care when they need it.

The NHS system operates as one overarching hospital system, one public insurance system, one employer (apart from private medicine) of clinicians, and one administrator of the entire system (with individual NHS trusts handling local oversight). In England and Wales, changes regarding entitlements are assessed via central organizations such as the National Institute for Health and Clinical Excellence (NICE) and are then rolled out across the entire system. Both the Canadian and UK systems, with universal and equal coverage for all, and with far less incentive to maximize profits, avoid a lot of the gamesmanship, waste, and resultant high costs seen in the US health care system. (Of course, there are budgetary struggles within both Canadian Medicare and the NHS, but these arise from a separate set of external forces – both systems operate on a set budget and must make hard choices about where to spend health care dollars compared with the US system where spending (at least for Medicare) is effectively unlimited.)

In both the United Kingdom and in Canada, constraints exist to rein in over-utilization of medical care as a means to increase physician compensation. The United Kingdom has moved away from fee-for-service reimbursement of physicians[68] and, within the NHS, effective guardrails are in place to prevent the provision of clinically ineffective care. NICE, which operates in England and Wales, makes recommendations regarding treatments that should not be available or should have only limited availability to certain patients – and these recommendations are based on scientific and clinical evidence.[69] NHS Commissioning Groups evaluate funding issues for treatments in general and also consider 'individual funding requests' from patients who claim that their medical situations justify

66 Wolfe et al., It Is Time to Liberate Hospitals from Profit-Centered Care.

67 The NHS Constitution (July 27, 2015), https://www.gov.uk/government/publications/the-nhs-constitution-for-england.

68 Miriam J. Laugesen & Sherry A. Glied, Higher Fees Paid to U.S. Physicians Drive Higher Spending for Physician Services Compared to Other Countries, 30 Health Aff. 1647–1656 (2011).

69 National Institute for Health and Care Excellence (NICE), https://www.nice.org.uk/.

exceptions to general non-funding decisions.[70] These and related mechanisms work to make evidence-based decisions about what treatments, tests, procedures, and medications are both cost effective and medically appropriate for patients. It is true that the NHS faces criticism for 'rationing', but much of this decision-making is based on evidence that certain types of medical care are either medically unnecessary or harmful to patients.[71] Whatever one may think of the United Kingdom's centralized system, it has the benefit of relieving physicians from pressure to provide all possible medical care for dying patients, including burdensome and ineffective interventions that will often increase patient suffering with little benefit or even a net effect of harm.

In Canada, fee-for-service reimbursement generally remains in place, but its effects are diluted by the inclusion of quality-based bonuses and bundled payments for certain types of medical care.[72] Moreover, Canadian law forbids higher fees for private physician services outside of Medicare, so there is little incentive for physicians to 'go private'.[73] The Canadian Institutes of Health Research provide evidence-based information designed to strengthen the health care system.[74] The private nonprofit Canadian Institute for Health Information (CIHI) monitors quality and provides data and analyses regarding many aspects of Canadian Medicare.[75] In the United States, the Centers for Medicare and Medicaid Services (CMS) perform oversight as well, but only of these publicly funded programs. There are interesting alternative theories as to how CMS could more effectively identify physicians who routinely provide unnecessary and unwanted medical care,[76] but, apart from identifiable fraud and abuse, these approaches are not (yet) part of the routine supervision of Medicare providers. The regulation of private health insurers is otherwise generally left to the fifty states (though the federal ACA now has some hand in this process); the resulting decentralization of oversight creates major systemic challenges for the improvement of quality of care for the dying.

LIABILITY FEARS

The United States is the land of the lawsuit, and physicians understandably worry about being sued. Conflict avoidance, together with a reluctance to communicate

70 Jonathan Herring, Medical Law and Ethics p. 65 (7th ed. Oxford 2018).

71 A broader discussion of the ethics of rationing is outside the scope of this book.

72 Laugesen & Glied, Higher Fees Paid to US Physicians Drive Higher Spending for Physician Services Compared to Other Countries.

73 Canada Health Act, https://laws-lois.justice.gc.ca/eng/acts/c-6/page-1.html.

74 Canadian Institutes of Health Research, https://cihr-irsc.gc.ca/e/37792.html.

75 Canadian Institute for Health Information, www.cihi.ca/en/about-cihi.

76 Isaac D. Buck, Overtreatment and Informed Consent: A Fraud-Based Solution to Unwanted and Unnecessary Care, 43 Fla. St. L. Rev. 901–950 (2016) (proposing a new enforcement strategy based on lack of informed consent to unnecessary care under the federal False Claims Act, which protects federal payers like Medicare and Medicaid from paying for substandard and unnecessary medical care).

bad news, has created a culture in which physicians may hesitate even to raise the question of withdrawal or withholding of therapeutic or life-sustaining medical care unless the patient or family initiates the conversation. In hospital care settings, whether in the emergency department or the ICU or elsewhere, family members have little opportunity to get to know and personally trust the health care team. If a patient is hospitalized more than briefly, multiple physicians will be responsible for the patient's care on different shifts and from different specialties, further hindering the family's ability to talk in any meaningful way about a plan of care. Frightened and grieving families may have even more doubts if a physician suggests de-escalating care or asks about a DNAR order. While the physician's hesitation is understandable, it is in fact well documented that poor communication by physicians about end-of-life issues actually increases the risk of litigation, while effective communication reduces conflict.[77] Although many physicians find end-of-life conversations with patients and families difficult, the risk of litigation in the absence of open and honest discussion about the 'end-game' plan should, in principle, incentivize physicians to talk about these issues.

Patients and families often misunderstand the ethics around withdrawal of life-sustaining medical technology. This misunderstanding is one primary source of confusion and conflict in end-of-life care, more so when physicians have difficulty explaining the ethics to families. In the United States, and in most other countries with developed medical systems, there is a clear distinction, both in ethics and in law, between killing a patient via euthanasia and allowing a patient to die. The former remains illegal in the United States and the United Kingdom,[78] but it is well established that allowing a patient to die by withholding or withdrawing life-prolonging technology, coupled with palliation of symptoms, is ethically and legally permissible. In the words of one poet, "Thou shalt not kill; but needst not strive / Officiously to keep alive."[79] In these cases, it is understood that patients die from the underlying medical condition that prevents the patient's body from sustaining itself without the help of medical technology.

Another aspect of end-of-life care also raises ethical questions among family members and sometimes health professionals. Despite the fact that there is consensus in medical practice and among relevant legal experts that 'aggressive symptom control' (e.g., large doses of opioids or sedatives to control pain, breathlessness, and other symptoms) is not a criminal act, even when it may hasten the patient's death,

77 Wendy Levinson et al., Physician-Patient Communication: The Relationship with Malpractice Claims among Primary Care Physicians and Surgeons, 277 JAMA 553–559 (1997).

78 Voluntary euthanasia (injection of a lethal substance at the request of the patient to end suffering) remains illegal in the United States and in the United Kingdom but is permitted in certain circumstances under Canadian law. The law in some US states permits 'medical aid in dying' as a distinct practice from voluntary euthanasia. Footnote 83 and accompanying text further explain these distinctions.

79 Arthur Hugh Clogh, The Latest Decalogue, The Poems of Arthur Hugh Clough (F. L. Mulhauser, ed. 2nd ed., Oxford University Press 1974).

physicians understandably worry about being sued and found liable for a patient's death. The data suggest that a significant number of physicians in the United States have been accused of, investigated for, and occasionally prosecuted for murder or euthanasia in circumstances in which they discontinued life-supportive measures, provided drugs for pain control, or sedated patients whose suffering they were unable to alleviate in other ways. With rare exceptions, these accusations are wildly inappropriate, but they do happen. In one survey looking back five years, more than half of respondents had been accused of attempted or actual euthanasia or murder by a patient, a patient's family member, or another clinician and 4 percent of those surveyed had been formally investigated for hastening a patient's death.[80] An older study of court opinions revealed that between 1990 and 1997, at least six physicians were criminally tried for allegedly killing patients.[81] Although the actual numbers of prosecutions are very low, the fact that they happen can have a chilling effect on palliative care at the end of life. These accusations are not benign – either for the accused physician or for the practice of palliative medicine. Physicians on the receiving end of these accusations experience anxiety, anger, depression, shock, sleeplessness, self-doubt, and embarrassment.[82] Reputational and professional damage is difficult to measure but surely afflicts some of those who are sued.

These accusations and investigations reflect a misunderstanding of the difference between palliative care and euthanasia. Euthanasia comes in two forms – voluntary (at the request of the patient) and involuntary (at the decision of the physician) – and is defined as the direct administration of a substance to a patient, usually via injection, with the intent of immediately ending the patient's life. Both voluntary and involuntary euthanasia are crimes in every US jurisdiction and throughout the United Kingdom, though Canadian law permits voluntary euthanasia under certain circumstances.[83] By contrast, palliative care is lawful medical care with the sole goal of symptom relief. Palliative care can help terminally ill (and other) patients with pain, breathlessness, nausea, depression, anxiety, and other common symptoms that

80 Nathan E. Goldstein et al., Prevalence of Formal Accusations of Murder and Euthanasia Against Physicians, 15 J. Palliative. Med. 334–339 (2012); Lewis Cohen et al., Accusations of Murder and Euthanasia in End-of-Life Care, 8 J. Palliative Med. 1096–1104 (2005) (describing examples of such accusations along with occasional prosecutions and providing data for rates of prosecution in end-of-life care cases).

81 Ann Alpers, Criminal Act or Palliative Care: Prosecutions Involving the Care of the Dying, 26 J. Law Med. Ethics 308–326 (1998).

82 Nathan E. Goldstein et al., Prevalence of Formal Accusations of Murder and Euthanasia Against Physicians, 15 J. Palliative. Med. 334–339 (2012).

83 In 2016, the Canadian parliament enacted a law that amended the criminal code to permit medical aid in dying, including voluntary euthanasia. That Act was further amended in 2021, https://parl.ca/DocumentViewer/en/43-2/bill/C-7/royal-assent. This practice is distinct from 'medical aid in dying' (popularly known as 'physician-assisted suicide'), permitted in some US states, in which physicians may, at the request of a terminally ill patient, prescribe a lethal dose of medication that the patient self-ingests orally (e.g., Oregon Death with Dignity Act, Oregon Revised Statutes Ch. 127). The distinction between voluntary euthanasia and medical aid in dying may strike some readers as inconsequential, but the US states that legalized 'death with dignity' permit only the latter practice.

accompany serious illness or are caused by medical treatments. While it is true that large doses of opiates, barbiturates, and other drugs may, in principle, hasten the death of an already dying patient, the important difference between palliative care and euthanasia is the intent of the physician. Physicians who provide palliative care to patients intend to relieve suffering at the end of life, not to cause their patients' deaths. This idea – that physicians can provide aggressive symptom management with the intent to alleviate suffering while at the same time acknowledging that it may hasten the inevitable death of the patient – is well recognized in philosophy and ethics as an example of the doctrine of double effect.[84] Unfortunately, laypeople may misperceive certain types of palliative care, particularly the administration of powerful drugs to relieve pain and breathlessness, as euthanasia and may respond with accusations. Only careful conversation with an explanation of these concepts can help allay doubt about the physician's intentions and the legality of the symptom relief that the dying patient receives.

Patients who suffer as they are dying have a right to effective palliative care, and physicians must be able to provide this care without worrying about accusations of euthanasia or homicide. US law protects this process. The Supreme Court's companion decisions in Vacco v. Quill[85] and Washington v. Glucksberg[86] considered whether state bans on physician aid in dying as part of broader bans on assisting in a suicide were inconsistent with the Due Process and Equal Protection clauses of the Fourteenth Amendment to the US Constitution. Although the Court concluded that these state laws did not offend the Constitution, some members of the Court separately offered a clear endorsement of palliative care, even when it may hasten death. Justice O'Connor, in her concurring opinion, emphatically stated: "There is no dispute that dying patients in Washington and New York can obtain palliative care, even when doing so would hasten their deaths."[87] The effect of this pronouncement, which was supported in varying ways by several other Justices, was to provide a foundation to challenge any state law that would interfere with the provision of medications to alleviate pain for dying patients. It was a very significant and welcome endorsement of palliative care practices.[88] Despite the apparent clarity in law and medical practice with respect to the ethics of aggressive symptom management at the end of life, physicians would be wise to discuss their intentions with the patient if

84 St. Thomas Aquinas (1225–1274) first suggested the doctrine of double effect in answer to the question of whether it is permissible to kill another person in self-defense. As he explained, "Nothing hinders one act from having two effects, only one of which is intended. . . . Accordingly, the act of self-defense may have two effects, one is the saving of one's life, the other is the slaying of the aggressor." Since the intention is to save one's own life, the slaying of the other is not unlawful. Thomas Aquinas, Summa Theologica, II–II, Qu. 64, Art.7 (Burns Oates & Washbourne, Ltd., 1922).

85 Vacco v. Quill, 521 U.S. 793 (1997).

86 Washington v. Glucksberg, 521 U.S. 702 (1997).

87 Vacco v. Quill (O'Connor, J. concurring).

88 Robert A. Burt, The Supreme Court Speaks: Not Assisted Suicide but a Constitutional Right to Palliative Care, 337 New Eng. J. Med. 1234–1236 (1997).

she is able, with the family, and with other members of the care team to avoid misunderstandings.

Another cause of overutilization of medical tests and interventions is the fear of making a medical error or failing to 'do everything', with the accompanying prospect of malpractice litigation.[89] Yet continuing inappropriate or burdensome care also poses risks of iatrogenic harm and of additional suffering, often with no discernable offsetting medical benefit. On the flipside, there is also potential liability for over-treating patients and causing harm by providing treatment that runs contrary to the patient's wishes. In the end-of-life context, physicians may face liability for failure to comply with advance directives or with the directions of surrogate decision-makers,[90] and for failure to provide adequate pain management and palliative care.[91] In this context, physicians may feel trapped between these competing concerns. The escape from this trap is, of course, to ask the patient or surrogate decision-maker for guidance, but this requires timely and frank conversation that one or more of the parties involved may wish to avoid.

Patients and families may demand all medical treatment and, unless it is scientifically, medically 'futile' – that is, it simply cannot accomplish its intended goal – physicians may be inclined to accede to these demands in order to avoid conflict and potential liability. As many treatments have at least a small chance of 'helping,' physicians often feel compelled to provide them on request, even if these treatments are not what they would recommend or would choose for themselves. Particularly in the case of patients who have lost the ability to make their own medical decisions, physicians may feel pressure to provide whatever care is demanded by the family member who prefers the most aggressive approach, even if that family member isn't the official health care agent or legal surrogate decision-maker, and so avoid exposure to a potential lawsuit (even one that would clearly be without merit).[92] There are laws designed to protect physicians from being forced to provide treatment that they believe to be medically inappropriate but, in practice, these laws provide little comfort or cover to physicians faced with the demands of family members that they 'do everything' to prolong life.[93]

While many misperceptions surround the American malpractice liability system that impact physician behavior,[94] fear of liability for malpractice or hastening death is very real. Physicians will often practice 'defensive medicine', including treatment that they believe to be medically inappropriate, to avoid litigation. As one physician

89 Alan Meisel et al., Seven Legal Barriers to End-of-Life Care: Myths, Realities, and Grains of Truth, 284 JAMA 2495–2501 (2000).

90 Alan Meisel et al., The Right to Die §§11.01[A]; 11.03[A] (3rd ed. Wolters Kluwer 2020).

91 Meisel et al., The Right to Die §11.03[C][2].

92 Marshall B. Kapp, Commentary: Anxieties as a Legal Impediment to the Doctor-Proxy Relationship, 27 J. Law, Med. & Ethics 69–73 (1999).

93 Thaddeus Mason Pope, Medical Futility Statutes: No Safe Harbor to Unilaterally Refuse Life-Sustaining Treatment, 75 Tennessee L. Rev. 1–81 (2007–2008).

94 Tom Baker, The Medical Malpractice Myth (University of Chicago Press, 2005).

wrote: "Most doctors are intensely risk-averse. We don't tolerate uncertainty. Not wanting anything bad to happen, we reflexively overtest and overtreat in order to protect our patients – and ourselves."[95] This sort of physician behavior – deliberately over testing and overtreating – runs counter to the exercise of sound medical judgment and adherence to the medical standard of care, even if it doesn't cause injury. Recent research has raised doubts about the validity of defensive medicine as a major explanation for physician behavior.[96] Even so, the evidence of defensive medicine is plentiful,[97] and there is also some evidence that physicians across multiple specialties who use more hospital resources are less likely to face malpractice litigation.[98]

It is important to remember that the filing of a lawsuit is not necessarily going to result in a finding of medical error or inappropriate practice and ultimate liability. Overall, physicians greatly overestimate their risk of general malpractice liability, and tort reform has done little to change physicians' perceptions. The risk of being sued for medical malpractice is not insignificant, but the chance of being found liable for medical negligence is much smaller than most physicians probably realize. In a study based on survey data, 34 percent of physicians have been sued over the course of their careers, but a finding of liability is comparatively rare. Survey data from the United States show that 7.4 percent of all physicians had a malpractice claim, but only 1.6 percent had a claim leading to a payment. In other words, 78 percent of all claims did not result in payments to claimants.[99] Interestingly, a small number of all physicians – just 1 percent – account for 32 percent of paid malpractice claims, with certain specialties at far higher risk of malpractice lawsuits.[100] While the risk of being sued is high across an entire career, malpractice risk also varies considerably by specialty, and most lawsuits do not result in the payment of compensation.[101] Nevertheless, the prospect of being sued and the worry that accompanies litigation weigh heavily on physicians, and it is probably small comfort that, statistically speaking, the chances of losing a lawsuit are very slim. Even in these rare cases, the physicians do not personally pay the damage award – their

95 Sean Palfrey, Daring to Practice Low-Cost Medicine in a High-Tech Era, New Eng. J. Med. e21(1–2) (10.1056/NEJMp1101392) (2011).

96 Michael J. Saks & Stephan Landsman, The Paradoxes of Defensive Medicine, 30 Health Matrix 25–84 (2020).

97 Michelle M. Mello et al., National Costs of the Medical Liability System, 29 Health Aff. 1569–1577 (2010).

98 Anupam B. Jena et al., Physician Spending and Subsequent Risk of Malpractice Claims: Observational Study, 351 Brit. Med. J. h5516 (2015) (studying resource utilization and malpractice claims in acute care hospitals in Florida).

99 José R. Guardado, Medical Liability Claim Frequency Among US Physicians. Chicago: American Med. Ass'n (2017) (using survey data from the AMA's 2016 Physician Practice Benchmark Survey).

100 David M. Studdert et al., Prevalence and Characteristics of Physicians Prone to Malpractice Claims, 374 New Eng. J. Med. 354–362 (2016).

101 Anupam B. Jena, et al., Malpractice Risk According to Physician Specialty, 365 New Eng. J. Med. 629–636 (2011).

malpractice insurer pays – but the disruptive effects of lawsuits on emotions and professional reputation are very real.

Compared with Canada and the United Kingdom, the US malpractice litigation and insurance system is unwieldy and dysfunctional, resulting in lengthy processes and delayed resolutions of claims.[102] In Canada, there appears to be less concern about potential liability in end-of-life care (or overall). The Canadian Medical Protective Association (CMPA) provides professional support, including assistance for physicians when they are sued. This support includes education to prevent and reduce medical errors and in response to a lawsuit, advice, support, and if required legal assistance. When a patient has been injured by medical negligence, the CMPA provides compensation on the physician's behalf.[103] The overall actual risk of malpractice liability in Canada appears to be even lower than in the United States, and malpractice lawsuits are comparatively even more rare. In 2019, there were just 775 total resolved legal actions, with only five judgments for patients, forty-seven judgments for physicians, and the remaining matters either dismissed or discontinued.[104] In the United Kingdom, the Medical Protection Society (MPS) provides similar guidance and support for physicians concerning prospective liability.[105] Both the CMPA and the MPS are paid membership services that support practicing physicians in both preventing medical errors and managing potential liability. By contrast, in the United States, physicians or organizations purchase medical liability insurance and retain private counsel or organizational counsel to manage claims. Without the backing of a medical protection organization such as those in Canada and the United Kingdom, US physicians no doubt feel even more vulnerable to litigation. Physicians in the United Kingdom and Canada may hesitate to initiate emotionally challenging conversations about prognosis and end-of-life decision-making, but this reluctance is far less likely to be driven by liability concerns.

PATIENTS ONLY DIE ONCE

Within this labyrinthine landscape of external pressures and stressors, physicians and patients must make complex and life-altering medical decisions. Even those physicians who acknowledge the limitations of their communication skills, the impact of professional culture, the effects of payment incentives, and the fear of malpractice liability exposure are somewhat captive to the system in which they practice. Asking physicians to seek out communication training, to self-police for the

102 William M. Sage et al., Another Medical Malpractice Crisis? Try Something Different, 324 JAMA 1395–1396 (2020).

103 Canadian Medical Protective Association, www.cmpa-acpm.ca/en/home.

104 Canadian Medical Protective Association Annual Report (2019), www.cmpa-acpm.ca/static-assets/pdf/about/annual-report/2019/annual-report-e.pdf. Of course, the population of Canada is far smaller than that of the United States.

105 Medical Protection Society, www.medicalprotection.org/uk.

unwanted influences of payment structures and liability fears, and to confront their own emotions and deficiencies with humility and a desire to do better is asking a lot. But unlike a patient who only dies once, physicians who regularly care for dying patients often know when a patient is on the doorstep of death. Every dying patient relies on her physician to do right by her. Many, but not all, physicians ably shoulder this high-stakes responsibility. While not every patient wants to hear the bald truth about what is coming, every patient needs a physician's expert guidance to avoid unnecessary suffering at the end of life.

7

Palliative and Hospice Care

Misunderstandings and Lost Opportunities

At last, tenderly,
From the walls of the powerful fortress'd house,
From the clasp of the knitted locks, from the keep of the well-closed doors,
Let me be wafted.

Let me glide noiselessly forth;
With the key of softness unlock the locks – with a whisper,
Set ope the doors O soul.

Tenderly – be not impatient,
(Strong is your hold O mortal flesh,
Strong is your hold O love).

—Walt Whitman, *The Last Invocation* (1819–1892)

Before the middle of the twentieth century, most people died rather abruptly of infection, or in the late stages of untreatable illnesses like cancer and heart disease, or in accidents or battle. It was comparatively rare to die slowly in old age. Now, in the age of modern medicine, protracted deaths from cancer, heart disease, dementia, and frailty are far more common, triggering an ever-increasing need for palliative and hospice care. The current health care system in the United States encourages high-intensity care and high utilization of technology at the end of life while reimbursing comparatively little for services such as coordination of care and advance care planning and counseling. The emphasis on technology and treatment makes sense when it is possible to cure or to prolong a life of acceptable (to the patient) quality. But, when death is approaching, the US system sometimes fails the patients who need it most.

The etymology of the word 'palliate' comes from Latin verb *palliare* meaning 'to cover with a cloak, to conceal'. It is related to the word 'pall' (also derived from Latin) which, by the fifteenth century, referred to a rich cloth or cloak that was sometimes draped over a coffin. Palliative care cloaks or alleviates symptoms of suffering. The word 'hospice' (from the Latin *hospes*) comes more recently from the French *hospice* meaning a hospital or almshouse and later referred to a 'house for the reception of travelers'.[1] In its modern usage, hospice (whether at home or in a dedicated facility) is the last stopping place – designed to provide rest and ease (and shelter) – before death. Every person who is ill and suffering symptoms from an illness or its treatments deserves to receive palliative care, and everyone who comes to the end of life deserves the rest and ease that hospice can provide. Why, then, do we systemically underutilize palliative care and hospice? The answer to this question, as with all matters concerning death and dying, is complicated. Lack of education about these services, access issues, communication reluctance, and an underlying unwillingness to acknowledge that death is approaching all play a role.

There is a lot of confusion about terminology, even within the medical profession. Physicians may misunderstand the role of palliative care and believe that it is only appropriate at the end of life,[2] and many patients themselves have never heard of the term. Palliative care is not only for dying patients. Patients with chronic illness and those with acute illness who recover fully may require palliative care during treatment, and there is evidence that palliative care is being utilized more frequently in these patient populations.[3] In the purely clinical sense, it refers to medical care intended to alleviate symptoms associated with illness and with side effects of treatment, whatever the patient's prognosis. Depending on the individual patient's circumstances, palliative care can address pain, shortness of breath, insomnia, depression, nausea, and lack of appetite, among other symptoms. In cases where recovery isn't possible, once a patient discontinues efforts aimed at cure or prolongation of life, palliative care continues for symptom management until death.[4]

Palliative care isn't solely about addressing physical symptoms of illness and side effects of treatment. The broader interdisciplinary concept of palliative care focuses on maximizing quality of life and enhancing patient participation in planning and decision-making. Key principles of palliative care include not just physical symptom management but also increased attention to the patient's emotional and spiritual needs, open and honest communication, and attempts to set medically appropriate goals.[5] Palliative care team consultations can include 'decision support' for patients and families, including assistance with advance directive completion, help with clarifying goals of care, and choosing among options with a better understanding of their risks and benefits. It is important to distinguish palliative care from end-of-life care, particularly hospice care. Although the two types of care naturally intersect for

1 Walter W. Skeat, An Etymological Dictionary of the English Language (Clarendon Press, 1882).

2 Mary K. Buss et al., Understanding Palliative Care and Hospice: A Review for Primary Care Providers, 92 Mayo Clinic Proc. 280–286 (2017).

3 Laura A. Schoenherr et al., Trends in Hospital-Based Specialty Palliative Care in the United States from 2013 to 2017, 2 JAMA Network Open 1–11 (2019).

4 Lise M. Stevens, Palliative Care, 296 JAMA 1428 (2006); Amy S. Kelley & Diane E. Meier, Palliative Care – A Shifting Paradigm, 363 New Eng. J. Med. 781–782 (2010).

5 Betty R. Ferrell et al., Integration of Palliative Care into Standard Oncology Care: American Society of Clinical Oncology Clinical Practice Guideline Update, 35 J. Clinical Oncology 96–112 (2017).

terminally ill patients, palliative care is a much broader concept that is distinct from and ideally should be implemented well before the end of life, though that time period before the active dying process begins is not always easy to predict.[6] Hospice by definition is a subset of and includes palliative care, but palliative care does not necessarily require that a patient enter a hospice program or even that the patient is terminally ill. When palliative care is limited to hospice patients and hospital inpatients, it misses the majority of patients, such as many cancer patients, who may have manageable but unmanaged physical symptoms and emotional needs from the earliest stages of their illness.[7]

Although access to palliative care services in the United States is improving, many hospitals still lack palliative care programs. About 72 percent of hospitals with fifty or more beds have an institutional palliative care program and 94 percent of hospitals with 300 or more beds have such a program. Unsurprisingly, nonprofit hospitals are more likely to have these programs than for-profits. In addition, palliative care programs are more prevalent in some regions of the country, such as the Northeast, than in others, leading to overall inadequate access to palliative care in certain regions of the country.[8] Finally, although the specialty of palliative care is growing, there is a documented shortage of palliative care specialists overall, which creates an additional hurdle to access for many patients.[9]

'Hospice' refers to care provided at the end of life and includes palliation of physical symptoms along with psychological, spiritual, and family support through an integrated team of professionals. Hospice care prioritizes the management of symptoms (such as pain, depression, or difficulty breathing) over the treatment of the disease itself. Hospice may include in-home care by trained nurses and physicians or inpatient care at a specialized facility or skilled nursing facility, as well as support for the patient's family through respite services and grief counseling.[10]

Unfortunately, hospice is not always the 'magic bullet' that wards off potentially inappropriate, high-intensity care at the end of life. Even when patients enroll in hospice, it is not uncommon for them to end up hospitalized, with some even receiving care in an ICU.[11] Transitions to hospital-based settings after hospice enrollment may lead to increased burdensome medical interventions and, for some patients, death in hospital rather than at home. Many patients and families

6 Bethel Ann Powers et al., Meaning and Practice of Palliative Care for Hospitalized Older Adults with Life Limiting Illnesses, *J. Aging Research* (2011).

7 Ravi B. Parikh et al., Early Specialty Palliative Care–Translating Data in Oncology into Practice, 369 N. Eng. J. Med. 2347–2351 (2013).

8 R. Sean Morrison & Diane E. Meier, Center to Advance Palliative Care, America's Care of Serious Illness: A State-by-State Report Card on Access to Palliative Care in Our Nation's Hospitals (2019), 2019-state-by-state-report-card-on-access-to-palliative-care-in-our-nations-hospitals (2).pdf.

9 Amy S. Kelley & R. Sean Morrison, Palliative Care for the Seriously Ill, 373 New Eng. J. Med. 747–755 (2015).

10 Brian Pace, Hospice Care, 295 JAMA 712 (2006).

11 Melissa D. Aldridge et al., The Impact of Reported Hospice Preferred Practices on Hospital Utilization at the End of Life, 54 Med. Care 657–663 (2016).

also misunderstand the meaning and intent of hospice, mistakenly believing that hospice kills patients or hastens death. This misunderstanding is unsurprising, given that many patients wait too long to access hospice care and so die shortly after beginning hospice. Spanish-speaking patients for whom English is a second language may also misunderstand what hospice entails because the term may have a different meaning in Spanish[12] (and in other languages).

RATES OF UTILIZATION

The palliative and hospice landscape in the United States is improving, with more hospitals implementing palliative care programs and more physicians specializing in palliative care. There is real cause for optimism that access to palliative care and hospice will continue to expand. Of course, expansion of services doesn't mean much if these services aren't used appropriately. For now, the United States still has rather low rates of palliative and hospice care utilization for seriously ill patients. For terminally ill patients, palliative and hospice care should function together seamlessly as a continuum of interventions appropriate to each stage of the illness rather than as two separate steps. Palliative care should commence as soon as it potentially can benefit the patient, even while curative or life-extending therapy is ongoing. Initiation of palliative care as soon as it is medically appropriate requires not only that physicians outside of the palliative care specialty receive training about its benefits but also that physicians learn to communicate better with patients about their choices for care during serious illness.

Although growing numbers of patients with serious and terminal illness now receive palliative care, hospice care for dying patients remains underutilized. The most common diagnosis for hospice patients is cancer, followed by heart disease and dementia. For cancer patients in particular, Medicare utilization data indicate that, in the last month prior to death, many patients received high levels of inpatient hospital care while only slightly more than half of cancer patients received any hospice care. There are also wide variations among different types of hospitals in rates of utilization that are not easily explained by expected variables such as for-profit status, size, or cancer center designation.[13] The most recent data from the National Hospice and Palliative Care Organization show that in 2017, just under half of Medicare patients (all causes of death) received one day or more of hospice care. Interestingly, substantially more women than men received hospice care (58.4 percent versus 41.6 percent) and more than 80 percent of patients were

[12] Hospice Foundation of America, Spanish Language Resources, https://hospicefoundation.org/Hospice-Care/How-to-Choose/Spanish-Language-Resources. In different Spanish-speaking cultures, the word *hospicio* is understood to mean a home where the poor are sent to die, a place for orphans, or a home for the destitute who have no one to care for them.

[13] Nancy E. Morden et al., End-of-Life Care for Medicare Beneficiaries with Cancer Is Highly Intensive Overall and Varies Widely, 31 Health Aff. 786–796 (2012) (54 percent of patients with cancer).

White, while only about 8 percent of patients were Black and about 6 percent Latinx. The length of hospice service is also revealing. While the Medicare hospice benefit is available to patients with a prognosis of six months or less of life expectancy, the average length of service in 2017 was only seventy-six days, and nearly 28 percent of hospice patients received care for only one to seven days, more than for any of the other length of service categories.[14] The numbers clearly demonstrate that patients in the United States are frequently referred to hospice only at the very end of life and so miss out on the multidimensional care and support that hospice can provide. Short-term hospice enrollment also may indicate a reluctance to cease curative care until the very end of life, which in turn suggests that the patient is either uninformed about the medical reality or refuses to acknowledge it.

The racial gap in utilization of palliative and hospice care provides another example of the profound disparities that Blacks and other people of color face within the US health care system, one that very much affects quality of care at the end of life. Multiple studies have demonstrated that racial and ethnic minority patients utilize hospice at a lower rate than White patients and that they receive more high-intensity treatment at the end of life.[15] Cancer patients who receive care at minority-servicing hospitals (hospitals with a high proportion of Black and Latinx patients) were also less likely to receive palliative care compared with hospitals serving a larger proportion of White patients, and Black and Latinx patients in particular received palliative care at lower rates.[16] Families of Black patients also report less satisfaction with the quality of care received by their family members at the end of life and express more concern about inadequate pain management and physician communication, particularly how well health care providers listen and share information.[17]

Education level and socioeconomic status also play a role in hospice utilization trends, and community outreach to underserved patient populations is essential to increasing utilization.[18] Because racial minority patients often distrust the medical system, they may interpret the offer of palliative or hospice care as being in some way substandard care and so may request high-intensity care because they distrust

[14] National Hospice and Palliative Care Organization, NHPCO Facts and Figures, 2018 Edition (Revised July 2, 2019) (a total of 48.2 percent of Medicare patients received one or more days of hospice care), https://39k5cm1a9u1968hg74aj3x51-wpengine.netdna-ssl.com/wp-content/uploads/2019/07/2018_NHPCO_Facts_Figures.pdf.

[15] Katherine A. Ornstein et al., Evaluation of Racial Disparities in Hospice Use and End-of-Life Treatment Intensity in the REGARDS Cohort, 3 JAMA Network Open DOI: 10.1001/jamanetworkopen.2020.14639 (2020); Jyotsana Parajuli et al., Barriers to Palliative and Hospice Care Utilization in Older Adults with Cancer: A Systematic Review, 11 J. Geriatric Oncol. 8–16 (2020).

[16] Alexander P. Cole et al., Association of Care at Minority-Serving versus Non-Minority-Serving Hospitals with Use of Palliative Care Among Racial/Ethnic Minorities with Metastatic Cancer in the United States, 2 JAMA Network Open DOI: 10/1001/jamanetworkopen.2018.7633 (2019).

[17] Kimberly S. Johnson, Racial and Ethnic Disparities in Palliative Care, 16 J. Palliative Med. 1329–1334 (2013).

[18] M. Courtney Hughes & Erin Vernon, Closing the Gap in Hospice Utilization for the Minority Medicare Population, 5 Geron. & Geriatric Med. 1–8 (2019).

physician recommendations. Given that racial minorities already experience, on average, poorer health and lower levels of insurance coverage prior to Medicare eligibility, this disparity is profoundly disturbing – it increases the likelihood that any given patient will receive potentially inappropriate high-intensity care at the end of life when they might prefer an emphasis on comfort and quality of life. In order to get there, however, Black and other racial minority patients must trust physician recommendations that they cease cure-oriented interventions in favor of comfort care. Interventions to increase Black and Latinx utilization of palliative care services do work, resulting in increased advance directive completion (including DNARs), increased attention to spiritual needs, and reduction of high-intensity care at the end of life.[19]

Interestingly, hospice utilization for residents in nursing homes, assisted living facilities, and other types of long-term care facilities rose significantly between 2014 and 2017, with more than 31 percent of residents receiving hospice care.[20] For patients with diagnoses other than cancer, hospice care in long-term care facilities resulted in lower utilization of various intensive interventions at the end of life. Utilization of hospice care in this setting has been shown to reduce ICU admissions, enteral feeding, and hospital transfers in the last three months of life. Nevertheless, the overall effect of increased hospice use has been to ramp up Medicare spending for the nursing home population, mainly because the growth of for-profit hospice providers has led to the enrollment in hospice of residents without cancer, whose life expectancy is more difficult to predict. This growth in for-profit hospice, coupled with a two-tiered per diem reimbursement rate for hospice care,[21] has actually resulted in a substantial average net increase in Medicare payments for residents who die in long-term care facilities, despite the decreased utilization of intensive interventions at the end of life.[22] The number of for-profit hospice companies is soaring,[23] leading to concerns about fraud in the hospice industry.[24] While hospice care can be of value for all terminally ill patients, the rapid increase of hospice enrollment in nursing homes (while hospice use for cancer patients lags) suggests that the profit motive is skewing the hospice industry toward patients whose hospice care needs are less labor intensive, which makes the per diem payment a better deal for hospice providers.

Despite this uptick in overall utilization of hospice care, concerns remain about high-burden care and poor symptom management in the final months of life. Recent

19 Sean O'Mahony et al., Preliminary Report of the Integration of a Palliative Care Team into an Intensive Care Unit, 24 Palliative Med. 154–165 (2010).

20 National Hospice and Palliative Care Organization, NHPCO Facts and Figures, 2018 Edition (Revised July 2, 2019).

21 Medicare's hospice payment system pays higher per diem rates on days 1–60 that then decrease for day 61 and beyond. More about palliative and hospice care reimbursement later in the chapter.

22 Pedro Gonzalo et al., Changes in Medicare Costs with the Growth of Hospice Care in Nursing Homes, 372 New Eng. J. Med. 1823–1831 (2015).

23 At last count, about 65 percent of hospice organizations are for-profit. National Hospice and Palliative Care Organization, NHPCO Facts and Figures.

24 Joshua E. Perry & Robert C. Stone, In the Business of Dying: Questioning the Commercialization of Hospice, 39 J. Law Med. & Ethics 224–234 (2011).

data suggest continuing problems with pain management, management of breathlessness (dyspnea), and attention to anxiety, depression, and the spiritual concerns of patients during the last month of life. Separately, there is some evidence that demand for both palliative care and hospice will exceed availability with the aging of the US population.[25]

THE BENEFITS OF PALLIATIVE AND HOSPICE CARE

The World Health Organization has called for access to palliative care as a human right.[26] The US Supreme Court also has recognized that current law effectively protects a patient's access to effective pain management and palliative care.[27] Other international health organizations concur, characterizing pain management as a fundamental human right. When pain and other symptoms are poorly managed, the patient suffers biophysical responses, reduced mobility and strength, disturbed sleep, and immune system consequences, among other things.[28] Providing access to quality palliative care as soon as it is medically appropriate is essential to improving patient outcomes and avoiding distressing symptoms. Earlier introduction of palliative care also leads to more timely referrals to hospice and reduced use of non-beneficial, high-burden care.[29] Although most studies of palliative and hospice care focus on cancer patients, there is good evidence that these interventions also provide benefits for patients with other illnesses.[30] In fact, a growing body of evidence demonstrates that a timely emphasis on palliative care, in conjunction with carefully considered therapeutic care, can improve patients' quality of life, reduce the burden on caregivers, and even prolong survival.

Timely integration of palliative care into standard cancer care provides enormous benefits for patients. One study of patients with metastatic lung cancer found that patients who received palliative care very early in the treatment process lived significantly longer and reported better mood and quality of life than the control group who received only standard therapy. Fewer patients in the early palliative care group received burdensome late-stage treatment compared with those in the standard therapy group, which suggested that the combination of palliative with standard

25 Dale Lupu et al., The Growing Demand for Hospice and Palliative Medicine Physicians: Will the Supply Keep Up? 55 J. Pain & Symptom Mgmt. 1216–1223 (2018).

26 World Health Organization, Strengthening of Palliative Care as a Component of Comprehensive Care Throughout the Life Course (2014) https://pubmed.ncbi.nlm.nih.gov/24779434/.

27 Washington v. Glucksberg, 521 U.S. 702 (1997). Justice O'Connor wrote: "There is no dispute that dying patients . . . can obtain palliative care, even when doing so would hasten their deaths."

28 Frank Brennan et al., Pain Management: A Fundamental Human Right, 105 Anesthesia & Analgesia 205–221 (2007).

29 Thomas J. Smith et al., American Society of Clinical Oncology Provisional Clinical Opinion: The Integration of Palliative Care into Standard Oncology Care, 30 J. Clinical Oncology 880–887 (2012).

30 Kieran L. Quinn, Association of Receipt of Palliative Care Interventions with Health Care Use, Quality of Life, and Symptom Burden among Adults with Chronic Noncancer Illness: A Systematic Review and Meta-analysis, 324 JAMA 1439–1450 (2020).

oncology care "may facilitate the optimal and appropriate administration of anticancer therapy, especially during the final months of life."[31] This is a powerful example of less-is-more in action. Making decisions that emphasize quality of life may not only preserve quality but also extend life.

Other studies add weight to the case for early introduction of palliative care. For example, another study of cancer patients found that palliative care that commenced more than ninety days before death resulted in lower rates of inpatient hospitalization, ICU admission, and emergency department utilization compared with late referrals to palliative care.[32] For ICU patients with various illnesses, early palliative care intervention led to more family meetings to discuss the patient's care and a shorter length of stay in the ICU or elsewhere in the hospital.[33] In yet another study of patients with various forms of advanced cancer, patients who received early palliative care as outpatients reported significantly improved quality of life and mood, providing yet more evidence that early palliative care intervention provides real benefits.[34] Based on these and other studies, the American Society of Clinical Oncology (ASCO) emphasizes the benefits of timely palliative care referrals and has issued a clinical opinion recommending that palliative care combined with standard cancer care should be considered early in the treatment of any patient with metastatic cancer.[35]

Here is the takeaway: contrary to popular belief, there is no evidence that enrollment in hospice shortens patient lives. In fact, the research makes a strong case that for certain types of cancers, early introduction of hospice care actually *prolongs* survival in addition to enhancing quality of life. More specifically, one study found that patients with lung cancer (279 versus 240 days) and pancreatic cancer (210 versus 189 days), as well as patients with congestive heart failure (402 versus 321 days), who received hospice care survived significantly longer than their non-hospice peers.[36] Similarly, in a study of Medicare beneficiaries with non–small cell lung cancer, hospice care did not shorten life and patients with a longer length of hospice care actually survived longer than those who received short-term hospice care only.[37] The

31 Jennifer S. Temel et al., Early Palliative Care for Patients with Metastatic Non-Small-Cell Lung Cancer, 363 New Eng. J. Med. 733–742 (2010).

32 Colin Scibetta et al., The Costs of Waiting: Implications of the Timing of Palliative Care Consultation among a Cohort of Decedents at a Comprehensive Cancer Center, 19 J. Palliative Med. 69–75 (2016).

33 Nicholas Braus et al., Prospective Study of a Proactive Palliative Care Routine Intervention in a Medical ICU, 42 Intensive Care Med. 54-62 (2016).

34 Marie Bakitas et al., Effects of Palliative Care Intervention on Clinical Outcomes in Patients with Advanced Cancer: The Project ENABLE II Randomized Controlled Trial, 302 JAMA 741–749 (2009).

35 Betty R. Ferrell et al., Integration of Palliative Care into Standard Oncology Care: American Society of Clinical Oncology Clinical Practice Guideline Update, 35 J. Clinical Oncology 96–112 (2016).

36 Stephen R. Connor et al., Comparing Hospice and Nonhospice Patient Survival among Patients Who Die within a Three-Year Window, 33 J. Pain Symptom Mgmt. 238–246 (2007).

37 Akiko M. Saito et al., Hospice Care and Survival among Elderly Patients with Lung Cancer, 14 J. Palliative Med. 929–939 (2011). Other studies reinforce these findings. Kelley E. Irwin et al., Early Palliative Care and Metastatic Non-Small Cell Lung Cancer: Potential Mechanisms of Prolonged Survival, 10 Chronic Resp. Disease 35–47 (2012).

value of hospice lies in reducing symptoms, managing pain, providing emotional support, and, crucially, helping patients and families understand that continuing curative care for an incurable illness exacts a cost on quality of life and stresses the body in ways that actually may shorten life.

The benefits of early palliative care and a timely transition to hospice extend beyond cancer patients. In a study of patients suffering from breathlessness (dyspnea) as a symptom of various advanced diseases, patients assigned to a support group that provided symptom palliation combined with physical therapy and breathlessness management techniques reported improved control over their symptoms and survived longer than the control group.[38] In another study of seriously ill patients with cancer, emphysema, or congestive heart failure, dyspnea improved among those patients who were randomly assigned to the usual care plus comprehensive care from a palliative care team. In addition, their spiritual well-being was reported as better than that in the standard care group, and more of the intervention group completed advance directives. There was no reported difference in pain, anxiety, depression, emergency department visits, hospitalization rates, or site of death.[39] Another similar study of outpatients reported greater patient satisfaction among the palliative care group, along with lower total average health care costs, higher advance directive completion, and longer hospice stays.[40] All of these measures indicate that early integration of palliative care (and timely transition to hospice) on an inpatient or outpatient basis improves patient satisfaction and mood, leads to lower rates of acute care utilization and hospitalization, and reduces costs. To the extent that this less intensive approach to care at the end of life comports with individual patients' goals and preferences, increased palliative care and hospice utilization for patients receiving therapeutic care have the potential to benefit patients and families, not to mention the health care system's bottom line.

STRUCTURAL BARRIERS TO ACCESS AND UTILIZATION OF PALLIATIVE CARE AND HOSPICE

The current system of 'silos' of specialists within the broader system of medical practice creates a false dichotomy between curative and palliative care,[41] but the patient and her body, her biological and emotional system, are one whole.

[38] Irene J. Higginson et al., An Integrated Palliative and Respiratory Care Service for Patients with Advanced Disease and Refractory Breathlessness: A Randomised Controlled Trial, 2 Lancet Respiratory Med. 979–987 (2014).

[39] Michael W. Rabow et al., The Comprehensive Care Team: A Controlled Trial of Outpatient Palliative Medicine Consultation, 164 Archives Internal Med. 83–91 (2004).

[40] Glenn Gade et al., Impact of an Inpatient Palliative Care Team: A Randomized Controlled Trial, 11 J. Palliative Med. 180–190 (2008).

[41] Kathy L. Cerminara & Barbara A. Noah, Removing Obstacles to a Peaceful Death, 25 Elder L.J. 197–233 (2018) (thank you to Professor Cerminara for her excellent analysis of the payment and structural barriers to increased utilization of hospice care, featured in this section).

Physicians who practice in the curative role tend to focus on clinical problem solving, may continue to advocate for therapy even when the prognosis is grim, and may often view death as a professional failure. Physicians who practice in the palliative care role focus on the patient as a whole person rather than as a disease diagnosis and will view unnecessary suffering at the end of life as a failure. When, however, care for a seriously ill patient *integrates* curative goals (for as long as they are clinically appropriate) with palliative goals, the patient, the family, and the physicians are all better off. There is no reason to keep these goals separate or to provide these two types of care only sequentially.[42] In a similar vein, the distinction between palliative and hospice care is artificial when the goal is to provide palliation of symptoms and psychological supportive care for patients and families throughout the entire course of terminal illness. As the empirical research demonstrates, it's important to avoid treating palliative care as something that one implements only when cure is unattainable. Instead, the goal should be to encourage physicians who are providing treatment to consult and include palliative care specialists in the care plan from the outset and to encourage dying patients to make a timely transition to hospice.

Unfortunately, there are several obstacles to the achievement of these goals. First, payment complexity can discourage physicians from introducing palliative and hospice care into the patient's care strategy. Medicare's hospice benefit provides payment on a two-tiered per-diem basis that is intended to capture all costs of not only medical professionals but also the rest of the interdisciplinary team.[43] The absurd complexity of coding, billing, and payment for health care services in the United States can present serious challenges, even to those many physicians who are aware of the benefits of palliative and hospice care and who seek to provide it in a timely fashion to their patients. Physicians find it vexing to deal with health insurers and so may subconsciously tailor treatment decisions to avoid or minimize frustration with reimbursement processes. In addition, traditional insurance payment and coverage rules, inspired by Medicare, erect barriers to appropriate utilization of palliative and hospice care.[44] There is also evidence that various insurance types and structures (fee-for-service, managed care, Medicare) are associated with different levels of palliative care and hospice utilization.[45] To be clear, none of these

[42] Laura P. Gelfman & Diane E. Meier, Making the Case for Palliative Care: An Opportunity for Health Care Reform, 8 J. Health & Biomedical L. 57–80 (2012); Marie Bakitas, et al., Oncologists' Perspectives on Concurrent Palliative Care in an NCI-designated Comprehensive Cancer Center, 11 Palliative Support Care 415–423 (2013).

[43] In 2016, Medicare adopted a new hospice payment system that pays higher per diem rates on days 1–60 that then decrease for day 61 and beyond (and allows additional retrospective payments in the last 7 days of life in some cases). Donald H. Taylor Jr. et al., Will Changes to Medicare Payment Rates Alter Hospice's Cost-Savings Ability? 21 J. Palliative Med. 645–651 (2018).

[44] Seung Jun Lee et al., Seeing the Forest for the Trees: Institutional Environment Impacts on Reimbursement Processes and Healthcare Operations, 47–48 J. Operations Mgmt. 71–79 (2016).

[45] Jyotsana Parajuli et al., Barriers to Palliative and Hospice Care Utilization in Older Adults with Cancer: A Systematic Review, 11 J. Geriatric Oncol. 8–16 (2020).

payment structures forbids the use of palliative care and hospice – they only in some cases create unnecessary complexity that in turn makes the referring physician's job (and that of the billing staff) more difficult.

Second, payment systems create an artificial dichotomy between palliative and hospice care and between therapeutic and hospice care.[46] Medicare currently pays for hospice services only for patients who are 'terminally ill', which regulations define as having a prognosis of six months or less of life expectancy,[47] though in many cases it's difficult to predict prognosis with any precision. It is particularly challenging to estimate life expectancy for patients with dementia and heart failure, yet many of these patients can benefit from hospice care if their goal is to focus on comfort care. For this reason, experts have suggested eliminating the six-month prognosis rule.[48] Most insurance, including Medicare, also requires patients to cease active therapy in order to become eligible for coverage of hospice,[49] a decision that patients may resist because it represents relinquishing hope for a cure or remission of disease. Once a terminally ill Medicare beneficiary enrolls in hospice, she usually must forgo coverage for certain other medical services: those "related to the treatment of the terminal condition for which hospice care was elected or a related condition."[50] This either/or approach to coverage is worrisome for multiple reasons. First, it's not always obvious where the line lies between treatment with curative intent and treatment with palliative intent. For some medical conditions, curative care can also provide relief from symptoms, so the requirement that patients renounce curative care may lead to more suffering. Additionally, a variety of cultural influences and beliefs, particularly among Latinx and Black patients, along with widespread mistrust in the medical system, may lead to an unwillingness ever to renounce curative care, even when these patients have accepted that death is near.

One bright spot on the horizon is the Medicare Choices Model, an option implemented in 2016 that allows Medicare beneficiaries to receive palliative care from a hospice provider while still receiving therapeutic care. Access to this program is limited geographically depending on hospice participation and is also limited to patients with advanced cancer, chronic obstructive pulmonary disease, congestive heart failure, and HIV/AIDS.[51] Many terminally ill Medicare beneficiaries will not qualify for or be able to access this program, due to either their diagnosis or geographical location.

On top of the either/or problem, there is the question of cost and profit. From an institutional perspective, profit always matters. A hospital considers questions of

46 Cerminara & Noah, Removing Obstacles to a Peaceful Death.

47 42 C.F.R. §418.3 (2019).

48 Muriel R. Gillick, How Medicare Shapes the Way We Die, 8 J. Health & Biomed. L. 27–55 (2012); Kathy L. Cerminara, Pandora's Dismay: Eliminating Coverage-Related Barriers to Hospice Care, 11 Fla. Coastal L. Rev. 107–154 (2010).

49 Cerminara, Pandora's Dismay.

50 42 C.F.R. § 418.24 (2019).

51 Medicare Choices Model, https://innovation.cms.gov/innovation-models/medicare-care-choices.

profitability just like any other business or nonprofit organization – even nonprofits have to consistently run with a surplus to survive long term. For this reason, incorporation of palliative care into a treatment plan concurrently with curative measures poses financial questions for a health care institution. The palliative care perspective, generally speaking, advocates a 'less is more' approach to late-stage, high-intensity treatments, focusing on actual quality of life instead of speculative potential to extend life. In a fee-for-service setting, this lower-intensity care generally will result in less billing, and thus less payment generated on a per-patient basis. While palliative care services also reduce institutional costs, it may be difficult to document these cost reductions when determining profitability line-by-line.[52] In other words, increased palliative care utilization initially may create concerns among facility administrators because it reduces higher-value reimbursements; they will fully recognize the benefits of palliative care only after also analyzing the concurrent cost reductions attributable to de-escalation of high-intensity care and a shift to symptom management.

Despite institutional profit concerns, the evidence is clear. Early integration of palliative care not only improves outcomes for patients (both the terminally ill and those diagnosed with life-threatening illness who have the potential to survive), it also saves substantially on hospital costs. Proactive symptom management prevents crises that would otherwise send patients to hospital emergency departments for care.[53] Across a range of empirical and nonempirical comparisons, there are consistent patterns of utilization of care in which palliative care frequently costs less than comparator approaches in both hospital and outpatient settings.[54] The challenge, then, is to break out of the piecemeal mode of care provision that our current billing and reimbursement practices encourage and move to a system that establishes a medically reasonable, patient-centered, and integrated plan of care for terminally ill patients.

ONCE AGAIN, HONEST COMMUNICATION REALLY MATTERS

There is a cartoon in which a physician informs his patient: "You've got six months, but with aggressive treatment we can help make that seem much longer."[55] Good palliative and hospice care really can ease suffering at the end of life, improve quality of life, and sometimes even prolong it. Terminally ill patients should receive palliative and hospice care in a timely manner when they can realistically benefit from it. For this to happen, the physician must understand the value of both

52 J. Brian Cassel et al., The Business Case for Palliative Care: Translating Research Into Program Development in the U.S., 50 J. Pain & Symptom Mgmt. 741–749 (2015).

53 Peter May et al., Economics of Palliative Care for Hospitalized Adults with Serious Illness: A Meta-Analysis, 178 JAMA Internal Med. 820–829 (2018).

54 Samantha Smith et al., Evidence on the Cost and Cost-Effectiveness of Palliative Care: A Literature Review, 29 Palliative Med. 130–150 (2014).

55 "Cornered" by Mike Baldwin (Andrews McMeel Syndication).

palliative care and hospice and must communicate this information to the patient. This in turn requires that the physician be honest with the patient about prognosis and, when it is time for hospice, about the possible wisdom of forgoing further efforts to cure in favor of a focus on comfort. The broader impediments to truthful and informative communication between physicians and patients about diagnosis, prognosis, and potential efficacy and adverse effects of treatment are therefore also partly responsible for underutilization of palliative care and, particularly, of hospice.

Physicians are taught in medical school to keep a professional distance between themselves and their patients, but it is possible to acknowledge the patient's struggle and connect with the patient as another human being while remaining professional. One palliative care physician writes of a patient who asked him to cross the "invisible line in medicine that marks the edges of professional behavior appropriate to our clinical roles." The patient, on discovering that the physician was also an opera singer, demanded that he sing for her. Eventually, unable to resist her entreaties, he sang (to their mutual delight). The encounter helped him understand the value of sharing something with a patient – a love of music – that resonated deeply with them both, and he continued to find ways to connect with patients over shared interests and experiences.[56] We all have experiences in life that tug at our hearts, that stir our emotions – these are the experiences that make life very precious, and hard to relinquish. Physicians are expected to possess and use a wide array of disease-oriented professional skills and at the same time demonstrate 'humanistic values' such as comprehension of the patient's emotions, compassion, and commitment to relieving suffering. This ideal is elusive in many physician-patient relationships. Many physicians exhibit an understandable emotional guardedness, but the ability to connect with patients also suffers from external pressures: time constraints, uncoordinated care, the need for data input into the patient's electronic medical record during the visit, and the overall culture of high-intensity, for-profit medicine. When physicians connect on a human basis with patients, listen to their stories, and directly address their worries with compassion, and when they acknowledge the limits of what medicine can achieve, patients are more likely to trust their physicians going forward.[57] In a relationship of trust and open communication – of shared humanity – patients may then seek out and follow (or at least be receptive to) advice based on professional experience that might help them avoid unwanted and burdensome care.

When physicians themselves misunderstand the concept of palliative care, it's not surprising that they're reluctant to discuss it with patients who are beginning or in the middle of an invasive and debilitating therapeutic regimen. To compound this problem, many oncologists, as well as other physicians, lack training in how to have difficult conversations, to break bad news, or to encourage advance care planning with

[56] Joshua Wales, Last Song – Sharing Humanity While Maintaining Boundaries, 381 New Eng. J. Med. 1894–1895 (2019).

[57] Ami Schattner, The Silent Dimension: Expressing Humanism in Each Medical Encounter, 169 Arch. Internal Med. 1095–1099 (2009).

seriously ill patients and their families. Recall from Chapter 6 that very few physicians report having had training in how to have these discussions and sometimes feel unsure of what to say during them. As the evidence in Chapter 3 suggests, many physicians avoid or postpone disclosing details about patients' prognoses and spontaneously initiating discussions about possibly ending therapeutic care and making the transition to hospice. They struggle with how and when to discuss palliative care and hospice with patients and families and so sometimes avoid the conversation altogether. One study found that only half of patients with stage IV lung cancer had any discussions with physicians about hospice in the final two months prior to death.[58] There are plenty of reasons for open and honest discussion of prognosis and the realistic potential that treatments will work to cure or slow the progression of disease. Here, the intercession of palliative care specialists is definitely beneficial. Talking with patients about end-of-life preferences while patients are still receiving therapeutic interventions can help patients wrap their minds around the possibility that they may not survive their illness and also can help patients make more informed choices about whether and how to proceed with treatment (while also focusing on palliation of symptoms). These discussions are absolutely essential when patients are not well informed about their prognosis and realistic options going forward.

The American Society of Clinical Oncology agrees that it's necessary for patients to understand their prognoses along with the benefits and risks of treatment. Its guideline on physician-patient communication recommends a number of items designed to improve communication with cancer patients.[59] As with the ASCO guideline, other guidelines for end-of-life conversation recommend that physicians begin by asking the patient what she would like to know about her illness and prognosis and then tell the truth in an understandable and clear way about the time that the patient may have left and what she can expect.[60] Another ASCO guideline focusing on the integration of palliative care with standard cancer care recommends a series of conversations with patients with terminal cancer diagnoses, with content to reflect the patient's evolving medical condition and her appetite for conversation beyond the minimum that she needs to know.[61] In addition to formal guidelines, there are resources identifying and illustrating effective communication techniques to help physicians initiate conversations and connect with patients about their concerns and emotions.[62] Chapter 11 explores these matters in more detail.

The 'how much care is enough' quandary plays a role here, of course. The idea of integrating palliative and hospice care with clinically appropriate therapeutic care

[58] Haiden A. Huskamp et al., Discussions with Physicians about Hospice among Patients with Metastatic Lung Cancer, 169 Archives Internal Med. 954–962 (2009).

[59] Timothy Gilligan et al., Patient-Clinician Communication: American Society of Clinical Oncology Consensus Guideline, 31 J. Clinical Oncology 3618–3632 (2017).

[60] Thomas J. Smith & Dan L. Longo, Talking with Patients about Dying, 367 New Eng. J. Med. 1651 (2012).

[61] Betty R. Ferrell et al., Integration of Palliative Care into Standard Oncology Care: American Society of Clinical Oncology Clinical Practice Guideline Update, 35 J. Clinical Oncology 96–112 (2016).

[62] Bernard Lo et al., Discussing Palliative Care With Patients, 130 Ann. Intern. Med. 744–749 (1999).

requires confronting the question of whether any particular test, treatment, or other intervention (apart from palliation of symptoms) is 'right' for a particular patient. Clinical guidelines can help answer this question, but the patient's wishes play a large role in whether or not physicians believe that continuing treatment makes sense in any given case. This dilemma arises more in some clinical scenarios than in others. For some treatable or potentially curable cancers, it may be obvious that initiating treatment is appropriate for most patients unless the patient has other serious conditions that would make treatment unwise, or the patient makes an informed decision to forgo treatment. For example, while trying immunotherapy for metastatic melanoma might make sense for the vast majority of patients, a patient with this condition who is already suffering from debilitating heart failure might decline treatment – or his physician might explain why immunotherapy with its risk of serious side effects is not an appropriate treatment option. Similarly, an older patient with a treatable condition might prefer to allow death to have its way without interruption. An octogenarian living in a skilled nursing facility, for example, might skip treatment for colon cancer rather than trying to endure the rigors of surgery or chemotherapy.

Patients whose cancer hasn't responded to standard chemotherapy regimens and who have a poor prognosis are unlikely to benefit from additional chemotherapy; to the contrary, additional treatment is unlikely to prolong life (and may well shorten it) and is very likely to reduce quality of life. ASCO recommends against chemotherapy for patients with poor 'performance status' (a measure of a patient's ability to take care of herself and manage other activities of daily living), but evidence suggests that these patients, including patients who have a recurrence of cancer, often receive chemotherapy.[63] Despite the ASCO recommendation, patients with terminal cancer often consent to chemotherapy at the end of life – which means, of course, that they either have been offered additional chemotherapy or have requested it. Remember from Chapter 3 that many patients *do* understand that they have an incurable disease but may nevertheless consent to burdensome treatments such as chemotherapy. Although lack of prognosis comprehension also is common, it is striking that of patients who actually understand that chemotherapy won't cure them and may not extend life, a large number of these patients still consent to chemotherapy. Patients who rank physician communication highly are *more likely* to have unrealistic expectations of treatment effectiveness.[64] It seems that the late-stage cancer patients in this study had more positive communication experiences when their physicians were optimistic and upbeat rather than truthful about the patients' poor prognoses and the lack of curative value of further chemotherapy.

63 Lowell E. Schnipper et al., American Society of Clinical Oncology Identifies Five Key Opportunities to Improve Care and Reduce Costs: The Top Five List for Oncology, 30 J. Clinical Oncology 1715–1724 (2012).

64 Jane C. Weeks et al., Patients' Expectations about Effects of Chemotherapy for Advanced Cancer, 367 New Eng. J. Med. 1616–1625 (2012).

In another study of terminally ill cancer patients with metastatic cancer that hadn't responded to chemotherapy, 56 percent of the patient group were receiving palliative chemotherapy (intended to reduce symptoms) at the time of study enrollment, which was a median of four months before death. The study demonstrated that the use of chemotherapy in this group was associated with higher rates of CPR, ventilator use, death in an ICU, and late referrals to hospice. All of these interventions can lead to a worse quality of life for dying patients and more distress and intense bereavement for their family members. Although a majority of patients in the study stated a preference for care that focused on relieving pain and discomfort, more than half of the patients said that they would agree to chemotherapy if it would extend their life by a week, including 60 percent of the patients who were not themselves receiving chemotherapy. There was no statistical difference in survival between those patients who received late-stage chemotherapy and those who did not.[65] Here, a dose of honesty from an oncologist or palliative care physician can help patients avoid suffering in their final days from unavailing chemotherapy.

In yet another study of patients with end-stage cancer (defined as having a life expectancy of six months or less), those who received chemotherapy did not fare as well as those who did not. For patients who were moderately disabled from the effects of their disease, chemotherapy did not improve their lives. Even worse, patients who were relatively well and able to perform most activities of daily living fared far worse with chemotherapy than those without it; there was no evidence that the treatment lengthened the lives of any of the patients.[66] In a study of patient willingness to participate in a Phase I clinical trial of an experimental drug, more than 90 percent of the patients said that they would try the drug, even if, in doing so, they had a 10 percent chance of dying, and only 12 percent of the studied patients found information about adverse effects of the drugs to be useful. Most of these patients indicated that they were aware of hospice but only a few had seriously considered it for themselves.[67] Other studies have similar findings – many cancer patients will accept proffered treatment that offers only a negligible chance of benefit and a high level of adverse effects. Researchers speculate that cancer patients think differently than healthy people: "Patients value even small benefits greatly, and believe that toxicity is less important than small gains or even the hope of small gains." The study authors were uncertain whether more and better information would change the calculus for these patients and observed that relevant information often isn't provided.[68] Americans are not alone in their willingness to continue toxic treatment at the end

65 Alexi A. Wright, et al., Associations between Palliative Chemotherapy and Adult Cancer Patients' End of Life Care and Place of Death: A Prospective Cohort Study, 348 Brit. Med. J. g1219 (2014).

66 Holly G. Prigerson et al., Chemotherapy Use, Performance Status, and Quality of Life at the End of Life, 1 JAMA Oncol. 778–784 (2015).

67 Manish Agrawal et al., Patients' Decision-Making Process Regarding Participation in Phase I Oncology Research, 27 J. Clinical Oncology 4479–4484 (2006).

68 Robin Matsuyama et al., Why Do Patients Choose Chemotherapy Near the End of Life? A Review of the Perspective of Those Facing Death from Cancer, 24 J. Clinical Oncology 3490–3496 (2008).

of life – studies document similar patterns in England, Canada, Norway, Italy, and Japan.[69]

Patients understandably hope for a miracle from experimental therapies, and the US Food and Drug Administration (FDA) has encouraged this hope with accelerated approval of certain cancer therapies. Unfortunately, only about one-fifth of cancer drugs approved on an accelerated basis later proved to statistically increase overall survival – and overall survival in cancer research only refers to extended survival until death from the cancer or any other cause.[70] Because accelerated approval relies on "surrogate endpoints" – such as shrinking or delaying the growth of tumors in some percentage of patients – rather than on overall length of survival, the true prospective benefit of these drugs at the time of approval is unknown. Physicians who prescribe and patients who receive treatment with accelerated approval oncology drugs therefore have even less information about harms versus benefits than with standard therapy drugs. The FDA permitted sale of ninety-three of these accelerated approval cancer drug indications between 1992 and 2017, though six were later withdrawn. Both England and Canada have reviewed cancer drugs approved by the FDA to decide whether to purchase and provide these drugs to their residents; both countries were far more skeptical about the prospective clinical benefit and cost-effectiveness of many of the drugs approved by the FDA, permitting the use of only a fraction of drugs approved in the United States.[71]

There are two problematic aspects of the US model. For individual patients, more chemotherapy at the end of life is rarely helpful and very frequently harmful, but the allure of something new nevertheless leads patients to try these drugs. At the system level, new chemotherapy drugs mean big money for pharmaceutical companies. While private insurers may be more discriminating about covering accelerated approval oncology drugs, Medicare pays for these drugs without any price negotiation. Pharmaceutical companies then enjoy significant profits from drugs that are not proven to help cancer patients.[72] Even when insurers will not pay, there is the option of crowdfunding for unproven therapies.[73] Some patients will try anything to survive, but sometimes an expert ought to step in and explain the downside risks.

69 Sarah Elizabeth Harrington & Thomas J. Smith, The Role of Chemotherapy at the End of Life: When Is Enough, Enough? 299 JAMA 2667–2678 (2008).

70 Bishal Gyawali et al., Assessment of the Clinical Benefit of Cancer Drugs Receiving Accelerated Approval, 179 JAMA Intern. Med. 906–913 (2019).

71 Avi Cherla et al., Assessment of Coverage in England of Cancer Drugs Qualifying for US Food and Drug Administration Accelerated Approval, *JAMA Intern. Med.* DOI: 10.1001/jamainternmed.2020.8441 (2020); Daniel E. Meyers et al., Evaluation of Clinical Benefit of Cancer Drugs Submitted for Reimbursement Recommendation Decisions in Canada, *JAMA Intern. Med.* DOI: 10.1001/jamainternmed.2020.8587 (2020).

72 Vinay Prasad & Myung S. Kim, Approval and Coverage of Cancer Drugs in England, Canada, and the US, *JAMA Intern. Med.* DOI: 10.1001/jamainternmed.2020.8587 (2021).

73 Jeremy Snyder & I. Glenn Cohen, Medical Crowdfunding for Unproven Medical Treatments: Should Gofundme Become a Gatekeeper? 49 Hastings Ctr. Rep. 32–38 (2019).

All of this evidence illustrates the need for oncologists to be more honest with patients about the implications of late-stage chemotherapy and other last-ditch treatments – that they will not cure their disease (or even prolong life, in many cases), and that the side effects will reduce the quality of life that remains. Most of all, physicians can help patients understand that stopping chemotherapy or other therapeutic treatment is not stopping medical care. Those who agree to endure toxic therapy at the very end of life, if they are Medicare beneficiaries, make themselves ineligible for hospice care. Of course, acknowledging that one has come to the end of life is hard, and a patient's visible struggle to face facts makes candor more difficult for physicians. Still, physicians, as repeat players, can help some patients have a gentler death – no chemotherapy, ICU, CPR, ventilator, and so on – if they explain, truthfully, what the patient is signing up for by consenting to more chemotherapy, including experimental therapies. If, after this explanation, the patient still wants to give it a go, then at least it is a more informed (though not fully informed) decision. The patient can never compare in advance what those last weeks of life would be like with more burdensome therapy versus without it, and the evidence strongly suggests that patients are better off saying no to additional chemotherapy and prioritizing comfort care.

A 'BETTER' DEATH IN BRITAIN?

The United Kingdom is both a pioneer and a model for palliative care and hospice services. The Economist Intelligence Unit's Quality of Death Index has twice ranked the United Kingdom first based on its comparative evaluation of the quality of palliative care around the world.[74] Palliative care is integrated into the NHS of each country (England, Scotland, Wales, and Northern Ireland), and there is a strong commitment to providing free palliative care education of clinicians, from medical students to mid-career practitioners. Through the NHS, palliative care consultation and medications are provided free of charge and hospices and specialized palliative care units are well subsidized.

That said, there are still inequalities and deficiencies in hospice care, even in the most highly ranked country on this measure. A recent evaluation of care provided in hospices and in long-term care facilities noted the problems with what is essentially a two-tier system of end-of-life care in England. Patients up to age 64, particularly those with cancer diagnoses, are most likely to receive care from specialized hospices. Patients with other conditions such as heart disease, stroke, and dementia are more likely to receive end-of-life care and to die in long-term care homes that provide suboptimal end-of-life care compared with hospices. While it is true that hospice is less well suited for patients who die after a slow decline with frailty or dementia, the fact remains that the much-touted end-of-life care in England is

74 Economist Intelligence Unit, 2015 Quality of Death Index, https://impact.economist.com/perspectives/sites/default/files/2015%20EIU%20Quality%20of%20Death%20Index%20Oct%2029%20FINAL.pdf.

unequally distributed, depending on the cause of death.[75] Overall, there is lively debate about whether hospitals or hospices provide more effective end-of-life care, but the fact remains that palliative and hospice care in the United Kingdom, when they are available, provide valuable comfort to patients and families.

In the past, efforts to provide consistently high-quality end-of-life care sometimes fell short – there have been difficult times for end-of-life care programs in the United Kingdom. In the late 1990s, the Liverpool Care Pathway (LCP) was adopted as a model of best practices in the care of dying patients. The LCP set out procedures that focused on the care of imminently dying patients, rather than the broader population of seriously ill patients that is the target of palliative care and, ultimately, hospice. The goal of the LCP was to ensure that all dying patients, and their relatives, received a high standard of care and emotional support in the last hours and days of life. Once a patient was placed on the care pathway, clinicians would then decide whether to continue artificial nutrition and hydration, whether sedation or cardiopulmonary resuscitation was appropriate, and how to manage pain and other symptoms. The LCP also required that the team reconsider the necessity of continuing with or initiating new tests and treatments, and it explicitly required physicians and others on the team to communicate with relatives and the patient, when possible, about these decisions, and to obtain consent from the patient if the patient retained decisional capacity. The overall goal of the care pathway was to support and guide health care professionals caring for dying patients, to keep these patients comfortable and maintain their dignity, while also offering information and emotional support to families.[76]

About a dozen years after its inception, the LCP was phased out, due primarily to a public backlash in response to instances of negligent or unauthorized implementation.[77] Among other problems, patients were mistakenly diagnosed as imminently dying who then went on to survive for some time, raising concerns about premature withdrawal of life-supportive measures.[78] The rise and demise of the LCP provides an informative case study that illustrates the challenges in implementing guidelines for care at the end of life that respect patient autonomy while providing humane and compassionate care. Despite the United Kingdom's advantages in the form of universal health care access and a centralized regulatory system for the practice of medicine, the LCP was thought necessary to promote best practices in end-of-life care. Unfortunately, the LCP suffered from implementation problems often enough to lead to its discontinuation, which suggests that the most significant causes of poor care at the end of life are less related to resources, access to care, or the

75 Diana Teggi, Care Homes as Hospices for the Prevalent Form of Dying: An Analysis of Long-Term Care Provision Towards the End of Life in England, 260 Social Science & Med. 113150 (2020).

76 Julia Neuberger et al., More Care, Less Pathway: A Review of the Liverpool Care Pathway (2013).

77 Krishna Chinthapalli, The Birth and Death of the Liverpool Care Pathway, 347 Brit. Med. J. 4669 (2013).

78 Neuberger et al., More Care, Less Pathway.

proliferation of consensus-based guidelines than to poor communication among physicians, patients, and families about end-of-life matters.

For England and Wales, the National Institute for Health Care and Excellence (NICE) has published guidelines requiring the development of individual care plans for all dying patients, which also extend more broadly to cover the care of patients with life-limiting conditions before they reach their final weeks and days.[79] The current system provides a structural opportunity for communication and planning engagement between physicians and patients and families, at least at the very end of life and, based on the ratings of palliative care in the United Kingdom, appears successful in reducing the frequency of high-burden/low-benefit care for dying patients. One might wonder what happens with a patient in the United Kingdom who requests ventilation, dialysis, or CPR to prolong life at the very end of life. This sort of request is less likely to be granted in the United Kingdom, particularly if the patient lacks capacity to make medical decisions. The physician typically serves as the decision-maker in these circumstances and is less likely to provide medical interventions that only prolong the dying process without any qualitative benefit to the patient. Is this a blow to patient autonomy? Perhaps, in some cases, but avoiding high-intensity, debilitating care at the very end of life is usually what dying patients prefer. Parts of Chapters 10 and 11 explore this scenario in more depth.

PALLIATIVE AND HOSPICE CARE ARE MEDICAL CARE

While palliative care and hospice services have expanded in the United States, there is no national strategy to ensure that these services are available to everyone, especially prior to Medicare eligibility. Private organizations continue to work toward this goal, but with an incoherent and fragmented insurance system and substantial numbers of uninsured individuals, not to mention geographical care deserts, many patients who could benefit from palliative care and hospice will not receive it. Yet, there is some cause for optimism. Recognition and accreditation of palliative care as a medical specialty began in 1996; by 2000, all medical schools included some coverage of palliative care in their curricula.[80] The benefits of palliative care and hospice are now well documented and recognized by many clinicians. There is a growing interest in the integration of the modifying influence of palliative care into the care and culture of the ICU,[81] and some evidence that ICU patients and their families are receiving more palliative support in the form of end-of-life discussion meetings, advance care planning, and the de-escalation of life-prolonging care.[82] There is also increasing

79 National Institute for Health Care and Excellence (NICE), End of Life Care for Adults: Service Delivery Guidance, NG 142 (Oct. 2019), www.nice.org.uk/guidance/ng142.

80 Economist Intelligence Unit, 2015 Quality of Death Index, Country Profiles US.

81 Center to Advance Palliative Care, Palliative Care Practices in the ICU Toolkit (2020), https://www.capc.org/toolkits/integrating-palliative-care-practices-in-the-icu/.

82 Christopher E. Cox et al., A Measured Dose of Optimism for the Evolution of ICU-Based Palliative Care, 322 JAMA 1655–1657 (2019).

integration of palliative care with standard oncology care, especially at National Cancer Institute's designated cancer centers.[83] That said, the trends in hospice utilization described in this chapter are less encouraging.

Successful utilization of palliative care as soon as it is medically appropriate requires that physicians outside of the palliative care specialty receive training about its benefits and – the harder bit – that physicians learn to communicate better with patients about their choices for care for life-threatening illness. Timely transition to hospice care – so that patients can reap its full benefits – requires the same. To facilitate these goals, policymakers should amend relevant law to harmonize the payment systems for palliative and hospice care and to avoid perpetuating the artificial dichotomy between therapeutic and palliative care (and, at the end of life, hospice care). Even then, the obstacles to integration are substantial and entrenched. Many physicians themselves misunderstand the goals and benefits of palliative care, even confuse or conflate it with hospice care, so it's not surprising that these physicians hesitate to discuss palliative care with patients who are beginning an invasive and debilitating therapeutic regimen.

When a seriously ill patient reaches the point where further curative care is not an option (or would make no medical sense to pursue), words matter. Rather than speaking of 'stopping or withdrawing care', the emphasis can shift to providing care that focuses on the comfort and dignity of the patient – the patient should always receive 'care' until the very moment that he dies. Physicians can explain that the time has come to stop therapeutic interventions or to consider ceasing life-prolonging measures, while reassuring the patient and family that care, in the form of palliative care and emotional support, will continue until the end. As one palliative care physician explained, it's a mistake to tell patients "There's nothing more we can do." There is always more – not with more burdensome and unavailing interventions but with de-escalation – that 'more' comes in the form of palliative and hospice care. One physician asks all of her patients this question: "If I had a magic wand, what is it you would wish for today?" And they tell her their wishes – not for a magical cure, but to see family, or sit in their garden or be at home.[84] Palliative care often (though not always) can alleviate suffering at the end of life, and it can also provide an impetus and opportunity for dying patients to express their final wishes, to speak with loved ones of previously unspoken things, and to say good-bye. Patients and families can still experience pleasures at the end of life (though only the French would think to open a wine bar in a hospital palliative care center).[85] There is the possibility of joy, even in the

83 David Hui et al., State of Integration of Palliative Care at National Cancer Institute-Designated and Nondesignated Cancer Centers, 6 JAMA Oncol. 1292–1295 (2020).

84 Dawn M. Gross, The Error in "There's Nothing More We Can Do," NY Times, July 15, 2015, https://opinionator.blogs.nytimes.com/2015/07/15/the-error-in-theres-nothing-more-we-can-do/.

85 French Hospital to Open Wine-Bar for Terminally Ill Patients, The Guardian (Aug. 1, 2014), www.theguardian.com/world/2014/aug/01/french-hospital-open-wine-bar-terminally-ill-patients-clermont-ferrand.

midst of suffering.[86] The essential requirement for this kind of 'good death' is information – in the form of gentle truths about prognosis and recommendations about scaling back burdensome interventions in favor of a focus on comfort and dignity, and maybe even a checkmark or two on a bucket list.

[86] Benzi M. Kluger et al., Joy, Suffering, and the Goals of Medicine, *JAMA Neurology*, DOI: 10.1001/jamaneurol.2020.4604 (Dec. 2020).

8

Rational Apathy and the Role of Uncertainty

[E]verything can be taken from a man but one thing: the last of the human freedoms – to choose one's attitude in any given set of circumstances, to choose one's own way.

—Viktor E. Frankl[1]

The vast majority of people diagnosed with a life-threatening illness want to survive that illness. (A few will take the position that they've had a good long life and that treatment to prolong that life further isn't necessary or desirable.) People in the striving for survival group – that vast majority – naturally want to make 'good' (i.e., rational) decisions about treatment to maximize their chances. Some patients will, early on in the process, consider the balance between surviving (increasing quantity of remaining life) and thriving (maintaining quality of life). The problem is that, as several of the preceding chapters have demonstrated, physicians and patients struggle mightily to have timely and honest conversations about the prognosis, the harms and potential benefits of treatment options, and the burdens of life-prolonging technology when the patient reaches the terminal stage of an illness. As laid out in detail in Chapter 3, decisions about whether and when to cease curative care and whether to initiate or to withdraw life-prolonging technology are often medically complex and are further hampered by limited or absent communication. Up to this point, this book has focused primarily on physician behavior and its underlying causes. This chapter considers the higher-order behavioral and cognitive phenomena that affect patients and that result in avoidance of end-of-life planning, communication, and decision-making (though much of what follows applies to physicians as well).

Even if we agree that rational end-of-life decisions reflect patients' preferences after a series of informative discussions with physicians, and even if physicians and patients are willing to have these conversations together, barriers to good decision-making remain. The impact of cognitive biases and related phenomena (not to

[1] Viktor E. Frankl, Man's Search for Meaning: An Introduction to Logotherapy (Ilse Lasch, transl.) p. 65 (Beacon, 1959).

mention existential terror) affect patients, family members, *and* physicians and make it quite difficult for patients in these circumstances to make robust decisions. These phenomena affect patients' ability to process and comprehend the strategic uncertainty and resultant risks and benefits of whatever therapy or life-prolonging technology physicians may offer. All of these factors combine to render the classic goal of 'informed consent' unachievable in all but the rarest of circumstances. Even so, these are all *alterable* barriers to rational decision-making – barriers that, in theory, can be overcome by some patients who behave in a highly rational or 'activist' fashion. These activist patients will attempt to set aside their emotions and, with scientific precision and logical reasoning, evaluate all of the available information on prognosis and potential risks and benefits of proposed treatment. With due deference to the limitations of statistical predictions, they will then calculate and decide based on this information and their personal goals (e.g., maximal life prolongation, maximal avoidance of suffering, or something in between). These patients can, with sufficient information, time, and persistence, make good medical decisions.

But only up to a point. Even these very determined, activist patients run into a wall in their effort to make the 'best' choice. Here, in addition to all of the obstacles to good communication described in prior chapters, deeper-layer cognitive challenges will continue to undermine physicians' willingness to communicate and patients' ability to comprehend and to decide what needs deciding. The added complexities of bounded rationality, clinical uncertainty, and overall Knightian uncertainty place insurmountable, unalterable roadblocks in front of rational decision-making. Knightian uncertainty refers to the idea that there are types of future contingent events and probabilities that are not capable of being quantified in advance. Therefore, they can't be reduced to quantifiable risks that could inform rational decision-making.[2] On top of the known unknowns about prognosis and prospective therapeutic benefit, unknown unknown variables are always present – and leave highly informed patients with the lurking realization that they don't even know (and cannot know) all of the things that they don't know about their individual medical situations.

KNIGHTIAN UNCERTAINTY, CLINICAL UNCERTAINTY, AND COGNITIVE BIASES

Patients and their physicians want to make the 'best' choices about medical care for life-threatening illness but obviously lack the omniscience needed to calculate all future possibilities without error. All human decision-making, including medical decision-making, occurs under conditions of irreducible uncertainty and resultant ambiguity. All of the well-recognized barriers to 'good' decision-making operate

[2] Frank H. Knight, *Risk, Uncertainty, and Profit* (1921).

within a broader realm of uncertainty and fallibility that is built into most medical decisions. And uncertainty creates ambivalence.

Medical decision-making is inherently subject to fallibility, which arises out of three distinct causes. As philosophers Samuel Gorovitz and Alasdair MacIntyre explain (in the context of discussing causes of medical error), the first cause is "ignorance" based on a limited understanding of the medical issue. In this situation, the physician has full access to relevant medical information but cannot subjectively understand it fully. The second cause of fallibility is "ineptitude" based on the physician's failure to find and follow available medical information – all of the information is available to arrive at a 'correct' diagnosis and treatment plan, but the physician, while capable of understanding the relevant information, fails to fully collect and process the information.[3] Both of these forms of fallibility can, in theory, be overcome with more skilled, careful, unbiased, and rational effort by the physician.

There is yet another layer of complexity that makes medical decision-making even more challenging. This is where Knightian uncertainty comes in. The Knightian 'unknown unknowns' inherent in medical decision-making fundamentally complicate the already very challenging conversations between physician and patient. Within this human realm of irreducible uncertainty, even highly rational decision-makers can never confidently calculate the highest-utility (i.e., best overall) treatment option.

Gorovitz & MacIntyre's third cause of fallibility is "necessary fallibility" in which that which must be understood scientifically to make the 'best' decision simply cannot be known in advance and therefore predicted. As they explain, "the best possible judgment may always turn out to be erroneous – and erroneous not merely because our science has not progressed far enough, nor because the scientist has been either willful or negligent, but because of the necessary fallibility of our knowledge of particulars."[4] In this respect, no physician – no matter how skilled, careful, conscientious, and rational – can provide a solution or best recommendation because what is 'best' is (at least, *ex ante*) unknowable due to the unpredictability of the many objectively unknown and unknowable variables involved in any single patient's prognosis or response to a particular treatment – in spite of the statistical averages or likelihoods that generally apply to patients with the same condition. This type of necessary fallibility applies to every patient and every prognosis because every patient's prognosis and future response to treatment remain subject to Knightian uncertainty.

All of these ideas are quite abstract, so let's consider an example of how Knightian uncertainty plays out in medical decision-making. Imagine that a patient is offered a late-stage cancer treatment. Let's assume that this treatment has a hypothetical

[3] Samuel Gorovitz & Alasdair MacIntyre, Toward a Theory of Medical Fallibility, Hastings Ctr. Rep. 13–23 (Dec. 1975). "Ignorance" and "ineptitude" are the authors' original words.

[4] Ibid.

60 percent chance of 'success' (defined as some prolongation of life) and a 40 percent chance of 'no success' (defined as failing to prolong life while subjecting the patient to severe side effects) based on past application and experience with similarly situated patients (but, of course, not this particular patient). It is known that this treatment kills cancer cells – this is an example of a knowable fact that is also actually known – a 'known known'. It is also known that this treatment will do damage to other parts of the body, including healthy organs, but it is not known how bad the damage and resulting adverse effects might be in a particular patient – this is an example of a 'known unknown' contingent outcome. Based on the known knowns and known unknowns, the patient must decide whether to consent to the treatment.

Here's the problem: the 60 percent chance of success only correlates with the known knowns and the known unknowns – and only as a statistical average for a homogenized group of *past* cancer patients (all of whom are unique and uniquely different, though grouped in the same category). These statistical averages are still useful in guiding decision-making, however; they can improve understanding of which treatments might be potentially inappropriate (not providing a benefit) in a given patient's case. As Lawrence Schneiderman has observed,

> Most of us probably would agree that if a treatment has not worked in the last 100 cases, almost certainly it is not going to work if it is tried again. . . . The experience of 100 cases is attainable in many areas of medicine. This proposal [to define futile medical care] is . . . one that seeks reasonable consensus where absolute certainty is impossible and therapeutic benefit is the goal.[5]

In our hypothetical case, we do know that the treatment 'works' in 60 percent of patients, so it would not be inappropriate to offer it (though the broader question of whether active therapy with potential side effects makes sense at a late stage in the patient's illness remains). But acknowledging these points is only the first step to accepting the full extent and impact of Knightian uncertainty (here, as a form of clinical uncertainty) in making medical decisions. A patient's decision based on the statistical 60 percent chance of benefit has to entirely ignore the additional category of 'unknown unknowns' – those variables impacting patient outcomes that are objectively unknowable and unquantifiable at the point of decision-making. To make as rational a decision as possible, physicians and patients should acknowledge that unknown unknowns may always exist and may substantially impact the prognosis calculus for a particular patient, and that they can't know the extent of the unknown unknowns or how they might apply to the patient's particular case. The 60–40 success ratio for past patients might have only a 10 percent relevance to this particular patient due to unknown unknowns unique to the patient (even though based on current knowledge she belongs in this group of similarly situated patients).

[5] Lawrence J. Schneiderman, Defining Medical Futility and Improving Quality of Care, 8 Bioethical Inquiry 123–131 (2011).

In other words, this patient, because of unknown and unknowable variables unique to her, could be 90 percent likely *not* to fall within the 60–40 benefit-harm calculus that derives from what is known about the broader population of past patients. Moreover, this aspect of clinical uncertainty might operate to her benefit or to her detriment. In spite of this non-quantifiable Knightian uncertainty, patients have to make decisions based on statistical averages and will develop expectations of outcomes, even though these expectations may be largely irrational.[6] Further complicating matters, to the extent that patients understand the idea of unknown unknowns that might be at work in their particular case, they may very well choose to embrace the upside possibility that their particular unknown unknowns make them far more likely than other patients like them to fare unusually well with the treatment.

The term "clinical uncertainty" refers to the idea that despite growing bodies of empirical evidence about particular medical conditions, their prognoses, and the potential efficacy of treatments, there is no way for a clinician to be entirely sure that the relevant evidence applies to or will predict the outcomes for any individual patient.[7] Patients facing terminal illness want their treating physicians to advise them as to the 'best' treatment for their illness or condition. The problem is that clinical uncertainty often makes it difficult to determine the medically 'best' approach for any particular patient at any particular time. In the specific context of medical decision-making, the concept of clinical uncertainty is one form of necessary fallibility. Clinical uncertainty limits the ability of physicians and patients to make rational calculations about the comparative desirability of alternative treatment options because predictive data on therapeutic response, adverse effects, and prognosis is always imperfect.[8] As two commentators have explained:

> The existence of an information mountain provides a myth of certainty for the patient, the public and perhaps for health care policy-makers. Certainty is an illusion. In most professional spheres the expert is more critical of the available evidence, than is the lay person. Hopefully, clinicians are taught to be more critical than patients but they are faced with a dilemma. They appear to be very well informed yet are acutely aware of the fallibility of the information that is expected to guide their practice. How do clinicians respond to this dilemma? Their day consists of a succession of points at which decisions have to be made on the basis of

6 Niklas Luhmann, Familiarity, Confidence, Trust: Problems and Alternatives, in Trust: Making and Breaking Cooperative Relations p. 97 (Diego Gambetta ed., Basil Blackwell, 1988). ("You cannot live without forming expectations with respect to contingent events and you have to neglect . . . the possibility of disappointment . . . because it is a very rare possibility, but also because you do not know what else to do. The alternative is to live in a state of permanent uncertainty.")

7 Stefan Timmermans & Alison Angell, Evidence-Based Medicine, Clinical Uncertainty, and Learning to Doctor, 42 J. Health & Soc. Behav. 342–359 (2001).

8 Jerome Groopman, How Doctors Think (Houghton Mifflin 2007); George A. Diamond, Future Imperfect: The Limitations of Clinical Predictive Models and the Limits of Clinical Prediction, 14 J. Am. C. Cardiologists 12A-22A (1989).

> incomplete and inadequate information and in a context in which risk, never mind error, is outlawed.[9]

On top of the impact of clinical uncertainty on decision-making, physicians and patients must keep in mind that what is 'best' depends at least to some extent on the patient's (possibly shifting) goals, values, and preferences – in the face of a suddenly shortened life-span. While one patient may be seeking maximal life extension no matter what the costs in terms of adverse effects, increased suffering, isolation from loved ones, or medical dollars, another patient may prefer to focus on maintaining physical and intellectual functionality even at the cost of a potentially shorter life-span. For this latter group of patients, the prospect of loss of meaningful ability to interact with the world might drive decisions to focus more on palliation of symptoms than on (hypothetical) life prolongation. Clinical uncertainty will always add to the cognitive and emotional load of both physician and patient in these situations.

So, clinical uncertainty (as a form of necessary fallibility) means that it's impossible to determine with any rational certainty a 'best' or 'optimal' treatment before the fact. Even after the patient has made a decision and it has been implemented, another kind of uncertainty remains – who is to say that a different decision might not have been better? Patients (and perhaps physicians) mistakenly view these sorts of decisions like forks in the road at which one can take a 'right turn' or a 'wrong turn'. However, complex medical decision-making is more like a river into which many tributaries flow but all of which end up in a single sea. Choosing the best treatment is very different from a financial investment (although there is plenty of uncertainty inherent in that activity as well). With stock investing, for example, we can look at past data and make an educated bet. If the initial money invested creates a return, we can assess retrospectively whether the chosen stock gave the best return on investment by comparing how the same money would have performed if invested in a different stock. With humans and medical treatment, by contrast, we can never look back and assess with any certainty whether a different choice would have been 'better' – because humans can only make the investment once and with no ability to compare alternative outcomes. There is no 'do-over'. Their decisions are perhaps informed to the extent that physicians provide information about likelihood of success, but the concept of 'informed' is greatly limited. All medical decision-making remains Knightian uncertain, even with the benefit of hindsight, when the outcome is not cure but death. Physicians, when they fail to acknowledge this uncertainty to themselves or disclose it to patients, become complicit in patients' demanding and receiving potentially ineffective and harmful care.

On top of uncertainty in all of its forms, bounded rationality and cognitive biases also play a role in decision-making. The ability to investigate, evaluate courses of action, and make decisions about complex medical care is limited by heuristic flaws

9 Andrew F. West & R. R. West, Clinical Decision-Making: Coping with Uncertainty, 78 Postgraduate Med. J. 319–321 (2002).

in collecting and processing information. Necessary fallibility also encompasses the idea of bounded rationality: the human ability to make truly informed decisions about end-of-life care is unavoidably limited by the cognitive ability to gather and process complex information perfectly and rationally.[10] In addition, cognitive biases affect both physicians and patients and further interfere with boundedly rational informed decision-making. In principle, these cognitive shortcuts are avoidable, but, in the reality of most human decision-making, they remain in place. At some point, patients have to make a decision to begin (or forgo) treatment, and they naturally crave reassurance that they are doing the 'best' thing. For this reason, patients engage in other decisional strategies to shore up their confidence, all of which are common human responses in critical illness situations.

For example, optimism bias often leads patients to overemphasize the positive aspects of a treatment decision, downplay the negatives, and overestimate the probability of positive outcomes.[11] Patients tend to think they will be among the fortunate 1 percent who greatly outlive the statistical prognosis for their disease or who respond unusually well to an otherwise non-curative therapy. Returning to the earlier example, patients will tend to place themselves, *ex ante*, among the 60 percent chance-of-success cohort, rather than the 40 percent no-success group. As explained in Chapter 3, patients frequently discount the likely non-curative value of certain invasive treatments, either because this information wasn't mentioned or, as is relevant here, because they do not (or do not want to) understand that it is impossible to predict with any accuracy the effects of the treatment in a particular case. In one study where participants in an early phase clinical trial understood that the treatment would not cure their cancer, a majority of those surveyed nevertheless exhibited an optimistic belief that the experimental drug would control their disease and that they would experience only benefits from the drug and no side effects.[12] Recalling a study mentioned in Chapter 7 in which large numbers of patients with lung and colorectal cancer professed not to understand that their disease was terminal and consented to additional chemotherapy, we see the effects of self-deception at work.[13] A commentary article about that study asked some very good questions: "Were the patients who were surveyed not actually told that their disease was incurable? Or were they not told effectively, did they choose not to believe the message, or did they fully understand the message but respond too optimistically to the questions posed by a stranger?"[14] It is

10 Herbert A. Simon, A Behavioral Model of Rational Choice, 69 Q. J. Econ. 99–118 (Feb. 1955); Daniel Kahneman, A Perspective on Judgment and Choice: Mapping Bounded Rationality, 58 Am. Psychologist 697–720 (2003).

11 John Chapin & Grace Coleman, Optimistic Bias: What You Think, What You Know, or Whom You Know? 11 N. Am. J. Psychol. 121–132 (2009).

12 Lynn A. Jansen et al., Unrealistic Optimism in Early-Phase Oncology Trials, 33 IRB: Ethics & Human Res. 1–8 (2011).

13 Jane C. Weeks et al., Patients' Expectations About Effects of Chemotherapy for Advanced Cancer, 367 New Eng. J. Med. 1616–1625 (2012).

14 Thomas J. Smith & Dan L. Longo, Talking with Patients About Dying, 367 New Eng. J. Med. 1651–1652 (2012).

likely that all of these explanations were in play among the various patients. Add to this that physicians also tend to overestimate the remaining life expectancies of seriously ill patients and to convey prognoses in overly optimistic terms, and there is plenty of fuel for optimism bias.

Once patients begin treatment, they may also adopt loss-aversion strategies: patients may prefer to avoid the chance of further loss of remaining lifetime through opting for *more* treatment intervention rather than considering the possibility of gaining more remaining lifetime (or improved quality of remaining lifetime) through opting for *less* intensive medical treatment.[15] Patients may also engage in confirmation-bias behaviors, in which they gather and remember information selectively while ignoring or discounting negative or discordant information to protect the confidence and optimistic outlook 'bought' through their optimism-bias behavior,[16] and physicians generally tend to back them up in all of this.

These behaviors and biases have modern names and empirical research to measure their prevalence and impact, but Leo Tolstoy understood them long ago. Both death denial and optimism bias afflicted Tolstoy's Ivan Ilych. Consider the following passages. First, the patient denies to himself that the disease was serious: "The pain did not grow less, but Ivan Ilych made efforts to force himself to think that he was better." "The progress of his disease was so gradual that he could deceive himself when comparing one day with another – the difference was so slight." Then the patient shores up his decision regarding treatment after hearing about an alternative: "I mustn't give way to nervous fears but having chosen a doctor must keep strictly to his treatment. That is what I will do. Now it's all settled. I won't think about it, but will follow the treatment seriously till summer, and then we shall see."[17] Later, when Ilych could no longer deny that he was dying, he cast off his mortality denial: "It's not a question of appendix or kidney, but of life and . . . death. Yes, life was there and now it is going, going and I cannot stop it. Yes. Why deceive myself?"[18] Finally, the patient became infuriated by the ongoing denial of others:

> What tormented Ivan Ilych the most was the deception, the lie, which for some reason they all accepted, that he was not dying but was simply ill, and that he only need keep quiet and undergo a treatment and then something very good would result. . . . This deception tortured him – their not wishing to admit what they all knew and what he knew, but wanting to lie to him concerning his terrible condition, and wishing and forcing him to participate in that lie.[19]

15 Daniel Kahneman & Amos Tversky, Choices, Values and Frames 39 Am. Psychologist 341–350 (1984).
16 Raymond S. Nickerson, Confirmation Bias: A Ubiquitous Phenomenon in Many Guises, 2 Rev. Gen. Psychol. 175–220 (1998).
17 Lev Nikolayevich Tolstoy, *The Death of Ivan Ilych* pp. 48–50 (trans. Louise & Aylmer Maude) (Hubris edition) (first published 1886).
18 Ibid. p. 57.
19 Ibid. p. 69.

The patterns of modern societal behavior toward the dying, and of physician and family participation in supporting denial, are not new. They have been with us for centuries.

Fear of death and denial of mortality constitute the flipside and ultimate drivers of unreasonable optimism. They make confronting these ineluctably imperfect choices, reasoning through them in the context of personal beliefs and goals of care, and then making an informed (but rationally never perfect) choice very difficult. Truly informed consent requires an understanding of the limits of knowledge, knowability, and rational decision-making – and a lot of courage. For all patients, the ethical value of autonomy is to some extent a construct that assumes that patients have endless time and ability to process endless amounts of perfect and complete information to make a perfectly rational end-of-life decision. This is simply never the case.

There are multiple cognitive and behavioral barriers to 'good' clinical decision-making. Only by acknowledging these barriers and working within the shifting boundaries of clinical uncertainty can patients and physicians make the 'best' choices. The first step in this process is to admit that we can never fully know, *ex ante* (or even *ex post*), which choice is, was, or would have been 'best'. It is true that, in many cases, the limited choices available under the clinical circumstances make it likely that the path chosen – with respect to treatment or care at the end of life – is a sensible one. But there will nearly always be a feeling of lingering doubt.

We all need to form some expectations about the future in order to function in the present,[20] but the trick is not to get too attached to these expectations. Those people who acknowledge on a regular basis during healthy times the uncertainty of the future and the precarity of life probably will be more prepared to accept the onset of terminal illness and to make treatment decisions that are both well informed (as to known knowns, known unknowns, and the unknowable impact of unknown unknowns) and consistent with their individual values and goals of care. Accepting uncertainty – about prognosis and efficacy of treatments – will be easier for patients whose physicians also acknowledge and discuss the uncertainty that is inherent and unavoidable in virtually all complex medical care decisions. Physicians themselves, by the very nature of their work, live with clinical uncertainty and life's precarity every day, and sharing this reality with their patients is more likely to bring patients and physicians together in a collaborative decision-making team than to destroy hope or leave patients feeling abandoned. For both decision-making and post-decision ambivalence, informed hope is better than overoptimistic hope. Accepting uncertainty can optimize the rationality of patients' informed consent and with it their confidence in having made good decisions under the most challenging of circumstances.

20 Luhmann, Familiarity, Confidence, Trust: Problems and Alternatives, in Trust.

If a physician understands that necessary fallibility is impossible to overcome, then she can also understand that she can never 'fail' to overcome it. The word "fallibility" has a negative connotation but, in the context of necessary fallibility, the use of the word is inapt and actually harmful. There is nothing wrong with necessary fallibility, and physicians should not let this sort of uncertainty inhibit them from either disclosing the limits of knowledge to patients or from acknowledging to themselves that these limits are okay and indeed inevitable. Both statistically and rationally, it is clear that in predicting the future, physicians can and will sometimes get it wrong without *being* wrong. Physicians are mortals with bounded rationality like the rest of us. In this sense, the whole idea of 'best' treatment is fundamentally misconceived (objectively with respect to medical data and subjectively with respect to a particular patient). Perhaps it is the lurking reality of this unavoidable fallibility that leads physicians and patients to want to 'do everything'[21] (and so unwittingly reinforce their optimism biases), but physicians must try to do their best. They have an ethical obligation to take the lead in initiating discussions about treatment choices, and acknowledging fallibility would be a good thing for both physicians and patients – if both can understand that this sort of fallibility does not also imply a lack of skill or care that might lead to loss of a chance of cure or extended life. Acknowledging the cognitive limitations – affecting both patients and physicians – that negatively impact care for the seriously ill is a useful step to acknowledging mortality. Maybe this is a chicken-or-egg problem. We need to acknowledge uncertainty in all of its forms, but it is easier to do if we already accept mortality. Yet, accepting mortality is what makes acknowledging uncertainty much easier.

RATIONAL PATIENT APATHY

In the context of complex medical decision-making, with its accompanying anxiety, asymmetric information and communication problems, the realities of clinical uncertainty coalesce into a perfect decisional storm. Even within what we *can* know, despite the confines of bounded rationality and clinical uncertainty, there is yet another phenomenon at work that hobbles good decision-making. It is psychologically and emotionally daunting to confront the absolute uncertainty inherent in mortality. For this reason, many people leave these ideas largely unexplored for most of their healthier decisional lives. We just don't think about mortality too much while we're healthy, but a life-threatening or terminal diagnosis upends the ability to 'cruise along' while generally avoiding thoughts of mortality – a kind of lifelong

[21] It isn't even clear what 'doing everything' under any given set of circumstances actually means. Worse, it also may oversimplify the decision to a choice between 'doing nothing' (a 'wrong' decision) and 'doing everything' (a 'right' decision). Complex end-of-life decision-making almost never fits that kind of binary model but rather requires physicians and patients to develop a plan to 'do something' that is right for the particular patient and that may be more than 'nothing' and will likely be less than 'everything'.

rational apathy. Reality crashes through like a wrecking ball. With the realization that life might come to an end in the not-too-distant future, the patient must suddenly begin to process unwelcome facts while carrying a new and much heavier cognitive load. The looming knowledge that the future will bring an unavoidable loss of both quantity and quality of life, including a possibly prolonged and painful dying process, means for the patient that the prior strategy of avoiding mortal thoughts is no longer workable. Since in many cases the active dying process won't yet have commenced at the time of diagnosis, and since prognosis is by definition uncertain, the patient enters a new realm (unprecedented in actual personal experience) where the idea of an open-ended future of surviving and thriving completely stops. Instead, quantity of remaining life and quality of remaining life become potentially antagonistic and, sometimes, mutually exclusive conditions.[22] The patient now may have to choose one over the other or discriminate in terms of more of one at the expense of less of the other.

In this situation, patient decision-making may overwhelmingly default to negative decision-making: an affirmative choice to *not* make any decision on the merits but rather to remain ignorant of some aspects of the choice situation. If the patient opts for the decisional default of 'deciding nothing' or 'waiting things out' (i.e., of not making an active decision for or against treatment or simply assenting to whatever the physician recommends), the patient is still making a choice that will affect his scarce future quantity and quality of life. Given the lack of practice in thinking about impending death, patients may tend to blind themselves to what they otherwise *could* know or learn about their medical situation, because this path tends to reduce both emotional suffering and cognitive load in the short term – it immediately reduces the burden of processing large amounts of complex information in the middle of an existential crisis. This path, a kind of 'rational patient apathy',[23] refers to the idea that some patients give up trying make the most informed decisions possible and opt to avoid acknowledging and getting to know what is actually knowable about their medical condition. The term rational apathy is not meant as a criticism of anyone – it's only a descriptive term, not a normative one. In many decisional contexts, rational apathy is highly effective and beneficial decisional behavior. It's reasonable and understandable to be a rationally apathetic patient in a normative sense.

The problem is that rational apathy will often have a subversive effect on the quality of end-of-life decision-making – it exacts huge opportunity costs on the patient that the patient might not want to pay, if she were aware of them. Even for

22 As one physician explains, "Patients' decisions become more difficult when they are asked to compare apples to oranges, metaphorically speaking of course. For instance, some decisions require patients to make trade-offs between length of life and health-related quality of life." Peter A. Ubel, Beyond Costs and Benefits: Understanding How Patients Make Health Care Decisions, 15 Oncologist 5–10 (supp. 2010).

23 Barbara A. Noah & René Reich-Graefe, Rational Patient Apathy, 49 Seton Hall L. Rev. 535–628 (2019).

the self-interested individuals that we are, the personal costs are substantial. (That part of ourselves that is other-regarding also may wish to think in terms of the 'bigger picture', whether it is the emotional stress that we put onto loved ones or the financial stress that we place on the health care system.) In the context of this persistent patient avoidance of substantive decision-making, the empirical evidence reviewed earlier demonstrates frequent reversion to a quantity-over-quality approach, allowing health care providers to 'do everything' until continued medical intervention reaches the point of obvious medical or economic futility. Rational patient apathy in the context of end-of-life decision-making not only negates the classic (and utopian) goal of informed consent, it also exerts tremendous costs – on patients, on loved ones, on health care providers, and on society – in the form of adverse effects of treatment, avoidable suffering, recurring decisional stress, and the wasting of scarce medical resources.

The denial of death – a kind of rational apathy with regard to one's future death throughout the healthy part of life – is normal and necessary. Setting aside thoughts of mortality and how one might cope with serious illness and the effects of aging certainly makes daily life more cheerful and livable. But lifelong rational apathy can also impact what we actually do and how we behave during our healthy time on the planet. We fear death but we may also fear life with its constant and unavoidable uncertainty all the while that we're living,[24] and so, as Chapter 4 explained, we may resist engaging fully with life as a form of self-protection, turning instead to busyness.

Imagine a person in middle age who has spent his life chasing wealth and all of its trappings – a large house with servants, luxurious clothing and decadent food, travel to all the best hotels and resorts – and has achieved this goal. He lives a life that is dedicated to leisure and pleasure. Now imagine that he is diagnosed with a form of cancer that is nearly always fatal. Suddenly, none of what he has accumulated or experienced matters any more, however much he may have enjoyed it all at the time. Worse still, if he is sufficiently self-aware, he realizes that it never meant much at all – that he has frittered away his life on things that are nice to have but that, without being enjoyed as part of a life of greater substance, lack personal and profound meaning. In the face of death, fine clothing, vintage champagne, endless vacations, and the rest not only lose their allure in the time-limited future, they also metamorphose into hollow experiences in the past. With this realization, no matter how much he may attempt to avoid it, come horror and regret and fury. Things start to coalesce. The patient may begin to think frantically backward and forward, about what he hasn't done and what he might yet do. He may have brief and very unsettling glimpses of his unlived lives. Ivan Ilych, too, experienced this regret. Describing his decades of chasing money and the trappings of a 'successful' life, the character realizes that "the longer it lasted the more deadly it became. 'It is as if I have been going downhill while I imagined I was going up. And that is really what it was. I was

24 Ernest Becker, Escape from Evil, p. 92 (The Free Press, 1975).

going up in public opinion, but to the same extent life was ebbing away from me. And now it is all done and there is only death.'"[25]

ACTIVIST AND PASSIVIST PATIENTS AND PHYSICIANS

Patients (and their physicians) fall along a continuum of willingness to acknowledge the fact of mortality – both at the time of a life-threatening diagnosis and for all of the life that precedes that time. At one end of the continuum are what we might call 'activist' patients, those who have acknowledged their mortality for all or most of their adult lives and who are willing and emotionally able to participate thoughtfully and in a fully engaged manner in the complex medical decision-making that will impact the course of their illness and (if they don't survive it) how they die. These patients do the best they can, within the strictures of (and with some awareness of) bounded rationality and clinical uncertainty, to make choices that comport with their goals and preferences. When it matters most, they attempt to pull their chin up over the bar of rational apathy and to battle their cognitive biases. In particular, instead of optimism bias, activist patients are more likely to start with skepticism about the efficacy of treatments and the length of life remaining – a kind of pessimism bias. The effort to discuss and evaluate strategic uncertainty, its reduction into risks and benefits, and alternatives to treatment, in order to optimize decisions, will have genuine intrinsic value only for those patients who are highly rational activists. Given the impact of clinical uncertainty, an activist patient always has to acknowledge to herself that neither she nor her physician can ever predict how incorrect a prognosis may turn out to be in a particular patient's case or to what extent a recommended medical treatment may prove useless or even harmful.

But most patients likely aren't deciding and proceeding in a highly rational, activist manner. At the other end of the continuum are 'passivist' patients, those who tuck away thoughts of mortality as much as possible and who resist acknowledging and accepting, for as long as possible, the frightening implications of a potentially fatal diagnosis. These patients are understandably shocked by the diagnosis and very frightened given all of the uncertainty and change that the diagnosis and recommended treatment will bring to all aspects of their lives. (Of course, activist patients will experience the same shock and fright.) The fight-or-flight response in this context means that flight – the instinctive decision to avoid confronting that which causes fear – is likely. Apathy toward active decision-making likely will follow. Fight would require flipping to activist mode, beginning with asking a lot of questions that may very well bring unwelcome answers and processing loads of complex medical information, all the while struggling with the unavoidable existential distress that comes with the diagnosis.

[25] Tolstoy, The Death of Ivan Ilych p. 85.

Some patients will cling to passivism, no matter what information might be available to inform decision-making, and no matter how much a physician may try to provide it. While still healthy, such a patient might say, "I want to die in my sleep." This patient wants no warning of impending death, no attendant fear or suffering, no dealing with the 'mess' that's inherent in concluding a life. The avoidance of fear, for these individuals, more than compensates for lost opportunities to get their emotional and logistical affairs in order and to say good-bye to those whom they love. For these individuals, death denial is only part of their method of operation – they are people who dislike all involuntary change. Everything must be as it always was; every day must follow its appointed rhythm in perpetuity. There's some logic in this way of thinking – if the person didn't die today and tomorrow can and must be like today, then he can't die tomorrow either. And so on. This thinking can play out in attachment to inanimate belongings, so that the house that shelters these things and their owners becomes a physical and emotional barrier to change. But the physical continuity of the structure itself, and of its contents, conveys a feeling of permanence that simply doesn't exist for our corporeal bodies. In a fascinating study of patterns of moving house in the United States, researchers were puzzled by the fact that mobility rates have fallen substantially over the past three decades. In 1985, nearly 20 percent of US residents moved, by 2019, just under 10 percent changed residence. The researchers found that psychological costs played an outsized role in many decisions not to move – and that these costs increase with age and length of residency.[26] The research suggests that, for some portion of the population, resistance to change drives decision-making in global ways that can harm the person, at least in terms of decisional 'elasticity' and the resilience to deal with unwelcome news.

Between the extremes of activist and passivist patients, there are patients who might be called 'persuadable passivists' (or maybe 'ambivalent activists'). These patients default generally to the passivist approach but, with the assistance of good physician communication and perhaps with the aid of palliative care consultation focused on aligning medical care with goals (survival, comfort, time without treatment, energy to get personal affairs in order), may more readily wade into activist waters. The personality and communication skills of the physician matter a lot in this context.

Physicians are humans like the rest of us and, like the rest of us, they vary in temperament and in their approach to difficult tasks such as communicating bad news to patients. In a fascinating study from Sweden that sought to understand how patients view their physicians' approach to these sorts of conversations, patient interviews revealed six types of physicians: (1) the inexperienced messenger (sent by a senior doctor to deliver bad news but lacking the experience to do so gently); (2)

[26] Gizen Kosar et al., Understanding Migration Aversion Using Elicited Counterfactual Choice Probabilities, Federal Reserve Bank of NY, Staff Report No. 883 (April, 2019), www.newyorkfed.org/medialibrary/media/research/staff_reports/sr883.pdf.

the emotionally burdened (described as kind and understanding but too emotionally involved and so adding distress to the situation); (3) the rough and ready expert (described as medically experienced but lacking empathy or communication skills, tending to deliver news rapidly and focused on medical facts); (4) the benevolent but tactless expert (described as sympathetic and competent but not sensitive to the patient's situation); (5) the distanced expert (described as formal, calm, and experienced but keeping patients at an emotional distance and uninterested in the patient); and (6) the empathic professional (described as balancing medical competence and empathy for the patient and as interested in both physical and psychological concerns). Patients emphasized how important the relationship with the doctor was in helping them cope with the information.[27] The physician who can communicate medical information clearly while expressing empathy for the patient, who can maintain the professional role and draw on experience but encourage the patient to express feelings, worries, and questions, sounds like the ideal 'type' to convey bad news and to guide complex medical decision-making.

Communication failures are a co-produced dilemma. Physicians, like their patients, fall along the passivist to activist spectrum. As we have seen, some physicians avoid communication about prognosis and potential treatment efficacy and withhold information or outright lie to patients. Just as patients don't want to hear bad news, some physicians don't want to tell it to them. Physicians also engage in other behaviors, including collusion with the patient to postpone acknowledging medical reality and confirmation of the patient's rational apathy and biases.

In a highly original ethnographic study seeking to understand the multiple causes of unrealistic optimism in patients, researchers in the Netherlands followed thirty-five patients with incurable small cell lung cancer to understand patterns of optimism, how they developed, and how physicians participated in supporting unrealistic optimism. The primary researcher in the study observed the patients from initial diagnosis to death – in the outpatient clinic waiting room, at clinic visits, at x-ray and other hospital services, in meetings with treating physicians, and at home. She also formally interviewed patients and staff, attended patients' funerals, and interviewed some of the bereaved spouses. As a result of this intensive in-person study of terminally ill patients, she witnessed many revealing exchanges between physicians and patients, and she reached a number of fascinating conclusions. From her observations, she identified five emotional stages in the trajectory of the patients' illnesses: an existential crisis at diagnosis, a focus on therapy during treatment, relative peace of mind when the cancer disappeared from x-rays, a second existential crisis at the point of cancer recurrence, and a final crisis upon the news that no further treatment was available. All of the patients studied had terminal lung cancer and all had received this information, but with little detail. Nevertheless, twenty-nine of the thirty-five patients

[27] Maria J. Friedrichsen et al., Breaking Bad News in the Transition from Curative to Palliative Cancer Care – Patient's View of the Doctor Giving the Information, 8 Support Care Cancer 472–478 (2000).

studied exhibited striking patterns of baseless optimism, which developed during the first treatment period, peaked at the point where the cancer was not visible and the patient felt 'cured', disappeared when the cancer recurred, and sometimes redeveloped during further rounds of chemotherapy.[28] All of these twenty-nine patients appear to have engaged in rationally apathetic behavior – accepting treatment without question or activist inquiry into the choices on the table, and shoring up that decision with a good dose of optimism, loss aversion, and confirmation biases.

The published study results include excerpts from conversations between physicians and patients that illustrate structural patterns of patient self-deception and the physicians' role in supporting it. In discussions of terminal prognosis, patients were usually told that they had incurable cancer, but this information often was immediately undercut with a statement to the effect that "it is extremely difficult to give any indication of the general prognosis because each patient is unique." (Again, we are each an n of 1, but this cuts both ways.) For a patient who hears what he wants to hear, this sort of statement provides an immediate escape hatch – *he* is the unique patient for whom this cancer, while supposedly fatal, will not cause death for a very, very long time. The type of cancer these patients had is terminal but usually responds well to a first round of chemotherapy, creating an initial full remission. When the cancer recurred, patients were again told that prognosis would depend on the results of future treatment, leaving them with an open-ended idea of the future. Kicking the prognosis can down the road in this way also subtly supports hope for a cure or at least another full remission or slower decline given that the cancer had responded 'so well' to the first round of treatment. In effect, instead of acknowledging Knightian uncertainty and the fact that it can cut both ways, the physicians here helped patients weaponize Knightian uncertainty ("each patient is unique") to encourage unrealistic hope.

Another pattern of communication emerged that encouraged optimism: physicians turned the focus of conversation from the terminal prognosis to the details and logistics of treatment as quickly as possible. Here, physicians (perhaps unknowingly) helped patients close the window of opportunity for a more activist decision-making approach. When patients later on failed to ask about prognosis or what to expect as the disease progressed, physicians assumed that patients didn't want to know and kept mum. The longer patients resisted prognostic information (even as they became sicker), the more unsettling it became for physicians – who then tended to try harder to help patients understand that death was approaching. Physician disclosure of this news was very much influenced by patients, especially those who made it clear that they just didn't want to know.[29] At the same time, it was influenced by physicians' reluctance to provide prognostic information in a more activist

[28] Anne-Mei The et al., Collusion in Doctor-Patient Communication About Imminent Death: An Ethnographic Study, 321 Brit. Med. J. 1376–1381 (2000).

[29] Ibid.

manner, even though physicians are repeat players in these specific conversations and even though patients, as nonexperts, generally trust their physicians to tell them all that they need to know to make good decisions.

In addition to this physician-patient collusion, physicians used ambiguous language. Even using the word "treatment," from the patient's perspective, meant that the cancer was treatable (which it is, but patients may interpret 'treatable' to mean 'curable' or at least indefinitely manageable). Physicians told patients in remission that "the therapy has had the optimal effect" and that "your lungs are clear," and patients believed that they were cured. One exchange of this nature was particularly jaw-dropping. The physician, looking at x-rays of the patient's lungs, said, "Marvellous, ... Complete remission! Look, I'll show you. This is where the abnormality was." The patient then asks, "So, it's looking good?" The physician replies, "Very good ... if I didn't know you, I wouldn't know where the abnormality had been. ... Of course, there could always be a little cell left somewhere that we cannot see in the picture. That's always possible. Only time will tell." The physician's approach to truth in this conversation would be comical if it weren't so terribly misleading. Calling a tumor an 'abnormality' ranks high on the euphemism scale but is understandable – people recoil at the word "tumor." But there is a difference between euphemism and delusionality – the physician appears to have gone to great lengths to support the patient's belief that he was cured, or at least to avoid reminding the patient of the terminal nature of his illness. The result of this sort of collusion is what the investigators called the "recovery plot" – that recurring narrative that the patient is sick but he will be better again with treatment – which ultimately places a great deal of pressure on the patient to maintain the fiction, especially later in the disease process. Overall, it leads to patients' feeling better about 'doing something' to address the illness, but it also puts patients in the untenable position of struggling to maintain an aura of hope when reality has finally broken through. Some patients expressed regret about choices they made – had they known earlier that death was approaching, they may have spent more time with family or rejected more burdensome treatment.[30] These lost opportunities are one of the most dispiriting results of communication avoidance (passivist patient-physician collusion) – the patient never gets the chance to do what she might have done.

The pattern of physician behavior observed in this study appears common. Many physicians seem willing to collude with patients to support unrealistic optimism or hope. Apart from the fact that patients may retrospectively regret their late acknowledgment of impending death or may accept more treatment late in the disease process than they would have if they had understood their prognosis, is collusion such a bad thing? After all, it appears to reduce the existential suffering of patients over the course of illness – at least superficially. (There are likely many patients who

[30] The et al., Collusion in Doctor-Patient Communication About Imminent Death.

outwardly participate in the recovery plot while a little voice is telling them that something doesn't seem right.)

One oncologist who is familiar with the Dutch ethnographic study and its conclusions appears to have recognized his own communication pattern in the study.[31] Acknowledging that he finds it hard to give accurate and honest prognostic information to patients, he then describes a style of communication that 'works' for him and his patients – creating a gradual arc of comprehension over time that he believes allows patients to cope better with the knowledge that they will die from their disease. He correctly points out the clash of values created by empirical evidence that patients want both accurate estimates of prognosis in a timely fashion and also want to maintain hope. (As explained in Chapter 3, these two desires are not necessarily as much in conflict as they may appear at first glance.) In a defense of his approach to communication, the oncologist argues that unless a patient openly requests "stark frankness," avoiding and delaying discussion of numerical prognostic estimates of life expectancy are necessary and ethically appropriate to preserve hope. As to the studies demonstrating that cancer patients want to know their prognosis, he notes that these studies include both patients with potentially curable cancer and those for whom treatment can only palliate disease or achieve temporary remission. Because many, *though not a majority*, of patients with *incurable* cancer do *not* want an estimate of how long they may live, he argues that withholding this information, when the patient doesn't specifically request the truth, is consistent with patient preferences. The author also suggests that given the inherent uncertainty in prognosis, "it seems wiser to avoid devastating (and often inaccurate) time frames until there are clear indications that the patient is ready to hear them." This, he suggests, preserves the "patient's sense of hope and open-endedness."[32] While this goal is commendable, the primary duty of an oncologist is not to preserve hope, particularly when it is likely false hope of a cure or long remission. The oncologist's first order of business is to provide medically appropriate and proportionate treatment for cancer. The patient's emotional well-being is also important, but not to the extent that it keeps patients ignorant of their prognosis (unless they expressly waive participation in their treatment decisions), which can result in consent to burdensome, toxic treatment that patients would not choose if they were better informed.

The problem is that taking a statistical approach to patient disclosure preferences when each patient is an n of 1 ignores each patient's unique and personal preferences. Instead of discussing what each patient would like to know about her situation and then helping the patient decide on a treatment plan that best aligns with that patient's goals, the oncologist avoids this inquiry and keeps the patient in the dark – in contravention to the patient's information preferences, at least in some cases. The oncologist's approach may 'work' for those patients who truly do not want to know

[31] Paul R. Helft, Necessary Collusion: Prognostic Communication With Advanced Cancer Patients, 23 J. Clin. Oncology 3146–3150 (2005).

[32] Helft, Necessary Collusion.

their prognosis, but it puts the onus of asking on the patients who *do* want to know. Patients who do want to know about prognosis and potential treatment efficacy may still hesitate to ask, for a variety of reasons (fear of the answers, overwhelming emotions, the physician's communication patterns – such as moving the conversation as quickly as possible to a treatment plan rather than dwelling on the implications of the diagnosis for the patient's future). The oncologist states that he will answer direct questions from patients "with as much specificity as one can honestly communicate" but leaves it to patients to ask questions. Don't ask–don't tell neither promotes patient autonomy nor is it in the best interests of most patients. It is the physician's obligation to proffer information to allow the patient to decide whether and what she wants to know or to decide to waive participation in decision-making or in receiving information about her condition. For example, the physician can ask, "Would you like to know about the usual progression of this sort of cancer?" If the patient says yes, the physician can give an honest answer (based on statistical life expectancy and with whatever additional patient characteristics might lead to a longer or a shorter time frame) and add a clinical uncertainty caveat.

As with physicians in the ethnographic study discussed earlier, the author turns to prognostic uncertainty as a justification for preserving hope and preemptively withholding information until a patient asks for it. He suggests that the oncologist can refine the patient's prognosis over time as the disease progresses, allowing patients the opportunity to digest and accept the terminal nature of their illness incrementally. He advocates "forecasting" – letting patients know that things are bad without offering specific estimates of life expectancy. In his view, patients will develop more trust in their physicians over time and will therefore more willingly believe and accept the prognosis when it is finally disclosed later in the treatment relationship. This all may be true for some patients, but there is also the possibility that patients will trust their oncologist *less* when, in the eleventh hour, the truth is revealed. Remarkably, he argues that preserving hope and a sense of open-endedness justifies physicians to "honestly outline a range of prognostic estimates and include descriptions of outcomes that are unlikely – even highly unlikely – as long as such outcomes are within the range of clinical possibility." The oncologist can then refine prognostic estimates as time passes.[33] Recounting the far outlier case – the rare medical miracle – to a frightened patient who is making medical decisions based on what the physician tells him – doesn't help most patients who will not experience these miracles. The focus of the ethical argument for this approach relies on the presumption that allowing both the physician and patient to 'feel good' for as long as possible is a valid goal. For some patients, this may be an acceptable way to proceed (if it is the result of the patient's informed choice to leave decision-making in the hands of his oncologist), but it fails to consider those who, while they may not explicitly request "stark frankness," rely on their physician to tell them what they

[33] Helft, Necessary Collusion.

need to know in a timely fashion so that they can make good decisions about consenting to burdensome interventions and more broadly about how to spend what's left of their lives. The idea of 'evolving prognosis' – while technically acceptable due to clinical uncertainty – underplays what *can* be known with some certainty about the progression of many incurable cancers. Patients can at least be told what percentage of patients with their disease live for one year or for two. Prioritizing the preservation of hope over the provision of patient-centered cancer care makes little sense. It also renders consent to treatment in these circumstances invalid, or at least not very meaningful.

Many physicians, oncologists in particular, seem to believe that blunt disclosure of numerical prognostic information is too brutal for patients to endure. They speak of specific prognostic disclosure in metaphorical terms that convey violence – 'hit someone in the face' with prognosis, 'force it down their throat', 'hammer' the patient, or 'beat the patient over the head'. But some form of less-than-blunt disclosure of terminal prognosis and life expectancy is ethically required to support the principle of autonomy and to help patients make treatment decisions that are consistent with their goals. In the absence of this information, cancer patients may consent to participation in early-stage clinical trials or other burdensome interventions that are highly unlikely to preserve life and highly likely to further impair quality of remaining life.[34] In his defense of 'collusion', the oncologist never explicitly acknowledges these points, although he mentions providing information to enable patients to decide how best to spend their remaining time. The reluctance to convey the stark reality of specific prognosis to the patient is understandable. It is unwelcome news for the patient and emotionally challenging for the physician. And because of clinical uncertainty, a numerical prognosis of life expectancy at the point of initial diagnosis makes no sense – at best, the data will provide a median and mean for overall survival in incurable cancers. Yet, how can it be ethically proper to preserve hope by withholding information from patients who will try anything, do anything, to live longer? Patients need timely information about prognosis and disease progression to make decisions about treatment – when to carry on and when to stop.

Mortality denial, rational apathy, and passivism are far from universal, but activism appears relatively rare. In the Dutch ethnographic study described earlier, only six of the thirty-five patients either declined treatment or accepted treatment (but without exhibiting false optimism) to buy time to reach an important milestone. Some people are more willing and able to look at death and say, "Okay, this will happen to me. With complete certainty, I will die. And, until I'm actually in the process of dying, I can never know when death will come. Maybe it will come for me early. And who is to say what is 'early'?" Some even acknowledge these truths early

34 Elisa J. Gordon & Christopher K. Daugherty, "Hitting You Over the Head": Oncologists' Disclosure of Prognosis to Advanced Cancer Patients, 71 Bioethics 142–168 (2003).

and often in life, though likely with the usual measure of disquiet that tends to accompany mortal thoughts. Others prefer to tuck the certainty of death away in a dark corner and to ignore it for as long as possible. Some people also prefer to face problems rather than to postpone or avoid them. These patients might say to their physicians, "Tell me straight – how bad is it and how long do I have? Is there any treatment and is the treatment worse than the disease?" These same activist types tend to prefer to know the worst as quickly as possible. They prefer information to uncertainty, wishful thinking and suboptimally informed choice. For these patients, wishful thinking and hope cannot exist in a state of ignorance – it is impossible to conceive of reasons for hope without first knowing what can reasonably be hoped for – and that requires knowledge of the facts.

The concepts of rational apathy and of patient activism or passivism (or something in between) only describe patient behavior and are not intended as a normative judgment. Being an activist is not necessarily a character strength, nor is passivism a flaw – it is simply how we are made, or how we are raised and educated. There is no right or wrong here – at least as to the effects on ourselves, although the passivist path can lead to patients accepting treatment that they would otherwise decline with better information. Rational apathy's effects on others, family members in particular, are another story. In any event, it's fairly clear that postponing thoughts of death carries with it some substantial disadvantages.

I have a childhood ritual to thank, in part, for my long-standing willingness to think about my impending demise. From the earliest age that I can remember, I was made to say a prayer at bedtime, which goes like this:

> Now I lay me down to sleep.
> I pray the Lord my soul to keep.
> If I should die before I wake,
> I pray the Lord my soul to take.
> God bless [insert exhaustive list of relatives in order of importance here].
> Make Barbara a good girl and bless her.
> Amen.

Being an excessively literal child, I spent some sleepless nights wondering if I *would* die before I woke. Would they just find me, cold and stiff, in bed the next morning? And, once I was dead, did I actually have a soul and, if so, where would the Lord take it? Had I been bad lately? I was glad to discover, in the course of reading for this project, that I was not the first to find this prayer unsettling.[35] Brahms's famous *Wiegenlied* (Lullaby) isn't very comforting for children either. In translation, it says, "Good evening, good night .... Early tomorrow morning, if God wills, you will awake again." And if God doesn't will?

[35] Charles W. Wahl, The Fear of Death in the Meaning of Death p. 24 (Herman Feifel, ed., McGraw-Hill 1959).

PORTRAIT OF AN ACTIVIST

In the culture of modern medicine, people may need to do a lot of advance thinking and planning to avoid landing on the medical conveyor belt and then struggling to get off. Even those who firmly reject life-prolonging treatment when they reach old age can still stumble into the medical vortex. The life and death of my dear friend Emma,[36] a schoolteacher and principal, is such a story. Our friendship began when she and her schoolteacher friend moved next door to my childhood home. I was about five years old at the time and Emma was fifty-eight, which seemed to me quite ancient. Though we were separated in age by more than five decades, we became lifelong friends. Throughout my childhood, she encouraged my enthusiasms and nurtured my fragile talents. Her house was filled with what seemed like wonders to my eyes – an upright piano, a cello (I was allowed to play, or rather play *with* both), a fur-covered koala bear that played *Waltzing Maltilda* when I wound its key. A vegetable garden with tomatoes and cucumbers and radishes that we ate after harvesting with our own hands, and where I learned that parsnips, another favorite, were best left in the ground all winter and dug up in the spring. A wooden bucket with an iron hand-crank churn for making ice cream in cold weather. Books of every sort, some so old that the leather bindings crumbled at the edges. *National Geographic* magazines that contained to my young eyes some rather startling images. Ancient mahogany furniture from Emma's long-dead family, full of little drawers and compartments and locks with keys. A tiny elephant, the size of a fingernail, carved of ivory. Deep claret-colored Persian carpets with intricate designs and tassels made of silk. The scent of baking apple pie and roasting ham. To all of these wonders I had open access – I needed only to knock on the door.

Emma never married, lost her parents early in adulthood, and had no siblings. Apart from a couple of cousins and her friends, she was alone in the world. She welcomed me into her wonderful and enchanting life. She and her schoolteacher friend travelled all over during summers and in retirement – to Australia, to China, around Europe, to Alaska and Canada, and to many of the fifty states. She enriched my life in many ways. We went to local music recitals, and to museums, to Audubon events, and to a book and art supply store (long closed) where I could spend my pocket money on books and calligraphy pens and India ink and paintbrushes. And so, I grew up and Emma grew older. She retired from teaching and her friend died, rather abruptly, from Alzheimer's disease. I left for college and then onto law school and marriage, law practice, a baby, and life in the wider world. Whenever I came back for a visit, I would knock on her door and we would catch up.

I never knew Emma to be anything but cheerful and welcoming. Once I was into my twenties and thirties, she would sometimes remark, in a thoughtful voice, that more of the people she'd known all her life were gone. She was a gregarious person, but comfortable with silence and with her own company. She was not an

[36] I have changed her name for reasons of privacy.

emotionally demonstrative woman, but, in her later years, she welcomed the brief hug and kiss on the cheek that I would offer on meeting and again when saying goodbye. And so our visits continued and our lives flowed on. She celebrated milestones with my family – graduations and weddings. I have a photo of Emma holding my infant daughter, her wide smile made wider with her customary bright fuchsia lipstick that matched the flowers on her printed dress.

At some point, Emma decided to sell her house and move to an assisted living apartment in the next town. No one admonished her that the house and garden were getting too much for her to handle, or warned her of the dangers of living alone. She simply looked around her and decided that this move was the next logical step in her life. She sorted out her things and brought along her favorite pieces of furniture, her favorite books, her fern-green printed Corel dinnerware. She let go of the rest and organized the entire transition herself. Eventually, I moved back to the area and so could see her more often. As we sat out in the sun on a bench one day, my ninety-year-old friend turned to me and said, "You know, I've had a good, long life and I've done everything I ever wanted to do. I am ready to go when the good Lord takes me." I nodded at her, not sure what to say but, Emma being Emma, left no room for ambiguity. "What I'm telling you, Barbara, is that when my time comes, just let me go. I don't want doctors and hospitals." On the receiving end of the stern schoolteacher look, I said that indeed I understood, and that I would remember what she'd said.

At some point after that, Emma passed out in her apartment, apparently from bradycardia – a slow heart rate. She was taken to a nearby hospital for assessment. I visited her there and she told me that she wanted to go home to her apartment, but that the doctor said she needed a pacemaker. She told me that she was having none of that. A few days later, she was still in the hospital and I visited again. She told me that the pacemaker would be placed in a couple of days. When I looked a bit baffled, she explained, "They say I have to have it if I want to go back home." After more than a week in the hospital bed, Emma was discharged to a local nursing home for rehabilitation. It doesn't take long for old folks to lose the strength in their legs. Emma never left that nursing home. She lived the remaining eight years of her life in a two-person room with a few bits of her own things and a lot of institutional furniture. She never complained, though sometimes I saw the sadness in her eyes. She appointed me as her health care agent and asked me to manage her bills. She only became distraught when she ran out of money and had to 'go on the State', something that really bothered her, with her self-reliant streak. In her final year, she became a bit confused, and when I visited on a weekday, she would ask why I wasn't in school. When I explained that I had finished school and now had a job, she would then ask with some asperity why I wasn't at work. She once became acutely ill with food poisoning and the nursing home staff called me to come quickly. I sat by her bedside; she was delirious. I picked up her hand and she opened her eyes and glared at me and said, "Barbara, why are you here? And why are you holding my hand?!"

When I explained, she tutted and said that she was fine. “This, too, shall pass” was one of her favorite sayings. Then one day, at ninety-eight years of age, Emma climbed into bed for an afternoon nap and never woke up.

Emma had a marvelous life, but it didn’t end as she intended. She was bullied into accepting a pacemaker that both prolonged her life and landed her in a long-term care facility. She made the best of it, but Emma, who had so definitely and firmly said no to life-prolonging measures, ended up saying yes, and regretted it. Despite her frank and spirited appreciation of life and her ability to face death with a measured calm and certainty, she died after the long, slow decline that she’d sought to avoid.

SO, WHAT NOW?

All end-of-life communication and decision-making occur within the broader reality of unavoidable uncertainty. The sooner we as patients and our physicians together acknowledge and accept this fact, the better that the collaborative decisions occasioned by serious illness will be. Clinical uncertainty, bounded rationality, and (to some extent) cognitive biases have an irremediable impact on medical decision-making. Of course, communication and informed consent to treatment, implemented with as much truth and compassion as possible, remain the goal. But it is worth acknowledging the multiple, and often insurmountable, obstacles to making a ‘perfect’ highest-utility decision regarding end-of-life care. Patients can only do their best to make the ‘right’ decision and, even then, with the knowledge that decision-making will unavoidably remain subject to uncertainty and to human limitations with regard to perfect rational choice.

Rational patient apathy and physician collusion have practical effects and implications – they can lead to unwanted treatment at the end of life and render the ideal of informed consent virtually meaningless. The cultural tendency to avoid thinking too much about mortality, even when one is terminally ill, together with physician avoidance of truthful and timely conversation about the risks, benefits, and alternatives to treatment and life-sustaining therapy, mean that many dying patients may make the choice to remain un(der)informed. When physicians take the path of least resistance and let this un(der)informed state continue, they do their patients no favors. Of course, these sorts of conversations are emotionally challenging, and more so if the patient exhibits reluctance or wrenching emotions. The philosopher Ivan Illich (not the Tolstoy guy) exhorts physicians to step up to the challenge:

> The ordinary person suffers from the inability to die. In an amortal society, the ability to die – that is, the ability to live – no longer depends on culture but on friendship. The old Mediterranean norm that a wise person needs to acquire and treasure an amicus mortis, one who tells you the bitter truth and stays with you to the

> inexorable end, calls for revival. And I see no compelling reason why one who practises medicine could not also be a friend – even today.[37]

Illich asks a lot of physicians but, in his opinion, it is an intrinsic part of the job.

In a strange way, uncertainty is our friend – but not because it provides a basis for withholding information from patients or supporting baseless optimism. Accepting uncertainty – about prognosis or potential efficacy of treatments – can free us from decisional paralysis and we can make better choices with no (or fewer) regrets – because there is no do-over, no ability to compare different outcomes, and therefore no reason to regret what might have been. Nietzsche wrote: "Not doubt but certainty drives one mad."[38] Embracing uncertainty will be easier for patients whose physicians also acknowledge and discuss the uncertainty that is inherent and unavoidable in virtually all complex medical decisions – in the service of promoting realism, not baseless optimism. There is a cartoon in which an interviewer asks a physician, "Doctor, how do you respond to critics who say that with this new procedure you are, in effect, 'Playing God'?" The doctor replies, "I strike them dead with a bolt of lightning."[39] Physicians can acknowledge to their patients that they are neither omnipotent – can't always cure – nor omniscient – can't always predict outcomes accurately. The best of these difficult conversations will acknowledge these points and then follow a model in which the physician asks the patient about what they value most at the close of life and then makes evidence-based predictions and explains the choices. Then, rather than leaving the ultimate decision to the patient, the physician can make a recommendation based on her own expertise and explain the reasons for it. In the words of John Stone, "For after you learn what to do, how and when to do it / the question will be *whether*."[40] This is much more than informed consent law requires, but it's what we patients and physicians should be aiming for.

37 Ivan Illich, Death Undefeated, 311 Brit. Med. J. 1652–1653 (1995).

38 Friedrich Nietzsche, Ecce Homo p. 35 (Clifton P. Fadiman, transl.) (Modern Library, 1927).

39 Cartoon by Don Piraro (1975).

40 John Stone, Gaudeamus Igitur, in On Doctoring: Stories, Poems, Essays pp. 326–330 (Richard Reynolds & John Stone, eds.) (Simon & Schuster 1995) (emphasis in the original).

9

The Crucible

Making Decisions for Incapacitated Patients

From caring comes courage.

—Lao Tzu

The many challenges to effective physician-patient communication and decision-making become even more intractable when patients are unable to make decisions for themselves. In ideal circumstances, patients can provide information about their preferences directly, but if the patient has lost the ability to make some or all medical decisions, physicians must try to figure out what the patient would choose based on advance directives, conversations with family members or surrogate decision-makers, and the context of the patient's known values and goals. Under this approach, the ideal is to make decisions that respect the patient's preferences even when he can no longer articulate them. In reality, this process often doesn't work well because insufficient evidence of the patient's preferences coupled with uncertainty about prognosis (and a lot of other variables) can leave physicians and family members in a quandary about whether to provide therapeutic treatment or life-prolonging care. Patients frequently are reluctant to discuss their preferences regarding end-of-life care or even to acknowledge to themselves or to their families the fact that they are dying. And remember that if physicians haven't actually disclosed pertinent facts, these patients and families are making choices in an even greater state of ignorance.

Let's begin with a case history that illustrates some common challenges:

Mr. H., a 75-year-old man, was admitted to the hospital complaining of progressive weakness and shakiness on his right side. A CT scan indicated lung cancer with metastases to the brain. Mr. H. refused further invasive tests, explaining that his wife died of the same disease and that he did not want any life-prolonging treatment. Several physicians pushed the patient to have a biopsy of the lung, to which he agreed. When the biopsy confirmed lung cancer, the patient refused surgery to resect the cancer in the lung and brain and was discharged after three weeks in the hospital with full-time care at home. Three months later, he was readmitted to the hospital after having several seizures. A CT scan showed that the brain mass had grown larger. Mr. H. continued to suffer seizures and could not talk. His son and other family requested a DNAR order based on his father's prior expressed wishes. The neurology team again recommended surgery to resect the tumor but the son declined. Over the next three weeks, Mr. H. received oxygen, fluids, drugs, multiple blood tests and additional CT scans, and was fed via a nasogastric tube. Although he was minimally responsive, he managed to remove the NG tube several times. He was then placed in restraints and, after 29 days of hospitalization, the family was persuaded to consent to a gastronomy tube for feeding. The tube was surgically implanted in Mr. H's stomach on the 29th day of hospitalization. The patient had a cardiac arrest and died the following day.[1]

In this case, the patient was able to clearly and repeatedly express his preferences at the time of his diagnosis, not just to his family but also to his treating physicians. He refused more testing and therapeutic interventions and even gave a reason for his refusal – the experience of watching his wife die of the same disease. Yet Mr. H. suffered unnecessarily, probably spent more on health care costs than if his preferences had been honored, passed many of his remaining days in the hospital and died there rather than at home and, most importantly, received care that was inconsistent with his expressed wishes. His family appears to have wavered between respecting his wishes and being persuaded to accept some (but not all) burdensome interventions to prolong his life. What combination of factors leads to this state of affairs – in which a patient's express refusal of care is ignored when he later loses the ability to make medical decisions?

In the final stages of terminal illness (or at the most acute stage of what may turn out to be a serious but survivable illness), many patients lose the ability to make medical decisions – usually referred to as 'decisional capacity'. Decisional capacity requires that the patient can understand the information relevant to his medical situation, can weigh options and alternatives in the context of a set of goals or values, and can communicate decisions.[2] A substantial percentage of seriously ill patients lose decisional capacity at the end of life. One estimate suggests that in the final weeks of life, approximately 42 percent of dying patients aged 60 or older require assistance with decision-making and, of that 42 percent, about 70 percent of those patients eventually lose decisional capacity entirely.[3] Another study places these numbers even higher, estimating that 75 percent of patients with life-threatening illness and more than 95 percent of patients in critical care units lost decisional capacity.[4] For these

[1] Adapted from R. Sean Morrison et al., When Too Much is Too Little, 335 New Eng. J. Med. 1755–1759 (1996).

[2] Paul S. Appelbaum, Assessment of Patients' Competence to Consent to Treatment, 357 New Eng. J. Med. 1834–1840 (2007).

[3] Maria Silveira et al., Advance Directives and Outcomes of Surrogate Decision Making Before Death, 362 New Eng. J. Med. 1211–1218 (2010).

[4] Nicholas G. Smedira et al., Withholding and Withdrawal of Life Support from the Critically Ill, 322 New Eng. J. Med. 309–315 (1990).

individuals, a surrogate decision-maker must make difficult choices on behalf of the patient about how much therapeutic and life-prolonging medical care to request or accept. As the proportion of older Americans increases, along with higher incidences of Alzheimer's disease and other forms of dementia, the need for surrogate decision-making will increase.

THE BASICS OF SURROGATE DECISION-MAKING LAW AND ETHICS

The person who serves in the role of surrogate decision-maker is typically the patient's family member or a legally appointed agent who often also is a family member. Because of the family relationship, surrogates are presumed to know more about the patient in the moment when decisions are required than a patient might be able to predict and document in advance via a living will or similar document. Surrogate consent laws in the fifty-one US jurisdictions vary, but most of these statutes grant a person the authority to make medical decisions for patients who have lost capacity. Many states have enacted surrogate consent laws that create a hierarchy of relatives who are granted the legal authority to make decisions, typically beginning with the patient's spouse, followed by adult children, parents, adult siblings, and sometimes a friend who has exhibited special care and concern for the patient. The person who is highest in the hierarchy and available and willing to make decisions for the patient has statutory authority to do so.[5] The statutes also vary in what authority is granted to the surrogate, with some states limiting surrogate decision-making to cases in which the patient is terminally ill or permanently unconscious, and with other states limiting what sorts of interventions can be withheld – particularly artificial nutrition and hydration.[6] Because these statutes vary widely, it's no surprise that both physicians and family members have little understanding of the rights and obligations of surrogates, and that no consistent or reliable process has emerged to manage disputes about care for incapacitated patients. Chapter 10 considers certain dispute resolution mechanisms in the United States, the United Kingdom, and Canada.

Once a patient has lost decisional capacity, physicians and surrogates must try to understand the patient's preferences through a process known as 'substituted judgment' – a term that can cause confusion for the surrogate because it seems to convey the idea that the surrogate should substitute her own choice for that of the patient. The law and underlying ethical principles actually require that surrogate decision-makers make choices based on what the *patient* would choose under the circumstances and then apply that knowledge to the decision at hand. When the patient's preferences are uncertain or unknown, the surrogate must decide according to the

5 Alan Meisel et al., The Right to Die § 8.04 (3rd ed. Wolters Kluwer 2020).

6 Ibid., § 8.07. For example, Missouri (where Nancy Cruzan resided and ultimately died) has enacted a statute that excludes artificial nutrition and hydration from the definition of "death-prolonging procedure." Rev. Mo.Stat. § 459.010(3).

patient's best interests.[7] Under this substituted judgment approach, the goal is to respect the patient's autonomy even when he can no longer articulate a preference. The process of substituted judgment is highly subjective, centered as much as possible on the particular patient and his values and goals rather than on what a majority might think is the 'best' decision. This principle of autonomy contains within it both the principles of self-determination – the ability to make and execute a choice – and of authenticity – the idea that the patient's choice may be unique to the individual based on her particular characteristics, beliefs, quirks, and ideals.[8] This all sounds good, but, for patients who have lost decisional capacity, an autonomy-based model of medical decision-making is all but useless unless patients were previously willing and able to confront their medical situation and then discuss their preferences with family and physicians in advance.

Despite the emphasis on the principle of autonomy, in situations where the patient's preferences are unknown or not adequately understood, both the law and the ethical principle of beneficence require that patients receive care that is in their best interests.[9] American law also generally favors continuing life-supportive measures when the patient's preferences are in dispute or unknown. As the *Cruzan* and *Schiavo* disputes and other litigated end-of-life cases illustrate, many individuals take the position that end-of-life laws should default to continued treatment whenever a patient's preferences or best interests are in dispute, and with little regard to the patient's quality of life or degree of suffering.[10] The goal then in making complex medical decisions for incapacitated patients is to evaluate whether medical care provided to individual patients comports with their values and preferences or is otherwise in their best interests using a combination of specific (subjective) information particular to the patient and general (objective) information about benefits and harms of the proposed medical care.

All of the usual operational and theoretical problems with the law of informed consent in the context of complex medical decision-making multiply when a patient loses capacity and a surrogate decision-maker must step in. The consent process becomes even more complicated and emotionally fraught. In a simple consent scenario for a patient with decisional capacity, the patient receives information about the purpose, benefits, and potential harms of a proposed intervention – like gall bladder removal – and then consents to the surgery, recovers, and returns to routine life. By contrast, when a dying patient has not expressed any preferences

7 Ibid., § 8.08.

8 Daniel Brudney, Choosing for Another: Beyond Autonomy and Best Interests, 39 Hastings Center Rep. 31–37 (2009).

9 E.g., Barber v. Superior Ct., 195 Cal. Rptr. 484 (Ct. App. 1983); In re Beth Israel Med. Ctr. for Weinstein, 519 N.Y.S.2d 511 (Super. Ct. 1987); In re Conroy, 486 A.2d 1209 (N.J. 1985). As explained previously in Chapters 3 and 5, determining what is in a patient's best interests is far from straightforward.

10 Cruzan v. Director, Missouri Dept. of Health, 497 U.S. 261 (1990); Guardianship of Schiavo, 780 So.2d 176 (2001). Chapter 5 discusses these cases, *Schiavo* in particular, in more detail.

about life-prolonging technology and has lost decisional capacity, the decision defaults to a surrogate who may, for various reasons, hesitate to refuse proffered life-prolonging care. In these cases, the surrogate decision-maker may agree to, for example, artificial nutrition and hydration via a gastronomy tube and may sign a consent form after receiving information about the purpose, risks, and benefits of surgically implanting the tube – but without a broader understanding of the implications of prolonging life with artificial nutritional support. The surrogate may consent not because she believes that this is what the patient would want, but rather because feelings of grief, guilt, or decisional inertia make it more difficult to refuse life-prolonging treatment on behalf of a loved one than to simply agree to it. In this situation, the surrogate provides facially valid consent but fails to understand and advocate for what the patient, if able, would choose (or, in the absence of information about the patient's preferences, of what would be in the patient's best interests).

The operation of the typical surrogate consent process means that for patients who do not clearly opt out of life-prolonging treatment before losing decisional capacity, the path of least resistance will often lead to decisions to initiate or continue life-prolonging care – that is often highly invasive and hospital based. Even when the patient has previously refused these measures, family members may struggle to shore up and implement that refusal – as the case study at the beginning of this chapter demonstrates. Grieving and anxious family members will sometimes request that physicians 'do everything' (or at least 'do something') even when further interventions have a very low chance of prolonging life or improving quality of life. It is difficult for physicians to refuse these requests. Physicians can, of course, simply decline to offer more therapeutic or life-prolonging options for dying patients when they think it's medically inappropriate, but the realities of our culture and of the culture of medical care make this path quite challenging. If the family or surrogate requests more interventions, physician liability concerns and, perhaps, a desire to avoid difficult conversations with family members will sometimes result in situations where the now-incapacitated patient receives burdensome interventions that provide little or no benefit and may increase suffering. The systemic pressures on physicians to offer and provide potentially inappropriate care, discussed in Chapter 6, make this default pathway even more difficult to avoid in the surrogate decision-making context.

What is underlying and driving these patterns of care? Physicians and families may disagree as to whether and when therapeutic care and life-sustaining measures cross the line into potentially inappropriate ('futile') care. Futility questions arise in two categories – questions about the subjective value of the medical intervention for the particular patient and questions about the probability that the medical intervention will actually be 'successful' in any objectively discernable way. Without information about an individual patient's preferences regarding continued life-supportive measures, it's difficult to know when to cease providing life-prolonging care to a patient whose condition will not improve. In these circumstances, physicians (and courts) may be reluctant to opine about an incapacitated patient's best interests and may instead err on the side of continued treatment.

WHY SURROGATE DECISION-MAKING IS SO DIFFICULT

Decision-making for incapacitated patients often poses heart-breaking dilemmas for family members. Critically ill patients (and non-critically ill patients with progressive cognitive and physical disability) who have lost decisional capacity depend on someone to make decisions that are consistent with their preferences or best interests, but a combination of emotions, ethical ambivalence, and lack of information makes the job difficult for many surrogates. As described in previous chapters, inadequate physician communication, including failure to initiate conversations about the reality of the patient's condition, overoptimistic estimates of prognosis or therapeutic efficacy, and the use of medical jargon can make the surrogate's job harder. When a patient is unable to make decisions herself, the surrogate must grapple with these issues, and with the added burden of choosing for someone else rather than for herself. Surrogates also often don't know much about their rights and obligations and have had little or no preparation or guidance as to their role – they are thrust into the situation and basically have to learn on the go. For these reasons, conversations about decisions for incapacitated patients also should include a broader contextual discussion of the role of the surrogate – which is to make decisions based on what the patient would choose if able. It is unclear how often this sort of discussion occurs, though the presence of a palliative care expert improves the odds. All of these factors can lead surrogates to consent to more care than the patient might have chosen, if he or she had the capacity to do so.

In the absence of a directly on-point advance directive or a very specific prior conversation with the patient that instructs the surrogate as to the precise question she is facing, it is understandable that surrogates will hesitate to decline care that may prolong the patient's life. Consider, for example, a situation in which a surrogate is asked whether the incapacitated patient would choose to remain on a ventilator. The surrogate may feel fairly confident that the patient would not choose to continue yet may struggle emotionally with the consequences of deciding on the patient's behalf to stop. Prior to the illness, especially if it was sudden (a stroke, for example), the patient may have been very functional at home. No one was thinking about death. Sometimes, the surrogate simply isn't ready to accept the loss of the loved one and so requests all interventions to postpone the loss. Surrogates need time to process and accept the information that physicians provide about diagnosis and prognosis – another reason why dying patients receive care that may not benefit them.

On top of this very human need for time to process, many surrogates, untrained in law and medical ethics, will believe (understandably) that a decision to discontinue life-supportive measures that are already in place makes them the agent or cause of the patient's death. Even in situations in which the medical concept itself is simple to comprehend (as in deciding whether to withdraw ventilator support), the broader ethical challenges inherent in such a decision are daunting. The burden is heavy – surrogates don't want to be the person who makes a 'wrong' decision that might prematurely end the life of someone they love, so they often will request or consent to interventions to prolong life. While removing a feeding tube or extubating a patient may be one factual cause of the patient's death, the true cause of death is the patient's underlying condition. Often it is only after a physician or other professional explains that the patient relies on the life-supportive technology *because* the disease renders his body unable to perform that particular function independently (for example, taking in nourishment by mouth or breathing) that the surrogate begins to understand that the true cause of death is the natural, inexorable process of the illness itself rather than the removal of artificial life-supportive measures.

All of these complexities may derail the operation of substituted judgment, which is rarely straightforward to begin with. Research confirms that surrogates consider the patient's preferences and best interests but also their own personal interests and preferences, personal religious beliefs, and feelings of guilt.[11] Surrogates may view their role not only as the voice of or advocate for the patient but also as an advocate for others and for themselves.[12] The evidence demonstrates that surrogate decision-making in practice does not always conform to the ethical ideals of respect for autonomy and consideration of the patient's best interests but is instead sometimes influenced by the needs and desires of the surrogate. This is neither surprising nor necessarily a bad thing – many patients express the wish to avoid becoming a burden on family members and may explicitly encourage surrogates to consider the totality of the circumstances in making decisions. In fact, some patients specifically prefer that the surrogate make decisions that balance patient preferences with what the surrogate thinks is best, rather than focusing exclusively on substituted judgment, and evidence suggests that this approach reduces surrogate stress.[13]

Even when surrogates *are* trying to decide according to what the patient would choose, evidence suggests that surrogates incorrectly predict patient preferences nearly one-third of the time.[14] These findings validate an older study, in which researchers used paired interviews to assess the accuracy of surrogate decision-makers' predictions, interviewing seriously ill patients and their surrogates about treatment preferences and predictions of patient preferences, respectively. Surrogates were correct two-thirds of the time and incorrect one-third of the

11 Jenna Fritch et al., Making Decisions for Hospitalized Older Adults: Ethical Factors Considered by Family Surrogates, 24 J. Clinical Ethics 125–134 (2013).

12 Lingsheng Li et al., How Surrogate Decision-Makers for Patients with Chronic Critical Illness Perceive and Carry Out Their Role, 46 Crit. Care Med. 699–704 (2018).

13 Daniel P. Sulmasy et al., The TAILORED Study: A Randomized Controlled Trial to Improve Surrogate Decision Making, 54 J. Pain Symptom Management 455–465 (2017).

14 David Shalowitz et al., The Accuracy of Surrogate Decision Makers, 166 Arch. Int. Med. 493–497 (2006).

time.[15] In another study that considered what factors cause surrogates to misunderstand prognosis as conveyed by physicians, the investigators found that in more than half of cases, surrogates misunderstood what they had been told due to comprehension problems *and* because they believed that maintaining optimism and focusing on the patient's individual strengths would help the patient's chances.[16] Surrogates also may fail to take into account the possibility that the patient's prior preferences and priorities can and do shift with serious illness – that patients can adapt to and enjoy life with disability.

Even when surrogates accurately express the goals of care of patients for whom they speak, there is still a real risk that these patients will receive aggressive life-prolonging interventions that they would not choose and that are contrary to the surrogate's instructions. Empirical data suggest that nearly half of patients receive at least one medical intervention that is inconsistent with their preferences. Refusal of CPR is the most often disregarded decision, prompting commentators to urge patients and surrogates to complete DNAR orders as soon as appropriate.[17] Timely and consistent communication between surrogates and clinicians – physicians, nurses, and others – is the best way to reinforce the preferences of incapacitated patients, especially given that medical staff in ICUs regularly change shifts and information may be lost in the transition.

Better informed surrogates, particularly with regard to prognosis, do better with the process overall – and they generally want to receive information that will help them in their task. In one study of the perspectives of surrogate decision-makers, 93 percent of those interviewed believed that withholding information about prognosis was an unacceptable means of preserving hope and instead emphasized the importance of timely, truthful information to help them prepare for the patient's death and to provide emotional support to the patient.[18] The evidence also suggests that family members who are well informed about a patient's poor prognosis are far more likely to opt for comfort care. For example, in a study of nursing home residents with advanced dementia, those whose surrogates understood that these patients had a poor prognosis and would likely experience distressing symptoms at the end of life were significantly less likely to consent to burdensome interventions such as artificial nutrition, parenteral therapy (IV hydration or antibiotics), emergency department visits, and hospitalization. While nearly all of the health care

[15] Daniel P. Sulmasy et al., The Accuracy of Substituted Judgments in Patients with Terminal Diagnoses, 128 Ann. Intern. Med. 621–629 (1998).

[16] Douglas B. White et al., Prevalence of and Factors Related to Discordance About Prognosis Between Physicians and Surrogate Decision Makers of Critically Ill Patients, 315 JAMA 2086–2094 (2016).

[17] Amber R. Comer et al., Assessment of Discordance between Surrogate Care Goals and Medical Treatment Provided to Older Adults with Serious Illness, 3 JAMA Network Open e205179 (2020) (finding that 46.6 percent of patients received treatment that was discordant with the goals expressed by their surrogate decision-maker).

[18] Latifat Apatira et al., Hope, Truth, and Preparing for Death: Perspectives of Surrogate Decision-Makers, 149 Annals Internal Med. 861–868 (2008).

surrogates in the study believed that the primary goal of care was comfort, only a few reported having received information about prognosis from the treating physician.[19] Taking the time to explain to surrogates the incapacitated patient's poor prognosis helps surrogates appreciate more fully how burdensome interventions may cause avoidable suffering. Without this perspective on the patient's situation, surrogates are more likely to consent to burdensome care – the opposite of their expressed goal of comfort care.

Empirical evidence demonstrates that surrogate decision-makers experience significant stress and grief during and after the process of making health care decisions for their loved ones. About one-third of surrogates actually experience posttraumatic stress disorder (PTSD) after a family member dies in an intensive care unit.[20] Interventions to provide emotional support to surrogates had limited effectiveness against stress, though surrogates appreciated the improved emphasis on communication, and patients in the intervention group had shorter ICU stays.[21] Surrogates also frequently face interpersonal conflict with other family members, which adds to their emotional burden at a time when all family members are already in distress.[22] The fact that the surrogate is highest in a statutory hierarchy of potential decision-makers or has even been formally appointed by the patient will not prevent other family members from voicing objections to the surrogate's choices. Decisional paralysis, or worse, may follow. In these situations, the treating physician may accede to the demands of the most vocal and aggressive (including litigation-threatening) family member, even if this means initiating or continuing life-prolonging measures or attempting CPR in contravention to the patient's preferences (as expressed by the surrogate). Those family members who have been least involved in the care of the incapacitated patient sometimes appear on the scene, in denial, and feeling guilty or angry about the patient's situation, and demand inappropriate and aggressive care. There is even a technical term for this pattern of behavior – 'the Daughter from California Syndrome'.[23] In this high-stress context, it is no surprise that surrogates find it quite challenging to weigh the risks and benefits of various medical options in the context of the incapacitated patient's values and preferences.

Occasionally, there is even cause to suspect that a surrogate deliberately fails to act out of good will and concern for the patient. A physician once told me a horrifying story: his elderly patient was terminally ill with multiple medical conditions and was

19 Susan L. Mitchell et al., The Clinical Course of Advanced Dementia, 361 New Eng. J. Med. 1529–1538 (2009) (96 percent versus 18 percent).

20 David Wendler & Annette Rid, Systematic Review: The Effect on Surrogates of Making Treatment Decisions for Others, 154 Ann. Intern. Med. 336–346 (2011).

21 Douglas B. White et al., A Randomized Trial of a Family-Support Intervention in Intensive Care Units, 378 New Eng. J. Med. 2365–2375 (2018).

22 Yael Schenker et al., I Don't Want to Be the One Saying "We Should Just Let Him Die": Intrapersonal Tensions Experienced by Surrogate Decision Makers in the ICU, 27 J. Gen. Intern. Med. 1657–1665 (2012).

23 David W. Molloy et al., Decision Making in the Incompetent Elderly: "The Daughter from California Syndrome," 39 J. Am. Geriatrics Soc. 396–399 (1991).

nearing death. The patient's two daughters took turns staying in her hospital room on a continuous basis and demanded every possible intervention to prolong their mother's life, including CPR, intubation, and other invasive and painful procedures. The physician explained that their mother was dying and that it would be kindest to let her die in peace. The daughters replied that they wanted everything done so that (to quote the physician's exact words) "the bitch would suffer for as long as possible." The physician requested a consult from the hospital's ethics committee but, after discussion with members of the committee, the daughters were unmoved. The patient died shortly after. Such a case goes beyond being wrong about what the patient would choose and moves into the surreal realm of using medical technology opportunistically, apparently for revenge. It certainly illustrates the value of formally appointing a trusted individual as a health care agent, especially because these documents also allow the patient to explicitly exclude from decision-making those whom she doesn't trust.

THE LIMITATIONS OF ADVANCE DIRECTIVES

If a patient has not in advance (and ideally in writing) opted out of further treatment or life-prolonging technology or expressed any specific preferences as to future medical care, the default often will be to continue whatever care and technology is in place, and it will be up to the surrogate whether to disturb the status quo. Advance directives can promote patient autonomy because they formalize an individual's preferences about treatment choices and provide both guidance and guide rails for family members and treating physicians. (Advance care planning can also reduce costs – physical and financial – by avoiding the provision of potentially inappropriate care.) While one patient may prefer to focus solely on comfort, another may request all measures to extend life, even if these interventions (such as CPR, artificial nutrition and hydration, ventilation, late-stage chemotherapy, and dialysis) may increase suffering and reduce quality of life. Most patients who complete advance directives do not want burdensome interventions such as resuscitation at the end of life.[24] Unfortunately, only about a quarter to a third of Americans have any sort of advance directive,[25] although elderly and seriously ill patients increasingly complete these documents.[26] The relatively new Medicare reimbursement for physicians who engage in advance care planning with patients may boost

[24] Melissa M. Garrido et al., Quality of Life and Cost of Care at the End of Life: The Role of Advance Directives, 49 J. Pain & Symptom Mgmt. 828–835 (2015).

[25] Jaya K. Rao, et al., Completion of Advance Directives Among U.S. Consumers, 46 Am. J. Prev. Med. 65–79 (2014); Kuldeep N. Yadav et al., Approximately One in Three U.S. Adults Completes Any Type of Advance Directive for End-of-Life Care, 36 Health Aff. 1244–1251 (July 2017).

[26] In the studied cohort of patients, 67.6 percent of patients who required surrogate decision-making had completed a living will, a durable power of attorney for health care, or both. Maria Silveira et al., Advance Directives and Outcomes of Surrogate Decision Making Before Death, 362 New Eng. J. Med. 1211–1218 (2010).

these numbers in the future, but the jury is still out.[27] In the absence of these documents or any detailed prior specific discussion, it can be difficult for surrogates to know what an incapacitated patient would choose, even for what appear to be straightforward, binary choices like whether or not to decline attempted resuscitation in the event of cardiac arrest.

Advance care planning documents (sometimes referred to collectively as 'individual instructions for health care') include living wills, values history forms, do-not-resuscitate orders, do-not-hospitalize orders, and POLST (Physician Orders for Life Sustaining Treatment) forms. Some states have no required living will form, but nearly all states have enacted statutes that permit individuals to formally appoint a health care decision-maker (called an agent, a proxy, or an attorney-in-fact).[28] The formally appointed health care agent must make decisions either based on the patient's separately executed advance directive or, if none is available, based on the patient's values and preferences as the agent understands them. Merely appointing a health care agent or proxy, however – even a spouse – doesn't ensure that the parties have communicated with any specificity about preferences regarding end-of-life care.

States vary widely in their approaches to advance directives, their enforceability, and even their desirability. Some states expressly forbid requiring patients to complete advance directives,[29] but others have taken a variety of steps to encourage their citizens to complete an advance directive by simplifying the process and recognizing the validity of out-of-state documents.[30] In recent years, some states have attempted to encourage health care providers to consult existing advance directives by creating registries that make these documents more easily accessible to providers, especially in emergencies.[31] Still other states have expanded the contexts in which advance directives are applicable, including legislation that recognizes various POLST forms, which allow patients to request that physicians withhold life-sustaining treatments and less aggressive interventions such as antibiotics and may also include patient preferences for resuscitation, intubation, artificial nutrition and hydration, and hospital transfer.[32] Patients with POLST forms in place are less likely to be admitted to an ICU or to receive burdensome interventions and are more likely to receive comfort care, though having a treatment-limiting POLST in place is no

[27] Kimberly Pelland et al., Assessment of First-Year Use of Medicare's Advance Care Planning Billing Codes, 179 JAMA Internal Med. 827–828 (2019).

[28] For an example of a proxy appointment form, see Massachusetts Medical Society, Health Care Proxy Information and Forms, which includes discussion questions to guide conversation between the patient and the appointed agent, www.massmed.org/Patient-Care/Health-Topics/Health-Care-Proxies-and-End-of-Life-Care/Health-Care-Proxy-Information-and-Forms/. Massachusetts has no official living will form.

[29] E.g., Conn. Gen. Stat. Ch. 368w § 19a-580b.

[30] For example, North Carolina's statute explicitly recognizes advance directives created in other states as long as they were valid under the law of the state where they were created. N.C.G.S. § 90–321(d1)(l).

[31] E.g., Or. Rev. Stat. § 127.666 (establishing a statewide registry for POLST documents).

[32] National POLST, https://polst.org/programs-in-your-state/.

guarantee of avoiding goal-discordant care.[33] States that have implemented POLST have created a structural opportunity for physicians to talk with patients or surrogates about the patient's prognosis and to make some in-advance collaborative decisions about life-sustaining treatments such as ventilator use, artificial nutrition and hydration, and CPR. At this point, the implementation of POLST is uneven, and it's too soon to tell whether it will lead to meaningful improvement in patient-directed care, but it shows some promise because POLST forms are usually readily available as part of the patient's medical record and carry the imprimatur of a formal, medical decision. In addition to these state law efforts, commentators have urged the development of a simple and effective form that will comply with the legal requirements of all states, and most who favor reform agree that legislatures should enact laws that make the execution of advance directives simple and affordable for their citizens. The federal government's separate effort to increase advance directive completion via the Patient Self-Determination Act (PSDA) (enacted back in 1990) hasn't had much of a positive impact on advance directive completion.[34]

Advance directives may have limited utility for many patients. Depending on the law of the state in which it was executed, an advance directive may apply only when a patient is terminally ill, or it may also apply to patients in persistent vegetative states, irreversible coma, or other nonterminal conditions.[35] About one-third of states exclude permanent unconsciousness as a condition for which advance directives can be drafted to direct the withdrawal of life-prolonging care. In these states, even if a patient like Theresa Schiavo had completed a written directive declining artificial nutrition and hydration in the case of permanent unconsciousness, the existence of the document would not guarantee care that complies with her preferences. Because states frequently restrict applicability of advance directives to terminal illness, patients who suffer from chronic and debilitating disease have more limited options to direct their care in the event of incapacity, such as the appointment of a health care proxy.

In some instances, physicians may be reluctant to implement the patient's wishes as expressed in an advance directive if the patient's relatives are protesting; understandably, physicians worry about conflict and potential legal liability. Family disagreement with documented preferences and physicians' concerns about litigation may leave physicians with the unpalatable choice – either following the directive or facing the wrath of some part of the patient's family. Since at least three-quarters of states allow individual health care providers to refuse to carry out a patient's wish for withdrawal or withholding of life-prolonging treatment, either for reasons of conscience or for no reason at all,[36] backing away from family dissent

33 Robert Y. Lee et al., Association of Physician Orders for Life-Sustaining Treatment with ICU Admission among Patients Hospitalized Near the End of Life, 323 JAMA 950–960 (2020),

34 General Accounting Office, Patient Self-Determination Act: Providers Offer Information on Advance Directives but Effectiveness Uncertain (Aug. 28, 1995) www.gao.gov/products/hehs-95-135.

35 Meisel et al., The Right to Die §7.07.

36 Stephen Arons, Current Issues in End-of-Life Care, in Berzoff & Silverman, Living with Dying p. 734 (Columbia University Press, 2004).

carries less legal risk. Empirical evidence also indicates that nearly half of a cohort of surveyed physicians would refuse to comply with a patient's prior stated preferences to withdraw or withhold life supportive technology under some circumstances.[37] While most state laws regarding advance directives insulate physicians from liability if they comply in good faith with the provisions of an advance directive, they do not compel that compliance,[38] allowing physicians to default to high-intensity care. Even so, there are sometimes penalties and legal consequences for ignoring advance directives.[39] While the role of physician conscience and the moral values guiding state legislatures deserve consideration, this state of affairs doesn't exactly encourage advance care planning.

Advance directives also are not necessarily accurate predictors of what an individual would actually choose under the particular circumstances when incapacitated by illness. Patients who complete these documents prior to the onset of serious illness must respond to hypothetical situations that they have not yet experienced.[40] They have difficulty predicting their preferences in advance because they misunderstand illnesses and treatments, underestimate (or overestimate) their ability to endure suffering, think about their choices only superficially, and may change their minds over time.[41] Decision science suggests that the complexity of future unknown contingencies and the unfamiliar nature of the choices that patients face coalesce in ways that make it difficult to form preferences that can then be documented via an advance directive.[42] For this reason, commentators have suggested strategically timing advance care planning discussions to optimize the likelihood that the decisions patients make will accurately reflect their values and goals – not too early in the disease progress and not too late.[43] Moreover, sometimes, what a patient chooses for the hypothetical future conflicts with what's in his best interests in that future reality, leaving physicians to place more decisional authority (and stress) on surrogates.[44] Despite all of these complexities, there is some evidence that when physicians discuss advance care planning with patients (still a relatively rare event), those patients receive less intensive therapies such as chemotherapy and intubation and

37 Neil J. Farber et al., Physicians' Decisions to Withhold and Withdraw Life-Sustaining Treatment, 166 Arch. Int. Med. 560–564 (2006).

38 Meisel et al., The Right to Die §7.10[E],[G].

39 Thaddeus Mason Pope, Legal Briefing: New Penalties for Disregarding Advance Directives and Do-Not-Resuscitate Orders, 28 J. Clinical Ethics 74–81 (2017).

40 Peter A. Ubel et al., Misimagining the Unimaginable: The Disability Paradox and Health Care Decision Making, 24 Health Psychol. S57–S62 (2005).

41 Angela Fagerlin & Carl E. Schneider, Enough: The Failure of the Living Will, Hastings Ctr. Rep., 30–42 (March/April 2004).

42 Amber E. Barnato, Challenges in Understanding and Respecting Patients' Preferences, 36 Health Aff. 1252–1257 (2017).

43 J. Andrew Billings & Rachelle Bernacki, Strategic Targeting of Advance Care Planning Interventions: The Goldilocks Phenomenon, 174 JAMA Intern. Med. 1085–1092 (2014).

44 Alexander K. Smith et al., When Previously Expressed Wishes Conflict With Best Interests, 173 JAMA Internal Med. 1241–1245 (2013).

are more likely to enroll in hospice. Paradoxically, these same patients were more likely to be hospitalized, though the researchers speculated that they may have required hospitalization because they tended to be sicker than those who did not discuss advance care planning with physicians.[45]

On top of these problems, advance directives sometimes may work to protect patient autonomy (i.e., they can announce a patient's choice to reject CPR, for example, or to decline artificial nutrition or ventilation), but they do little to promote *authenticity* in decision-making. Authenticity means more than documenting a choice – it means exercising that choice in a meaningful way that reflects holistically the patient's values, preferences, and beliefs within the context of her current, and evolving, life circumstances. Authenticity also requires that patients understand the difference between desire and choice – we may desire some things that we may choose not to act on.[46] Diligently considering these future scenarios and discussing them in detail with family members or in writing is unappealing to many people. Those individuals who *do* confront end-of-life questions and document their preferences still may be influenced, consciously or unconsciously, by family and societal expectations about what medical interventions the patient should accept (or decline) and when. They may also hurry through the uncomfortable thought process that form completion requires. These are not the sorts of questions that can be answered in an attorney's office or at a hospital admissions desk with a few moments of reflection – they require far more than simply ticking boxes on a one-size-fits-all form. An authentic decision requires a reasonably detailed understanding of the relevant options and their potential impact on the patient's prognosis and quality of life in the context of the patient's values and goals. To achieve authenticity, the patient must think carefully about the various possible scenarios and make some decisions about what sort of medical care he is willing to endure and what life-prolonging measures he might wish to avoid. Advance directives drafted with these goals in mind, therefore, must speak with specificity about the patient's instructions for care when he suffers from a self-defined 'intolerable indignity' as a result of a medical condition.[47] This process requires the confrontation of death, its inevitability, and perhaps eventually its desirability.

For all of their potential promise, advance care planning documents are frequently inaccessible at key decision-making points, irrelevant or insufficiently specific to address the actual medical decision at hand, overruled by family members, or ignored by health care providers. When physicians do communicate with their patients about advance care planning, evidence suggests that they spend little time

45 Deepshikha Charan Ashana et al., Advance Care Planning Claims and Health Care Utilization among Seriously Ill Patients Near the End of Life, 2 JAMA Network Open, DOI: 10.1001/jamanetworkopen.2019.14471(2019).

46 Daniel Brudney, Choosing for Another: Beyond Autonomy and Best Interests, 39 Hastings Ctr. Rep. 31–37 (2009).

47 Norman L. Cantor, Making Advance Directives Meaningful, 4 Psychol. Pub. Pol'y & L. 629–652 (1998).

discussing patients' values and attitudes, particularly toward uncertainty in medical decision-making.[48] The fact remains that most end-of-life decisions are made based on conversations between physicians, patients (when able), and families at the point of the serious illness – and so, these conversations become very important as a means to providing care that is consistent with patient preferences. For all of these reasons, commentators have suggested abandoning efforts to encourage the utilization of advance directives.[49]

Despite the limitations of advance directives, the inherent and immediate benefit to the individual of thinking about and executing an advance directive or discussing preferences with a health care proxy is worth a mention. The completion of any advance directive – at any point in life – provides an opportunity for individuals to make an effort to consider and articulate to themselves and others what is most important to them in the face of life-threatening illness. Engaging with these documents provides a structural context in which individuals also can address their mortality more broadly, and an opportunity for each individual to reorient himself individually to his goals and approaches to life (including quality of life) that have meaning on a personal level. When advance care planning shifts from filling forms to substantive discussion about a patient's wishes, fears, and preferences, an advance directive, coupled with a well-informed surrogate, can help patients avoid burdensome and unwanted care at the end of life. A number of patient- and family-directed initiatives, such as The Conversation Project[50] and Death Over Dinner,[51] are designed to promote discussion of end-of-life matters. While it's likely that those who participate in these types of activities are a self-selected bunch who are already inclined to address the fact of mortality, it's encouraging to see these programs gaining popularity in the United States.

In addition to efforts like the PSDA that focus on regularizing the process of making advance directives and promoting interstate recognition, states can publicize the purposes and availability of these documents and could promote them as part of the daily business of being a citizen of the state. In La Crosse County, Wisconsin, a program called Respecting Choices has succeeded in doing just that.[52] Although the idea of *mandating* advance directives raises serious concerns about privacy and autonomy, there seems no reason to discourage states from promoting the execution of these documents. Just as in the United States, we ask people to indicate on their driver's licenses their willingness to be organ donors, general practitioners could similarly make an annual inquiry about memorializing end-of-life preferences (though physicians already have way too much to accomplish

48 James A. Tulsky et al., Opening the Black Box: How Do Physicians Communicate About Advance Directives?, 129 Arch. Int. Med. 441–449 (1998).

49 Fagerlin & Schneider, Enough: The Failure of the Living Will.

50 The Conversation Project, https://theconversationproject.org/.

51 Death Over Dinner, https://deathoverdinner.org/.

52 Respecting Choices has now joined the Coalition to Transform Advanced Care (CTAT), www.thectac.org/.

with their patients during the limited time allocated for an annual exam). States also can educate their citizens about the value of periodic review and encourage individuals to revisit their choices as their values, experiences, and circumstances change.[53] States might even consider including information about end-of-life law and ethics in their public school health curricula. Teaching young adults about these issues (along with safe sex practices and good nutrition and the rest) would likely help improve their comfort level with thinking about and discussing these matters throughout their lives. Intergenerational contact between the very old and the very young also can help make aging and death less of a frightening unknown. There are programs in the United States that offer child care at long-term care and assisted-living facilities. Both the old and the young benefit enormously from this sort of mixing.[54] Over time, education about advance care planning and regularizing inquiries and updates could make advance directives a natural part of citizenship, like obtaining vehicle registration stickers or paying property taxes. More broadly, all of these interventions could, perhaps, help demystify the prospect of death.

All that said, advance directives may give patients who complete them a sense of control (or at least a sense of peace) over their future health care should they lose decisional capacity, but, in multiple respects, this sense of control is an illusion. Advance care planning creates a false sense of control over the dying process, because it addresses (and more often in theory than in practice) the externalities of dying, not the emotions and inner struggle of the person approaching death.

THE EXTRA LAYERS OF CLINICAL AND ETHICAL UNCERTAINTY

Various manifestations of uncertainty, along with cognitive biases and bounded rationality (discussed in Chapter 8), combine to make decision-making even more difficult for surrogates to navigate. First, *clinical uncertainty* affects the entire decision process from the perspective of both the physicians and the patient and family members, including the surrogate. For example, uncertainty about prognosis in the case of terminal illness adds to the complexity of decisions about withholding or withdrawing treatment or life-supportive measures, and surrogates may therefore hesitate to make choices that will theoretically shorten life, even when the patient's hope of recovery is gone and his quality of life is poor.[55]

Consider again the example from Chapter 8: A patient is offered a late-stage cancer treatment. This treatment has a hypothetical 60 percent chance of 'success' (defined as prolongation of life) and a 40 percent chance of 'no success' (defined as

53 For example, New York created a program to educate the public about the need for advance care planning and other health-related matters. N.Y. Pub. Health Law § 207.

54 Tiffany R. Jansen, The Preschool Inside a Nursing Home, The Atlantic (Jan. 20, 2016).

55 Portions of this section of the chapter draw on previously published work. Barbara A. Reich, Surrogate Decision-Making: Clinical Uncertainty, Rational Apathy, and the Problem of Trust, 15 Ethics Med. & Pub. Health 100523 (2020) (used with permission).

failing to prolong life while subjecting the patient to terrible side effects) based on past application and experience with similarly situated patients (but, of course, not this particular patient). It is known that this treatment kills cancer cells – this is an example of an in-advance knowable fact that is also actually known – a 'known known'. It is also known that this treatment will do damage to other parts of the body, including healthy organs, but it is not known what or how bad the damage and resulting adverse effects might be in a particular patient – this is an example of an *ex ante* 'known unknown' contingent outcome. Based on the known knowns and known unknowns, the surrogate must decide whether to consent to the treatment on behalf of the incapacitated patient.

With the responsibility for another person's life looming, the surrogate must make decisions within the realm of these uncertainties about the patient's future and, perhaps, also while processing what the patient's experiences portend for the surrogate herself one day. The surrogate carries the burden of the patient's rational apathy (putting aside future thoughts of death) as well as her own. As the surrogate has been told that the treatment works in 60 percent of patients, she may feel pressure to try it, regardless of what the patient may previously have said. Also, recall from the prior discussion in Chapter 8 that acknowledging these points is only the first step to understanding the full extent and impact of clinical uncertainty in making medical decisions. A surrogate's decision based on the statistical 60 percent chance of benefit described earlier also has to entirely ignore the additional category of 'unknown unknowns' – those variables impacting future individual patient outcomes that are objectively unknowable and unquantifiable at the point of decision-making. To make as rational a decision as possible, surrogates and physicians should acknowledge that unknown unknowns always exist and may substantially impact the prognosis calculus for a particular patient, and that they can't know the extent of the unknown unknowns or how they might apply to the patient's particular case. Notwithstanding this non-quantifiable Knightian uncertainty, the surrogate will have to decide based on statistical averages, unless the now-incapacitated patient has done her the favor of clearly directing her to decline the proposed treatment.

Similar to rationally apathetic patients, surrogates are likely to consent to or acquiesce to continuing medical interventions – even when the statistical likelihood of 'success' is far less than the 60 percent in the hypothetical example – because of an intuitive belief or hope that the patient will fall into the success group and despite the fact that there may be no scientific or medical basis for that hope. Surrogates tend to disbelieve grim prognostic estimates from physicians and to believe that their family member's particular strengths will lead to a better-than-predicted outcome. In a study of surrogates for critically ill patients in the ICU, well over half of those who were told that a *hypothetical* patient had a 5 percent chance of survival interpreted the prognosis optimistically. As one surrogate explained in a follow-up interview, "And we are talking about my father in this case, not just any patient. I know that my father could do better than what the doctor is saying . . . and I think he will." The study authors observed a high incidence of overly optimistic expectations, particularly when the estimated chances of survival were very low.[56] This desire to retain hope at all cost and to therefore discount poor prognostic estimates is only human. The problem is that these feelings can skew the surrogate's thought processes as to whether the patient himself would in fact desire any of the medical interventions being offered.

It is quite understandable that if even a small possibility of cure or significant life prolongation exists, surrogates will rather want to acquiesce to all interventions that might help, no matter what the statistical likelihood of success might be based on past clinical evidence. This is especially the case in the absence of clear instructions from the now-incapacitated patient. Proactively deciding to the contrary requires more, emotionally and cognitively, of the surrogate than accepting on the patient's behalf all care that is offered. In principle, acquiescing to continued medical care will nearly always be easier for surrogates in terms of cognitive and emotional load than declining it, and a decision to withdraw life-prolonging technology already in place may also *feel* more difficult than a refusal to initiate new forms of life support. The old saying, "When in doubt, do nothing" nicely illustrates the effects of the status quo bias – the cognitive effect caused by our standard preference in the face of unwelcome news. When faced with difficult decisions, people tend to stick with the status quo because they feel overwhelmed, fear losing what they currently have, and fear that they will regret decisions that implement a change in circumstances.[57] There is also evidence that having to decide among multiple options, compared with considering a single choice, further increases status quo bias.[58]

The status quo bias seems to play an outsized role not only in the cognitive processes of patients but also in those of their surrogates. If the surrogate, as part of the discussion, is made aware of this normal and common bias in favor of the status quo, it may become easier to consider alternatives, even difficult choices such as discontinuing life-prolonging technology. A physician could explain that, "I know it can seem easier to just keep doing what we're doing, but that may not be the best thing under the circumstances." Again, this is asking even more of physicians as part of the discussion process – to recognize and explain the impact of various cognitive biases in others and in themselves.

On top of these complexities, within this milieu of clinical uncertainty, surrogates also must process uncertainty as to the accuracy of their prediction of what the incapacitated patient would choose (separately and apart from the clinical uncertainty inherent in various treatment choices). Even when the patient has previously

56 Lucas S. Zier et al., Surrogate Decision Makers' Interpretation of Prognostic Information: A Mixed-Methods Study, 156 Ann. Intern. Med. 360–366 (2012).

57 Stephen M. Fleming, et al., Overcoming Status Quo Bias in the Human Brain, 107 Proc. Nat'l Acad. Science (PNAS) 6005–6009 (2010).

58 Donald A. Redelmeier & Eldar Shafir, Medical Decision Making in Situations That Offer Multiple Alternatives, 273 JAMA 302–305 (1995).

instructed the surrogate, it's sometimes impossible to know whether a medical decision is consistent with the patient's preferences or is even in a patient's best interests. The patient may merely have said, "Don't let them keep me alive if I won't be able to enjoy life," leaving the surrogate to the messy job of forecasting survival and quality of life based on imprecise instructions. (Of course, a *too* precise set of instructions – as in "Don't let them keep me alive if I can't do the *New York Times* crossword anymore" – may separately leave the surrogate struggling with whether *any* further intervention – even something that might seem otherwise sensible to try – would meet the high standard set by the patient.) Uncertainty about this substituted judgment process may lead surrogates to err on the side of continued treatment or life-sustaining measures. Since empirical evidence suggests that surrogates incorrectly predict the choice of incapacitated patients fairly often, this is a separate burden on surrogates – the fear of or at least ambivalence about getting the decision 'wrong'.

This in turn raises a broader question: is the sole goal of surrogate decision-making to ascertain what the incapacitated patient's preferences would be under the circumstances and to make decisions accordingly? If we focus on implementing the prior preferences of now-incapacitated patients by looking for an accurate representation of what the patient would choose, then the answer is "yes." Perhaps a highest-utility surrogate decision is one that represents the best and most authentic approximation of what the patient's preferences would be in a given situation. But this answer overlooks the underlying struggle that surrogates may experience when they disagree, based on their own preferences or beliefs, with what they perceive would be the incapacitated patient's choice. As the evidence discussed earlier in this chapter suggests, this disagreement is not uncommon and does in fact motivate some surrogates' choices.

There is a clear distinction between accuracy in substituted judgment and ethical 'correctness'. The problem with the narrow focus on accuracy is that, for some surrogates, announcing and carrying out the patient's preference may feel normatively wrong, particularly when the surrogate disagrees with what she thinks the patient would choose – an *ethical uncertainty* scenario. Accurate decisions as to what would be the patient's choice are not necessarily ethically correct decisions (and the ethically 'correct' decision in some scenarios is not always obvious). For example, a surrogate might express the patient's wish to receive all life-prolonging treatment, even when the patient is permanently unconscious, and this might be an accurate surrogate decision, but one of questionable ethical validity (considering, for example, ethical values of dignity or just utilization of medical resources). A surrogate may believe that it is wrong to request all life-prolonging care on behalf of the incapacitated patient in a situation where the benefit to the patient is only life extension in a permanently unconscious state. Alternatively, a surrogate may also believe that the patient would be wrong to refuse life-prolonging care when in a permanently unconscious state because, for her, all life is valuable and only nature (or a deity) should determine when someone dies. Empirical evidence suggests that surrogates who attend religious services of any denomination are more likely to request continued treatment for their incapacitated family member, perhaps out of a sense of altruism or guilt.[59] This sort of decisional dissonance no doubt contributes to the struggle that some surrogates experience, particularly in declining therapeutic or life-prolonging care in a situation that will lead to the incapacitated patient's death from the underlying terminal condition.

Adding to the problem of uncertainty about patient wishes, it is well documented that people often underestimate their future tolerance of illness, including their willingness to live with decreased quality of life and increased disability.[60] For this reason, surrogates might believe that although the patient's prior expressed wishes to discontinue treatment were clear, the patient could have been wrong about his limited willingness to tolerate burdensome medical care in exchange for extended life and would now decide differently. On that basis, the surrogate might authorize additional treatment to preserve the life of the patient. These scenarios provide just a few examples of the substantive complexity and uncertainty inherent in the surrogate decision-making process. Physicians who suspect that the surrogate is not being honest or accurate face a dilemma: to abide by the surrogate's expressed view of the patient's wishes or to probe the validity of the surrogate's views.

The impact of all of these forms of uncertainty can lead surrogates to consent to more care than the incapacitated patient might have chosen, prolonging suffering at the end of life. Even in situations where the medical concept itself is simple to comprehend, the broader ethical and cognitive challenges inherent in the decisional process are daunting. In such cases, surrogate decision-makers may default to a binary, all-or-nothing approach rather than engaging more actively in what is really a shades-of-grey, incremental, ethically and factually complex, and constantly evolving medical dilemma (with multiple decision points). Recognition of the role of uncertainty and resultant decisional apathy (deciding not to decide – in advance or at the point of decision) in health care decision-making may help physicians (who, again, are repeat players) to more effectively guide surrogate decision-making. This in turn may help surrogate decision-makers in their quest to make good decisions on behalf of patients and may provide surrogates with some comfort that they have done well (and can never 'do perfect') in the face of an emotionally and ethically challenging dilemma. Surrogate decision-makers may, in fact, find it quite liberating that, given clinical uncertainty, there is sometimes no single correct decision possible in *absolute* terms. In this context, surrogates can only aim for a satisfactory decision – not a best choice – while being fully cognizant that the decision may still differ from what the patient would actually have chosen if given the ability, information, and opportunity to decide.

59 Daniel P. Sulmasy et al., The Accuracy of Substituted Judgments in Patients with Terminal Diagnoses, 128 Annals Internal Med. 621–629 (1998).

60 Marsha N. Winntink et al., Stability of Preferences for End-of-Life Treatment After 3 Years of Follow-Up: The Johns Hopkins Precursors Study, 168 Arch. Internal Med. 2125–2130 (2008).

RACE AND SURROGATE DECISION-MAKING

What do the overall inequalities, biases, and lack of trust among Black and other racial minority patients and families mean for surrogate decision-making? The inherent racism in health care delivery that creates a profound level of distrust in the medical system may further exacerbate all of the difficulties inherent in surrogate decision-making. All of the obstacles to and burdens of good surrogate decision-making discussed here are made worse – unavoidably so – when patients and their surrogates, justifiably, lack threshold trust in the veracity and beneficence of physicians and in the health care system. Clinical uncertainty (and related forms of uncertainty) looms large in the context of surrogate decision-making. Physicians themselves understand that uncertainty as to diagnosis, test results, proposed treatments, and prognosis requires the exercise of clinical discretion. They may be less aware, however, that this discretion as to what treatments or life-sustaining measures to offer may be influenced by stereotypes and unconscious biases.[61]

On top of these problems, the White cultural presumptions about the primacy of autonomy and the role of the family in medical decision-making may not fit well with the approaches to these matters in other cultures. Calls for greater cultural sensitivity, when properly implemented, may lead to improvement, but the complexities of understanding other cultures and how they impact a patient's medical decision-making can't be easily addressed with a quick bit of training.[62] Neither can racial bias and structural racism in health care. While it is always emotionally challenging to decline or discontinue potentially life-prolonging treatment for an incapacitated loved one, it must be even more difficult when the surrogate distrusts the information she is receiving about the patient's medical condition and prognosis. As the evidence in Chapter 7 suggests, this broken trust dynamic appears to reduce rates of hospice utilization for Black and other racial minority patients, causing avoidable suffering at the end of life.

WITH CARING COMES COURAGE

As explained in Chapter 1, at the system-wide level, there is ample evidence of a major misalignment between the kind of medical care at the end of life that most patients say they prefer – a focus on comfort care – and what many patients actually receive – high-intensity, high-burden therapeutic and life-prolonging care, which tends to produce more suffering than comfort. At least some of this misalignment arises because physicians offer medical care that incapacitated patients would, if they could, refuse – and that family members agree to, for all of the reasons described here. Patients with life-threatening illness and, indeed, all adults would do their loved ones a favor by

61 Ana I. Balsa et al., Clinical Uncertainty and Healthcare Disparities, 29 Am. J. Law & Med. 203–219 (2003).

62 Insoo Hyun, Waiver of Informed Consent, Cultural Sensitivity, and the Problem of Unjust Family Traditions, 32 Hastings Ctr. Rep. 14–22 (2002).

having periodic discussions about their end-of-life wishes and worries. The act of considering and discussing end-of-life choices, whether via a formal document-completion process or simply as conversations with family members and physicians, will do more to prevent conflicts and overutilization of life-sustaining technology than any state statute or medical association guideline. While this suggestion may not appeal to many (or most) people, there are some for whom the idea has merit. Still, there are at least two obstacles to these discussions – discomfort with discussing mortality and a lack of information and education about these topics, especially prior to whatever event lands the patient on the medical conveyor belt.

Surrogate decision-makers understandably struggle with their own emotions – the impending loss of a dearly loved person can make clear-eyed consideration of the choices at hand quite challenging. Grief, especially at its freshest, can make the sufferer lose sight of the broader arc of life – that of the dying patient and his own. W. H. Auden captured this feeling well in 'Funeral Blues', which begins with "Stop all the clocks, cut off the telephone," and ends with this:

> The stars are not wanted now: put out every one;
> Pack up the moon and dismantle the sun;
> Pour away the ocean and sweep up the wood;
> For nothing now can ever come to any good.[63]

In the face of this kind of ineluctable grief – which affects at least some surrogates – we ask a person to make decisions that will in many cases lead to the rapid demise of a much-loved person. It is hardly surprising that surrogates struggle with the task. The process of surrogate decision-making brings death up close and personal because the surrogate must confront not only the patient's death but also his own mortality.

Making decisions for seriously ill and dying patients is rarely simple or emotionally and cognitively costless for the surrogate. Systemic factors contribute to the burden on surrogate decision-makers, and various forms of uncertainty lie beneath the surface of most decision scenarios, adding to the burden for both surrogates and physicians. For minority-race patients and surrogates, distrust in the medical system will often contribute to added uncertainty about the optimal choice, even if the surrogate in these situations feels fairly confident in her assessment of what the patient would choose. None of this is going to get easier any time soon. In these times, with a large segment of the political system that seeks to reduce rather than protect access to health care in general (and so to high-quality end-of-life care more specifically), there is little cause for optimism, and the impact of mortality denial continues unabated. The system – governmental and health care – is not going to save us. Instead, it is up to individual patients, surrogates, and physicians to have the candid, factually based, and emotionally difficult conversations necessary to make decisions on behalf of the most vulnerable among us, which is all of us as we approach the end of life.

[63] W.H. Auden, Funeral Blues, The Year's Poetry (London, 1938).

10

Resolving Conflicts at the End of Life

It is not conflict of opinions that has made history so violent but conflict of belief in opinions, that is to say conflict of convictions.

—Friedrich Nietzsche[1]

Disputes about care for dying patients are rife with emotions. They are also, unfortunately, quite common.[2] In the event that a patient has not made and documented end-of-life decisions in advance and loses the ability to make those decisions, the baton passes to her surrogate decision-maker. When that surrogate elects to go against the tide of family (or professional medical) thinking, or some other conflict flares up, then the worst-case scenario arises. Disputes about the care of the patient move from the bedside to a more formal setting. The incapacitated patient's very private dying process becomes the focus of an institutional dispute resolution procedure. All of the patient's intimate struggles – the details of her unfortunate medical plight and perhaps her family's conflict – become public and open to discussion and debate.

The vast majority of medical care disagreements in the United States are resolved in the clinical setting. In the event of conflict, most US hospitals have hospital ethics committees (HECs) – an informal dispute resolution mechanism – but, if the ethics consultation process fails, the parties usually must resort to the courts. Judicial dispute resolution involves a process that is often slow, stressful for family members, and ultimately reliant on the ability of medical experts to effectively convey information to judges who usually lack medical expertise. The judicial process also varies depending on state law. Other countries have adopted specialized approaches to decision-making and dispute resolution for the care of incapacitated patients. In Ontario, Canada, the Consent and Capacity Board offers a locus and process for resolving conflict in the care of incapacitated patients. In England and Wales, the

1 Friedrich Nietzsche, Human, All Too Human: A Book for Free Spirits pp. 199–200 (R. J. Hollingdale, transl.) (Cambridge University Press, 1986).

2 Ann C. Long & J. Randall Curtis, The Epidemic of Physician-Family Conflict in the ICU and What We Should Do About It, 43 Crit. Care Med. 461–462 (2014).

Court of Protection and other courts supervise the implementation of provisions of the Mental Capacity Act in cases of disagreement or uncertainty about how to care for patients who can no longer make medical (or other) decisions. Both the centralized nature of these latter mechanisms and the uniformity of standards applied illustrate a different attitude and approach to achieving optimal care for incapacitated patients.

THE UNITED STATES: HOSPITAL ETHICS COMMITTEES AND JUDICIAL RESOLUTION

In most cases, physicians accept the surrogate's decisions regarding life-sustaining treatment for an incapacitated patient, but there are some situations that require review, and the US system offers two primary options to resolve disputes. A hospital ethics committee may be asked to guide discussion and facilitate consensus. Although ethics consultation can, and often does, facilitate agreement between parties, these committees have no formal decisional authority and can only offer recommendations.[3] Even when the patient has clearly designated a surrogate decision-maker in writing, other family members may disagree with either the designation itself or with the surrogate's decisions. When there is no family member available to serve as surrogate or when there is a dispute among family members and no clear designation of a decision-maker in an advance directive, the American Medical Association (AMA) recommends seeking some form of institutional or judicial review. In cases where a physician believes that the surrogate's choice doesn't align with what the patient would choose or is not in the patient's best interests, the AMA similarly recommends ethics committee consultation and review.[4] Should this process fail to resolve the disagreement, the dispute may land in court.

Hospitals are not required by the law of most states to operate ethics committees, but the private accreditation process under the nonprofit Joint Commission on Accreditation of Healthcare Organizations (JCAHO) considers whether and how hospitals handle ethical issues when they arise in providing medical care.[5] Since hospitals want and need JCAHO accreditation, most form and maintain ethics committees, whether or not mandated by state law. These multidisciplinary committees are typically composed of physicians and other clinicians from multiple specialties, social workers, chaplains, and members with ethics and legal expertise. The ethics committee's mission is twofold: to educate hospital personnel about

3 Glenn McGee et al., A National Study of Ethics Committees, 1 Am. J. Bioethics 60–64 (2001).

4 American Medical Ass'n, Opinion 2.1.2 – Decisions for Adults Who Lack Capcaity, www.ama-assn.org/delivering-care/ethics/decisions-adult-patients-who-lack-capacity.

5 A few state statutes require hospitals to establish ethics committees to resolve patient care disputes. Thaddeus Mason Pope, Legal Briefing: Healthcare Ethics Committees, 22 J. Clinical Ethics 74–93 (2011).

ethical principles and situations in which medical care raises ethical questions and to assist with the resolution of disputes between clinicians and patients or family members of patients. In the latter role, the usual practice involves ethics consultation, in which a couple of members of the committee meet with clinicians and family members (and the patient, if she is able) to discuss disputes relating to medical care and attempt to resolve them.[6] (Separately, family meetings between clinicians and the patient's family members can help keep the family informed and proactively prevent misunderstandings and disagreements.[7]) The ethics committee may also advise clinicians against taking steps that are questionable, not permitted by law, or arise out of inappropriate motivations. The informal nature of ethics committee review, usually conducted in the vicinity of the patient and her medical team, can help with hard choices while providing a more supportive and less intimidating environment than a courtroom. When ethics committees succeed in resolving a dispute to the satisfaction of all interested individuals, the result can reduce potential institutional liability and help the physicians involved learn how to address similar situations in the future.

Critics of ethics committees note their deficiencies – that the inherent nature of inter-peer advising means that physician members of the committee lack neutrality toward others in their shared profession, while the 'cloak of anonymity' allows individual committee members to hide behind the collective decisions of the group.[8] Despite these concerns, ethics consultation really does help resolve disputes in many cases, in no small part because members of these committees have the training, the experience, and the self-selected interest to engage in conflict resolution. Avoiding litigation via ethics consultation or other forms of alternative dispute resolution offers the possibility of an informal but professional option, with a more subtle understanding of disputes and more emotionally satisfactory solutions to intractable medical conflicts.[9]

In the United States, courts can make decisions for incapacitated patients, but the process is unwieldy and often time consuming and varies in substance and procedure across state jurisdictions. The United States also lacks a consistent definition of capacity in the first place – capacity is sometimes defined by state statute for particular legal purposes but usually is left to the judgment of the physician in the context of medical decision-making. Laws concerning decision-making for incapacitated patients differ significantly from one jurisdiction to the next. Among states with a mandated hierarchy of surrogate decision-makers, a few states include an

6 Am. Med. Ass'n, Guidelines for Ethics Committees in Health Care Institutions, 253 JAMA 2698–2699 (1985).

7 Eric Widera, Family Meetings on Behalf of Patients with Serious Illness, 383 New Eng. J. Med. e71(5) (2020).

8 Alan Meisel et al., The Right to Die: The Law of End-of-Life Decisionmaking §3.25[A] (3rd ed. Wolters Kluwer, 2020 supp.).

9 I. Glenn Cohen, Negotiating Death: ADR and End of Life Decision-Making 9 Harv. Negotiation L. Rev. 253–330 (2004).

extra-judicial dispute resolution provision[10] to enable challenge of the default surrogate (either to whether she is the appropriate decision-maker or to her actual decision) and, even in those states, further challenges will land in court. In most other states, if someone in the family wishes to challenge the default surrogate under a state's statutory hierarchy, he can appeal directly to the court.[11] When a court does review a decision to forgo life-prolonging treatment, it may either review the clinical decision-making process to determine whether the decision was made according to the correct substantive standard (patient's wishes or best interests) and procedural requirements or the court may actually make the substantive decision itself. Courts in these circumstances may defer to family requests to continue life-sustaining care, even when physicians argue that this care is inappropriate.[12] Finally, some state laws specifically grant ethics committees the authority to make decisions in the role of alternative dispute resolution bodies,[13] rather than serving purely in an advisory capacity. Texas, for example, enacted a statute with a series of procedural requirements to address disagreements between surrogates and physicians about the appropriateness of continuing life-sustaining treatment. Under the statute, when a physician refuses to honor a patient's advance directive or the treatment requests of a surrogate, a non-judicial review process kicks in to evaluate that decision. Ultimately, if the ethics committee review supports the physician's position, the patient's family has ten days to locate another facility that is willing to accept transfer of the patient. If the family objects to the decision and needs more time, the statute also provides for judicial review to extend the ten-day period while a search for a willing transfer facility continues.[14] The Texas statute has both champions and critics, but Texas is one of the few states that have attempted to expedite review of certain end-of-life care disputes.

Experts have championed regional ethics committees as a preferable dispute resolution process, noting their superiority to hospital ethics committees in several dimensions. Regional ethics committees can sidestep the inherent institutional conflicts of interest that single-institution committees consistently face. Also, while some members of hospital ethics committees may have genuine expertise in law and biomedical ethics, many others will not, resulting in decisions that are not only potentially arbitrary or biased but also based on incorrect or limited understanding of medical law and ethics. Regional ethics committees and multi-institutional ethics

10 For example, the relevant statutory provision in Maine states that in cases of disputes among or within a class of decision-makers in its statutory hierarchy, "The health-care provider may refer the members of the class or classes to a neutral 3rd party for assistance in resolving the dispute or to a court of competent jurisdiction." Maine Revised Statutes Title 18-A § 5–805(e).

11 Erin S. DeMartino et al., Who Decides When a Patient Can't? Statutes on Alternate Decision Makers, 376 New Eng. J. Med. 1478–1482 (2017).

12 E.g., Betancourt v. Trinitas Hospital, 415 N.J. Super. 301 (2010).

13 Diane E. Hoffmann & Anita J. Tarzian, The Role and Legal Status of Health Care Ethics Committees in the United States, in Legal Perspectives in Bioethics (Ana S. Iltis et al. eds., Routledge, 2008).

14 Tex. Health & Safety Code §§166.046; 166.052; 166.053.

committees can ameliorate many of the failings of hospital ethics committees by sidestepping institutional conflicts and ensuring multidisciplinary expertise in membership and can increase both depth of experience and consistency in decision-making across similar cases.[15] It is difficult to predict whether and to what extent the medical community will embrace this approach on a widespread basis, but committees currently in operation offer a genuinely useful alternative to the long, slow process of litigation.

CANADA: ONTARIO'S CONSENT AND CAPACITY BOARD

As explained in Chapter 2, the law of informed consent in Canada is quite similar to that in the United States, and both include end-of-life decisions within the realm of medical decisions requiring informed consent. As in the United States, once a patient loses the ability to make medical decisions and provide consent, a substitute decision-maker (the Canadian term for surrogate decision-maker) must make decisions according to the patient's wishes or, if these wishes are unknown, based on the patient's best interests. Canadians face many of the same challenges that we in the United States do with respect to surrogate decision-making, including lack of advance care planning – although rates of completion of advance directives appear higher than here, at least in some provinces. In a survey of residents of Nova Scotia, more than half of the patients who died had an advance directive and about two-thirds of these patients had completed a durable power of attorney for health care.[16] In a slightly older survey, two-thirds of a surveyed population had been advised to discuss their health care preferences, and about 70 percent of respondents had actually done so. Slightly less than half of those surveyed had also completed a written form – either appointing a substitute decision-maker or completing a document expressing health care preferences.[17] About 75 percent of Canadians living in long-term care facilities have a DNAR order and 20 percent have executed a Do Not Hospitalize Order.[18]

The province of Ontario, Canada has implemented a well-developed process for supporting surrogates and for testing the wisdom and accuracy of their decisions. In 1996, as part of a broader initiative to describe rights and duties under the law of informed consent in Canada's Health Care Consent Act and its Mental Health Act, the provincial government of Ontario created the Consent and Capacity Board

15 Thaddeus Mason Pope, Multi-Institutional Healthcare Ethics Committees: The Procedurally Fair Internal Dispute Resolution Mechanism, 31 Campbell L. Rev. 257–332 (2009).

16 Christian Digout et al., Prevalence of Having Advance Directives and a Signed Power of Attorney in Nova Scotia, 34 J. Palliative Care 189–196 (2019).

17 Gina Bravo et al., Are Canadians Providing Advance Directives About Health Care and Research Participation in the Event of Decisional Incapacity? 56 Can. J. Psychiatry 209–218 (2011).

18 Canadian Institute for Health Information, Care in Canadian ICUs (2016), https://secure.cihi.ca/.

(CCB), an independent governmental body located in Toronto. The CCB's mission is to promote "fair and accessible adjudication of consent and capacity issues," and its "key areas of activity are the adjudication of matters of capacity, consent, civil committal and substitute decision-making." The CCB is composed of psychiatrists, lawyers, and members of the general public appointed by the provincial government. Hearings may involve one, three, or five members and are generally open to the public. (The trade-off between transparency and privacy is a tough call – but private medical disputes in the United States also become fully public during litigation.) Decisions of the CCB are appealable in the Canadian courts.[19]

As in the United States, Canadian medical decision-making law seeks to protect the ethical value of patient autonomy via the legal doctrine of informed consent.[20] The CCB's role is neither mandatory nor automatic; it only begins when a family member or health care provider requests a hearing. The board attempts to hold a hearing within seven days of receiving the request. Hearings can focus on a variety of issues including challenges to a determination that a patient lacks capacity to make medical decisions, appointing a substitute decision-maker, requests for treatment directions based on a patient's prior capable wishes, requests to depart from a patient's prior capable wishes, and a review of a substitute decision-maker's compliance with the rules for substitute decision-making. The board's role is to ensure that medical decisions reflect incapacitated patients' values and preferences when known, or that the medical care provided is otherwise in the patients' best interests.[21] Canadian commentators argue that the CCB hearings make for a less confrontational and ultimately more robust decision-making model. The option to have disputes resolved via a board rather than in court also offers a less formal and therefore less intimidating process for families. Ontario's board provides prompt resolutions to disputes, often reaching a final decision within days after hearings,[22] which is a far superior procedural outcome compared with the months- or even years-long litigation process that is typical in US courts.

The selection process for CCB members is designed to ensure the quality of membership and its resultant decisions. The Ontario CCB members are appointed by a provincial government official (the lieutenant governor) using a "competitive, merits-based selection process" that includes an appointment advertisement on the government website, review of applicants' experience and knowledge of the matters that come before the board, the candidates' "aptitude for impartial adjudication," an interview process, and enhanced reference checks.[23] The board's appointment and

19 Ontario Consent and Capacity Board, www.ccboard.on.ca/scripts/english/index.asp.

20 Udo Schuklenk et al., End-of-Life Decision-Making in Canada: The Report by the Royal Society of Canada Expert Panel on End-of-Life Decision-Making, 25 Bioethics 1–73 (2011).

21 Ontario Consent and Capacity Board, www.ccboard.on.ca/scripts/english/index.asp.

22 Jocelyn Downie & Michael Hadskis, In Defence of Consent and Capacity Boards for End-of-Life Care, 61 J. Can. Anesth. 899–904 (2014).

23 Ontario Public Appointments Secretariat, www.pas.gov.on.ca/scripts/en/BoardDetails.asp?boardID=876.

participation process means that potential board members will have the interest and emotional appetite, already developed through professional experience or community background, to go through a substantial vetting process and to participate in the board's challenging work.

A board similar to the CCB, implemented in US states that are politically and culturally receptive, would have the potential to improve the quality of medical decision-making for incapacitated patients, to relieve the burden that surrogate decision-makers feel when choosing for incapacitated loved ones, and to optimize the process and substance of dispute resolution when disputes arise. A similar model in US states could also draw on voluntary applicants with relevant professional qualifications who express interest in board membership and who are appointed after a careful, merit-based appointments process. As in the Ontario version, US state board members should receive appropriate per diem compensation and members should serve limited terms. Although, the remit of such a board would be limited to situations where families or physicians request its intervention, the benefits of independent board decision-making in these cases would have the potential to encourage incremental change in the culture of US end-of-life care over time. It would offer all of the benefits of regional ethics committees but would, in addition, help leverage and improve legal certainty for common but highly difficult medical decision-making scenarios, providing support to patients, their surrogates, and their medical teams.

As in the Ontario model, a US state board would not make all decisions for incapacitated patients. Instead, it would provide decision support and dispute resolution in cases of conflict about the appropriateness of an individual to serve as a surrogate, requests for treatment decisions based on a patient's prior expressed wishes, requests to depart from a patient's prior stated preferences, determinations of a patient's best interests, and a review of a surrogate's compliance with the statutes and ethical standards governing surrogate decision-making. As in Ontario, these disputes would be submitted to board jurisdiction first, and board decisions would be binding on the parties. If, after board review, a party were dissatisfied with the result, the matter could then also be subject to judicial review. Finally, any US state board, like the Ontario CCB, would be subject to open hearings and public reporting and monitoring, ensuring transparency and full accountability.

An independent board modeled on the Ontario CCB but focusing exclusively on surrogate decision-making for critically ill patients who have lost decisional capacity, implemented in the United States on a state-by-state basis, has the potential to offer practical improvements to the surrogate decision-making process at both the individual and systemic levels. This decision-making model offers several potential benefits compared with the existing US approach. These boards would be multidisciplinary – with members of multiple professions including critical care medicine, psychology and psychiatry, law, bioethics, and religion, as well as members of the local community. The multidisciplinary model replicates that of institutional review boards (IRBs) in the United States that review and supervise clinical research in human subjects.[24] Hospital ethics committees are also typically multidisciplinary, with membership that often includes physicians, nurses, clergy, attorneys, and social workers. Although both IRBs and ethics committees have been the subject of well-deserved criticism regarding their effectiveness in harm prevention, the perspective of multiple disciplines, including nonmedical disciplines and community representation, reliably enhances the quality and depth of discussion in complex decision-making.

Compared with decision-making by a single judge, or even a panel of judges, the multidisciplinary decision-making model of the CCB is inherently superior. Judges typically hear a wide variety of cases and have no expertise in medical matters or in the complexities of surrogate decision-making, whereas CCB members receive training and can draw on their individual expertise in medicine, law, psychiatry or psychology, and the mores of the community in making decisions for incapacitated patients. Boards are specialist decision-making bodies and, as repeat players, will develop expertise and best practices, whereas judges are generalists who lack relevant bioethics training and may not see surrogate decision-making disputes very often. Also, in many US states, judges are elected, making them susceptible to political pressure in cases where their decisions might offend political forces or voters in the state. Finally, rather than making decisions in an adversarial proceeding where trial judges often operate more like procedural umpires than substantive decision-makers (as is frequently the case with court interventions in end-of-life disputes), a CCB-style board offers a more collaborative, deliberative, supportive, non-hierarchical process that can focus entirely on the needs of the patient, instead of which party to the dispute is 'right' and, with enough evidence, may prevail. This sort of board can also, over time, develop and follow a canon of best practices that will elevate it above the idiosyncrasies of individual disputes.[25] CCB members, as expert repeat players, can over time form the institutional memory to make decisions that are consistent with ethical standards, even as every next decision will continue to refine decision quality, institutional practices, and acquired wisdom.

In the vast majority of cases, patients suffering from terminal illness are *not* repeat players – they will have no prior experience of their situation, and they are nearly always emotionally vulnerable. Similarly, the family members of dying patients also will rarely be experts either in medical matters or in navigating the intellectual and emotional complexities of medical decision-making with and for their loved ones (along with any intra-family complications that may exacerbate the emotional complexity of the situation). In many surrogate decision-making scenarios, the parties' emotions, arising out of anxiety, grief, guilt, intra-familial conflict, or clinical

24 Carl Coleman et al., The Ethics and Regulation of Research with Human Subjects (Matthew Bender & Co., Inc. 2005).

25 Jocelyn Downie & Michael Hadskis, In Defence of Consent and Capacity Boards for End-of-Life Care, 61 J. Can. Anesth. 899–904 (2014).

uncertainty, will impact the objectivity and reliability of the surrogate decision-making process, all, at least in principle, at the expense of the parties' (and especially the patient's) welfare. Physicians *are* repeat players and medical experts but still suffer from communication challenges, conflicts of interest, and external pressures that can interfere with the provision of sound medical advice and proportionate medical care to dying patients.

There are additional reasons to believe that a CCB-type mechanism would result in better substantive outcomes for both the patient and the surrogate decision-maker. From the patient's perspective, the goal of surrogate decision-making is to attempt to reach a decision that accurately reflects the patient's values and preferences, if known, or that is in the patient's best interests, if there isn't enough information available as to patient preferences. As explained earlier, it is often impossible to know *ex ante* what is the 'best' choice, but an impartial, expert, and well-informed board can more objectively take into account the potential adverse impact of invasive medical technology on a dying patient and will have substantial expertise and experience in facilitating complex medical decisions. The board's impartiality and its lack of family or other emotional connection offer the potential to relieve some of the stress that surrogates regularly endure. When physicians and families have more confidence in the decision process and therefore also in its outcome, there is some potential to reduce tensions and to build trust among the surrogate decision-maker, the family, and the health care team.

Despite all of these potential benefits, the barriers to adopting a dispute resolution mechanism that was developed in a different cultural, political, and historical context are significant. The CCB model would face tremendous challenges in approval and implementation in most, if not all, US states. These challenges can be expected to fall into two categories. First, the rather radical decision to take end-of-life decision-making disputes away from courts as the primary, formal, and binding resolvers of disputes and to place them into the hands of a governmentally appointed panel will be met with a combination of skepticism and inertia. Currently, there appear to be no such boards addressing end-of-life decision-making operating in any of the US states, though some states have boards that address issues relating to involuntary civil commitment for mental health treatment.[26] Americans find it difficult to accept and implement major changes quickly. It is likely that, as with other changes to medical decision-making such as the POLST paradigm,[27] a CCB-type board would begin with a pilot project, probably in a single state that is politically amenable to major change, and running in parallel with the continuation of primary judicial dispute resolution. Second, the highly polarized political culture

26 E.g., Neb.Rev.St. § 71-915: Mental health boards; N.Y. State Justice Center for the Protection of People With Special Needs, www.justicecenter.ny.gov.

27 National POLST Paradigm, www.polst.org (describing the paradigm of Physician Orders for Life Sustaining Treatment forms that represent patient or surrogate decisions with respect to various types of life support and that become part of the patient's medical record).

in the United States will present a major obstacle to board implementation, even in states that have the interest and the will to overcome inertia and implement major systemic change. These boards also risk being labeled as "death panels,"[28] because, by definition, they will sometimes decide to withhold or withdraw certain types of medical care, to the extent that such withholding or withdrawal is required by an incapacitated patient's values and preferences or their best interests.

Opponents of institutionalized decision-making also will label the resultant decisions as a form of cost-driven rationing[29] and will object vehemently to any sort of committee or board making these decisions. Perhaps more than any other Western society, the United States emphasizes the individual interest over that of the collective. Any attempt to move the decision-making process for incapacitated patients toward a process that might also consider the needs of, egalitarian rights of, and costs to the collective (even indirectly) will likely be met with furor. Critics will claim that board decisions to withhold or withdraw life-prolonging care are contrary to pro-life values and individual choice. Although a surrogate decision-making board modeled on the CCB would focus on the wishes of individual patients for whom it is making medical decisions, such a board will also, by definition, try to make good decisions across a population – focusing on the values of autonomy and beneficence – but in ways that may be perceived as taking a collectivist approach to end-of-life decision-making. Given that the US system regularly makes these sort of collectivist decisions, for example, in deciding how to provide health insurance coverage and to whom, where to build and operate hospitals, how to regulate physician-patient relationships by law, and other forms of global regulation, all of which directly impact individual health in times of need, objections on this basis seem unpersuasive. Unfortunately, recognition of this sort of fundamental logical inconsistency is unlikely to penetrate or sway the political discourse among those who oppose all governmental intervention in medical care (even as they participate as current or future beneficiaries in the government-funded and administered Medicare system).

As William Blake once wrote, "The man who never alters his opinion is like standing water, and breeds reptiles of the mind."[30] For the time being, it remains likely that political and cultural obstacles will prevent implementation in the United States of state governmental boards to resolve disputes regarding decisions for incapacitated patients at the end of life. Even so, the process of evaluating the potential benefits of these boards is a worthwhile exercise because it holds a mirror up to the US culture and the health care system that is born of this culture and exposes its deficiencies. On the other hand, if a CCB-type board *were* to begin operation in one or more states, physicians and families (if not society generally)

28 Jim Rutenberg & Jackie Calmes, False 'Death Panel' Rumor Has Some Familiar Roots, N.Y. Times (Aug. 13, 2009).

29 Elizabeth Weeks Leonard, Death Panels and the Rhetoric of Rationing, 13 Nev. L. J. 872–887 (2013).

30 William Blake, The Marriage of Heaven and Hell, The Complete Illuminated Books (Thames & Hudson, 2001).

might quickly learn to appreciate its benefits, just as many in the United States have come to appreciate the benefits of the Affordable Care Act.

ENGLAND AND WALES: THE MENTAL CAPACITY ACT

In England and Wales, although patients' wishes play an important role in deciding whether to initiate or continue life-prolonging measures for seriously ill or dying patients, this principle is supplemented with a strong emphasis on best interests, particularly when the patient's wishes are unknown or unclear, when the physician questions the wisdom of the patient's choice on medical grounds, or when resource constraints become relevant. The Mental Capacity Act (MCA), which guides these decisions, reflects a heavier and more explicit emphasis on the patient's best interests and quality of life compared with the autonomy-dominated model of medical decision-making in the United States. The MCA was first enacted in 2005, and applies to all people in England and Wales aged 16 and older. The Act provides substantive standards relating to decision-making for incapacitated individuals and it established the Court of Protection, which is charged with making decisions relating to the financial and health and welfare interests of these patients under the auspices of the MCA. The Act also established national, uniform standards of practice for the care of patients who cannot make their own decisions.[31]

In 2010, the General Medical Council (GMC) published a *Guidance for Doctors on Treatment and Care Towards the End of Life* that describes a more formal and quite different approach in the United Kingdom to end-of-life decisions compared with that of the United States. It is worth noting that, although the publication is called a 'guidance' and contains a disclaimer that it is not a statement of legal principles or a substitute for legal advice, it has the effect of a series of regulatory statements. Physicians are informed that in cases where the guidance states "you must," this creates an "overriding duty or principle" of practice.[32] The GMC published another relevant guidance, *Decision-Making and Consent*, in 2020 that, as its name suggests, focuses primarily on consent to medical care for patients with and without decisional capacity.[33]

In the absence of an advance directive or other prior statement to guide the decision and in the absence of an appointed legal proxy decision-maker, GMC guidance makes the physician the responsible decision-maker,[34] which is obviously quite different from the official role of the physician in the United States and in

[31] Mental Capacity Act (2005, as amended), https://www.legislation.gov.uk/ukpga/2005/9/contents.

[32] General Medical Council, Treatment and Care Towards the End of Life: Good Practice in Decision-making (May 20, 2010). The British Medical Association also has issued guidance on end-of-life issues. Brit. Med. Assn., Clinically-Assisted Nutrition and Hydration (CANH) and Adults Who Lack Capacity to Consent: Guidance for Decision-Making in England and Wales (2018).

[33] General Medical Council, Decision Making and Consent (Nov. 9, 2020).

[34] General Medical Council, Decision Making and Consent §§ 88-89 (Nov. 9, 2020).

Canada. Physicians in the United Kingdom, pursuant to the MCA and guidance documents for physician practice, are expressly charged with the responsibility to determine whether initiating or continuing life-sustaining medical treatment is appropriate for patients who lack decisional capacity. The MCA and related guidance documents also include provisions that require physicians to act in the best interests of incapacitated patients.[35] The patient's family must be consulted, but the physician retains the ultimate authority to make treatment decisions. In situations where there is uncertainty about next steps in the care of patients who lack capacity, the GMC's guidance strongly emphasizes the patient's best interests and recognizes that many patients have not formally stated their wishes concerning care under these circumstances. The guidance instructs physicians to use their own "specialist knowledge … and clinical judgement, together with evidence about the patient's views (including advance statements, decisions, or directives), to identify which … treatments are clinically appropriate and are likely to result in overall benefit for the patient."[36] "Overall benefit" is defined as "the ethical basis on which decisions are made about treatment and care for adult patients who lack capacity to decide for themselves. This involves weighing up the risks of harm and potential benefits for the individual patient of each of the available options, including the option of taking no action."[37] In England and Wales, although the physician retains ultimate treatment decision authority, GMC guidance also requires the physician to request the appointment of an advocate to participate in the decision-making process when there is no legal proxy or close relative who is willing to stand in that role for the patient.[38] This requirement ensures (or attempts to) a more collaborative and balanced decision-making process for the incapacitated patient.

Where there is disagreement about whether a particular treatment or intervention would be of overall benefit (either between physicians or among the physician, the patient, and the patient's family or proxy), the *Treatment and Care* guidance sets out a process to resolve the dispute. In anticipation of care disputes, the guidance

[35] Mental Capacity Act, §4. Section 4(6)(a)–(b) adds that the doctor must, in evaluating the patient's best interests, also consider "the person's past and present wishes and feelings (and, in particular, any relevant written statement made by him when he had capacity), [and] the beliefs and values that would be likely to influence his decision if he had capacity"). According to guidance documents, if a patient does not have a relevant advance directive, the physician may consider withdrawing life-sustaining treatment "based on a range of clinical criteria, including unresponsive physiological deterioration, overwhelming and irreversible pathology such as brainstem death, and progression of co-morbidity against a background of significant impairment of quality-of-life prior to the critical illness." General Medical Council, Treatment and Care Towards the End of Life: Good Practice in Decision-Making (2010).

[36] General Medical Council, Treatment and Care Towards the End of Life.

[37] General Medical Council, Decision Making and Consent § 87 (Nov. 9, 2020).

[38] General Medical Council, Treatment and Care Towards the End of Life (explaining that the Mental Capacity Act of 2005 requires the appointment of an Independent Mental Capacity Advocate (IMCA) in such circumstances). The IMCA has "authority to make enquiries about the patient and to contribute to the decision by representing the patient's interests but cannot make a decision on behalf of the patient."

specifically addresses situations in which the proxy or decision-maker requests treatment that the physician believes would not be clinically appropriate or of overall benefit to the patient. In these circumstances, the physician should explain the reasons for this opinion and discuss it with the patient's family but is not obligated to provide the treatment. The decision-maker or proxy can at this point request a second opinion or seek review from an appropriate court. In disputed cases, the guidance recommends various extra-judicial approaches as a first step, including involving an independent advocate, seeking advice from a more experienced colleague or obtaining a second opinion, holding a case conference, or using local mediation services to work toward consensus. If none of these steps effectively resolves the disagreement, the guidance instructs physicians to seek legal advice by applying to an appropriate court for an independent ruling.[39]

The *Treatment and Care* guidance expressly addresses particularly complex end-of-life scenarios as well, including questions about the provision of artificial nutrition and hydration, and issues arising with patients in PVS or other disorders of consciousness. With respect to adults who lack capacity and who are not expected to die within hours or days but who are in the end stage of a disease or condition, the guidance instructs physicians to provide artificial nutrition and hydration if it would be of overall benefit to the patient and to take into account the patient's wishes and values: "The patient's request must be given weight and, when the benefits, burdens and risks are finely balanced, will usually be the deciding factor." In these circumstances, if the physician believes that artificial nutrition and hydration would not be of overall benefit to the patient, it can be withheld or withdrawn, but she must obtain a second opinion from another physician who is familiar with the patient's condition but is not directly caring for the patient.[40] For patients in PVS or similar conditions, the guidance instructs physicians to approach the appropriate court for a ruling before withdrawing nutrition and hydration,[41] though a recent court decision removed the requirement for judicial review in certain circumstances where there is no dispute with the family about withdrawal of life-prolonging care.[42]

Overall, physicians in England and Wales have significant authority to decide that artificial nutrition and hydration and other life-prolonging technologies are not of overall benefit for particular patients. As the saying goes, with great power comes great responsibility. Placing the decision in the hands of physicians allows for a more dispassionate and professional judgment about the patient's best interests, particularly if the physician takes into consideration the patient's wishes, as expressed by the family. There is certainly the potential for physician overreaching in this system, and the guidance warns against making value judgments about

39 Ibid.
40 Ibid.
41 Ibid.
42 Re M (Withdrawal of Treatment: Need for Proceedings) [2017] EWCOP19.

quality of life,[43] but the checks and balances appear designed to minimize this risk, and judicial review is available when necessary.

PATIENT PREFERENCES, WITH A DOSE OF BEST INTERESTS

In contrast to the centralized and heavily guidance-based system of end-of-life medical care and decision-making in England and Wales, US physicians are regulated in the state in which they practice by state boards of medicine, which occasionally work with state legislatures to promulgate specific standards of practice (often addressing discrete concerns like the overprescribing of addictive drugs). Boards of medicine also sometimes discipline physicians who violate standards or mistreat patients. The US state boards of medicine do not, however, routinely promulgate general standards of practice for end-of-life care (or any other area of medical practice). The nearest equivalents in the United States are professional organizations such as the American Medical Association or the National Hospice and Palliative Care Organization and private ethics organizations such as The Hastings Center. These private groups publish professional standards, statements of practice, and principles of treatment,[44] but they are not binding on physicians, even on those who are members of the organizations.

By expressly and deliberately incorporating an additional layer of consideration of a patient's best interests in situations where there is little or nothing known about the patient's actual wishes, US physicians can, consistent with existing law, initiate more effective conversations about desired versus realistic goals of care and can reduce harm from burdensome and potentially inappropriate end-of-life care. Because patient preferences are still very much part of the conversation here in the United States, those surrogates who believe that any life, even permanently unconscious life, is preferable to death can continue to request and often succeed in maintaining life-prolonging measures for an incapacitated patient. However, adding explicit consideration of the patient's best interests – the benefits and burdens of continued treatment (including a concept of burdens that includes dignitary harm) – can help the physician and surrogate better understand the implications of continuing life-prolonging care. For example, in the *Bland* case, it was argued, in support of discontinuing artificial nutrition and hydration, that continuing such treatment would be of no benefit because it could not reverse the patient's condition and that keeping him alive under these circumstances when he would most likely not wish it diminished his dignity. In response to those who object that it cannot burden

43 General Medical Council, Treatment and Care Towards the End of Life. ("You must be careful not to rely on your personal views about a patient's quality of life and to avoid making judgements based on poorly informed or unfounded assumptions about the healthcare needs of particular groups, such as older people and those with disabilities.")

44 Nancy Berlinger et al., The Hastings Center Guidelines for Decisions on Life-Sustaining Treatment and Care Near the End of Life (Oxford University Press 2013).

a person's dignity to be kept alive if he cannot feel pain or humiliation, commentators have pointed out, quite persuasively, that this argument assumes that our interests end with our consciousness. Most people will disagree with this assumption – we still retain all of our rights, including dignity-based rights when we go to sleep each night.[45]

This is not to suggest that a US physician should unilaterally impose her assessment of the patient's best interests and then dictate the course of treatment (or non-treatment) accordingly. But US physicians can learn to move beyond discussion of patient preferences to articulate the facts about the patient's chances for meaningful improvement and the benefits and burdens (both physical and dignitary) of continued treatment and life-prolonging measures for patients at the end of life. They can offer a firm opinion. While some physicians discuss these matters with surrogates, the frequent use of high-intensity interventions for dying patients suggests that many others do not. Ultimately, if the permanently unconscious or dying patient has no relevant advance directive and the surrogate is unable or unwilling to make a decision about continued treatment or life-supportive measures, the physician or medical team can take more initiative in having the necessary conversations. But in some circumstances, this is a big ask. Although it is also the case in the United States (as in the United Kingdom) that physicians have no ethical or legal obligation to provide clinically inappropriate treatment, the combined force of disagreement about what might be clinically appropriate, liability concerns, and emotional pressure from a family can often lead to continued treatment. In other words, in the United States, the doctor may take the path of least resistance, particularly in the absence of uniform guidance and a culture of adherence to it to provide a backstop of support.

Completely abandoning the principle of patient autonomy in US end-of-life decision-making law would be unwise and unnecessary, not to mention highly controversial. It is essential, however, to recognize that the principle of patient autonomy alone provides an insufficient basis for end-of-life decision-making in many instances. Physicians know this very well. Sharing this truth with patients and families rather than deferring to 'what the patient or family wants' and getting explicit about the medical realities can help incapacitated patients avoid unwanted and burdensome interventions at the end of life. It may even reduce conflict. While it is true that, in the end, we each confront death individually in our own way, the 'good death' envisioned by most requires that we surrender control over the externalities of our medical care at some point and trust that those who provide that care will do what it takes to de-escalate at the right moment, to ease the pathway at the end of life, to cease doing futile and burdensome things.

45 Charles Foster, Human Dignity in Bioethics and Law, p. 102 (Bloomsbury, 2011).

11

At the End of the Day

There is always an easy solution to every problem – neat, plausible, and wrong.
—H. L. Mencken[1]

Two broad categories of stressors influence complex medical decision-making, including end-of-life decision-making. System-wide and external factors like payment incentives, liability fears, and institutional productivity demands pressure physicians from the outside to behave in ways that can run contrary to patient interests. Meanwhile, relational and internal causes – communication failures, death denial, and various forms of uncertainty – do the same. Impediments to good communication and decision-making often exert their impact silently – physicians and patients may not consciously acknowledge their effects, and may even be unaware of their existence.

Everyone – physicians, patients, and family members – reacts to stress and pressure. It's no surprise that many patients and families resist and delay difficult medical decisions. To quote Al Pacino (somewhat out of context) "it's too damned hard."[2] And so, patients and families end up making these hard, emotional, death-laden decisions at the last minute, or bit by bit when absolutely necessary, like the slow drip of a leaky faucet. With each drip comes the unwelcome realization that time is getting on and death is approaching. There is no medicine to make this situation better in its largest sense, but the support and advice of repeat-player physicians and other health professionals who convey what patients and families need to know, with tact and empathy, can help quite a bit.

The idiosyncrasies of the US health care system create nearly insuperable hurdles to system-wide improvement that are either unique to this country or that operate as more potent forces here than elsewhere. Other barriers, like rational apathy and clinical uncertainty, cross borders and affect us all. So, if it is virtually impossible collectively to 'fix the problem' of end-of-life communication and care at a systemic

1 H. L. Mencken, A Mencken Chrestomathy (Vintage, 1982).
2 Al Pacino, Scent of a Woman (Universal Pictures, 1992).

level, should we just throw up our hands? Despite the discouraging content of prior chapters, all is not lost. While it is difficult to eliminate the many costs (physical, emotional, financial) of treatment that is inconsistent with patient preferences and best interests, there are still things we can do, as individuals, to avoid or minimize these costs and to provide high-quality care for the dying. There are some solutions to the problems identified in this book, but they are not "neat," and they can ameliorate but certainly will not eliminate dysfunctionality in communication and medical decision-making at the end of life.

THE FEASIBILITY OF SYSTEM-WIDE CHANGES

To recap, many Americans receive a lot of burdensome medical care at the end of life, despite evidence that most patients – when asked – say that they would choose to focus on comfort care. Multiple aspects of the US health care system incentivize the provision of medical interventions when they will no longer benefit the patient. Physicians and patients don't talk with each other – at least not sufficiently for seriously ill patients to understand the reality of their situations. In the fog of missing information about prognosis and the likely efficacy or benefit of late-stage interventions, patients and surrogates acquiesce to more care than may be consistent with the good death and dying process that most seek – and the health care system profits from it all. Changing the structures that promote these patterns remains hugely difficult in the US's complex, fragmented, and politicized health care system. Cultural forces such as the pro-life movement and societal and individual denial of mortality cement us even more into the status quo. So, are we stuck? As the preceding chapters demonstrate, it's a complex problem with no systemic solution in sight.

There is no easy top-down solution to the problems described in Chapters 1 through 7 and in Chapter 9. In certain respects, there are no global remedies *at all* for the problems of bounded rationality, cognitive biases, clinical and Knightian uncertainty, and rational apathy described in Chapter 8. Canada appears to face many of the same challenges as we do in the United States but at least has the advantage of a federal/provincial health care delivery system and a more communitarian approach to health care that can implement reforms more efficiently than we in the United States can, even in the context of our Medicare program. While there is plenty of controversy and discussion about end-of-life matters in Canada, our neighbors to the north *appear* less burdened by reactionary efforts to interfere with any policies to reduce unnecessary and unwanted care at the end of life. The collective popular support for universal health care brings with it an acceptance of governmental authority in the health care context, including respect for governmental decision-making in matters such as hospice care and medical aid in dying. People in Canada may disagree on these matters substantively, and they may protest certain governmental policies, but Canadians respect the fundamental structure of federal and provincial health care delivery with its built-in governmental guidance. The moral imperative to provide health care for all is well engrained in the Canadian psyche. The same is true in the United Kingdom. The British may complain about the National Health Service and some of its policies, but they revere it deeply, and most do not question the fundamental rightness of providing access to health care for all, or of the government's role as steward of the health care system. I hope that I've refrained from portraying Canada and the United Kingdom as health care paradises. Both systems suffer from delays for non-urgent medical care, and each has had its share of failures and scandals. But both systems are structurally better able – in theory and in practice – to make system-wide changes that improve quality of care at the end of life.

Of course, the US health care delivery system and societal and medical cultures are quite different from those in the United Kingdom or Canada. Making system-wide changes to a single-payer system such as the NHS or to the various provincial plans in Canada is complicated. Truly multidimensional improvement to end-of-life care in the United States depends on health policy makers' willingness to consider more radical change, including looking at models from other countries' health care systems. The US system still lacks two key elements found in all other first-world health care systems – universal access to health care and attention to the financial bottom line. The lack of egalitarian access to health care in the United States prior to Medicare eligibility perpetuates health disparities and broader inequalities, and the simultaneous lack of fiscal discipline (necessary to ensure access to high-quality care for all rather than the more fortunate) leads to over-utilization of inappropriate or unnecessary care.

The cumulative effects of the fragmented US health care financing and regulatory systems, political balkanization on key questions of universal insurance coverage and the ethics of complex issues such as withdrawal of care from permanently unconscious patients (or even simple issues such as reimbursing physicians for advance care planning) make national reform very difficult to achieve. Instead, we're left to consider individual steps with different constituencies – physicians, medical schools, and state governments – that may incrementally reduce the impact of the system's dysfunctionalities and improve quality of care for the dying. Because the US system is so fragmented, we can only pursue fragmented solutions. Whatever reforms *are* implemented in the future will primarily affect system-wide issues – how physicians and hospitals are paid, for example. In the cobbled-together world that is US health care, these sorts of reforms can help improve care for the dying, but not in any dramatic fashion. Reform in the United States is a lot like pushing a very large rock up a very steep hill, with the real risk that a new federal administration that doesn't support reform will let the rock roll down again, or even give it an extra shove.

The structural deficiencies in the US system, together with cultural and political resistance among some in the United States to changes that would benefit the collective, mean that incremental and targeted change to address specific problems in the delivery of end-of-life care is likely the only realistic path forward. Earlier chapters mentioned some of those possible changes, but this chapter focuses primarily on the problem of how to improve physician-patient communication in ways that might result in end-of-life care that more consistently comports with patients' goals and preferences – which requires that patients actually form and articulate goals and preferences, which requires that these patients understand their medical situations more fully, which requires that physicians tell them about their prognosis and what can and cannot be achieved, which requires that we all accept that at some point we will die.

CULTURE MATTERS

The highly polarized political culture in the United States presents a major obstacle to implementation of system-level improvements at the federal level. The Institute of Medicine's report, "Dying in America," urged the overhaul of health care at the end of life, noting that many of its recommendations could be implemented without legislation. Some of the recommendations, however, like restructuring Medicare to pay for home health services (perhaps reducing spending on acute hospital care), would require legislative amendments to Medicare's implementing statute and regulations. Realistically, however, making changes to entitlements that affect patients at the end of life, especially to federal laws like Medicare, will bring on 'death panel' accusations and other sorts of unproductive rhetoric. By definition, reforms that insert the government or payers and insurers into the physician-patient relationship in a way that may influence a decision to withhold or withdraw certain types of medical care (to the extent that withholding or withdrawal is consistent with the patients' values and preferences or best interests) always will be controversial. Of course, the same withholding or withdrawing of treatment occurs many times every day in undisputed cases and all without any transparency, monitoring, or accountability. But cultural and religious conservatives in the United States embrace the idea that no one but patients and families should have the ability to make medical decisions that potentially hasten death or even promote the taking of these decisions. In the same way, these groups nearly always believe that in cases of uncertainty about an incapacitated patient's wishes, it is best to err on the side of continuing all available medical care, no matter what the costs in terms of patient suffering and dignity. And it appears almost unseemly to consider any questions of economic impact on the health care system (despite the fact that many individuals in this country still lack access to basic health care).

To the extent that it is politically feasible, we can implement mechanisms that incentivize physicians to communicate with patients and that discourage the provision of unnecessary care by continuing to reimburse physicians for advance care planning conversations and providing more training in communication skills and in palliative care. Unfortunately, even small steps like these toward the goal of reducing the use of unwanted and inappropriate medical treatment face cultural, political, and of course financial pushback. The death panels lie is still being repeated on a regular basis by conservative politicians, and a Republican representative in the US House has, for example, introduced a bill to remove the provision from the Medicare statute that authorizes payment of physicians for having advance care planning discussions with their patients. The name of the bill is the "Protecting Life Until Natural Death Act."[3] Conservative politicians, whatever their religious persuasions, frequently go along with this sort of thing to avoid running afoul of the pro-life base.

There isn't much to be done about US conservative culture and its symbiotic relationship with politics. Without a functional government to enact reforms to health care, we are left with protecting what's in place, perhaps shoring it up here and there, and hoping for the future. Recent events in the federal government (along with amplifying social media) have exacerbated a gathering wave of conservative discord, grievance, and 'alternative facts'. In an era where people in the United States cannot agree that even scientifically proven or otherwise well-documented facts are true, there's not much left to say. When it comes to death and dying (a human experience for which there will never be a politically convenient alternative fact), maybe all of that noise doesn't matter – at least as long as access to the basics of end-of-life care remains available to all. (Of course, these basics are not, as of this writing, available to all – at least until the age of 65.) Pain medications and other palliatives, along with skilled and humane clinicians to prescribe and administer them, will not (one hopes) disappear anytime soon. Because dying is ultimately an individual and personal experience, people in this country (at least, the lucky ones who have access to good health care) can still make choices about life-prolonging technologies, place of death, and all the rest.

THE COMMUNICATION CONUNDRUM

Physicians know that it's important to talk with patients about their medical condition, benefits and harms of treatment, and prognosis. They know that patients and families place a high value on quality physician communication. And they know what's at stake: physicians who undertake these conversations acknowledge that they are difficult, and that it is sometimes easier to let the patient be swept away by "the powerful momentum of modern medicine."[4] Timely, truthful, humane, and

3 H.R. 520, 116th Congress (2019–2020), introduced by Representative Steve King, a Republican from Iowa, seeks to exclude coverage of advance care planning services under the Medicare program. The euphemistic naming of the bill has an inherent logic problem: a 'natural death' means that a human body can no longer independently maintain itself and therefore expires. All medical treatment that interferes with this natural dying process and supports the living human body in an effort to avoid death (including life-sustaining technology that a person might otherwise refuse via an advance directive) interferes with 'natural death'.

4 Mark Vierra, Death Panels, 156 Arch. Internal Med. 394–395 (2012) (describing a case in which he explained to a dying patient's wife why he would not recommend additional life-prolonging surgery

empathetic conversations about dying can have a tremendous positive impact for the patient, the family, and the physician. Moments of connection, of honest sharing of raw emotions, and of active listening and engaging with patients can provide comfort and relief for dying patients and their families. When daily guardedness against our own mortality and future death comes to the end of its useful 'life', conversation and connection (and the introspection and resilience they help produce) are ultimately the only means left to allow us to move past guardedness and to learn to accept (or at least accommodate) the unwelcome news of impending death. Physicians can help patients make this move.

The ideal of fully informed, authentic, and autonomous choice is unrealistic for many, if not most, patients. Autonomy only gets us so far. At some point, whether or not patients lose capacity along the pathway of terminal illness, respect for human dignity and the obligation to avoid and relieve suffering assume more prominence within the physician's broad duty to the patient.[5] When a patient reaches a point where additional invasive treatments are unlikely to further her cause, physicians can speak up and advise against doing more. When a patient is permanently unconscious or at the end of life and life-prolonging measures are the only thing standing between that patient and a natural death, physicians can do more to protect patients' interests and dignity as human beings by having truthful conversations about prognosis and quality of life. Physicians must remember that many patients prior to the end of life consistently formulate two fundamental preferences – a preference for comfort care and a desire to die with dignity intact. In the light of these preferences (as and when they reflect the preferences of particular patients), physicians are the experts as to which interventions will contribute to comfort and dignity and which may not or definitely will not.

Guidelines for the care of dying patients exist for every specialty and in the form of generally applicable principles of professional practice. Physicians require guidance in two primary dimensions – appropriate utilization of treatments and life-prolonging technologies at the end of life and communication about these matters with patients and families. The Hastings Center, a well-regarded private bioethics research institute, has published evidence-based advice concerning the use of treatments and technologies at the end of life, including a step-by-step process for evaluating whether to initiate or stop life-sustaining technologies.[6] It also provides communication guidance for patients (and their families) who suffer from brain injuries, neurological conditions, and disorders of consciousness.[7] It covers a host of

and adding that "[e]very one of my patients is going to die one day. Like it or not, I should have these conversations earlier, more often, and more comfortably").

5 William T. Branch Jr., The Ethics of the Ordinary Doctor, 44 Hastings Ctr. Rep. 15–17 (Jan./Feb. 2014).

6 Nancy Berlinger et al., The Hastings Center Guidelines for Decisions on Life-Sustaining Treatment and Care Near the End of Life, p. 155 (Oxford UniversityPress 2013).

7 Ibid. pp. 157–161.

other technological interventions, including mechanical ventilation, CPR, dialysis, nutrition and hydration, and treatment for advanced cancer.

The Hastings Center guidelines also articulate and explain the ethical goals at end of life, including relieving suffering, respecting the experience of living and supporting the process of dying, promoting well-being, respecting persons, respecting dignity, and respecting difference.[8] (There are more goals on the list, but these are the most patient-centered among them.) The commentary on these goals emphatically states the need to avoid burdensome treatments at the end of life:

> To respect a life is to support the quality of that life to its end . . . . All medical treatments carry burdens . . . . Because any intervention has the potential to add to a patient's burdens, no treatment option should be characterized as or considered harmless . . . . While patients, loved ones, or professionals may perceive the possibility of prolonging life as a potential benefit of continuing treatment, extending the length of life is not an ethical imperative in and of itself, regardless of how young or old a patient is. Each treatment decision should be guided by patient preferences and well-being.[9]

No health professional would, I think, dispute this advice. Yet, returning to where this book began, the evidence of high utilization of burdensome interventions for dying patients suggests that adhering to these professional obligations is neither easy nor consistently achieved. The barriers to de-escalating care at the end of life are substantial.

Learning how to initiate conversation and engage with the patient and family requires time, training, and emotional and cognitive resilience – and it will not come naturally to many physicians (or other people, for that matter). Physicians, however, have a professional obligation and an ethical duty to learn and implement this essential skill. Even then, there will be patients and families who cannot comprehend or will not want to hear what the physician has to say, let alone accept the news and make decisions accordingly. This is especially true when the medical arsenal geared toward cure is empty and the physician must instead refocus the conversation on quality of remaining life and de-escalating care. It takes two to have a meaningful conversation, and there is only so much the physician can do to inform and guide decision-making. Even so, when a physician's efforts have been frustrated in this regard with a previous patient, they are still owed – unabridged and in full – to the next dying patient.

The medical literature is full of articles and commentary about physician-patient communication and making decisions for treatment and care at the end of life. In addition to communication skills, physicians need a better understanding of legal and ethical standards for withdrawal and withholding of life-sustaining care to avoid situations where they may dissent from requests for withdrawal of care because of

8 Ibid. p. 12.
9 Ibid. p. 13.

misguided liability or ethics concerns.[10] In fact, the ethics culture of an individual hospital, particularly its ICU, can have a significant impact on interprofessional communication and consensus building regarding the care of critically ill patients. When certain physicians or other clinicians believe that a particular patient is receiving excessive medical care, they are more willing to raise concerns in ICUs that have a climate that encourages these sorts of discussions. When physicians and others believe that it's safe to speak up about perceptions of inappropriate or burdensome care, patients receive more preference-based, proportionate, and appropriate medical care.[11] In this sense, there appears to be substantial variation in the culture of individual ICUs (and the hospitals that house them), and institutional culture will, to some unquantifiable extent, impact how individual physicians who work there behave.

Numerous training modules, medical publications, and communication initiatives offer the opportunity for physicians to improve their skills in all of these dimensions. The Academy on Communication in Healthcare and the American Psychological Association are two of many organizations that have developed evidence-based programs and trainings designed to improve the physician-patient relationship.[12] Physicians and medical students who complete these sorts of courses can learn to incorporate empathy and listening skills into their relationships with patients. They can learn how to prepare for and structure difficult conversations (even in urgent situations), how to deliver information effectively, how to discuss unwelcome news, and how to avoid ad hoc approaches to these repeat communication tasks that may create confusion or lead to conflict. Most importantly, physicians can learn how to carry this long-term communication burden as part of everyday practice without inflicting on themselves a cognitive and emotional toll that cumulatively erodes resilience. These efforts should also reach beyond physicians to other nonphysician health care providers, as well as social workers and related professionals. Some of this is happening already, but making this type of training routine (or mandating it for certain specialties) may help accelerate a change of culture and practice. If multiple members of a team or department incorporate these values into their interactions with patients and families, it can reinforce better practices and model them for any providers who remain reluctant.

Timely and honest discussions can help patients make more informed choices about whether and how to proceed with treatment versus focusing on palliation of symptoms. The American Society of Clinical Oncology (ASCO) has noted the importance of patients' understanding of their prognosis and the benefits and risks

10 Neil J. Farber et al., Physicians' Decisions to Withhold and Withdraw Life-Sustaining Treatment, 166 Arch. Int. Med. 560–564 (2006).

11 Dominique D. Benoit et al., Outcome in Patients Perceived as Receiving Excessive Care Across Different Ethical Climates: A Prospective Study in 68 Intensive Care Units in Europe and the USA, 44 Intensive Care Med. 1039–1049 (2018).

12 Acad. of Communication in Healthcare, https://achonline.org/; Am. Psych. Ass'n, www.apa.org/pi/aging/programs/eol.

of treatment. Its guidelines on physician-patient communication recommends a number of items regarding goals of care, prognosis, and treatment that physicians should discuss with cancer patients.[13] Among other things, the guidelines recommends the following:

1.2 At the beginning of conversations with patients, clinicians should explore the patient's understanding of their disease and collaboratively set an agenda with the patient after inquiring what the patient and family wish to address and explaining what the clinician wishes to address.

1.4 Clinicians should provide information that is timely and oriented to the patient's concerns and preferences for information. After providing information, clinicians should check for patient understanding and document important discussions in the medical record.

2.1 Clinicians should provide diagnostic and prognostic information that is tailored to the patient's needs and that provides hope and reassurance without misleading the patient.

2.4 When providing bad news, clinicians should take additional steps to address the needs and responses of the patients.

3.1 Before discussing specific treatment options with the patient, clinicians should clarify the goals of treatment (cure *v* prolongation of survival *v* improved quality of life) so that the patient understands likely outcomes and can relate goals of treatment to their goals of care.

3.3 Clinicians should discuss treatment options in a way that preserves patient hope, promotes autonomy, and facilitates understanding.

4.2 Clinicians should initiate conversations about patients' end-of-life preferences early in the course of incurable illness and readdress this topic periodically based on clinical events or patient preferences.

Guidelines are only useful to bring about necessary change if they are evidence based and reflect clinical reality, and if physicians are willing to follow them. As an aspirational list of conversation topics, processes, and goals, these guidelines are a good start, and the publications on which the guidelines were built provide empirical support for the recommended practices. The implementation advice accompanying the recommendations is also helpful. For recommendation 1.2, for example, physicians are encouraged to use open-ended questions to encourage patients to talk about their concerns. For recommendation 1.4, physicians are told to "avoid unnecessary delays in providing information," which only restates that advice should be timely, but it also reminds physicians to orient the patient to the topic of the meeting and to ask the patient what she knows and what she would like to discuss. (Offering the patient or an accompanying family member pencil and

[13] Timothy Gilligan et al., Patient-Clinician Communication: American Society of Clinical Oncology Consensus Guideline, 31 J. Clinical Oncology 3618–3632 (2017).

paper might also be useful.) For recommendation 2.1, the implementation strategies include asking the patient whether she desires explicit information, is ambivalent, or doesn't want information. For ambivalent patients, it recommends discussing "pros and cons of knowing" but doesn't mention the pros and cons of *not* knowing (which are not merely the flip side of the former). With respect to fostering hope, the strategies include assuring the patient that the physician "will do everything possible to get the best possible outcome" and will support the patient. This language may foster baseless optimism ("best possible outcome" may sound to the patient like remission or cure), and it may put the patient into the position of feeling obliged to accept every intervention that the physician offers in the quest to "get to the best possible outcome."

For recommendation 2.4, on conveying bad news, the strategies are quite specific and include step-by-step instructions regarding setting, timing, the use of succinct and plain language, pausing to let the patient absorb the news, waiting for the patient to respond, using empathy in response to patient distress, not minimizing the bad news or changing the subject, asking for questions and concerns, discussing next steps, and affirming support of the patient. For recommendation 3.1, the advice includes language that asks whether the patient's thoughts on continuing treatment have changed (in situations where therapy is not going well). What it does not include is any suggestion that the physician consider a patient's changed preferences and recommend that the patient discontinue or avoid therapeutic treatment in appropriate circumstances. Recommendation 3.3 reminds physicians to focus on what can be done, and to acknowledge uncertainty, to use decision aids where relevant, and to have an involved nurse who may contribute to the conversation and "will often be present for patients when questions and emotions arise after the physician has left the room." Finally, recommendation 4.2 emphasizes that physicians should initiate conversations about patients' end-of-life preferences early in the course of incurable illness and should discuss prognosis and advance care planning. Although these communication guidelines for cancer patients provide very useful talking points and standards for physician-patient communication, the evidence in Chapter 3 makes it clear that they aren't followed consistently.

Other guidelines advise what *not* to do in talking with patients about their medical situations. In one observational study of recorded physician encounters with patients, the researchers found that physicians "elicited the patient's agenda" – that is, asked about and understood the patient's concerns – in only 36 percent of patient visits and, among those agenda-setting conversations, interrupted patients as they stated their concerns 67 percent of the time – within an average of eleven seconds.[14] The takeaway message? Listen more, listen better, talk less, and let the patient finish speaking. In another example, the authors discourage the following:

[14] Naykky Singh Ospina et al., Eliciting the Patient's Agenda – Secondary Analysis of Recorded Clinical Encounters, 34 J. Gen. Intern. Med. 36–40 (2018).

blocking (redirecting conversation away from uncomfortable topics), lecturing (just what it sounds like, especially using medical jargon), collusion (what the ethnographic study in Chapter 8 describes), and premature reassurance (telling patients that all is okay before understanding what the patient is truly worried about).[15] It is striking how well the authors of this article acknowledge and describe the problematic patterns of communication with seriously ill patients. They follow up with what they call "behaviors to cultivate," including asking the patient to describe her understanding of her medical situation, telling her what she needs to know (including bad news), and then asking her whether she has understood (the classic 'ask – tell – ask' model of physician-patient communication). The authors also neatly unpeel the three levels inherent in most of these conversations – what is happening with the patient, how she feels about these events, and what the new information will mean for the patient going forward. They also urge physicians in their specialty to respond to the patient's emotions by accepting them rather than offering some countermeasure in the form of reassurance or rebuttal.[16] The question remains – how many physicians, oncologists in particular – adhere to these excellent recommendations? Given the rates of late-stage chemotherapy for terminally ill cancer patients, either oncologists aren't providing the information needed or patients aren't willing to heed the information and act accordingly.

It's worth noting here the common situation in which multiple physicians are involved in a single patient's treatment, including (for hospitalized patients) the effect of rotating shifts and 'on call' physicians. This structural model can perpetuate problems of inconsistent messaging and passing the buck – leaving these difficult discussions to other physicians and clinicians who are involved in the patient's care.[17] In ICUs, the responsibility to initiate conversations about end-of-life preferences with the patient's family often falls on the attending physician in charge. When various specialists evaluate a critically ill patient and conclude that the patient may not survive a particular intervention, or when a surgeon concludes that no further surgical procedures will help the patient's cause, the attending physician in the ICU often takes on the necessary conversations, letting surgeons and other specialists off the hook. As a matter of expediency, this pattern of communication lets the repeat player (the attending in charge in the ICU) conduct discussions with patients and families, but it may also mean that other specialists miss the opportunity to learn how to communicate effectively in the highly fraught setting of the ICU. Also, in many of these scenarios, it may be helpful to the patient to not only talk with the messenger but also with the specialist because more opportunities for patients to listen, digest information, and ask questions are better. It may also help avoid misunderstandings and differences of opinion.

15 Anthony L. Back et al., Approaching Difficult Communication Tasks in Oncology, 55 Cancer 164–177 (2005).

16 Ibid.

17 Lisa Rosenbaum, The Not-My-Problem Problem, 380 New Eng. J. Med. 881–885 (2019).

These sorts of conversations take more than just training. They require careful preparation, lots of time with each patient and family, and empathy and nuance. The rapid pace of medical practice together with the constant pressure to do more and to 'be productive' make the physician's time precious – and scarce. In the context of the ICU in particular, exhorting physicians to communicate better with families beyond the bare minimum of information transfer and decision-making may, in some circumstances, be unrealistic. Physicians who work in intensive care medicine routinely confront death (including the death of younger patients), trauma from accidents and violence, horrible disfigurement, and patients who experience intense pain, shortness of breath, or other agonies. When patients are dying in the ICU, physicians often are forced to assume an active role in deciding questions of withdrawal or withholding of potentially life-prolonging treatment. In these circumstances, physicians experience depression, grief, guilt, inadequacy, and frustration, among other emotions. Support from other disciplines, including nursing, social work, pastoral care, and palliative care, can help ICU physicians cope with these emotional challenges and can also assist with patient and family communication.[18] Even before the COVID-19 pandemic, many physicians felt rushed or burned out. Now, with the added pressure of the pandemic on hospital space and staffing, it feels quixotic to ask so much of physicians – particularly those with hospital-based practices. But the ASCO guidelines and others of its ilk are there for good reason, and widespread adherence to their recommendations would likely improve physician-patient communication and quality of care for patients with cancer, as would adherence to similar guidelines in other specialties that care for critically ill patients.

'How to' articles, guidelines, and courses provide a useful tool for training but cannot fully bridge the gap between theory and practice. The translation of abstract knowledge about improving end-of-life care into the actual practice of physicians remains a formidable challenge. Physicians still may hesitate to take the lead. A culture shift is needed so that these conversations happen consistently (and unhurriedly) as part of a professional norm, and that the recommendations presented continue to evolve as appropriate and to rest on sound scientific evidence. Evidence from multiple studies of interventions with physicians to improve communication and decision-making suggests that these interventions can significantly improve the quality and timing of end-of-life communication, but they have to be put into routine practice. Research suggests that despite clinical guidelines recommending end-of-life planning conversations with patients who have a life expectancy of less than one year, these conversations often are delayed until shortly before the patient's death. For patients with terminal cancer, discussions about end-of-life preferences occur on average only one month before death, and usually in

[18] Susan D. Block, Helping the Clinician Cope with Death in the ICU, in Managing Death in the Intensive Care Unit: The Transition from Cure to Comfort (J. Randall Curtis & Gordon D. Rubenfeld, eds, Oxford University Press, 2001).

a hospital setting rather than with the patients' treating oncologists. In fact, in one study, only 27 percent of oncologists had these discussions with their patients at all.[19] Training physicians and providing them with communication tools and reminders can substantially increase the frequency and improve the timing of these conversations.

When physicians have evidence-based training for discussing patient preferences and potential de-escalation of care with patients and families, they may feel more comfortable doing so. For example, in the context of CPR, researchers tested several decision models to see which model most accurately predicted which patients would survive attempted resuscitation with no or minimal neurological deficits and be discharged. The best of the models provided physicians with a sound basis for counseling patients about their DNAR status.[20] However, hospitals and physicians still need to study and implement this sort of model consistently for it to effectively reduce the incidence of unwanted and inappropriate resuscitation attempts. More generally, there is an ongoing effort to identify which patterns of medical practice should focus on de-escalation of medical care – identifying scenarios in which less is generally better.[21]

Various expert organizations recommend earlier discussion with all seriously ill patients, and they urge the conversations to venture beyond specific decisions about resuscitation and life-prolonging technology into a broader understanding of the patient's goals, hopes, and preferences. A recent study of a communication intervention at a major cancer care center provides encouraging news on the benefits of communication training. The study compared one group of oncologists who received communication-focused clinical tools and training with one control group. The intervention group also received email reminders before patient visits. The interventions led to marked improvements in that group: a significantly higher percentage of documented end-of-life care planning discussions with patients, with these conversations occurring much earlier before patient death and with much more focus on the patient's values, goals, and life-sustaining treatment preferences.[22]

Training and tools actually work, though it is less certain whether physicians will continue practices learned as part of any research study when they return to routine care of patients after the study ends. Evidence-based decision-making tools can help physicians guide patients and families, but only when physicians know of and utilize

[19] Jennifer W. Mack et al., End-of-Life Care Discussions Among Patients with Advanced Cancer: A Cohort Study, 156 Ann. Intern. Med. 204–210 (2012).

[20] Mark Ebell et al., Development and Validation of the Good Outcome Following Attempted Resuscitation (GO-FAR) Score to Predict Neurologically Intact Survival After In-Hospital Cardiopulmonary Resuscitation, 173 JAMA Internal Med. 1872–1878 (2013).

[21] Eve A. Kerr et al., Identifying Recommendations for Stopping or Scaling Back Unnecessary Routine Services in Primary Care, 180 JAMA Internal Med. 1500–1508 (2020) (providing a process to identify useful de-escalation recommendations in the primary care context).

[22] Joanna Paladino et al., Evaluating an Intervention to Improve Communication Between Oncology Clinicians and Patients with Life-Limiting Cancer, 5 JAMA Oncol. 801–809 (2019).

the tools, are willing to discuss the resulting prediction with the patient and family, and when the patient and family can accept the advice and decide accordingly. All the while, the broader problem remains – physicians are being asked to adhere to de-escalation recommendations while practicing in a system that incentivizes the provision of high-intensity medical care, whether or not it is necessary and wanted.

SOME PROMISING DEVELOPMENTS

For some while now, there have been efforts to improve physician-patient communication by moving to a 'shared decision-making' (SDM) model. Rather than viewing informed consent as a rigid two-step process in which the physician provides information and the patient then makes a decision and consents to treatment – a burdensome and not very effective process for many patients – the shared decision-making model emphasizes back-and-forth discussion of interrelated facts and values. Under this approach, patients share values and preferences while physicians share medical options and recommendations based on the information that the patient provides. Because the physician is the medical expert, it is her responsibility to make recommendations to the patient about how to achieve the patient's goals.[23] Shared decision-making recognizes that the patient is the expert about what is important to her and the patient's ultimate right to make choices and simultaneously acknowledges the physician's responsibility for the patient's well-being. SDM attempts to include the patient more actively in the process of making complex medical decisions, including choices about end-of-life care. As a result, even though the informed consent unilaterally given is still the decision of the patient, relationally the patient consents to a shared reality – a mutual understanding by patient and physician of relevant information and a shared agreement about the 'right way' forward for the particular patient based on her values and preferences. This process shows a genuine respect for patient autonomy because it helps patients (or surrogates) understand the consequences of decisions about end-of-life care. In the absence of physicians making recommendations based on patients' values, patients (or surrogates) often may not understand what they're agreeing to – they're making decisions in the dark.[24]

SDM gets a lot of support from medical and health policy experts, but it's not clear whether SDM consistently reduces rates of unwanted or potentially inappropriate care. SDM is particularly well suited to help patients make decisions about 'preference-sensitive' medical care – in which there is no single 'best choice' but rather an array of choices that may be 'best' depending on the patient's values and tolerance

[23] J. Andrew Billings & Eric L. Krakauer, On Patient Autonomy and Physician Responsibility in End-of-Life Care, 171 Arch. Intern. Med. 849–853 (2011).

[24] Recall from Chapter 3 that patients misunderstand the potential effectiveness of CPR and frequently incorrectly believe that chemotherapy for metastatic cancer is potentially curative, among other examples.

for risk.[25] It does appear to promote better decision-making in cases of complex medical care; however, because of the complexity of physician-patient encounters, it is hard to untangle and measure the effect of SDM on physicians versus patients.[26] For that matter, it isn't easy to measure what constitutes a good medical decision in the first place, especially in cases rife with clinical uncertainty and no obvious 'right' choice.[27] There is evidence, however, that SDM reduces costs and utilization of medical care. One investigation found that patients who received enhanced decision support (including support from trained "health coaches") had lower medical costs, significantly lower rates of hospital admission, and fewer preference-sensitive surgeries.[28]

SDM, when done well, can help patients and families make realistic decisions consistent with the patient's goals and values, but SDM has clear limitations. The power imbalance and informational asymmetry between physicians and patients may inhibit patients from speaking up about their preferences, even when they have a better knowledge base for making decisions after talking with physicians. It's also difficult to know whether the SDM model helps patients make decisions that reflect consideration of the physician's honest views (or whether the physician is being as candid as the model would require). One SDM-focused study, which evaluated audio recordings of actual instances of family decision-making in the ICU, considered how well physicians and families integrated patient values and preferences into end-of-life decisions. The study authors found that in one-quarter of these meetings, there was no discussion of the patient's values and preferences whatsoever. There was some exchange of information about these matters in about 68 percent of the meetings, but focused discussion about the impact of the patient's values and preferences on the decision at hand occurred only in 44 percent of the meetings. And physicians actually made specific treatment recommendations based on the patient's values in only about 8 percent of the meetings.[29] Other evidence also suggests that physicians may not be doing as well with SDM as they think they are. One recent study demonstrated a significant gap between the physicians' beliefs that they had conveyed prognosis or that they had discussed focusing on comfort care, and blind reviewers' evaluations of the transcripts concluded in many instances that these ideas had not been sufficiently discussed.[30]

25 Elliott S. Fisher & John E. Wennberg, Health Care Quality, Geographic Variations, and the Challenge of Supply-Sensitive Care, 46 Perspectives in Biology & Med. 69–79 (2003).

26 Stephen J. Katz & Sarah Hawley, The Value of Sharing Treatment Decision Making with Patients: Expecting Too Much? 310 JAMA 1559–1560 (2013).

27 Jada G. Hamilton et al., What Is a Good Medical Decision? A Research Agenda Guided by Perspectives from Multiple Stakeholders, 40 J. Behav. Med. 52–68 (2017).

28 David Veroff et al., Enhanced Support for Shared Decision Making Reduced Costs of Care for Patients with Preference-Sensitive Conditions 32 *Health Aff.* 285–293 (2013).

29 L. P. Scheunemann et al., Clinician-Family Communication About Patients' Values and Preferences in Intensive Care Units, 179 JAMA Internal Med. 676–684 (2019).

30 Scott T. Vasher et al., Physician Self-Assessment of Shared Decision-Making in Simulated Intensive Care Unit Family Meetings, 3 JAMA Network Open DOI: 10.1001/jamanetworkopen.2020.5188 (2020).

Medicare rules now *require* SDM for a few procedures, such as the use of implantable cardiac defibrillators, and commentators – while acknowledging the value of SDM – are wary of the burdens placed on physicians.[31] Still, the shared decision-making model, when fully and effectively implemented, looks like an improvement over the traditional model of binary informed consent. At the end of life, shared decision-making as a way of structuring the physician-patient encounter can help the parties engage more fully with one another, to take the time for the patient to understand what choices remain and what is achievable, and for the physician to understand what matters most to the patient. That said, SDM requires a nuanced understanding of what the process entails, and it requires time – which is often limited, given the demands on physicians.

As another practice to improve outcomes in complex medical decision-making, decision aids have been in use since the 1990s. They come in multiple forms, including videos, interactive web-based programs, and print. They have several goals: to help patients understand options and risks and benefits, using adequate detail and jargon-free language; to help patients understand and formulate what outcomes and goals are most important to them; and to guide patients in making choices consistent with their goals.[32] Decision aids can address complex medical decisions like navigating treatment for cancer and heart disease, and they're especially useful in helping patients make decisions about preference-sensitive care for medical conditions in which there are multiple reasonable treatment options. Here, shared decision-making using decision aids can help physicians and patients move beyond the medical-based information about what would be the 'right' or 'best' treatment choice and help them focus on the larger patient-based concerns that would lead to a 'good' decision for the particular patient.[33] There's evidence that decision aids improve the quality of decision-making across an array of medical specialties and situations such as early-stage breast cancer treatment[34] and colon cancer screening.[35]

In the context of life-threatening and terminal illness, decision aids can help patients and surrogates make more informed decisions by improving patient understanding of the benefits and harms of potentially life-prolonging interventions like CPR, mechanical ventilation, and dialysis. They can also help patients understand medical terminology commonly used in cancer treatment. Cancer patients

31 Faisal M. Merchant et al., Mandatory Shared Decision Making by the Centers for Medicare & Medicaid Services for Cardiovascular Procedures and Other Tests, 320 JAMA 641–642 (2018).

32 Annette M. O'Connor et al., Toward the "Tipping Point": Decision Aids and Informed Patient Choice, 26 Health Aff. 716–725 (2007).

33 Michael J. Barry & Susan Edgman-Levitan, Shared Decision Making – The Pinnacle of Patient-Centered Care, 366 New Eng. J. Med. 780–781 (2012).

34 Sarah T. Hawley et al., Decision Involvement and Receipt of Mastectomy Among Racially and Ethnically Diverse Breast Cancer Patients, 101 J. Nat'l Cancer Inst. 1333–1347 (2009).

35 Robert J. Volk et al., Patient Decision Aids for Colorectal Cancer Screening: A Systematic Review and Meta-Analysis, 51 Am. J. Prev. Med. 779–791 (2016).

frequently do not understand common terms including maintenance, palliative, toxicity, radiation, chemotherapy, and biopsy.[36] There is now quite a bit of evidence that end-of-life video decision aids have a significant impact on decisional robustness, making patients more likely to prefer comfort care, to reject CPR, and to reject intubation.[37] Moreover, video decision aids in particular not only inform patients about the options but also increase the probability that patients and physicians will have a conversation about prognosis and end-of-life decisions. Decision aids may also help patients feel better and more confident about their decisions – to reinforce their sense of control, clarity, and acceptance.

There is cause for caution, however, in concluding that decision aids are an easy solution to physician-patient communication problems. Although there is a strong correlation between watching end-of-life video decision aids and choosing comfort care, the studies cannot prove that adding decisional input from decision aids and the decisional outcome (a more common preference for comfort care) are causally connected. In most of the published studies, researchers compared two sets of patients – those who heard an oral presentation of information about end-of-life choices and goals of care and those who heard both the oral presentation *and* watched a video. Here, it may be that simple repetition improves comprehension, leading patients in the video group to choose comfort care and to reject CPR and other burdensome interventions more frequently than the patients in the oral presentation group. The other problem with decision aids is not that they fail to impact patient decision-making – it's that they may skew it in ways that don't accurately reflect pre-existing patient values. These videos, while designed to be neutral rather than value laden or outcome driven, may provoke strong emotions in patients who are already struggling with the reactions that come with life-threatening illness. There's also a real risk that decision aids will oversimplify or bias the outcomes of decisions by framing options in ways that encourage refusal of burdensome interventions or by triggering negative responses by portraying unsettling images of, for example, advanced dementia or the violence that is necessarily part of CPR.[38] Still, these videos can clearly have a positive influence on the decision-making process because they focus patients' attention more effectively on the relevant information compared with only oral or written presentation of information. Overall, experts support the utilization of well-designed, evidence-based

[36] Rebecca D. Pentz, Videos Improve Patient Understanding of Misunderstood Chemotherapy Terminology, 125 Cancer 4011–4018 (2019).

[37] Angelo E. Volandes et al., A Randomized Controlled Trial of a Goals-of-Care Video for Elderly Patients Admitted to Skilled Nursing Facilities, 15 J. Palliative Med. 805–811 (2012); Angelo E. Volandes et al., Augmenting Advance Care Planning in Poor Prognosis Cancer with a Video Decision Aid: A Pre-Post Study, 188 Cancer 4331–4338 (2012).

[38] Barbara Noah & Neal Feigenson, Avoiding Overtreatment at the End of Life: Physician-Patient Communication and Truly Informed Consent, 36 Pace L. Rev. 736–799 (2016) (thank you to Professor Feigenson for his excellent analysis of the evidence on efficacy and cognitive impact of video decision aids).

decision aids. Empirical research suggests that they improve end-of-life decision-making, resulting in more alignment between what medical interventions patients prefer and what they actually receive (though measuring this question presents its own complexities).[39]

Shared decision-making and the use of decision aids promise some progress beyond the minimum required by informed consent law and toward the goal of more robust and meaningful consent to treatment, but these measures may still not improve the authenticity of end-of-life choices.[40] The ideal of authenticity requires that the patient not only understand intellectually the nature of the treatment and its risks and benefits but also has the emotional ability to make difficult decisions, as well as a functional value system through which to evaluate a multiplicity of choices for herself. Shared decision-making and decision aids can play an important part in trying to reorient physicians and patients toward better-informed (and perhaps even more authentic) choice. The Affordable Care Act encourages the use of decision aids in the context of preference-sensitive care,[41] and some states, such as Washington State, also encourage the use of decision aids in certain contexts.[42] These are promising developments, but no legal reform can require that patients confront their own mortality or that physicians help them do so.

It is difficult to assess how often patient decisions reflect this sort of authenticity, but it is probably relatively uncommon because so many barriers exist. Patients often don't know what questions to ask either their physicians or themselves. Even when patients have important questions to ask, fear and denial of illness or deference to physicians may inhibit them from asking. The ability to talk openly requires that both patients and physicians acknowledge what they are feeling and undertake these conversations despite their inherent emotional challenges. This process can actually improve the quality of care *and* protect the physician's own well-being.[43] But there is no way to mandate, implement, or enforce this level of emotional engagement between any individual physician and patient. It will, if it occurs, depend entirely on the inclinations of the individuals in question. From the physician's perspective, authenticity requires physicians to be emotionally self-aware enough to recognize when they are avoiding or abridging difficult conversations with patients and families and to be able to correct for this avoidance. Physicians also need sufficient experience and emotional resilience to manage these conversations with patients and families whose own part in the conversation is very likely hampered by fear, regret, or grief. Many physicians very capably engage in these conversations but,

39 Justin J. Sanders et al., Achieving Goal-Concordant Care: A Conceptual Model and Approach to Measuring Serious Illness Communication and Its Impact, 21 J. Palliative Med. S-17–S-27 (2018).

40 Daniel Brudney, Choosing for Another: Beyond Autonomy and Best Interests, 39 Hastings Ctr. Rep. 31–37 (2009).

41 Affordable Care Act § 3506.

42 Rev. Code Wash. § 7.70.060.

43 Diane E. Meier et al., The Inner Life of Physicians and Care of the Seriously Ill, 286 JAMA 3007–3014 (2001).

because people vary so much in temperament and in their ability to acknowledge and discuss difficult emotions, it is unrealistic to expect all physicians (and patients) to behave this way.

In end-of-life care, relying on the patient's exercise of his autonomy-based right to choose is often insufficient to promote sound medical decision-making and, in particular, to avoid care that is excessive, whether measured by its objective benefits or its consistency with the patient's values and preferences, properly discussed and understood. Fear, denial of death, deference to physician authority, lack of trust, and simple ignorance often make patients and families reluctant to initiate or engage in discussions about the uncertain and unwelcome future. Physicians can try to step outside the comfortable confines of the traditional model of informed consent and initiate conversations that provide honest information, advice, and deeper insight about end-of-life choices while seeking better insight into the patient's values and preferences. The process of shared decision-making, if well implemented, represents a significant step forward, but it requires willingness on the part of individual physicians and patients to undertake it. Courage and diligence in the face of adversity and death are qualities that education and practice can encourage but never compel.

Patient decision-making reflects a complex mix of intuition, emotion, and the subjective and objective contemplation of future benefits and harms. While shared decision-making can improve patient satisfaction by enhancing understanding of treatments and alternatives, increasing patient involvement and preserving quality of life, for some patients, too much information or too much responsibility for complex medical decisions can result in decisional regret. In one study, about one-fifth of women with breast cancer believed that they had too much decisional responsibility. The population studied was racially diverse, and it appears that Latinx women were most likely to feel overwhelmed with responsibility for their treatment decisions, either because they were culturally more inclined to leave decisions to physicians or perhaps because they struggled with comprehension difficulties that are more common among non-native English speakers. In this same study, Black patients were most likely to report that they hadn't enough responsibility for their own decision-making, probably reflecting their ongoing lack of trust in health professionals.[44] There is clearly no one-size-fits-all approach to decision-making, which of course adds to the bundle of responsibilities that physicians face when sitting down with patients and families to discuss options. Physicians not only have the responsibility to initiate these conversations, to exchange information, to inquire about values and goals with patients, and to advise patients how to best proceed based on these exchanges – they have to start with an understanding of how much

44 Jennifer C. Livaudais et al., Breast Cancer Treatment Decision-Making: Are We Asking Too Much of Patients? 28 J. Gen. Int. Med. 630–636 (2012).

a patient (or family member) wants to participate in this intricate decisional process in the first place.

FORCING PHYSICIANS TO HAVE 'THE TALK'

I'm not advocating mandated disclosure here. Informed consent law can sometimes serve as an enforcement mechanism to disclosure, at least in the breach. But mandating disclosure of prognosis, of the limited utility of treatment options, of the undesirability of prolonging the dying process with life-supportive technologies simply will not solve the problem of inadequate physician-patient communication. The law requires physicians to inform patients of certain items of information. However, without context and an honest and elaborate discussion of the import of that information and what it means for the particular patient's experience, mandated disclosure gets us nowhere. Many patients cannot recall and apply to themselves what they have heard from the physician, and many are averse to making decisions at all when faced with life-threatening illness, all of which undermines any value of forcing physicians and patients to communicate.[45]

Some states, such as New York, have enacted legislation requiring physicians to proactively offer to discuss the subject of end-of-life options with their patients. New York's Palliative Care Information Act went into effect in 2011 and requires physicians and nurse practitioners to offer counseling and information about end-of-life options to terminally ill patients or their surrogate decision-makers. The language of the statute requires that this information be offered to all patients with a predicted six-month or shorter life expectancy. If the patient (or surrogate) accepts the offer, clinicians must explain to the patient her prognosis, the range of options available to her, the risks and benefits of those options, and the patient's "legal rights to comprehensive pain and symptom management at the end of life."[46] Although patients' rights groups celebrated the provision, physicians have not taken kindly to this sort of legislative interference with the independent exercise of professional judgment. In addition to pointing out the difficulty of identifying the 'terminal' phase of many illnesses, critics decried "the law's heavy-handed intrusion into the doctor-patient relationship" and the state's attempt to "prescribe legislatively what should be a subtle, intimate conversation between doctor and patient that often happens over time."[47] The authors of an article criticizing the legislation urged a focus on the real reasons why end-of-life conversations do not occur, noted that communication skills can be learned, and bemoaned the statute as another legalistic box that would need to be checked. But the statute only requires that physicians *offer*

[45] Omri Ben-Shahar & Carl E. Schneider, The Failure of Mandated Disclosure, 159 U. Pa. L. Rev. 647–749 (2011).

[46] N.Y. Laws Ch. 331 § 2997-c.

[47] Alan B. Astrow & Beth Popp, The Palliative Care Information Act in Real Life, 364 New Eng. J. Med. 1885–1887 (2011).

patients and surrogates this information (who can, of course, refuse it), and some – perhaps many – patients may be unaware that they have the right to palliative care at the end of life and the right to direct their own care, including refusal of life-sustaining treatment. They may instead believe that a family member has the primary right to make decisions, or that refusal of life-prolonging care amounts to suicide. They also may be temporarily overwhelmed by the situation and need some help thinking it through. All that the statute does is ask physicians not to abandon these patients in the decisional process and leave it to others who are less experienced and knowledgeable about what choices remain on the table. A thoughtful conversation about these matters – with patients or surrogates who are interested in having it – could be a gift to many. Silence in the face of death does not happen by accident. It is the role of the physician to offer and, where accepted, to have that conversation, whether or not a statute mandates it.

AN OPPORTUNITY FOR PHYSICIANS

Does the United Kingdom, with its top end-of-life care rankings, do better when it comes to physician-patient communication and care that is consistent with patient wishes? It's difficult to say in the case of any individual physician-patient encounter, but there are structural factors that increase the likelihood that physicians in the United Kingdom will discuss end-of-life decisions and provide useful information to their patients. The NHS not only provides access to medical care for all, it also has created a culture in which palliative and hospice care play an important role at the end of life. Whether a 'better' health care system produces a better end-of-life care culture or whether the British culture (that supported the creation of the NHS) generally seeks to avoid overutilization of burdensome end-of-life treatments is ultimately an unanswerable question. Given that these questions involve large-scale dynamic processes at the level of whole societies and cultures, it's probably some of both, forming a virtuous circle of sorts. Similarly, whether the British more willingly acknowledge fear and vulnerability at the end of life isn't obvious (or reliably measurable). I'll stick with the evidence and not attempt to answer these questions.

Although there are many differences between the US and the UK law governing patient decision-making, a few things stand out. US physicians have the right to refuse, based on conscience, to implement a patient's or proxy's request to withdraw care, as well as the right to refuse to provide requested care that they do not believe is medically indicated. However, the primacy of the autonomy principle in the United States means that physicians are not routinely asked to make the actual decision about whether to withhold or withdraw life-sustaining medical treatment. In the ICU, physicians may be more directive or may even assume decision-making responsibility at the request of a family member or surrogate. There is evidence that in the context of decisions about CPR, patients regularly delegate the particular decision about whether to attempt resuscitation in the case of cardiac arrest to their physicians or family members.[48] Overall, US physicians are asked to *implement* decisions made by patients (directly or via advance directives) or their surrogate decision-makers – but they rarely possess the responsibility or authority to decide themselves.[49] The legal structure in the United States fundamentally requires patient or family consent. There is a lively debate about whether US physicians can or should unilaterally decide to withdraw or withhold inappropriate life-prolonging treatment for terminally ill patients, but the matter is far from settled.[50] As the evidence in this book suggests, there is plenty of countervailing professional, cultural, and legal pressure for physicians to defer to patients and families.

In contrast, physicians in England and Wales, guided by the Mental Capacity Act and accompanying guidance documents, are expressly charged with the responsibility to determine whether continuing life-sustaining medical treatment is appropriate for patients who lack the ability to make their own health care decisions.[51] Patients with decisional capacity do, of course, participate in treatment decisions, including decisions about end-of-life care, but the physician generally assumes a prominent role in guiding decision-making.[52] Physicians also are clearly instructed under General Medical Council guidance that they have no obligation to provide a treatment simply because the patient (or surrogate) demands it.[53] Given that there are fewer incentives to provide inappropriate care, it appears that physicians don't provide it – at least not often and not for long. The fact that UK physicians are the primary decision-makers for incapacitated patients may also mean that they are

48 Christina M. Puchalski et al., Patients Who Want Their Family and Physician to Make Resuscitation Decisions for Them: Observations from SUPPORT and HELP, 48 J. Am. Geriatrics Soc'y S84–S90 (Supp. 2000) (most patients prefer to leave resuscitation decisions to their family and physicians rather than asserting their own preferences – 70.8 percent in one study group and 78 percent in another).

49 The Texas statute discussed in Chapter 10 is one exception. A handful of other state medical associations have expressed support for similar legislation. Douglas B. White & Thaddeus M. Pope, The Courts, Futility, and the Ends of Medicine, 307 JAMA 151–152 (2012).

50 J. Randal Curtis & Constantine A. Manthous, Point/Counterpoint Editorials, 132 Chest 748–756 (2007); Eric Gampel, Does Professional Autonomy Protect Medical Futility Judgments? 20 Bioethics 92–104 (2006).

51 In the absence of an advance directive or other prior statement to guide the decision and in the absence of a legal proxy to make decisions, GMC guidance makes the physician the responsible decision-maker. General Medical Council, Decision Making and Consent §§ 88–89 (Nov. 9, 2020). The physician, when deciding for an incapacitated patient, must still consider the patient's past and present wishes and beliefs (to the extent they can be known) and must consult with the patient's health care team and anyone who cares for the patient or is interested in his welfare. Mental Capacity Act § 4(6)-(7) (2005).

52 General Medical Council, Treatment and Care Towards the End of Life: Good Practice in Decision-Making §§ 15–16 (2010), www.gmc-uk.org/ethical-guidance/ethical-guidance-for-doctors/treatment-and-care-towards-the-end-of-life.

53 Ibid., §14d. The American Medical Association includes a similar opinion, but it is unclear how much impact the opinion has on actual practice. Am. Med. Ass'n Code of Ethics Opinion 5.5, Medically Ineffective Interventions, www.ama-assn.org/delivering-care/ethics/medically-ineffective-interventions.

more comfortable as a matter of routine with asserting opinions about best options for care and declining to provide potentially inappropriate care.

In our autonomy-focused milieu, US physicians may refrain from explicitly introducing best interests considerations into conversations and decision-making with patients or surrogates, whereas the best interests principle plays a more prominent role in the United Kingdom – for all patients but particularly for incapacitated patients. The concept of best interests is interpreted to include the values and preferences of the patient.[54] The UK approach therefore adds a layer of pragmatism into the decision, by routinely taking into account the best available information about the patient's prognosis and the likely effectiveness and potential harms of proposed therapeutic interventions. Interestingly, there is no exact parallel in England and Wales to the US law of informed consent – the law only requires that the patient understand "in broad terms the nature of the procedure which is intended."[55] Patients there do have the clear right to participate in their medical decision-making, and court decisions[56] and guidance documents[57] have very much emphasized the principle of autonomy in patient decision-making, making the prior, more paternalistic models outdated, at least for patients with decisional capacity. As in the United States, patients also have a well-recognized right to refuse medical care, even if refusal will lead to death.[58] However, courts have also made it absolutely clear that autonomy does not outweigh all other considerations – physicians are not obligated to offer treatments that they believe to be inappropriate.[59]

Finally, the empirical evidence discussed in Chapter 3 and elsewhere illustrates that many physicians in the United States do not adhere to practice guidelines and other recommendations that promote timely and truthful communication with seriously ill patients. The commodification, commercialization, and market competition aspects of medical services in the United States may explain why physicians here feel less obligated to comply with practice guidelines regarding communication and consent. UK physicians also express unease with discussing death with patients,[60] especially choosing the right time for discussion,[61] and sometimes have met with resistance or litigation from family members about discontinuing

54 Mental Capacity Act § 4(6) (2005).

55 Jonathan Herring, Medical Law and Ethics §6.9 (7th ed. Oxford University Press, 2018).

56 Montgomery v. Lanarkshire Health Board, USKC 11 (2015).

57 General Medical Council, Decision-Making and Consent, https://www.gmc-uk.org/-/media/documents/gmc-guidance-for-doctors---decision-making-and-consent-english_pdf-84191055.pdf (2020).

58 Pretty v. the United Kingdom, European Court of Human Rights (4th Section) (2002).

59 Anne-Maree Farrell & Margaret Brazier, Not So New Directions in the Law of Consent: Examining Montgomery v. Lanarkshire Health Board, 42 J. Med. Ethics 85–88 (2016) (discussing Montgomery v. Lanarkshire Health Board).

60 Jacqui Wise, Dying Remains a Taboo Subject for Patients and GPs, Finds Survey, 344 Brit. Med. J. e3356 (2012) (finding that 35 percent of GPs have not initiated a discussion with a patient about end-of-life preferences).

61 Helen Salisbury, Talking About Death, 365 Brit. Med. J. l4346 (2019) (noting the inhibiting problem of uncertain illness trajectory and its impact on the timing of these conversations).

therapeutic and life-prolonging care.[62] Even so, the high-quality rankings of end-of-life care in the United Kingdom suggest that physicians there communicate more effectively and in a more timely manner about initiating or scaling back burdensome and often non-beneficial medical interventions.[63] Guidance documents from the National Institute for Health and Clinical Excellence (NICE)[64] and the General Medical Council (GMC)[65] addressing end-of-life care quality emphasize the need to communicate with patients and families at the end of life. The recently updated NICE quality standard for end-of-life care requires that clinicians discuss prognosis with dying patients and their families and formulate an individual care plan that includes discussion of CPR. While NICE certainly has its critics (particularly with respect to its systemic health care rationing practices),[66] the requirement of individual care plans creates a valuable structural opportunity for physicians, patients, and families to discuss end-of-life preferences and to make hard choices. Guidance documents that apply to all specialties in the system help create a culture of shared respect for the value of evidence-based guidance.[67] So, what can perhaps be more generalized in comparison is this: whereas the US system promotes more subjective and idiosyncratic decisions and resulting practices, the UK system defaults more prominently to objective and pragmatic practices.

IT'S ALL UP TO US

From the moment of birth, we're all "up the Styx without a paddle."[68] There are limited opportunities to control what happens at the end of life, and those often require early or at least not-too-late acknowledgment of mortality. Patients, as nonexperts, need the help of physicians who can provide the information and support (medical, cognitive, and emotional) necessary to formulate and try to achieve realistic goals. Unfortunately, as inventorized in prior chapters, a lot of stressors that affect physicians, patients, and families routinely stand in the way of achieving a good death. Everything that burdens end-of-life communication is

62 Medical Protection, Survey of Members (March, 2019), www.medicalprotection.org/uk/articles/end-of-life-care.

63 Economist Intelligence Unit, 2015 Quality of Death Index, https://eiuperspectives.economist.com/healthcare/2015-quality-death-index (ranking the United Kingdom first on quality and delivery of palliative care).

64 National Institute for Health Care and Excellence (NICE), End of Life Care for Adults, www.nice.org.uk/guidance/qs13 (2011, updated 2017).

65 General Medical Council (GMC), Treatment and Care Towards the End of Life; Good Practice in Decision Making (2010).

66 Richard Smith, The Failings of NICE, 321 Brit. Med. J. 1363–1364 (2000).

67 It is worth noting, however, that the UK guidance describes optimal communication at the very end of life – there is less in the guidance documents about communication at earlier decision points in life-threatening illness, when patients may need to make informed decisions about whether to pursue high-burden treatments.

68 Quoting a senior law colleague who wishes to remain anonymous.

interconnected, and this interconnectivity creates a massive and complex ecosystem that physicians, patients, and families must navigate to make decisions together as they confront illness, aging, and dying. What we have here is an enormous collective action problem – and these types of problems are never easily solved. Perhaps, at a societal level – at least in the United States – these problems are insuperable. The problem of over-provision of medical care at the end of life is long recognized in the literature, but the solutions considered to date have had, at best, a marginally ameliorating effect.

All of this talk of structural reform and improvements to medical education and communication skills, more advance care planning, and the rest only go part of the way to addressing the inevitable personal and collective struggle to make difficult decisions at the end of life. The real impetus for improved communication must come from within – from physicians, from patients, and from families who find the courage to be open to these sorts of discussions. Evidence-based training to improve communication skills can certainly help, but, in the end, it will all come down to individual physicians and patients who are willing to push themselves out of the delay/deny mode in the service of a better death. A broader professional culture shift is needed. Patients who are diagnosed with a clearly terminal condition (as opposed to something that is potentially curable or at least manageable on a chronic basis) require timely, honest, and compassionate guidance from physicians and the treatment team to avoid inappropriate and burdensome care. Rather than a technocratic focus on disease mitigation (though that should happen too, along with appropriate palliative care), physicians can play a tremendously important role to guide and support the patient and family through the frightening process of terminal diagnosis, treatment, decline, and the active dying process. This process can give patients real hope – for a more comfortable final chapter of life and a more peaceful death.

The broader, unanswered question is what else, outside of the legal and medical system, can encourage individuals to address these questions on a personal level before the critical moment arrives? Autonomy does not have much meaning without the courage and foresight to think about what is important to us as individuals – whether it is achieving the longest life possible, minimizing life with disability or loss of dignity, or perhaps tolerating disability so long as cognitive abilities remain unimpaired – and to develop and memorialize these preferences through serious conversations with family members or via a written document. Of course, there is also the option to ignore reality and hope for immortality. But in denial, we harm ourselves and those around us – physicians and family and friends who ultimately are under pressure to participate in a charade. So, it's not just physicians who need to step up. Patients, their families, and all of us who are not yet patients or the family members of patients have the opportunity to think – in advance, profoundly, and before the added burdens and distractions of crisis interfere – about the reality of mortality and about what is important as death approaches. We can take responsibility to prepare for that moment that, when it comes, is ours alone to face.

12

Coda

Freude ist die einfachste Form der Dankbarkeit.

("Joy is the simplest form of gratitude.") —Karl Barth (1886–1968)

There is nothing new under the sun, and so much of what this book contains is nothing new, only perhaps a somewhat different and more systematic way of thinking about what is already known. It's impossible to develop any collective majoritarian default method for how best to deal with death on an individual level. Thinking carefully about how we live – in preparation for how we will die – is an ongoing and iterative process, an opportunity to be seized rather than postponed. Of course, no one of healthy mind actually wants to die, and it is normal and necessary to avoid dwelling continuously on mortality, but persistent denial of the *un*deniable fact of mortality harms more than it helps. Pausing from time to time to contemplate death may not make its impending arrival any more welcome but, like developing calluses from hard manual labor, it can toughen up the emotions a bit. Without occasional labor of this sort, the result is not calluses but painful blisters. Much of what we ultimately experience at the end of life is within our exclusive control – our inner lives remain ours alone. As for our outer lives, specifically our bodies and the prospect of suffering, taking some control of this aspect of dying also requires an initial willingness to confront what lies within. It is never too late to start thinking about the end of life, even when it's already getting late.

To be very clear, none of the argument throughout this book is intended to suggest that patients should be rushed into making decisions, denied medically necessary and appropriate care, or prevented from continuing to pursue standard and experimental therapies. There is rarely the need to rush decision-making (unless decisions have been avoided for so long that the key questions at the end of life are only addressed at the last moment). The goal is an unhurried thinking process. A patient's robustly informed choices will usually require that the patient will have time to contemplate the options and that the patient – when pursuing standard and experimental therapies or accepting life-prolonging measures – will have opted into these treatments with eyes wide open. Patients and families can and should take the time they need to understand holistically the implications of different options so that, when a patient or surrogate ultimately makes decisions, that person can feel reasonably confident that she has attempted, if not succeeded, to do the best that she can in a very difficult situation. This process at least increases the odds that the patient will receive medical care that aligns with her preferences and best interests.

The impact of bounded rationality and clinical uncertainty on complex medical decision-making means that most proposed 'solutions' or improvements to existing practices will only penetrate the surface layer of the complexities inherent in end-of-life communication and decision-making. Without deliberate acknowledgment of the deeper layers – that death is certain, that there likely will be pain of one sort or another, that along the pathway to death some decision-relevant facts will remain Knightian unknown unknowns – patients, families, and physicians will be attempting in vain to mitigate the effects of suboptimal decision-making in what is often a partial medical and emotional knowledge vacuum. In that moment of looking mortality square in the face, the values of candor, empathy, and courage in individual physicians *and* their patients may be the only pathway through the daunting but ultimately very ordinary task of dying.

As P. L. Travers wrote, "We are all made of the same stuff, remember, we of the Jungle, you of the City. The same substance composes us – the tree overhead, the stone beneath us, the bird, the beast, the star – we are all one, all moving to the same end."[1] Speaking of stardust, the famous photograph of Earth known as 'Pale Blue Dot' was taken by Voyager 1 in early 1990. As it happens, I was finishing my final year of law school, and the photo was featured in the major newspapers at the time. It caught my attention because the distances involved were so mind-blowing. At the time of the photograph, the Voyager spacecraft was on the edge of our solar system, about 4 billion miles away, and Earth appeared as a tiny blue spot of light. Carl Sagan, who had requested the image, summed it up:

> Look again at that dot. That's here. That's home. That's us. On it everyone you love, everyone you know, everyone you ever heard of, every human being who ever was, lived out their lives. The aggregate of our joy and suffering, thousands of confident religions, ideologies, and economic doctrines, every hunter and forager, every hero and coward, every creator and destroyer of civilization, every king and peasant, every young couple in love, every mother and father, hopeful child, inventor and explorer, every teacher of morals, every corrupt politician, every "superstar," every "supreme leader," every saint and sinner in the history of our species lived there – on a mote of dust suspended in a sunbeam.[2]

Sagan really got it – maybe we can all think more like astronomers. We are a speck in the vastness of space and time. On that pale blue dot lived dinosaurs and Socrates – and now physicians and patients, and you and me. Or maybe we can try to think like physicists. Richard Feynman, a theoretical physicist who shared the Nobel Prize in

1 P. L. Travers, Mary Poppins (HarperCollins 1934).

2 Carl Sagan, Pale Blue Dot: A Vision of the Human Future in Space (Random House 1994).

1965, described our situation as follows: "The world is a spinning ball, and people are held on it on all sides, some of them upside down. And we turn like a spit in front of a great fire."[3] At that highest level of cosmic infinitude, all that we hope for in life is just a delusion of grandeur. We are nothing of much cosmic consequence and yet, for each one of us, life is everything. Maybe when the time comes to stare death in the face, remembering that we are a speck on a pale blue dot (on a rotisserie spit in front of the sun) can provide some perspective and, with it, comfort.

About 164,000 people die every day,[4] which amounts to about 114 people per minute. For much of the world, the average age of death, otherwise known as 'life expectancy' (a phrase that itself connotes not only expectation but a smidge of entitlement), is significantly lower than that of high-wealth countries like the United Kingdom, Canada, the United States and much of continental Europe and Scandinavia. In most African countries, for example, life expectancy averages in the low to middle 60s.[5] US baby boomers, born between 1946 and 1964, have experienced the benefit of exponential gains in modern medicine, relatively little foreign and domestic strife, and the most stable, luxurious food supply in the history of humanity. They are living longer in consequence. The average age of death in the United States is now about seventy-six years for men and eighty-one years for women.[6] But no one is entitled to make it to the average age of death or, as many people wish, well beyond that age. We are in no way special or different from people in the rest of the world or our ancestors in the rest of human history. We are only lucky to have been born in modern times and in a wealthy country, to have survived infancy and maybe war, and to have the privilege of growing old.

Chapter 3 laid out different scenarios for death along a spectrum of foreseeability and predictable progression, pointing out that some death scenarios allow patients more opportunity to come to terms with mortality and to make plans and decisions. There is another type of death distinction worth mentioning here – the distinction between death as a tragedy and death as a natural result of late-age disease or decline. The death of a child or younger adult from accident or illness is truly a tragedy. The death of a person who has lived his or her three score and ten is much less so. These latter deaths are normal and to be expected; they are part of life's natural cycle and, while we may miss the person very much, these deaths are not tragic.

3 Richard P. Feynman, Excerpts from The Meaning of It All: Thoughts of a Citizen-Scientist (Perseus 1963). I have read that despite his professional achievements, Dr. Feynman did not behave well in his personal and professional life, but, that said, his perspective on our place in the universe resonates, and so I include it.

4 Oxford University, Our World in Data, https://ourworldindata.org/grapher/number-of-deaths-per-year. (These are pre-COVID-19 pandemic numbers.)

5 World Health Organization, African Health Observatory, https://aho.afro.who.int/data-and-statistics/null.

6 Elizabeth Arias and Jiaquan Xu, 69 Division of Vital Statistics, National Vital Statistics Report 12 (November 17, 2020).

Five years ago, my father died without a word or a warning. He was a kind, honorable, and gentle man with a love of dogs and crosswords, and a wicked sense of humor. He was supposed to come over for dinner that night. We didn't say good-bye. Others die protracted deaths, in a 'battle' against the foe that is disease or a slow surrender to the relentlessness of aging. In the end, death is what awaits us all and, in that sense, it's nothing special. That said, whenever we lose someone we love, even someone who has lived a long and contented life, death stings, and the prospect of death, even for someone who has lived to a healthy old age, naturally remains unwelcome. Even so, any healthy years around or beyond life expectancy seem like cause for gratitude rather than complaint.

Michel de Montaigne wrote, "It is uncertain where death looks for us; let us expect her everywhere: the premeditation of death, is a forethinking of liberty. He who hath learned to die, hath unlearned to serve. . . . To know how to die, doth free us from all subjection and constraint."[7] Not that we should spend *all* of our time contemplating impending death. As the editor of The Oxford Book of Death observed, "I cannot say that I share the thanatologists' missionary urge to bring death out into the open. Much of the time, as a subject of conversation or even of solitary thought, it belongs elsewhere – standing to one side of life, which being so much shorter deserves to be given priority."[8] With that wise acknowledgment, it's still useful to remember that we don't come with a guaranteed life span or a known expiration date, so we really must prioritize and not postpone to later. We have all heard the counternarrative. For me, it was a much revered mentor who lamented his mother's death in her late sixties, after she had 'done everything right', with good diet and healthy habits. Another person, whose diagnosis in her early seventies with a form and stage of cancer that is almost invariably fatal within six months, prompted someone who heard the news to exclaim, "She should have had ten more years." To somehow imply that these deaths were unfair or 'too soon' reinforces the fallacy that any of us deserve to live a given length of time. To say that someone 'did everything right' and so to suggest that the person's death was premature also implies the flip-side assumption – that there are others in our first-world realm who 'did something wrong' – in the form of mistreating their bodies, being born poor, becoming addicted, and so on, and therefore somehow deserve (or are at least responsible for) their own early demise. The idea of fairness in death is a fallacy and one that we would do well to abandon as quickly as we can.

As should be obvious at this point, this is not intended to be a 'how to live' book – I would never presume to write such a thing.[9] (In the Preface, I suggested that this is a book about how to think well about dying.) However, there are a couple of points about how we *do* live that seem to bear directly on how well we're able to confront

[7] Michel de Montaigne, *Essays* (1603).

[8] D. J. Enright, ed., The Oxford Book of Death p. xiii (Oxford University Press, 1983).

[9] For a couple of good ones, see Sarah Bakewell, How to Live – or – A Life of Montaigne (Chatto & Windus 2010) and Pema Chodron, Start Where You Are (Shambala Classics, 1994).

death. Appreciating the life we have and making something of it can make letting go of life easier. The opposite of gratitude is greed. Greed, in all of its forms – wanting more money, a better car, that dream vacation to post about on Instagram, fame and legacy, and most of all wanting more life – continuously undermines the enjoyment of what we have. This is not to say that we should never wish for anything or strive to achieve something or to acquire things that make life more pleasant or enjoyable. But as all of the sages have said, we should seek such things in moderation. All of that 'stuff' loses its transitory value anyway, when death approaches. Gratitude can make it easier to avoid wanting more, including wanting to know, when the time comes, whether we've made the 'best' choices in medical care, whether we've maximized our time on the planet. Ideally, it will be possible to say that what we had was 'enough', and that it was as good as a feast.

Caring for others provides an essential foundation for appreciating life. One of my friend Emma's former students came to her burial service and told the story of how she slipped him some lunch money when he'd forgotten it. She'd spotted his plight and quietly rectified the situation, without letting anyone know what she'd done and certainly without seeking out any kind of kudos for it. This student remembered her for this quiet act of kindness many years after he'd left middle school; it made enough of a mark on him that, decades later, he attended her burial in the middle of a working day to say good-bye and to share his memories of her.

People who live with gratitude understand that finding and maintaining equipoise in life (and medical care) is an existential yet daily task in which future nonexistence must always be part of the equation. The concept of gratitude includes, of course, an appreciation of what is good in life, but it also demands action at times. Gratitude requires living with integrity, and in a way that is other-regarding. Sticking with a code of moral values is just the beginning. Someone once said: "Integrity is doing the right thing even when no one is looking." I'll add to that – integrity is doing the right thing even when everyone seems opposed, and the cost may be personally high. It's doing one's best by others, avoiding the easy way out. Sometimes the right path isn't obvious, but when there is that unsettled feeling in the conscience, it's time to consider that disquiet and to act accordingly. In the end-of-life context, integrity may even require helping to protect a loved person from his worst impulses. We may not succeed in the effort to facilitate better decision-making and outcomes, but we're not responsible to succeed – only to try.

I was out one day when I met my favorite handyman, a sturdy old fellow, standing on his driveway tinkering with his meticulously maintained truck, his hands deeply callused from six decades of work. We've known each other for sixteen years, and I stopped for a catch-up chat. He spoke of things that many people would find difficult to put into words. He told me of the recent death of his closest friend since childhood, of the death of his brother, and of other people gone from his life. Along the way of this catalogue of loss, he chuckled and joked about himself and the state of the world. He mentioned that he had been referred for spinal surgery but added that he would ask the doctor a lot of questions before going "under the knife." He leaned on his truck to ease the pain in his back and turned his face up to the sun. Then he said that, at 80 years old, if his doctor told him that he had a month to live, he would be okay with that. He would put his affairs in order for the sake of "the missus." His childhood friend – that very best friend – in similar circumstances had made sure that his wife had all of the papers that she would need in one place. The friend had then asked his wife to drive him one more time around the town where he'd lived for his entire life. He and his friend had said good-bye, and the friend died shortly thereafter. As he talked, he periodically gave a sharp nod of his head – "I mean what I'm saying." It was a bright autumn morning when we had this conversation, and I was glad that my sunglasses masked the tears in my eyes. Winter was coming.

At the end of the day, the relentless drumbeat of life and death and the rapid passing of the years leave us with uncomfortable thoughts and questions – among them, whether we have used our limited days well. Our individual lives are just a brief moment of existence in between otherwise endless eons of nonexistence. We weren't here. Then we are born, and we live – some of us luckier and longer than others – and then we're gone again – every one of "[u]s, the most transient."[10] Intimations of mortality are scary, hence the denial. We all suffer attacks of *timor mortis* from time to time, growing more frequent with age. One response is to cultivate gratitude – for our lives, our loves, our work, and our leisure. Now I'm heading out to buy a couple of tubes of toothpaste.

[10] Rainer Maria Rilke, The Ninth Elegy, in Duino Elegies (University of California Press 1963).

Index